Country Bazaar

by
Andy Pittaway
and
Bernard Scofield

Fontana/Collins

First published by The Architectural Press
Ltd 1974
First issued in Fontana 1976
Copyright © Andy Pittaway and Bernard
Scofield 1974

Printed in Great Britain by
William Collins Sons & Co. Ltd, Glasgow

Contents

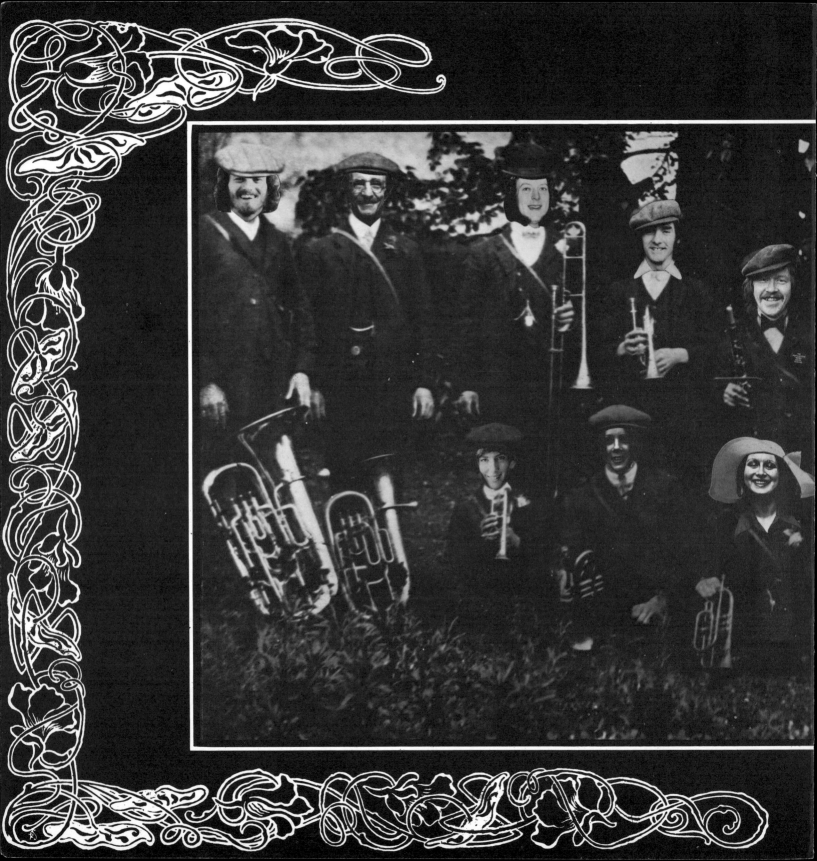

THE COUNTRY BAZAAR BRASS BAND

Acknowledgements

Our warm thanks and appreciation go to the following people who have contributed in one way or another to the creation of this book: to Irene; to Edwin (Neddy) Cooke for his illustrations which appear on pp. 36, 92, 150 and for other services rendered!; to Lisa and Lara for their drawings on pp. 62, 192–194, 197 and to their parents Jethro and Jackie Large for all their kindness; to Liz and Gavin Gault for providing the illustrations and photographs on pp. 76, 81–84, 232 and especially for their help and support; to Malcolm (Tiny) Chile who provided the photograph of his self-made silver brooch 'The Cottage' which appears on p. 127; to Mr and Mrs E. Frost for all their help and encouragement and in particular to Mr Frost who took the photographs which appear on pp. 50, 112, 210; to Marie and Alan Jenkins for lending us a number of their books and for providing the illustration which appears on p. 78; to Stephen Jenner for lending us his engravings by Stanley Anderson which appear on pp. 100, 105, 152, 223; to Betty Swanwick A.R.A. for her continued support and in particular for providing the photograph of her watercolour 'The Approach' on p. 179 and to Joan Gibson for permission to reproduce this painting which she owns; to Christopher Walker for his pen and watercolour picture 'The Children of Albion' which is on pp. 230–231; to John Shelley for supplying the photograph of his oil painting 'The Old Mill' which appears on p. 117; to Dr. Richard St. Barbe Baker for supplying the photographs of trees on pp. 140, 143; to Lawrence Whistler for supplying the photograph of his engraved goblet 'And Summer And Winter' on p. 182; to Ron Wilson for his article 'The Living Hedge' on pp. 151–153; to Peter Brown for his article 'Starting a Pottery' which appears on pp. 27–32; to Ray Moller for photographs which are featured on pp. 15, 246; to Gordon for lending us his engravings by Gustav Doré which are reproduced on pp. 22, 122; to Linda Wheeler of the Smile Design Group for her pen illustration on p. 240; to Tim and Sally Rodwell for supplying the information in 'Wayside Wines and Other Delights' pp. 183–191; to Bridget St. John for her poems which appear on pp. 61, 135; to Owen Stanier for the pottery photographs pp. 26, 28–35; to John Allen for his information on tree tapping pp. 144–145; to Frank W. Lane for his Agfacolorfilm photograph of lightning on p. 138; to *International Times* for the illustration on p. 166; to Michael Wills for his photograph from the Wills Family Album featured on p. 23; to Janet Bord for her tree photograph on p. 146; to Tin Pan Alley Music Ltd. for the poem on p. 156; to the Royal Society for the Protection of Birds for giving us permission to reprint extracts from their booklet *The Birds in Your Garden*; to the Council for the Protection of Rural England for granting us permission to reproduce extracts from their leaflets *Making a Hedge Survey* and *Making a Tree Survey*; to J. M. Dent & Sons Ltd. for permission to reproduce the photograph 'Thank you for the Clouds Above' from *A Child's Grace* which appears on p. 168; to the Ramblers' Association for permission to reproduce several of their Fact Sheets; to the Shirley Institute, Manchester for kindly supplying the photograph of the silk moth's life-cycle on p. 58; to Collins Sons & Co. Ltd. for permission to reproduce the illustration by J. Yunge-Bateman on p. 207 from their book *Shining Hours*; to Bob Hall for his work in correlating design and for his photographs on pp. 48, 52, 53, 54, 55, 94, 99, 204.

Our gratitude must also be extended to the following organisations from which we obtained help and information:
Banbury School of Art; Goldsmiths School of Art; Crafts Advisory Committee; Design Centre; Silk Education service; Irish Linen Guild; West Dean College; Cranks Vegetarian Restaurant; Burfield House School; CoSIRA; the Forestry Commission; Nature Conservancy; Frendz Magazine.

THE COUNTRY BAZAAR BRASS BAND

Back row, left to right: **Ray Moller** euphonium and photographs; **Mr E. Frost** tuba and photographs; **Malcolm (Tiny) Chile** slide trombone and illustrations; **Edwin (Neddy) Cooke** cornet and drawings; **Andy Pittaway** clarinet and co-author; **Bob Hall** bass drum and production; **Bernard Scofield** horn and co-author; **Godfrey Golzen** valve trombone and management; **Gavin Gault** tea urn, spoons and illustrations; **Sally Rodwell** second horn and wine know-how; **Richard St Barbe Baker** collecting box and tree photographs; **Christopher Walker** painting; **John Allen** tree-tapping notes.
Front row, left to right: **Bridget St John** bugle and poems; **Liz Gault** trumpet and illustrations; **Alexandra Artley** trumpet and editorial; **Betty Swanwick A.R.A.** trumpet and painting; **Lara Large** triangle and drawings; **Stephen Jenner** trumpet and engravings; **Lisa Large** penny whistle and drawings; **Tim Rodwell** collecting box and information.

Where should a man live? In solitude, or in society? In the green stillness of the country where he can hear the heart of nature beat; or in the dark, grey town where he can hear and feel the throbbing heart of man?

I fear, however, that in towns the soul of man grows proud. He needs at times to be sent forth, like the Assyrian monarch into green fields, a wondrous wretch and weedless, to eat green herbs and be awakened and chastised by the rain shower and winter's bitter weather.

LONGFELLOW

Introduction

About three years ago, a small magazine appeared in some London bookshops for the first time. The magazine was called *The Country Bizarre* and appeared seasonally, filled with a peculiar patchwork of country matters ranging from conservation, folklore and craftwork, to nature, poetry, stories and pictures. From its humble beginnings, *The Country Bizarre* grew into a well-loved publication and so it was only a matter of time before a book based on the magazine and preserving its unique atmosphere should appear.

Although the book contains a number of articles taken from the magazine, the majority of what lies within is quite new. Craftwork had always been an integral part of *The Country Bizarre* and so there are many articles in the book on country crafts: crafts that can be pursued without an expensive outlay in equipment and materials, and where the countryside itself provides the basics of the craft. There is a vast amount of information on sources of materials, making one's own equipment, outlets for finished work, education and courses, grants, financial aid and further reading. Also

mentioned are sources of supplies in the USA for the benefit of our American friends.

When setting out initially on the production of *The Country Bizarre's Country Bazaar*, we were haunted by the hundreds of other publications already on the market. Most of them, we felt, were stereotyped, uninspiring and in general, divorced from the world of creative art and design. In trying to avoid these faults, we have compiled a book which we hope not only overflows with information, but will delight and inspire the reader with beautiful drawings, engravings, illustrations and photographs by many artists, not just from our own times, but from historical periods long before our own. Only by studying and appreciating all kinds of art can the quality of design in craftwork be raised from the generally low standard it has fallen to today.

Finally, we must express warm thanks to our friends at the Architectural Press for having taken such an interest in the magazine and for giving us help and advice whenever needed. In particular, our thanks must go to Ted Cooke, who got the whole idea going, for without him

this book would never have happened. There are many others who must be equally thanked for their help, information and contribution and a fitting tribute to their collective effort appears on pages 4 and 5.

So here is *The Country Bizarre's Country Bazaar* and we sincerely hope you all get as much pleasure out of owning it as we did in creating it.

Love and best wishes

Andy Pittaway

Bernard Scofield

Of all the many monuments to be found in our churches and cathedrals, beautifully engraved brasses are frequently the most overlooked. Not only are they fine examples of the metal-worker's craft from the 13th to the 17th centuries, but they also serve as a pictorial guide to the development of fashions in armour and ecclesiastical gowns. They are also a commentary on the way of life in medieval England with such characters as monks, ladies, bishops, servants and knights all rigidly portrayed in brass as their contemporaries saw them.

Even today their value as a source of historical information has been increased by the simple techniques available to reproduce their exact designs, capturing the different textures and qualities in wax on paper.

Although one normally thinks of a church as belonging to the people, permission must in fact be sought from the priest of the church concerned, stating the time and date that you wish to make your rubbing. You must also contact the people responsible for the church's ornaments as sometimes a brass may be located under a pew or, in one case, behind an organ. CROCKFORD'S CLERICAL DIRECTORY (available in most public libraries) lists hundreds of names and addresses of these people. A small fee of probably no more than 25p may also be required to help with the up-keep of the church.

EQUIPMENT

The basic materials needed for brass rubbing consist of detail or lining paper, heelball wax or crayons, black ink, strong adhesive tape, a soft brush and rags. Before starting on your rubbing, dust and brush the brass carefully to remove any grit that might be wedged between the grooves and roll out the paper onto the brass, securing it firmly with the tape.

A Guide to Brass Rubbing

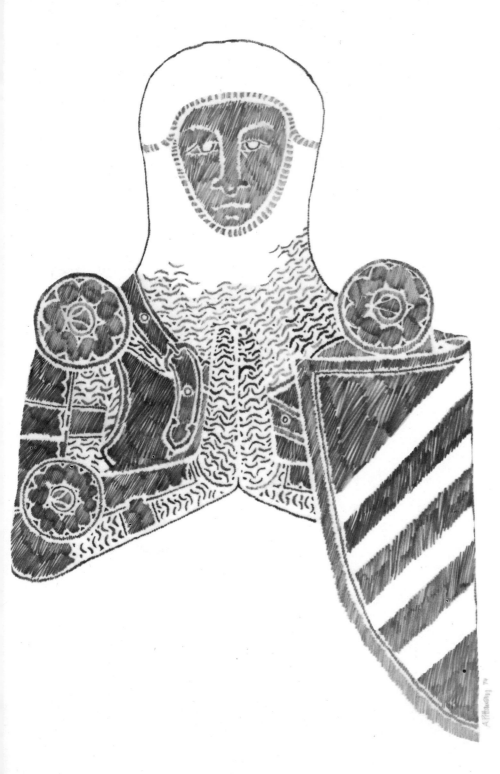

So that you know the area of the paper for rubbing, gently bring out the outline of the plate by rubbing the paper with a clean piece of cloth.

METHOD

There are three recognized rubbing methods which produce differing results. The first is with either sticks or cakes of black heelball which is a mixture of beeswax, tallow and lamp black. This method needs hard rubbing to produce an even black image and for good results a dull point should be kept on the sticks. When a brass is too detailed for the heelball to define it, a second method will have to be used: this is the dabbing technique.

Make a pad from a piece of chamois leather wrapped round some cotton wool and dip it into a paste of graphite mixed with linseed oil. Wipe off the surplus paste from the pad and dab it with medium pressure onto the surface of the paper. As very little friction is caused, thin paper, like tissue paper can be used. This process is ideal if you also want a fine impression of the stone surrounding the brass.

The third technique is based on the heelball process and is used solely for decoration. Instead of using a black heelball, a brown or yellow one could be used. The rubbing is made in the same way as before but after completion, wipe the paper with waterproof black ink. The ink will stain only the parts not touched by the wax and will give a white-on-black image. The rubbing is then cut out and mounted on coloured board.

Altogether there are some 2,000 brasses scattered throughout Great Britain, the most numerous being in the counties of East Anglia, the Home Counties and the Thames Valley, Kent, Essex, Norfolk and Suffolk contain a large amount followed closely by Buckinghamshire, Oxfordshire, Berkshire, Surrey and Hertfordshire.

9

Instead of listing every location, we think it best to mention only those brasses of high interest and good quality:

Bedfordshire:
BROMHAM: A Man in armour (1435) plus 2 Wives.
WYMINGTON: A Man in civilian dress with Wife (1391); Sir Thomas Brounflet in armour (1430); a Priest with chalice (1520); a Lady (1407).

Berkshire:
BLEWBURY: John Balam: priest (1496); a Man in armour plus 2 Wives (1515); Sir John Daunce in armour and tabard of arms with Wife (1523).
BRAY: Foxley in armour with 2 Wives (1378); a Judge (1475); a Man in civilian dress plus 2 Wives (1490).
CHILDREY: A Priest with chalice (1490); a Lady in a shroud (1507); a Man in civilian dress with Wife in shroud (1516); a Priest in academical dress (1529).
SHOTTESBROOKE: A Priest with civilian (1370); a Lady (1401); a man in armour (1511); a Man in civilian dress with 3 Wives (1567).
SPARSHOLT: A Priest (1353); a Civilian (1495); a Lady (1510).
WINDSOR: *(St Georges' Chapel)* A Child in a cradle (1630).

Buckinghamshire:
DENHAM: A Man in armour with 2 Wives (1494); a Lady (1545); a Priest (1560).
DRAYTON BEAUCHAMP: A Man in armour (1368); a Priest with a small chalice (1531).
ETON COLLEGE: *Chapel:* A Fellow with a small chalice (1509); a Fellow kneeling with 11 inscriptions (1636).
STOKE POGES: Sir William Molyns with Wife (1425).
TAPLOW: A Cross and Man in civilian dress (1350); a Man in armour with 2 Wives (1540).
THORNTON: Robert Ingylton dressed in armour with 3 Wives (1472); a Lady (1557).

Cambridgeshire:
BALSHAM: A Priest (1401).
ELY CATHEDRAL: Bishop Goodrick (1554); Dean Tyndall (1614).
HILDERSHAM: Robert de Paris; a Man in civilian dress with Wife kneeling (1379).
TRUMPINGTON: Sir Roger de Trumpington (1289).
WESTLEY WATERLESS: Sir John de Creke with Wife (1325).

Cheshire:
MACCLESFIELD: Roger Legh in civilian dress (1506).
WILMSLOW: Sir Robert del Bothe dressed in armour with Wife (1460).

Cornwall:
CALLINGTON: Nicholous Assheton (1465).
MAWGAN-IN-PYDER: A Lady (1578); a Man in civilian dress (1580).

Cumberland:
CARLISLE CATHEDRAL: Bishop Bell (1496); Bishop Robinson (1616).

Derbyshire:
MORLEY: Sacheverell dressed in armour with Wife (1525).
TIDESWELL: Holy Trinity for Sir Sampson Meverell (1462); A Man in civilian dress with Wife (1483).

Devonshire:

DARTMOUTH: *(St Saviour)* John Hauley dressed in armour with 2 Wives (1408); a Lady (1470).

STOKE FLEMING: John Corp dressed in civilian clothes (1391).

Durham:

SEDGEFIELD: Two skeletons in shrouds (1470).

Essex:

BOWERS GIFFORD: Sir John Gifford dressed in armour (1348) (mutilated).

CHIGWELL: Archbishop Harsnett (1631).

DAGENHAM: Sir Thomas Urswyk (1479).

OCKENDON: Sir Ingelram Bruyn (1400); a Lady (1602).

PEBMARSH: Sir William Fitzralph sitting cross-legged (1320).

WYVENHOE: Elizabeth, Countess of Oxford (1537).

Gloucestershire

CHIPPING CAMPDEN: Wool-merchant with Wife (1401).

CIRENCESTER: 12 brasses of Wool Merchants with Wives (1400–1626).

DRYHAM: Sir Morys Russel and Wife (1401).

NORTHLEACH: 7 brasses of Wool Merchants with Wives (1400–1526).

Hampshire:

CRONDALL: A Skeleton (1641).

RINGWOOD: A Priest with Saints (1416).

THRUXTON: Sir John Lysle (1425).

Herefordshire:

HEREFORD CATHEDRAL: Bishop Trilleck (1360); a Priest in head of cross (1360).

Hertfordshire:

BERKHAMSTEAD: Lady in a small shroud (1520).

CLOTHALL: John Wynter (1404); Priest with chalice (1519); a Lady (1572).

ST ALBANS ABBEY: Abbot Delamere (1360); 4 Monks (1450).

Kent:

CHARTHAM: Sir Robert de Setvans (1306); a Small Lady (1530).

COBHAM: A Lady (1320); a Man dressed in armour (1354).

HORSMONDEN: A Priest (1340); a Lady (1604).

MARGATE: Heart and scrolls (1433); a Skeleton (1446).

SEAL: Lord William de Bryene dressed in armour (1395).

STONE: A Priest in head of cross (1408).

WICKHAM: A Yeoman of the Guard with 3 Wives (1568).

Leicestershire:

BOTTESFORD: Henry de Codyngtoun with Saints (1404).

DONINGTON CASTLE: Robert Staunton dressed in armour (1458).

Lincolnshire:

BOSTON: A Man in civilian dress (1398).

CROFT: A Man dressed in armour (1300).

LINWOOD: John Lyndewode with Woolman and Wife (1419); a Woolman (1421).
STAMFORD: *(All Saints)* : Woolman with Wife (1475).

Middlesex:
HARROW: A Man in civilian dress with 3 Wives (1488).
HILLINGDON: Lord Le Strange with Wife (1509).
LONDON *(All Hallows Barking, Tower Hill)* : A Woolman with Wife (1437); The Resurrection (1510). Westminster Abbey: Bishop John de Waltham (1395); Archbishop Robert de Waldeby (1397).

Norfolk:
BURNHAM THORPE: Sir William Calthorpe dressed in armour (1420).
ROUGHAM: Judge with Wife (1470).
SHERNBOURNE: Sir Thomas Shernborne (1458).
UPWELL: Henry Martyn (1435); a Lady (1631).

Northamptonshire:
NEWTON-BY-GEDDINGTON: John Mulsho dressed in civilian clothes with Wife kneeling to cross (1400); a Lady (1604).

Northumberland:
NEWCASTLE-UPON-TYNE *(All Saints)* : Merchant with Wife (1429) (foreign).

Oxfordshire:
BRIGHTWELL BALDWIN: English inscription to John the Smith (1370).
DORCHESTER: Abbot Bewfforeste (1510); a Lady (1490).

Rutland:
LITTLE CASTERTON: Sir Thomas Burton (1410).

Staffordshire:
OKEOVER: Zouch and 2 Wives (1447) altered to Oker and Wife (1538).

Suffolk:
GORLESTON: Man dressed in armour, of Bacon family (1320).
PLAYFORD: Sir George Felbrigg dressed in armour (1400).

Surrey:
HORSLEY: Man in civilian dress (1400); Bishop Bowthe kneeling (1478).
LINGFIELD: Lady Cobham (1374).

Worcestershire:
FLADBURY: Man dressed in armour with Wife (1445).
KIDDERMINSTER: Sir John Phelip (1415).

Yorkshire:
TOPCLIFFE: Thomas de Topclyff dressed in civilian clothes with Wife (foreign) (1391).
WENSLEY: Simon de Wensley (1360).

There are no outstanding brasses in Ireland, Scotland, or Wales. The Channel Islands and the Isle of Man possess no known brasses at all.

SOURCES OF MATERIALS

Detail paper can be obtained from stationers, artshops or from:
WINDSOR & NEWTON LTD, Wealdstone, Harrow, Middlesex.
Shelf paper from:
BOOTS CHEMISTS, WOOLWORTHS, W. H. SMITH & SON.
Heelball, cobbler's wax, astral wax, available from:
PHILIPS & PAGE & SONS, Ltd, 50 Kensington Church Street, Kensington, London W8.

SOURCES OF MATERIALS IN THE USA

OLDSTONE ENTERPRISES, 77 Summer Street, Boston, Massachusetts.

SOCIETIES

MONUMENTAL BRASS SOCIETY, c/o The Society of Antiquarians, Burlington House, Piccadilly, London W1. *For the study and preservation of brasses and their care and repair. Gives free advice to churches.*

SERVICES

THE CHURCH OF ENGLAND ENQUIRY CENTRE, Church House, Dean's Yard, London SW1P 3NZ. *Has a directory of brasses to be found in churches in London.*

BIBLIOGRAPHY

BEGINNERS GUIDE TO BRASS RUBBING, by Richard J. Busby/Pelham Books Ltd.
BRITISH MONUMENTAL BRASSES, by Richard Strange/Thames & Hudson Ltd.
THE CRAFT & DESIGN OF MONUMENTAL BRASSES, by Henry Trivick/John Baker (Publishers) Ltd.
CREATIVE RUBBINGS, by Laye Andrew/B. T. Batsford Ltd.
CROCKFORDS CLERICAL DIRECTORY/Oxford University Press. *(Consult this in your nearest reference library for the names and addresses of clergymen whose permission you will have to ask.)*

MONUMENTAL BRASSES, by Herbert W. Macklin (revised by Charles Oman)/Allen & Unwin Ltd.

MONUMENTAL BRASSES, by J. P. Philips/Allen & Unwin Ltd.

MONUMENTAL BRASSES IN SOMERSET, by A. B. Connor/Kingsmead Reprints, Rosewell House, Kingsmead Square, Bath, Somerset.

MONUMENTAL BRASSES OF CORNWALL, by E. H. W. Dunkin/Kingsmead Reprints, Rosewell House, Kingsmead Square, Bath, Somerset.

THE PICTURE BOOK OF BRASSES, by H. Trevick/John Baker (Publishers) Ltd.

RUBBINGS AND TEXTURES, by John Bodor/Van Nostrand Reinhold Co., New York.

Many people may suffer discomfort from using brand-name soaps which contain harmful chemicals and perfumes. Rashes and unhealthy complexions can occur with the use of modern cosmetics so that alternative types composed of natural ingredients are the only answer. We have therefore compiled a list of the more important herbs which have been used traditionally in cosmetics, followed by a collection of recipes for simple soap, shampoo and face cream etc. which are completely harmless to delicate skins and will help to naturally enhance the beauty of face, skin, hair and scalp.

Beauty Without Cruelty

CHAMOMILE (Matricaria chamomilla)
Keeps blonde hair healthy. Good for ageing skin and helps soothe and heal inflammatory areas. Infuse in water and apply hot.

COLTSFOOT (Tussilago farfara)
Helps relieve the effects of dilated facial veins (sometimes known as thread veins). Infuse in water and apply cold only.

ELDER FLOWERS (Sambucus nigra)
One of the finest cures for sunburn, wrinkles and freckles. Also good for cleansing, softening and whitening the skin. Use infused in water, applied cold or in a cream.

EYEBRIGHT (Euphrasia officinalis)
Has been used for centuries in relieving tired eyes and inflamed eye-lids. Use infused in water and apply cold.

FENNEL (Foeniculum vulgare)
Good for smoothing out wrinkles and relieving tired eyes. Use infused in water and apply cold.

HORSE TAIL (Equisetum arvense)
An excellent herb for improving the condition of both hair and nails. Use infused in water and either take internally as a tea or applied warm as a hair rinse.

LIME FLOWERS (Tilia europaea)
Very good for eliminating wrinkles, whitening the skin, bleaching out freckles and stimulating the growth of hair. Use infused in water and apply hot or cold.

LOVAGE (Levisticum officinalis)
A herb best known for its deodorant qualities when taken internally, infused in water as a tea.

MARIGOLD PETALS (Calendula officinalis)
Helpful in reducing inflammation, smoothing rough skin and reducing acne and other skin complaints. Use infused in water and apply hot or cold.

NETTLE (Urtica dioica)
An excellent tonic for hair and equally good as a skin conditioner. Use infused in water and take internally hot or cold, or apply externally the same.

PEPPERMINT (Mentha piperita)
A skin conditioner and tonic, as well as having disinfectant qualities. Use infused in water and take internally hot or cold.

ROSEMARY (Rosmarinus officinalis)
Perhaps the finest herb for strengthening and beautifying the hair. Use infused in water and apply as a warm hair rinse.

SAGE (Salvia officinalis)
A good herb for improving the quality of hair. Use the same as rosemary.

SALAD BURNET (Sanguisorba minor)
For cleansing and beautifying the skin. Use infused in water and apply hot or cold.

VERBENA (Lippia citriodora) *Lemon Verbena*
A herb which has soothing qualities and is best used in relieving inflamed eyelids and tired eyes. Use infused in water and apply cold.

RECIPES

Simple Soap: 1 lb caustic soda, 35 oz. olive oil (or any other vegetable oil) and 3 pints of water. Put the soda and water into a large cooking pot and heat slowly, dissolving the soda by stirring gently. Allow the solution to cool until lukewarm and then add the oil. Stir for a couple of minutes and then pour the mixture into shallow metal trays lined with cotton or muslin. Keep the trays in a warm place for one day and after cutting the soap into bars, leave them to solidify in a cool place for *at least* six weeks. (Oil for simple soap can be obtained from grape seed and sunflower seed etc, simply by crushing with a mortar and pestle.) If desired, a little natural oil of geranium, rose or lavender etc., may be added during the mixing stage.

Irish Moss Cream: 1 oz Irish moss, 2 oz glycerine, 1 dram boracic acid; 1 oz eau de cologne and 10 oz of distilled water.

After washing the moss in water, gently boil it in the distilled water in a saucepan or some other pot with a lid. When cool, strain the mixture and add the glycerine and boracic acid (borax). Mix thoroughly and finally add the eau de cologne. Put the cream in little pots and cover them.

Witch Hazel Cream: $\frac{1}{2}$ oz sodium carbonate, 4 fluid oz glycerine, 20 fluid oz distilled extract of witch hazel, 4 oz stearic acid and 16 fluid oz of water.

Using only an enamel or stainless steel pot, add the sodium carbonate and the glycerine to the water and thoroughly stir. Add the stearic acid and gently heat the solution until all the effervescence has disappeared, leaving a clear liquid. Keep the solution on the heat and near to boiling point for an hour, continually stirring. Take off the heat, add the witch hazel and stir until a good cream has been made. Store in small pots.

Skin Softeners: Rub potato slices over the skin first thing in the morning and last thing at night. Equally as good is to fill a small bowl with half a cup of hot milk. Drop a slice of lemon in and let the mixture stand for a few minutes. Strain and throw away the curd. Wash your skin first with ordinary warm water and then apply the liquid gently massaging into the skin. Wipe off the surplus and allow the rest to soak into the skin.

For Large Pores: To close large pores and liven up the skin do the following: put four tablespoonfuls of bran and the shredded rind of two lemons into a flannel bag. Place in a pot of boiling water for a few seconds and then apply to the face, as hot as can be tolerated, gently squeezing the bag as you go.

Rough Skin Lotion: Put $\frac{1}{2}$ pint of milk into a pan and add $\frac{1}{2}$ oz of bicarbonate of soda, $\frac{1}{2}$ oz of glycerine, $\frac{1}{4}$ teaspoonful of powdered borax just before boiling. Remove immediately from the heat and when cold, apply freely to the skin.

Sunburn Protection: Firstly let it be said that sunbathing in large amounts has a severe and detrimental effect on the skin. It ages the skin like nothing else and stops the skin absorbing the sun's vital vitamin A content that is essential for a healthy complexion. If you are out in the hot sun for any length of time it is advisable to rub one or two slices of cucumber over the face, arms and neck and allow the juice to dry. Not only will this protect you from sunburn but it is a very good skin conditioner. A good sun oil can be made from olive oil with the addition of a little vinegar. Use liberally over exposed parts.

Freckle Cure: Freckles are not shaming in the least, but if you want to clear them, the following should be done. Pour ½ pint of boiling milk over 2 tablespoons of freshly-scraped horse-radish root. When cold, apply all the mixture to the face as thickly as possible and leave it to dry for half an hour. Wash off with rainwater if possible and repeat each day until the freckles disappear. Another way is to rub the leaves of an elm tree over the face just after a heavy dew or rain. It will clear freckles and make the skin beautiful.

Skin Fresheners and Other Advice: To revitalize the skin, take two handfuls of scented rose petals and put them into an earthen pot. Pour two pints of hot or cold water and ¼ lb sugar over them, leaving the mixture for an hour. Take an empty jug and pour the mixture back and forth until the scent is abundant in the water. Strain and apply freely to the skin.

To clear pimples more effectively than with any shop preparation, pick a dandelion flower and squeeze the stem until a milky juice appears. Apply the juice to the pimples and they will soon dry up and disappear. This remedy is unfortunately limited to Spring and Summer as the dandelion loses its cunning qualities in the Autumn and Winter.

Complexion Lotion: Into a large bowl put 1 oz of spirits of camphor, 2 oz sea salt, 1 oz spirits of ammonia and ¼ pint of unsweetened gin. Add boiling water to make 1 quart of liquid. Stir until the salt has dissolved and bottle, corking well. Shake the bottle before use and apply to the skin freely. This lotion has an amazing effect on the feel of the skin and its appearance.

Eye Preparations: The latter-day medical profession has scorned the use of the herb eye-bright as having no positive effect on eye care, but you never see a gypsy with glasses and eye bright was their herb. Put a teaspoonful of the dried herb in a teacup and infuse with boiling water. After allowing the solution to cool, strain and bathe the eyes with it. This preparation reduces tension in the eyes and makes them sparkle.

Nail Care: Never cut nails to shorten them as this makes them brittle. Instead use an emery board or file. If your nails are brittle rub them with slightly warm Lucca Oil (from any chemist).

Hair Tonics and Preparations: Add cat-mint to your rinsing water after washing your hair as this promotes bright shiny hair. Chamomile is equally good and keeps fair hair light and golden. To keep naturally blonde hair its natural colour, and to prevent it darkening, boil half an oz of chamomile flowers in a pint of water for 20 minutes. When cool, use it as a hair rinse after washing the hair with the following shampoo.

Chamomile Shampoo: Into a basin put 1 tablespoonful of pure soapflakes, 1 teaspoonful of borax and 1 oz of powdered chamomile flowers. Add ½ pint of hot water and beat till a thick lather appears.After wetting the hair with warm water, add the lather and massage well into the scalp. Rinse thoroughly and repeat.

Healthy Teeth: For sparkling, healthy teeth, rub them with fresh sage leaves. This freshens the teeth, hardens the gums and improves the state of your mouth immensely.

Rosemary Hair Rinse: Infuse a teacupful of boiling water with 1 desertspoonful of dried or fresh rosemary leaves. When cool add to your rinsing water and you can expect to have lovely hair if used continually. Verbena, columbine and lad's love are other good rinses which perfume and condition the hair in a wonderful way.

To Help Stop Hair Falling Out: This condition is generally caused by stress, worry or by such deficiencies as anaemia. A tonic of Peruvian bark will help to cure this malady. Into 1 pint of cold water place ½ oz Peruvian Bark (from a good herbalist) and after bringing to the boil, simmer for 10 minutes. Strain when cold and take half a cupful every day before going to bed and first thing in the morning. For hair that is in a serious condition, take a handful of green artichoke leaves and cook them (as with spinach) in their own juice mixed only with a little water. Cook gently for three hours, do not strain, then rub well into the hair two or three times a week.

Dandruff Cure: In a cupful of warm water dissolve a thimbleful of powdered borax. Wet the hair first and then brush in this solution, rubbing well into the scalp. Repeat daily.

Woodland Hair Tonic: Obtain from a good herbalist the following extracts: ½ fluid oz of skullcap, ½ fluid oz mistletoe, ½ fluid oz valerian root, ½ fluid oz wahoo bark, 1 fluid oz of hollyhock root, ½ fluid oz gentian root, 2 fluid drachms of golden seal root and 8 oz distilled water. Mix together and take 1 teaspoonful three times a day.

SOURCES OF MATERIALS

Many of the ingredients mentioned in this chapter can be obtained from your local chemist, herbalist or hardware shop. For a list of recommended herbalists see the end of the POT POURRI *and* POMANDERS *chapter (p. 181).*

BIBLIOGRAPHY

FEED YOUR FACE, by Dian Buchman.
THE HERBALIST, by Joseph E. Meyer/The Oak Tree Press Ltd.
HERBS FOR HEALTH AND COOKING, by Claire Loewenfield and Phillipa Back/Pan Books Ltd. *Contains recipes for cosmetics and food.*
THE ROOTS OF HEALTH, by Leon Petulengro/Pan Books Ltd.

Come, let us daub, my crazys,
Surrealize the thrill.
Of soapsuds on the daisies
And skylarks in the swill.

LEONARD FEENEY

Three Corn Dollies

The art of making corn dollies is very old indeed and is almost untracable in its origins. It has always been centred around the need to express hope for a good harvest and to give thanks at that time of year to goddesses of the earth and fertility, such as Ceres and Demeter. One of the most common symbols in harvest rituals is that of the cornucopia on the Horn of Plenty which is thought to have strongly inspired the traditional English corn dolly. As to the name 'dolly', this is subject to much discussion, but seems to be more akin to an idol or female deity to be worshipped, than a child's doll.

When the harvest was over, dollies were always carried round the fields to celebrate the year's sowing and reaping and there was much joy and thanksgiving. It is a sad tribute to our times that the harvest festivals which were once an accepted ceremony are now slowly disappearing.

Before the days of the combine harvester, which has virtually killed off the craft, there were rituals involving corn dollies all over the country, varying from region to region, though all having much the same things in common. A man was selected from the farm labourers and was elected 'Lord of the Harvest'. The

'Lord' was then to be respected above all the other men and it was he who would lead the pace in the harvest. Usually he was a man with much experience and the fastest worker, for the other men could then try to match his ability. His job also, was to see that each man was fairly paid for his work. At the end of the harvest, a procession of all the farm wagons, gaily decorated with flowers and ornaments, made a tour of the fields. The horses were at their best: groomed and wearing bells and trinkets, and the men and women were none the less gaily dressed. As they moved round the field, ancient songs were sung, bells rung and there was much fun and laughter. More often than not, the prettiest girl of the village was chosen to ride the leading horse and she was a frequent excuse for the young men to partake in kissing and horseplay. After

the procession came the feast—an enormous affair of the like that our ancestors were famous for. No doubt the old songs were sung year after year, such as:

Harvest home, Harvest home,
We have ploughed, we have sowed,
We have reaped, we have mowed,
We have brought home every load.
Hip! Hip! Hip! Harvest home.

There is a wide variety of corn dollies, one or two being peculiar to a county and each type usually had a beautiful name. We have listed a few for you: 'The Suffolk Horn', 'The Cornucopia', 'The Norfolk Lantern', 'The Durnham Chandelier', 'The Corn Neck', 'The Vale of Pickering Chalice', 'The Cambridgeshire Bell', 'The Mother Earth', 'The Horn and Whip', 'The Essex Teret', and 'The Five Straw Plait'.

When mechanisation came in, there was coupled with it the introduction of wheats that had a pithy-centred straw which unfortunately led to a general decline in the craft. Today, however, new wheats are being grown with a hollow straw such as Maris Widgeon and Elite Lepeuple and these are excellent for corndolly making. Should you be unable to get hold of these wheats, rye and oats will do, but barley is unsuitable.

18

COLLECTING

First find a farmer who is growing the type of grain you require and get permission from him to cut some of the straw when it is nearly ripe and the first joint below the ear is still green. If the straw is used within a week of collecting, dampening will not be required.

STORING

Straw tends to mildew rather easily so your first job must be to dry it, either in the sun, an airing cupboard, or in a slow oven with the doors open. It is then advisable to store the straw loosely packed in boxes until needed and this way will enable you to keep it for years.

TRIMMING

You will notice, on observing an individual straw, that it is made up of a number of joints at varying lengths up the stem. Each straw should be cut off above the top joint, just below the ear, and also just above the bottom joint nearest the base of the straw. The sheath should also be removed, i.e. the leaf that grows up and out of either the bottom or the second joint.

SELECTION

Your straw will probably be of varying shapes and sizes and you should grade them into bundles of fine, medium and thick straw.

MAKING THE CORN DOLLIES

Three types of corn dollies will be explained, and one finishing plait. These are:
THE FIVE-STRAW PLAIT, THE CORN NECK, THE CORNUCOPIA, AND THE FOUR-STRAW PLAIT.
These are all basic types and are the basis of more complicated dollies. If, on mastering these techniques, you feel that you would like to progress to the more advanced aspects of the craft, we suggest that you get hold of the books listed at the end of this chapter (p. 21).

The Five-straw plait *(the basis of most dollies)*
Take a bundle of graded straws and secure a rubber band round the thick ends. Pull up one straw and hold it so that you can hold the straws, five ends downwards into a bowl (fig 1) and pour boiling water over them. Roll the straws up in a damp cloth and always remember to keep those straws not being used immediately covered during working operations to keep them damp. This damping operation is necessary for all types of dollies being made as it renders them pliable for use.

METHOD

(a) Take five dampened straws and tie together tightly with a strong linen thread at the five ends using a clove-hitch knot for preference *(fig 2)*.
(b) With the short ends held between the left hand thumb and middle fingers, bend four of the straws down at right angles and bend the fifth straw right so that it is on top of straw 1 *(fig 3)*.
(c) Taking straw 1, move it under straw 5 and towards straw 4 *(fig 4)*.
(d) Bend straw 1 up and over straw 5 very closely so that it now lies beside straw 2 *(fig 5)*.
(e) Whilst holding these two straws together with the right hand, release the grip with your left and turn the whole thing clockwise so that you are back at the beginning again—*(as in fig 3 when straw 5 was lying over straw 1—the starting position)*.
(f) Repeat the operations using straw 2 this time, and then straw 3, etc., etc., using each straw in turn.

You will see that a definite shape begins to arise *(fig 6)*, which is a spiral consisting of a square section. The size of the square section will be seen to determine the size of the whole work and can be increased or decreased to the fancy of the craftsman and it is this variance that gives this particular dolly its character. To increase the diameter of the spiral (i.e. by increasing the square section) you simply place the moving straw at the right of the straw it kinks over *(figs 7 and 8)*. However, should you wish to keep the work of a uniform size, it is advisable to work around a round object such as a pencil.
ADDING STRAWS: If you are re-working a dolly of some size, or if one or more of your straws snaps or fractures, you just simply cut off that particular straw at the corner of the square section and insert the new straw into the old one, pushing it in as far as it will go—then simply carry on working.

The corn neck
This is basically the five-straw plait worked round a bundle of straws with the ears still intact (fig 9) or round a core and a head of ears inserted afterwards. You will need for this some Sellotape and florist wire 12 inches long as well as your straw.

METHOD

(a) Insert one piece of wire down a straw and around this, bind another six straws about $\frac{1}{2}$-inch further along the wired straw, each in turn so that you form a taper, using the cellotape as a binder. Insert more straws down the centre of the taper until you have a nice firm taper as a mould *(fig 10)*. Finally wedge a fat pencil down the centre—this is to create a hole for the head to be inserted into later.
(b) Make another taper, only this time it should be about 6 inches long. This is known as the false 'tail' and is made simply to make the starting off of the plaiting easier.
(c) Now we begin the plaiting. Grade your straws into fine, medium and thick, and taking the finest first, use five straws and begin plaiting around the false tail. Do this for about 3 or 4 inches and then remove it and insert the real tail *(fig 11)*. As you work up to it (as close as you can) gradually work in the medium straws and then the thick nearest the top.
(d) When the top is reached, aim to have a good 6 inches of each straw left as there must be no joins at this stage. You can judge this when you are about 2 inches from the top. Remove the pencil, and poke down the hole, all that remains of your plaiting straw.
(e) To make the head *(fig 12)* take a bunch of the best ears you can find, tie them firmly together (best to bind with Sellotape) and then insert in the hole left by the pencil.
(f) To finish off, you can tie ribbon just below the neck to hang up the dolly. Also the thin end can be bent round into a hook which is the traditional shape for this dolly.

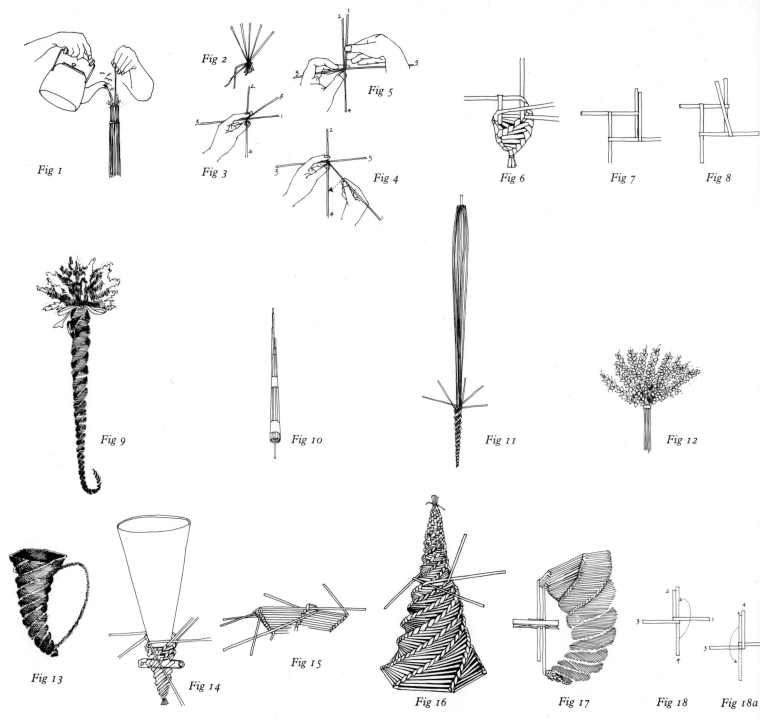

Fig 1

Fig 2

Fig 3

Fig 4

Fig 5

Fig 6

Fig 7

Fig 8

Fig 9

Fig 10

Fig 11

Fig 12

Fig 13

Fig 14

Fig 15

Fig 16

Fig 17

Fig 18

Fig 18a

The cornucopia

This again is plaiting round a cone but this time you use seven straws instead of five and you double plait; that is you work from the point of the cone to the open top and then double back again to the point. It is a more difficult dolly to make well, so take your time and don't worry if you can't do it properly at first *(fig 13)*.

METHOD

(a) Using thin cardboard, make a cone 6 inches deep with a hole 3 inches wide.

(b) Tie seven straws very tightly together and spread six of them out in an even circle with the seventh straw on top and to the right of the first straw.

(c) Using exactly the same principle as the five straw plait, work each straw in turn, the only difference being that you end up with a six-sided figure instead of four. When you have done a few turns, insert the cone and hold it in turn with a safety pin *(fig 14)*.

(d) When you reach the top, make sure you don't end up with any joins but have ample straw length to begin doubling back.

(e) Tend to work out at the top of the cone which will form the rim.

(f) To double back, simply take your working straw and bend it right round the adjacent straw instead of over it *(fig 15)* and back to the left to be beside this straw.

(g) Turn the whole thing upside down and plait back to the start, tying the ends very tightly on finishing and removing the cone *(fig 16)*.

(h) Insert six of the seven straws (now at the point and tied through the dolly) through the bottom of the cone and into the centre which forms a neat finish. If you have a lot of straw length left, shorten each one to about 3–4 inches.

(i) Dampen the dolly and bend it to a bow shape very slightly and then, using the seventh straw, insert it through the bottom of the cone and back up, fixing it with a peg *(fig 17)*. At the same time, pull the straw into a tighter bow shape. Allow to dry.

(j) After drying, cut off the seventh straw and make a length of four straw plaiting and tie at both ends to hang up your dolly. The method of the four straw plait is as follows.

The four straw plait

This is a finishing plait and can be used for hanging your dollies up as loops or ends.

METHOD

(a) You must have long straws for this and fine straws at that. Tie them up at the fine end and spread them out at right angles in an even circle.

(b) As in *fig 3*, bend straw 4 over straw 1 to lie beside straw 2.

(c) Bend straw 2 down over straw 3 to take the empty place left by straw 4 *(fig 18 and 18a)*.

(d) Turning the whole thing round one quarter of a circle clockwise, repeat the procedure.

(e) Carry on working until you reach the required length.

SOURCES OF MATERIALS

For those of you who may have difficulty obtaining the right sort of straw, there is now a substitute on the market which will be suitable to practice with until the right materials become available. The substitute is a long drinking straw which sells at approximately £1 for 2,000, available from :

SWEETHEART STRAWS, College Road, Fishponds, Bristol.

BIBLIOGRAPHY

CORN DOLLIES AND HOW TO MAKE THEM, by L. Sandford and P. Davis/Hereford FWI.
DECORATIVE STRAW WORK, by L. Sandford and P. Davis/B. T. Batsford Ltd.
A GOLDEN DOLLY: THE ART, HISTORY AND MYSTERY OF CORN DOLLIES, by M. L. Lambert/John Baker (Publishers) Ltd.
MAKING CORN DOLLIES, by Emmie White/available from the author at High Willows, Vineyards Road, Northaw, Potters Bar, London EN6 4PE.

COURSES

WEST DEAN COLLEGE, Chichester, Sussex: *Provides short courses on corn collies and decorative straw-work.*

CORN-DOLLY CRAFT STUDIOS TO VISIT

MRS P. ELAM, 'Gleanings', Rectory Lane, Ashdon, Saffron Walden. Tel Ashdon 344
Maker of traditional and modern corn dollies.
Living on the premises. Visitors welcome at any reasonable hour.

ANGELA GIBSON, 9 Park Street (rear entrance), Stow-on-the-Wold GL54 1AQ. Tel. Stow 30259
Corn dollies. Modern and traditional, from small favours to large Corn Maidens. Member of the Craftsmen of Gloucestershire.
Please write or telephone for appointment.

WINIFRED NEWTON-SEALEY, NDD, Straw Plaiter, Perton Croft, Stoke Edith, Hereford
Traditional corn dollies and cut straw work.
Most times.

JAQUIE BAKER, 54 The Avenue, Yeovil. Tel. Yeovil 22751
Traditional and modern corn dollies—special designs to order.
Any time by appointment, just off dual carriageway, behind hospital.

JAN WILKINS, Mullions, South Street, Walton Street
Corn dollies and straw work. Variety of traditional and modern designs, including: Cornucopia, Corn Maiden, Welsh Fan, Yorkshire Spiral, Staffordshire Knot, Horseshoes, earrings and lavender dollies. Any particular design, large or small made to order. Member of the Somerset Guild of Craftsmen.
Resident. Visitors welcome.

TINA PEACOCK, The Willows, Earl Soham, Woodbridge IP13 7SA (3 miles from Bramlingham). Tel. Earl Soham 418
Traditional and modern corn dollies including Suffolk Horseshoe and Whip, Norfolk Lantern, Essex Terret, Cambridge Umbrella, Shepherd's Crook, Cornucopia, bells, rattles, fans, stars and angels.
Visitors welcome but telephone first please!

Collecting Shells & How To Use Them

Within the British Isles alone there are about 350 different types of shells to be found, the colour, pattern and shape of each varying immensely. Every venture into the countryside or to the seashore may yield new specimens or exciting variations within each variety.

The inland shell most likely to be found will belong to the snail family and there are about 40 different types of these. Although most of them will be found between April and December, it is not unusual to pick up specimens at most times of the year. Unless you enjoy killing creatures (which we hope sincerely you don't) your collection will rely on empty shells which are mostly to be found amongst rubbish heaps, tree roots and under leaves and logs etc.

With regard to salt-water shells, there will invariably be a dozen or more types to be found on any stretch of coastline. Rockpools are often a veritable treasure trove, as well as high-tide lines on the beach and underneath seaweed patches.

You may feel that the shells you have

collected are beautiful as they are, kept perhaps in a nice box or jar, in which case read no further. But for those who may like to make something out of the shells, there are lots of ways to incorporate them, whether it be for jewellery, trinkets or purely decorative purposes. Most examples of shell craft tend to be found in trashy souvenir shops in Margate or Blackpool, but there are superb examples of shell craft in many of our museums such as the Victoria & Albert and the British Museum, as well as the odd folk museum around the country. The thing is to get around and have a look at as many examples as possible, for in this way, you will collect ideas for your own work.

USING THE SHELLS

Never use damaged shells but select only complete unbroken specimens. It is also advisable to sort them out into types and sizes, keeping them separately in bags or, preferably, boxes. When actually using the shells in a design, for example, a jewel box, it will be better to use groups of shells of the same type and size together, as they tend to look more effective this way. If all the shells are mixed up higgledy piggledy and stuck on ad-hoc, the results are not so good. Another good point to remember is that the shells must be stuck closely together when using the embedding technique, i.e. embedding the shells in a layer of plaster or 'Polyfiller'. With this method, boxes, flowerpots, candle holders, vases, lampstands and mirror surrounds etc., can be decorated. The shells can also be stuck on with a glue, such as 'Bostik'.

Whatever the object to be decorated, it must be cleaned so that the 'Polyfiller' will take to the surface. Mix up a good quantity of 'Polyfiller' and cover the surfaces to be decorated with a layer about $\frac{1}{8}$-inch thick. With boxes, or large objects it will be easy to do one side or one part at a time as the 'Polyfiller' may begin to go hard. The shells can now be embedded gently into the surface according to your own design. (It is a good idea to have the shells laid out ready in the design intended so that sticking them on correctly is made easier.) With very tiny shells, tweezers can be used to embed them in the surface.

When the filler is dry, a coat of clear varnish over the surface will greatly enhance the beauty of the finished object. Water-colour paint can be brushed on to add interest to the design if needs be, but this must be done before varnishing.

Other uses of shells include the making of jewellery such as necklaces, bracelets or individual shell brooches. With necklaces and bracelets, a tiny hole should be drilled in each shell so that a strong linen or wax thread can be passed through to string them together. For this purpose, there are a number of small drills available on the market. Great care must be taken when drilling as the shells will crack very easily. It will be found advantageous to hold them gently in a vice whilst drilling.

Clasps can be bought to finish off the necklace or bracelet, or they can be attached to a choker or strap.

SOURCES OF MATERIALS

Beaches:
A shingle beach will produce a good quantity of shells but only the sandy patches may have perfect specimens as shells easily become broken when lying amongst pebbles. Some suitable specimens to look out for are as follows :
THE AUGER SHELL (Turritella communis).
THE BLUE-RAYED LIMPET (Patina pellucida): a greenish-grey shell with vibrant blue spots, usually found amongst seaweed off-shore.
THE ELEPHANTS' TUSK SHELL (Dentalium entalis): a lovely long tusk-shaped shell, usually white and about 30 mm long.
THE EUROPEAN COWRIE (Trivia monacha): a lovely spotted shell up to 10 mm across in size.
THE FLAT TOP (Gibbula umbilicalis): a dark red shell, striped with grey.
THE ROUGH WINKLE (Littorina saxatilis): a common shell, usually brown, white or yellow and occasionally marked with darker bands.
THE SLIPPER LIMPET (Crepidula fornicata): a mottled pink and brown shell, white inside.
THE THIN TELLIN (Tellina tenuis): an orange, white and pink shell.
THE TROUGH SHELL (Mactra corallina).
THE WEDGE SHELL (Donax vittatus).
THE WENTLETRAP (Clathrus clathrus).

The following list gives stretches of seashore where a good variety of marine shells can be found :
ALLONBY BAY, Cumberland.
ABERDEEN BAY, East Lothian.
ABERLADY BAY, East Lothian.
BANGOR, Caenarvon.
BLACKWATER ESTUARY, Essex.
BLYTH, Northumberland.
BORTH, Cardigan.
CAMBER SANDS, Sussex.
CREAGORRY, Hebrides.
CROMER, Norfolk.
CRACKINGTON HAVEN, Cornwall.
DRIGG, Cumberland.
EASTBOURNE, Sussex.
GAIRLOCH, Ross and Cromarty.
HARLECH, Merioneth.
KISHORN, Ross and Cromarty.
MARLOES SANDS, Pembrokeshire.
NEWPORT, Pembrokeshire.
NEWQUAY, Cornwall.
PORT ST MARY, Isle of Man.
PORT ERIN, Isle of Man.
PETERHEAD, Aberdeenshire.
SALCOMBE, Devon.
SANDEND BAY, Banff.
SCILLY ISLES (St Martins Flats, St Mary's Rocks, Tresco Sands).
SCARBOROUGH, Yorkshire.
SENNEN COVE, Cornwall.
ST ANTHONY, Cornwall.
SHELL BAY, Dorset.
STUDLAND BAY, Dorset.
TONGUE, Sutherland.
TOR BAY, Devon.
WEYMOUTH, Devon.
WHITBY, Yorkshire.
WHITSTABLE, Kent.
ROBIN HOOD BAY, Yorkshire.
PORTHCURNO, Cornwall.
ALNMOUTH, Northumberland.

Inland Water Areas:
Apart from the seashore and estuaries, other sources of shells are rivers, lakes and canals. Areas of water such as reservoirs, gravel pits and the Norfolk Broads are perfect for searching out freshwater species. Look out for the following :
THE BLADDER SNAIL (Physa fontinalis).
THE COMMON BITHYNIA (Bithynia tentaculata).
THE DWARF POND SNAIL (Lymnaea truncatula).
THE EAR POND SNAIL (Lymnaea auricularia).
THE FRESHWATER NERITE (Theoduxus fluviatilis).
THE HORNY ORB SHELL (Sphaerium corneum).
THE LAKE LIMPET (Acroloxus lacustris).
LEACH'S BITHYNIA (Bithynia leachii).
THE MARSH SNAIL (Lymnaea palustris).
THE RIVER LIMPET (Ancylus fluviatilis).
THE WANDERING POND SNAIL (Lymnaea peregra).

Inland Habitats:
There are five main areas of habitat where land snails are best sought :
(a) HEDGEROWS Old tree stumps and beneath shrubs and leaves will always produce one or two species.
(b) WOODS Mixed woods will provide a greater variety of snails than other types of woods, such as those featuring only one species of tree, i.e. pine wood, birch wood.
(c) DOWNS Found living amongst the grass and low growing perennials.
(d) GARDENS A number of 'wild' snails can often be found in the garden, some of which live mainly underground while others live beneath low growing perennials such as the plants featured in rockeries.
(e) ROCKS AND WALLS.

Look out for the following species :
THE COMMON SNAIL (Helix aspersa).
THE DOOR SNAIL (Clausilium): cigar-shaped shells varying from fawn-grey to brown in colour.
THE GARDEN SNAIL (Helix hortensis): a pale yellow shell with darker coloured bands.
THE KENTISH SNAIL (Monacha cantiana): a whitish shell often tinged with red.
THE GLASS SNAIL (Retinella and Oxychilus): whitish almost transparent shells.
THE GROVE SNAIL (Helix nemoralis): varies between fawn, pink and yellow with darker bands.
THE ROCK SNAIL (Pyramidula rupestris): a deep brown to dark grey, tiny shell.
THE ROUNDED SNAIL (Discus rotundatus): a brown shell with red patches.
THE STRAWBERRY SNAIL (Hygromia striolata): a reddish brown shell sometimes varying to white.

THE TREE SNAIL (Balea perversa): a fawn grey shell.

Apart from picking them up yourself, shells may be bought from the following people :

AFRASIAN ARTCRAFTS, 2 Kneesworth Street, Royston, Hertfordshire.

ARTS & CRAFTS, 10 Bryam Street, Huddersfield, Yorkshire.

CLARISSA CLARKE, Ruxley, Rectory Road, North Fambridge, Chelmsford.

THE EATON BAG CO. LTD, 16 Manette Street, London W1.

THE NATURAL HISTORY MUSEUM, Godshill, Isle of Wight.

SAROGNY ART PRODUCTS, 11 Craneford Way, Twickenham, Middlesex.

KOLLECTA SHELL, 4 Melrose Avenue, Bristol.

SHANTY SHELL PRODUCTS, 173 The Headrow, Leeds 1, Yorkshire.

THE SHELL SHOP, 7 Totnes Road, Paignton, Devon.

TURKWISE MAIL ORDER SUPPLIES, 7 Totnes Road, Paignton, Devon.

WORLD OF NATURE, Knaresborough.

Winkle shells, mussel and other scallop shells, as well as cockleshells, can be got for nothing from certain fishmongers. Try out your local man.

SOCIETIES

CONCHOLOGICAL SOCIETY, c/o Hon. Sec., Mrs E. B. Rands, 51 Wychwood Avenue, Luton, Bedfordshire LU2 7HT.

CONCHOLOGY SOCIETY OF GREAT BRITAIN & IRELAND, 58 Teignmouth Road, London NW2.

BIBLIOGRAPHY

JOURNAL OF CONCHOLOGY, Conchological Society, c/o 51 Wychwood Avenue, Luton, Bedfordshire LU2 7HT.

BRITISH BIVALVE SHELLS, by N. Tebble/The British Museum.

BRITISH FRESHWATER BIVALVE MOLLUSCS, by A. E. Ellis/The Linnean Society.

BRITISH SHELLS, by Nora McMillan/Frederick Warne & Co. Ltd.

COLLECTING SEA SHELLS, by F. D. Ommanney/Arco Publications Ltd.

COLLECTING SHELLS, by Stella Turk/W. & G. Foyle Ltd.

COMMON BRITISH SEA SHELLS, by W. S. Forsyth/A. & C. Black Ltd.

DISCOVERING SEA SHELLS, by Barry Charles/Shire Publications Ltd, 12B Temple Square, Aylesbury, Buckinghamshire.

HOW TO MAKE THINGS FROM THE BEACH, by John Portchmouth/Studio Vista.

KEY TO THE BRITISH FRESH AND BRACKISH WATER GASTROPODS, by T. T. Macan/The Freshwater Biological Association, Ferry House, Far Sawrey, Ambleside, Westmorland.

LIFE ON THE SEASHORE, by A. J. Southward/Heinemann Ltd.

MOLLUSCS, by H. Janus/Burke Publishing Co. Ltd.

POCKET GUIDE TO THE SEASHORE, by J. Barret and C. M. Yonge/Collins, Sons & Co. Ltd.

THE SEA SHORE, by C. M. Yonge/Collins, Sons & Co. Ltd.

THE SHELL BOOK OF BEACHCOMBING, by Tony Soper/David & Charles Ltd.

SHELL COLLECTING, AN ILLUSTRATED HISTORY, by S. Peter Dance/Faber & Faber Ltd.

SHELL LIFE, by Edward Step/Frederick Warne & Co. Ltd.

SHELL-LIFE AND SHELL COLLECTING, by S. B. Murray/Avenel.

YOUR BOOK OF SHELL COLLECTING, by L. W. Stratton/Faber & Faber Ltd.

SHELLCRAFT STUDIOS TO VISIT

'SHELLCRAFT by Kay Wilson', 'DRIFTWOOD SCULPTURE by Karen Wilson'. Mary's Cottage, Vicarage Lane, Frodsham, Cheshire. Tel. Frodsham 33375

Wide selection of animals made from British shells. Abalone shell jewellery. Tropical shells for collectors. Driftwood collection includes bracelets, pendants, cuff-links and rings, etc.

Open 11 am–5 pm except Thursday, advisable to phone first. Enquiries by letter (enclose S.A.E.).

SEA CREATURES (John Aitchison), 'West Winds', Burnmouth, Eyemouth, 200 yards off A1 at Burnmouth, road no. 1107, Berwickshire, Scotland. Tel. Ayton 283

Real shellfish preserved for ornaments and displays, lobster, hermit, spider, green crabs, etc., world-wide shells, mother-of-pearl, tropical shell and gemstone jewellery.

MUSEUMS TO VISIT

The following list gives museums which contain important and interesting collections of shells, as well as specimens of shellcraft and curios. You may have to enquire to view any specific collection which isn't on public display :

BATH, Victoria Art Gallery and Municipal Galleries, 18 Queen Square.

BIRMINGHAM: University Museum and City Museum.

BRIGHTON: Art Gallery and Museum, The Royal Pavilion, Church Street.

BRISTOL: City Museum, Queens Road.

BRITISH MUSEUM (Natural History): Cromwell Road, SW7.

CAMBRIDGE: University Museum of Zoology, Downing Street.

CARDIFF: National Museum of Wales.

DEVIZES: Devizes Museum, Long Street.

DUBLIN: National Museum of Ireland, Kildare Street.

EDINBURGH: Royal Scottish Museum.

EXETER: Exeter Museum.

GLASGOW: Department of Zoology, The University.

LEEDS: City Museum, Municipal Buildings.

LEWES: Lewes Museum.

LINCOLN: City Library, Free School Lane.

LIVERPOOL: City Museum, William Brown Street.

MANCHESTER: The Museum, The University.

NEWCASTLE-UPON-TYNE: Hancock Museum, Claremont Road.

NOTTINGHAM: University Museum.

OXFORD: University Museum.

PAISLEY: Paisley Museum and Art Gallery.

PLYMOUTH: City Museum and Art Gallery.

PORTSMOUTH: Natural History Department, Cumberland House, Eastern Parade, Southsea.

RYDE, ISLE OF WIGHT: Shell Museum, Binstead Hill.

SALFORD: Science Museum, Buile Hill Park, Pendleton.

SCARBOROUGH: Museum of Natural History, Wood End, The Crescent.

TENBY: The Museum, Castle Hill.

WARRINGTON, Warrington Museum.

Starting a Pottery

It isn't difficult to set up a full-time pottery using local materials and improvised equipment.[1] After all, the pre-industrial potters did just that, and in many ways it's easier now than it was then. Appreciation of hand-made ware is high in this country, and centralized industry is now so inefficient that your prices may compare surprisingly well with the mass-produced (and lifeless) article. Some of the wasted material of industry can be put to good use in your workshop.

A large workshop is pleasant but not essential: it is not impossible to make a living in a shed 10 feet by 15 feet (I do). If you want to make large pots you need a larger workshop, but it must be frost-proof in winter. Medieval potters only made and fired pots in the summer months: the Winter was spent digging and weathering clay. In Winter, the wet pots would be frosted or else they would not dry out quickly enough. Also, kiln sites became waterlogged and fuel, which needed to be tinder-dry, would only be in that condition in the summer months.

CLAY The arguments for using a local clay are overwhelming: two to five hard days digging with a friend will yield a year's supply of clay. Every clay is unique, and a new pottery started on a new clay will produce a distinctive local ware, unique without gimmickery. Also, local diggers do not despoil the countryside, as do the big firms which sell clay; so there are spiritual reasons for digging it, too.

PROSPECTING Useable potting clay is to be found on the surface in almost every county in Britain, and is to be had for nothing. To find it, consult local people such as farmers, ditch-diggers, and builders, etc. Brickyards indicate the presence of clay and will often give, or sell large quantities very cheaply. Consult local libraries, archaeological societies (for kiln sites are always on clay) and geologists. There are also geological maps and surveys of your area. Explore fast-running streams, quarry floors, cuttings, post-holes and toppled tree roots for clay is as likely on hillsides as in valleys.

TESTING Clay is not always soft when dug. Any material which becomes sticky when wetted, and can be kneaded with a little water into a plastic mass, should be test fired. For this, charm a local art teacher or headmaster. Fire thin bars of the material, supported at each end, until they bend from the heat and record the temperature. This may be your eventual glazing temperature. Failing a school kiln, try a blowlamp, but gently at first.[2]

Explosions of the sample indicate too fast heating, *not* bad clay. Record temperatures with miniature cones.[3] When cool, the clay should be dense and hard; if it is porous and easily scratched, fire it higher. If it is hard but blistered, fire it to a lower temperature. As a last resort, send me a small sample with an exact map reference.

Always aim to fire your finished pottery as high as it will go, in order to develop its maximum strength. Surface clays mature at 1,000°C to 1,100°C, to make 'earthenware', but you may be lucky enough to find one which will go much higher: 1,200°C or more, to give you 'stoneware'. Such clays are usually found in or around coalfields (N.B. a coalfield does not necessarily contain any coalmines), and if you are near one it is worth a thorough search.

Clay is often thrown out on the spoil heaps of coal mines, however, or perhaps you can persuade the local mining authorities to get you some. Clays which seem very slimy and crack or warp badly when drying, may be improved by adding up to 20% of local lime-free sand. Clays which are 'short', i.e. crumbly and non-plastic, can often be made workable by additions of bentonite (up to 7%) or 'ball clay' (up to 30%) and long ageing or 'souring'.

DIGGING Wherever you get your clay, be sure you can get more later. Take off the turf, topsoil and subsoil and put them aside separately. Take the clay as soon as it looks clean, and reject any material which looks different from the rest. When finished, refill the hole immediately with local rubbish, replace the soils and turf in their correct order leaving a 'tump' to settle. Plant a tree as a marker and never leave open holes. A hole about 10 feet by 6 feet deep, excavated and refilled in 2 days by 2 men, will yield several tons of clay.

TREATMENT OF CLAY Ideally, clay-making has a yearly cycle: dig at Christmas, weather 3 months, paddle and seive, settle 3 months, sour

---

[1] *This chapter was written for us by a potter, Peter Brown, of The Snake Pottery, Green Street Cottage, Cam Green, Dursley, Gloucestershire GL11 5HW, and we are extremely grateful to him for all the work he has put in on our behalf.*

[2] See: *A Potter's Book*, by Bernard Leach/Faber & Faber, p. 245, for a description of a simple blowlamp test kiln.

[3] Ibid.

for 6 months. (The paddle used should have several 5 inch long lines of $\frac{1}{4}$ inch diameter mild steel projecting out of the bottom for maximum efficiency.) But to begin with you will have to shorten this process to get some useable clay quickly. Few clays are clean enough to use when dug, so you will probably have to puddle-and-sieve to remove grit and lime particles, as follows. First weather your clay (artificially if you are in a hurry by alternately drenching and drying it), turning it with a shovel after each frost. Next, soak in a tub of water (for small quantities in a hurry, hot water), stirring with a paddle to a creamy 'slip'. Pour from a height through a 40-mesh potters' sieve, then leave it to settle for as long as possible. This process may seem laborious at first but with practice it takes up only a few hours a month. For those clays that are clean, tread them with a little water on a firm floor until they are plastic.

The next job is drying the slip, and this is often a bottleneck. Syphon off the water and dump the slurry into large earthenware flower-pots, or boxes made from porous tiles, to dry in the wind. For larger quantities of stiffer slurry, the job is best done in a box built of unmortared common bricks, standing on legs in an exposed place. Any leaks can be stopped with clay from the inside. (Frost will help this device to work, whereas it cracks flowerpots.) In Winter the slip can be alternately frozen and thawed in metal containers and this method is very efficient.

Finish it off on large plaster slabs and store it in bins away from the frost. (For small quantities in a hurry, pour the slip on to newspaper, then plaster.)

POT-MAKING Knead your clay thoroughly

just before use. Beautiful, saleable dishes may be made by rolling out or slicing clay $\frac{1}{4}$ inch to $\frac{1}{2}$ inch thick on hessian or plaster, and laying it into 'depression' moulds or over hump moulds. Allow it to stiffen and then decorate with contrasting slips.

Many other pots can be made without a potters' wheel, but for sheer productive power the wheel beats even modern automation. If you lack the skill, enrol at an evening institute and behave like a fanatic. Refuse anything but an electric (that's important) wheel; squash up everything you make; eat and sleep and think 'throwing' for about two months and you may then have enough skill to continue on your own.

MAKING A WHEEL This is easy. Although you will learn quickest on an electric wheel, the crudest kickwheel will start you off in your own workshop, but avoid the crack-and-treadle type (unless you are given one). Good designs for a crude wheel running on a single post are given in David Green's book (listed in the bibliography, p. 34), and here is a description of a solid wheel I have used. Take any fairly straight, sound stick 2 inches or more thick and about 3 feet long, and sharpen the bottom to a rounded point. Fill a recessed wine-bottle with cement, up-end it firmly in the ground and fill the recess with grease. This forms the bottom bearing.

Next, fix a heavy flywheel about $2\frac{1}{2}$ to 3 feet in diameter to the stick, about 6 inches from the pointed end. Any wheel with a centre hole larger than the stick may be secured true-running with wedges all around. Wedge it from above and below, and nail wedges to the stick. Best of all, a reinforced concrete flywheel can easily be cast onto the stick, by driving it into the ground plumb upright, and carefully excavating a 'mould' around it about $2\frac{1}{2}$ feet in diameter, the floor of which should be dead level. Drive some large nails halfway into the stick in the area of the casting, check for uprightness, put some reinforcing (wire netting, fencing wire etc.) in place and pour in concrete to a depth of 5 or 6 inches. Leave this for at least a week, protected from frost if necessary. Then, raising it with great care, ease it into place over the bottle. Next, rough

carve or file a top bearing area on the stick as true as you can, just below the top. Now drive in four strong stakes around the wheel and fix rigid cross-pieces, with carved 'clamps' to accommodate the top bearing. Face these with hard leather, anoint them with grease and tighten until the assembly just turns freely.

Make a wheel-head from two pieces of 1-inch plank clinch-nailed together with the grain crossed, or from two discs of thick plywood. Attach this securely to top of the stick with brackets, taking care that it runs true.

Make your pots on removable asbestos tiles (bats) which attach to this wheelhead. This way you will have no trouble removing your pots after throwing.

This type of wheel is turned by kicking the top surface of the flywheel while sitting with your behind at wheelhead level.

More sophisticated bearings are better if you can get them—I'm told a car axle with wheel is very good. A 1-inch diameter steel shaft through a greased hardwood hole, with the bottom point resting on a dented (old) penny, will never wear out.

Electric wheels are expensive to buy. A simple but first-class electric wheel can be made easily from standard industrial parts at a cost of about £35 including the motor. I will send a copy of the plans (free) to anyone who sends me a stamped addressed envelope.

FIRING YOUR POTS The potter's worst problem is the large amount of energy needed for firing, and in the past they have been guilty of deforestation. The ideal solution is a waterwheel driving a dynamo, but until you are given a watermill you will have to make do with something less perfect. (At a rough estimate, an average waterwheel generating continuously for, say, 3 small kilns heated in rotation, could fire the output of 2 or more potters, with power left over for machinery. Workshops would be heated by the cooling kilns. In time, such local sources of energy may become a necessity for small workshops.) If your conscience allows you to make use of waste wood, then vast amounts of off-cuts may be had for nothing from local sawmills, where they are otherwise burnt as rubbish. Get as much coniferous wood as you can. You will

need more wood than you think for a firing, and you must dry it thoroughly before use. It is the traditional potters' fuel, it gives wonderful results and great satisfaction, but is very laborious. There are, however, good alternatives to wood which are as follows:

OIL involves very much less labour in use. It costs much less than electricity, and lends itself to improvisation more than gas.

GAS, both piped and bottled, is economical for potters.

ELECTRICITY is expensive, convenient, trouble-free and quite, quite soulless. (I use it, but many potters despise it.)

PEAT is a possible fuel if you can dig it, and if you can invent a burner which will cope with sawdust you'll fire cheaply.

KILNS You will have to decide which fuel you are using before building the kiln.

Although it is possible to fire pottery in holes in the ground or even in bonfires, to make a saleable ware it is necessary to make a fairly respectable kiln, lined with firebricks and built to a plan. The down-draught type is by far the best.

Vast quantities of used firebricks are thrown on industrial tips ($1\frac{1}{2}$ million tons a year in Britain) and large amounts can be had for nothing if you know where to go. Try foundries, demolished brickworks and scrapyards in industrial towns where they are just regarded as rubbish. Learn to recognise a firebrick and distinguish the various types: all firebricks are light in colour, yellow or pinkish, though some have dark spots all over them. They never have a 'frog' like building bricks do. The solid ones are very heavy, but you may be lucky enough to find 'insulating' firebricks, which are porous and light in weight and quite soft. These are particularly valuable to the potter, as a kiln lined with insulating bricks may cut down the use of fuel by half.

It is possible to make fairly good insulating firebricks if you have time. Take five parts (by volume) of sawdust, and mix it *very thoroughly* with four parts of 'N6 fireclay, ground 16's down', and one part of 'crude grog $\frac{1}{8}$ inch to dust'. (The last two items are available cheaply from Potclays Ltd, see p. 33.) Mix in enough water to make a dryish dough, and press it into a frame measuring about $6 \times 6 \times 4$ inches deep. To help drying, make nine equally-spaced holes $\frac{1}{2}$ inch in diameter going about two-thirds of the way down, before pressing or shaking each brick out of the frame on to a board. Turn them frequently when drying. When thoroughly dry, stack the bricks in a loose 'chequer' and build a simple, temporary kiln around them with bricks, carefully sealed with a sand and mud mixture. Seal over the top but leave a hole for some sort of chimney. (This

can be supported by angle-irons across the top, provided you arrange for them not to get too hot.) Leave two fireholes at the bottom (if you use solid fuel remember to dig a large fire pit for the embers) and fire the stack slowly and thoroughly, *getting it as hot as you can*. Nothing less than bright red heat (1,000°C) is any good. You may have to re-shuffle and re-fire when the stack has cooled, as up-draught kilns are notorious for uneven heating. (Oil is probably

the best fuel for this job.)

For really first-class insulation, build your actual potting kiln as follows:

The outside skin should consist of 9 inches of common brick; then a 5-inch cavity, then your home-made firebricks. A mortar of 4 parts sawdust, 2 parts grog, 3 parts N6 is used to set the bricks. The firebricks are laid *on edge*, with the perforated side facing the cavity. Fix 'bridge' bricks across the cavity at intervals to stabilise the structure, and fill the cavity as follows. Put some vermiculite into a tub and mix with it a small quantity of N6 fireclay, then a small quantity of water, until the vermiculite will just bind if compressed in the hand. Fill the cavity with this mixture, lightly pressing it down. At the top of the wall you must bridge the cavity solidly all round to support the roof arch or dome. Make the roof arch from cones of insulating firebrick about 4 inches long, 2 inches in diameter at one end and $2\frac{1}{4}$ inches at the other, or square if you wish. Cover the arch with 6 inches or more of the vermiculite mixture, then asbestos (no bricks) and protect it from the weather. The outside of this structure will remain stone cold throughout a firing and I bring my own kiln to 1,150°C with only 2 cwt of wood.

Temporary small kilns may be built from common house bricks bonded with fireclay and this is adequate for an uncertain number of earthenware firings.

Electric kilns are best bought ready-made unless you are an electrician.

Begin with a small kiln, of say 1–2 cubic feet, which will allow you to experiment frequently without loosing too much ware. A small kiln in the workshop will keep you warm, and dry pots as it cools.

GLAZES The appeal of your pottery depends more than anything else on the quality of your glazes. When beginning, or passing through a bad patch, it is excusable, but expensive, to buy ready-made glazes. As soon as possible, progress to mixing your own recipes from ready-ground bought minerals, i.e. flint, feldspar and whiting, and thence to using the highest possible proportion of local materials in the glazes. But this process is an uphill job, *and must not be hurried on at the expense of glaze quality*.

If you fire to stoneware temperatures you may soon be able to use 100% local materials (cost nil!), but earthenware potters will be lucky to use 70%, the addition being a soft borax 'frit' to flux the glaze. Below 1,120°C you may also have to add increasing proportions of lead frit, but keep the proportion of this as low as you possibly can. (N.B. *on no account* use lead ore, 'galena', from local lead mines.)

LOCAL MATERIALS Wood ash of any kind is particularly good for stoneware glazes, and needs little preparation. Whether you make earthenware or stoneware, try quarry stone of any kind except slate. If the quarry has a crusher, ask to take away a few hundred-weight of the very fine powder (it must be fine) which accumulates under the machine. Find out what sort of rock it is and look up its chemistry. Gromite and other igneous rocks are useful, but tend to contain iron, giving only dark glazes. Igneous rocks will replace flint and feldspar in conventional recipes. Sandstones will replace flint (quarty), and limestones will replace whiting. Some limestones contain magnesium ('dolomite') which is good for stoneware.

Any very fine natural deposit may be usable, including fine sand or silt, marl (crumbly material), river mud (Severn River mud is very good), some impure fusable clays, and a few crystaline minerals (in particular feldspar if you can find it) but *not* galena or barytes. Useful small pockets of volcanic ash, lava or pumice occur in many counties.

At the lower temperatures, say below 1,050°C, the proportion of local material which can be melted falls away sharply. The best plan then is to raise the maturing temperature of your local clay by adding fireclay, or not more than 20% of china clay.

NOTE: Always 'biscuit low, glaze high', as the old potters did. Fire your ware standing upright on the shelf, on sand. Fire as high as your clay will go, and counter any distortion by heavy ribbing and curving shapes. If you can use the 3-pointed stilts beloved of art-schools, then you are not firing high enough.

PIGMENTS Iron (brown, reds, yellows),

copper (blues, greens) and cobalt (blue) are the potter's main pigments. Stoneware potters get a whole range of colours from iron alone. Iron-rich rocks are fairly common. Copper oxide can be got by burning scrap copper wire in the kiln. Cobalt will have to be bought.

BALL MILL This is vital for the final grinding of glaze materials. It can be made fairly easily from two rubber-coated wringer rollers, mounted 6 inches apart and running freely in wood or brass bearing-holes. Attach a bicycle wheel to the end of one and drive it with a 'belt' of cord from a $\frac{1}{4}$ h.p. motor. The jar, which can be a glass wine jar, a small hooped wooden barrel or a polythene or stoneware jar, etc., is filled with water, any hard pebbles from the beach (but not slate stones), and the material to be ground. The jar turns on the rollers for 12 hours.

BLUNGER A rotary paddle driven *slowly* by a $\frac{1}{4}$ h.p. motor mounted on the lid of a large waterbutt can do your clay puddling for you.

ROCK CRUSHER This is immensely useful, but difficult to scrounge. Invent one (an eccentric and jaws housed inside a slotted oak log, powered by hand via heavy cast flywheel?).

MACHINERY The potter is able to salvage a great deal from the scrapheaps of the throwaway society. Cars, washing-machines and so on yield many useful parts. In particular collect bearings, belts, pulleys and quiet electric motors of all sizes.

DOUGH MIXER This large machine is often thrown out by bakeries. It will mix and knead large quantities of clay.

WASHING MACHINES Old ones make excellent blungers and slip mixers.

CORN MILL Old hand-powered corn mills, once used by farmers, must be rusting in many barns. They are good for powdering clays, marls, and rock already small in preparation for the ball mill. A small mill, 'Atlas No. 1', may be bought at a reasonable price from Hunt & Co., Earls Colne, Essex.

SELLING YOUR POTS This is something the books never mention! Price your pots to give yourself a living wage, plus expenses, plus a margin for trouble. You will need to work hard to offer reasonable prices. One golden rule is to keep your work out of conventional shops, although this may be difficult at first. A lively and individual ware of good quality will sell itself, and direct contact with the customer can be a very valuable asset.

Should the need arise, some financial help can occasionally be got from CoSIRA (Council for Small Industries in Rural Area), 35 Camp Road, Wimbledon Common, London, SW19 (see p. 222 for grant information).

SOURCES OF MATERIALS

Most suppliers of pottery equipment charge highly for their products hence the reason for the chapter you have just read. However, many of these big firms produce excellent catalogues which often contain extremely useful information for the potter, such as glazing temperatures etc. Send off for a few and see.

ACME MARLS, Clough Street, Hanley, Stoke-on-Trent. *Sells kiln furniture.*

E. J. ARNOLD & Son Ltd, Butterfly Street, Leeds. *Sells kilns.*

BELLMAN, IVEY & CARTER, 110a Mill Lane, West Hampstead, London NW6. *Sells plaster, sieves, scrapers, pressers and tools.*

BIRCH ENGINEERING, 14 Ludgate Hill, Wotton-under-Edge, Gloucestershire. *Sells cone and disc drive Cotswold pottery wheels.*

BRITISH CERAMIC SERVICE CO. LTD, Bricesco House, 1 Park Avenue, Wolstanton, Newcastle, Newcastle, Staffs. *Sells kilns (electric).*

PETER BROWN, The Snake Pottery, Green Street Cottage, Cam Green, Dursley, Gloucestershire GL11 5HW. *Will supply a copy of the plans for a simple but good electric wheel. Free, but please enclose a S.A.E.*

CAFFERATA LTD, Newark-on-Trent. *Sells plaster.*

R. M. CATTERSON SMITH LTD, Adams Bridge Works, South Way, Exhibition Grounds, Wembley, Middlesex. *Sells electric kilns.*

THE CRAFTSMENT POTTERS ASSOCIATION, William Blake House, Marshall Street, London W1.

Sells potters' accessories and books.

CROMARTIE KILNS LTD, Dividy Road, Longton, Stoke-on-Trent. *Sells kilns, particularly cheap electric kilns.*

THE FULHAM POTTERY, 210 New Kings Road, London, SW6. *Sells potters' wheels, kilns clays, glazes and accessories.*

GIBBONS BROS LTD, Dibdale, Dudley, Worcestershire. *Sells gas kilns.*

HARRISON & SONS (HORNLEY LTD), Phoenix Chemical Works, Stoke-on-Trent. *Sells various materials for the potter.*

HARRISON MAYWE LTD (Craft & Education Division), Mier, Stoke-on-Trent. *Sells prepared clays, glazes, oxides, slip & glaze stains, kilns, kiln furniture and sundries.*

LEN HUXLEY, 30 Pyrton Lane, Watlington, Oxfordshire. *Sells individual craftsman-built electric potter's wheels designed by Bill Read.*

MILLS & HUBBALL LTD, Dept H, Victoria Rise, Clapham Common, London SW4. *Sells kilns and wheels.*

MOIRA POTTERY CO. LTD, nr Burton-on-Trent, Staffordshire. *Sells stoneware and tenacott, clays and glazes.*

PIKE FAYLE LTD, Wareham, Dorset. *Sells clays.*

PILLING POTTERY, School Lane, Pilling, Lancashire. *Sells potters' wheels, kilns, clay and sundries.*

PODMORE AND SONS, Caledonian Mills, Shelton, Stoke-on-Trent. *Sells clays and glazes, but service is sometimes slow.*

POTCLAYS LTD, Copeland Street, Stoke-on-Trent. *Sells clays.*

TIRANTI, 72 Charlotte Street, London W1. *Sells turntables, scrim and modelling tools.*

BERNARD WEBBER LTD, Webcote Works, Alfred Street, Fenton, Stoke-on-Trent. *Sells kilns, both electric and gas.*

WENGERS LTD, Etruria, Stoke-on-Trent. *Sells glaze materials, oxides, turntables, scrapers, pressers and tools.*

ROSEMARY & DENISE WREN, Potters Croft, Oakshade Road, Oxshott, Surrey. *Will supply introduction plans for a coke furnace.*

SOURCES OF MATERIALS IN THE USA

A. D. ALPINE, INC., 353 Coral Circle, El Segundo, California.

ALLEN STONEWARE, 2507 N. Randolph Street, (Box 3951) San Angelo, Texas 76901.

AL 'N' DOL CERAMICS, 9517 Georgia Avenue, Silver Spring, Maryland 20910.

ARTISTIC CERAMIC SHOPS, INC., 10201 W. Oklahoma Avenue, Milwaukee, Wisconsin 53227.

ART SHOP, 1410 Patterson Avenue, Levittown, Pennsylvania.

A.R.T. STUDIO, 3512 Church Street, Skokie, Illinois 60203.

BELTSVILLE CERAMICS, 11104 Baltimore Avenue, Beltsville, Maryland 20705.

BETTY'S CERAMIC STUDIO, 840 South Central, Lodi, California.

BLAKELEY CERAMIC STUDIO & SUPPLY INC., 1500 Evergreen Avenue, Pittsburgh, Pennsylvania.

BOB BRENT POTTERS WHEELS, 527 S. Fair Oaks Avenue, Pasadena, California.

ROBERT BRENT CO., 128 Mill Street, Healdsburg, California.

ELAINE CARPENZANO, 745 Rebecca Avenue, Pittsburgh, Pennsylvania.

CATHY'S CERAMICS, 983 Drake Avenue, Marin City, California.

CEE AND KAY CERAMIC STUDIO, Rehoboth Highway, Milford, Delaware.

CERAMIC CENTER, 95 Mitchell Boulevard, San Rafael, California.

CERAMICS AND THINGS, INC., 5585 Paradise Drive, Corte Madera, California.

CERAMIC WORLD, 13320 Wilkins Avenue, Rockville, Maryland 20853.

CHIN'S CRAFT CENTER, 511 Warwick Avenue, Warwick, Rhode Island 02888.

CLAY PEOPLE, 3345 N. Halsted, Chicago, Illinois 60657.

CLAY PIGEON, 707 E. 6th Avenue, Denver, Colorado 80203.

CLAY POTTERY WORKSHOP, 517 N. 6th Avenue, Tucson, Arizona.

CLAY SHOP, 4363 W. Charleston Boulevard, Las Vegas, Nevada 89102.

CROCKERY SHED & GAIL CHASE GALLERY, 10416 N.E. 17th Bellevue, Washington 98004.

RUTH CUTLER, Farmington Valley, Creative Arts Center, Avon Park North, Avon, Connecticut 06001.

DEE'S CERAMICS & CHINA STUDIO, 5244 Colfax, Lincoln, Nebraska 68504.

EASERN MARKET POTTERY, 7th and C. Sts. N.W.

33

Washington, D.C. 20003.

EARTHSHINE POTTERY, Box 474 AA R.F.D. 2 North Scituate 02857.

EXPRESSIONS CERAMIC WORKSHOP, Farmington Valley Creative Arts Center, Avon Park North, Avon, Connecticut, 06001.

MAGGIE JOHNSON, Farmington Valley Creative Arts Center, Avon Park North, Avon, Connecticut 06001.

SHARYN LEE CERAMICS, 5646 Annapolis Road, Blandesburg, Maryland 20710.

LEON'S CASA DE ARTE, 13001 Las Vegas Boulevard S., Las Vegas, Nevada 89119.

JOEL LIFSHIN POTTERY, 4109 N. 39th Street, Phoenix, Arizona.

LYN'S VILLAGE CERAMICS, 5632 Parking Street, Greendale, Wisconsin 53129.

MARCELLA'S CERAMICS, INC., 1150 Inman Parkway, Beloit, Wisconsin 53511.

MARSHALL CRAFT, 1031E. Duanne Avenue, Sunnyvale, California.

MILLIE'S TIFFANY SHADE GALLERY, 459 2nd Street, Country Square, Lake Oswego, Oregon 97034.

MUD PALACE, 8 North Main, Camden, Delaware.

INEZ NORMAN POTTERY STUDIO, 3613 Labadie Drive, Fort Worth, Texas 76118.

OLLA PODRIDA POTTERY WORKSHOP, Olla Podrida, 12205 Coit Road, Dallas, Texas 75240.

OUTER BANKS CRAFTS, Manteo, North Carolina.

PACIFICA CRAFTS, P.O. Box 1407, Ferndale, Washington.

OSCAR PAUL CORPORATION, 522 W. 182nd Street, Gardena, California.

PEG'S CERAMICS, Smyrna, Delaware.

THE POT SHOP, 356 Bowery, New York 10012.

POTTERS BROWN, P.O. Box 781, Edom, Texas 75756.

POTTERS STUDIO, 842 N. Fulton, Fresno, California.

POTTERS' WORKSHOP, Tom Burdett 1840 Clement, San Francisco, California.

JAMES RILEY, 2779 Hilgard Avenue, Berkeley, California.

WORDEN ROBINSON ART POTTERY, 715 8th Street, S.E. Washington, D.C. 20003.

ROVIN CERAMICS, 6912 Schaefer Road, Dearborn, Michigan.

SOLDNER POTTERY EQUIPMENT, P.O. Box 90,

Aspen, Colorado.

ISHMAEL H. SOTO STUDIO, 306 Eanes Road, Austin, Texas 78746.

NANCY SPINA'S CRAFTS, 280 Emerystone Terrace, San Rafael, California.

STEWART CLAY CO., INC., 133 Mulberry Street, New York.

TALLE DE LOZA CERAMIC STUDIO, 1451 So. La Canada, Green Valley, Arizona.

TAYLOR MAID CERAMICS, 4550 E. Kentucky, Denver, Colorado 80222.

TINA'S CERAMICS, 813 Grant Avenue, Novato, California.

V-R CERAMICS, RD 1, Hartley, Delaware.

WEST BANK POTTERY, 901 W. 10th Street, Austin, Texas 78703.

WESTWOOD CERAMIC SUPPLY CO., 14400 Lomitas Avenue, City of Industry, California.

WILLOYD ENTERPRISES, P.O. Box 1301, Boulder, Colorado 80302.

SOCIETIES

BRITISH CERAMIC RESEARCH ASSOCIATION, Queens Road, Penkull, Stoke-on-Trent, Staffordshire. *Research in all fields of ceramics.*

BRITISH CERAMIC SOCIETY, Shelton House, Stoke Road, Stoke-on-Trent, Staffordshire.

THE CRAFTSMEN POTTERS ASSOCIATION, William Blake House, Marshall Street, London W1. *Aims to encourage the production of creative ceramics. Members co-operate to sell their work as well as make themselves more widely known. The Association produces a bi-monthly illustrated magazine entitled 'Ceramic Review' which is both interesting and useful to anyone interested in the ceramic art.*

ORNAMENTAL POTTERY ASSOCIATION, Federation House, Station Road, Stoke-on-Trent.

STONEWARE POTTERS ASSOCIATION, Federation, 102 Friar Gate, Derby.

BIBLIOGRAPHY

CERAMIC DIGEST/Ceramic Digest Ltd, 34 Townsend Drive, St Albans, Hertfordshire. (Quarterly) Price: 15p.

CERAMIC REVIEW/The Craftsmen Potters Association, William Blake House, Marshall Street, London W1. (Bi-monthly.)

CERAMICS/Turret Press Ltd, 65–66 Turnmill Street, London EC1M 5RA. (Monthly) Annual subscription: £3.20.

POTTERY QUARTERLY/Murray Fieldhouse, Northfields Studio, Northfields, Tring, Hertfordshire. (Irregular) Price: £1.85 for 4 issues.

BEGINNERS' BOOK OF POTTERY, by H. Powell/ Blandford Press Ltd.

CARVING IN PLASTER OF PARIS, by Edward Phelps/Dryad Press.

CLAY & GLAZES FOR THE POTTER, by Daniel Rhodes/Pitman & Sons Ltd.

CREATIVE CLAY CRAFT, by E. Rottger/B. T. Batsford Ltd.

THE ENGLISH COUNTRY POTTER, by P. C. D. Brears/David & Charles Ltd.

ENGLISH SLIPWARE, by Dorothy Kemp/Faber & Faber Ltd.

EXPERIMENTING WITH POTTERY, by David Green/Faber & Faber Ltd.

KILNS, by Daniel Rhodes/Pitman & Sons Ltd.

MAKING POTTERY, by Judith & Roy Christie/

Penguin Books Ltd.
PIONEER POTTERY, by Michael Cardew/Longman Ltd. (*Recommended although expensive.*)
A POTTER'S BOOK, by Bernard Leach/Faber & Faber Ltd. (*A classic by one of Britain's greatest living potters.*)
THE POTTERY HANDBOOK OF CLAY, GLAZE & COLOUR, by Harold Powell/Blandford Press Ltd.
POTTERY IN THE MAKING, by Dora Lunn/Dryad Press.

POTTERY & THE ONCE-FIRED METHOD, by A. T. White/Dryad Press.
POTTERY: THE TECHNIQUE OF THROWING, by John Colbeck/B. T. Batsford Ltd.
POTTERY WITHOUT A WHEEL, by Keith Tyler/Dryad Press.
PRACTICAL POTTERY AND CERAMICS, by Kenneth Drake/Studio Vista.
SIMPLE POTTERY, by Kenneth Drake/Studio Vista.

SLIPCAST POTTERY, by A. T. White/Dryad Press.
THE TECHNIQUE OF POTTERY, by Dora M. Billington/B. T. Batsford Ltd.

Relevant Geological Publications

BRITISH REGIONAL GEOLOGY HANDBOOKS/ H.M.S.O. (*Rather technical.*)
GEOLOGICAL ORDNANCE SURVEY MAPS.
THE OBSERVER'S BOOK OF BRITISH GEOLOGY/ Warne.

COURSES

ADULT EDUCATION CENTRES *Check out which courses are available in London in* Floodlight Magazine.
BURLEIGHFIELD HOUSE, Lowdwater, Buckinghamshire. *Provides a whole range of pottery courses at various times during the year for both children and adults, and accommodation is available. Send for a catalogue.*
THE CAMDEN ARTS CENTRE, 54 Arkwright Road, London NW3. *Pottery classes are available at about £10 a year.*
THE CHELSEA POTTERY, 13 Radnor Walk, London SW3. *Offers complete facilities to both amateurs and professionals at a fee of £1 an hour, plus payment of a yearly membership fee. All materials and the cost of firing are extra.*
CLOCKHOUSE ART CENTRE, Bruiseyard, Saxmundham, Suffolk. *Provides courses in pottery for beginners.*
CRAFTS UNLIMITED, The Old Mill, Nannerch, nr Mold, Flintshire. *Provides 5-day courses in the summer for beginners.*
FOURNIER POTTERY, Lacock (266), Chippenham, Wiltshire. *Provides short summer courses specialising in bonfire, sawdust and raku firings.*
JO & GERRY HARVEY, Shroton Creative Workshops, Sheriffs Mead Shroton, Blandford, Dorset. *Provides 1-week courses for beginners, set in the glorious Dorset countryside.*
SUSAN MEYER-MICHAEL, 99 North End Road, London NW11. *This lady runs classes for both children and adults at just over £1 for 2 hours, usually on a Saturday but also weekdays by appointment.*
MOUNTAIN STUDIO, Penian Cwmdu, Crickhowell, Breconshire, Wales. *Provides courses from May to September for beginners and advanced students.*
PILLING POTTERY, c/o J. Cross, Pilling Pottery, Pilling, Preston, Lancashire. *Send S.A.E. for details of courses.*
RIDGE POTTERY, Douglas Philips, Ridge Pottery, Warmbrook, Chard, Somerset. *Provides short 5½-day courses in pottery and accommodation is available. Send for details.*
JOHN SOLLY, 36 London Road, Maidstone, Kent. *A weekly course for 7 students is run at varying times through the Summer and early Autumn, basically for beginners. The fee is about £16–£20. We understand that grants from local education authorities can be applied for.*
WEST DEAN COLLEGE, Chichester, Sussex. *The college provides courses at various levels of involvement.*

VOCATIONAL, DEGREE AND POST-GRADUATE COURSES

BATH ACADEMY OF ART, Corsham, Wiltshire.
BRISTOL POLYTECHNIC, Faculty of Art and Design, Clanage Road, Bower Ashton, Bristol BS3 2JU.
BOURNEMOUTH & POOLE COLLEGE OF ART, Royal London House, Lansdowne, Bournemouth.
CITY OF BIRMINGHAM POLYTECHNIC ART AND DESIGN CENTRE, Corporation Street, Birmingham B4 7OX.
CAMBERWELL SCHOOL OF ART AND CRAFTS, Peckham Road, London SE5.
CARDIFF COLLEGE OF ART, Howard Gardens, Cardiff CF2 1SP.
CENTRAL SCHOOL OF ART AND DESIGN, Southampton Row, London WC1.
CORNWALL TECHNICAL COLLEGE, REDRUTH SCHOOL OF ART, Clinton Road, Redruth.
CROYDON COLLEGE OF ART, College Road, Croydon, Surrey.
DERBY & DISTRICT COLLEGE OF ART, Kedleston Road, Derby.
GOLDSMITHS COLLEGE SCHOOL OF ART, New Cross, London SE14.
HAMMERSMITH COLLEGE OF ART AND BUILDING, Lime Grove, Shepherds Bush, London W12.
HARROW SCHOOL OF ART, Northwick Park, Harrow.
HORNSEY COLLEGE OF ART, Crouch End Hill, Hornsey, London N8.
CITY OF LEICESTER POLYTECHNIC, P.O. Box 143, Leicester.

Berkshire

ALDERMASTON POTTERY, Aldermaston. Tel. Woolhampton 3359
Tin-glazed decorated earthenware and lustre-ware, tableware, ovenware, tiles and individual pots.
9 am–6 pm week-days except Tuesday.

PAULINE THOMPSON, Ginge Brook Pottery, East Hendred. Tel. East Hendred 484
Hand-made pottery to fill any need—domestic or decorative.
Open to visitors by appointment. Please write or phone.

TOUCHEN END POTTERY (Bill & Laddie Akroyd), Touchen End, nr Maidenhead (3½ miles from Maidenhead on A330 to Ascot). Tel. Maidenhead 27680
Hand-made earthenware with coloured glazes—dinner-sets, coffee-sets, ramekins, jugs, bowls, vases, lamps, etc.
Open daily 10.30 am–6 pm except Mondays.

ANN WRIGHTSON, THE POTTERY, 11a Washington Road, Caversham, Reading. Tel. Reading 479344
Stoneware, slipware and majolica tableware, ovenware and individual pieces.
10 am–6 pm Monday to Friday.

MICHAEL & SHEILA CASSON, Pottery Workshop, High Street, Prestwood, Great Missenden. Tel. Great Missenden 2134
Stoneware, some porcelain, individual pieces, table and ovenware.
Shop open for sales: Saturday only (except by appointment). Every day during the month of December.

CLAYCUTTERS STUDIO (BILL & VICKI READ), Sheep Street, Winslow. Tel. Winslow 2663 (main A413 road)
Hand-made reduction fired stoneware. Domestic and individual pieces.
Showroom. Resident.

DANNY KILLICK, School House, Mentmore, nr Leighton Buzzard. Tel. Cheddington 668436
Hand-made pottery, stoneware, domestic ware and individual pieces.
Visitors welcome any time. Advisable to telephone first.

Cambridgeshire

ABINGTON POTTERY, 26 High Street, Little Abington (on road A604). Tel. Cambridge 891-723
Stoneware pottery by David Lane. Also a large selection of work by other East Anglian potters. Resident showroom open every day except Thursday. Abington pottery is available from their stall at Cambridge Market on Wednesdays and Thursdays.

'THE CRAFTSMAN', 15 Magdalene Street, Cambridge CB3 0AF. Tel. Cambridge 62515
Stoneware pottery made on premises adjacent to Craft Shop, on sale, together with varied and interesting crafts.
Visitors welcome. Open 6 days a week, 9 am–5.30 pm.

Cheshire

M.B. POTTERY (Margaret Beaumont), 11a Heathfield Park, Grappenhall, nr Warrington. Tel. Warrington 65678
Hand-painted and decorated china and porcelain, including wall-plates, tea- and coffee-sets, fruit- and salad-bowls, children's named mugs, ceramic tiles, etc. Items styled to individual customers' requirements.
Open 10 am–5.30 pm except Monday. Please telephone first if possible.

Cornwall

AVALON POTTERY (S. J. & V. R. Boundy), Tintagel (showrooms at Bossinney Road, Tintagel). Tel. Tintagel 415
Genuine hand-made pottery, including coffee-sets, condiment-sets, vases, jugs, egg-cups, etc. A wide variety of shapes and colours. Special orders taken.
Open all day, every day.

CLIVE BLACKMORE, The Cottage, Old Hill, St John's, Helston.
Hand-made earthenware, stoneware and majolica. Range includes: mugs, wine-sets, vases, coffee-sets, jugs, etc.
Workshop is situated close to Old Mills Pottery where work is on show but some individual pots are available from the workshop itself.

BOSCEAN POTTERY (Scott Marshall), St Just, Penzance.
Hand-thrown stoneware pottery. Domestic ware and individual pieces.
Workshop open all the year round.

JOHN BUCHANAN, Anchor Pottery, The Sloop Craft Market, St Ives. Tells. St Ives 6051, Hayle 2106.
Hand-thrown stoneware pottery including coffee-sets, mugs, jugs, teapots, wine-sets, etc. Also individual and art pieces of every description.
The craft is demonstrated on the premises throughout the season.

DENNIS BULLOCK, Pottery Workshop, 4 Tamar Street, Saltash PL12 4EJ. Tel. Saltash 3864
Stoneware pottery. Domestic range, catalogue available. Limited number of personal commissions accepted.
Open daily 9 am–5 pm, Saturday until 1 pm. Closed Sunday.

JUNE CALVERT, Studio Potter, Trewellard Hill Farm, Pendeen, nr Penzance. Tel. St Just 708
Hand-thrown earthenware range of mugs, jugs, plates, bowls, coffee- and tea-sets, etc. All made on the premises.
Showroom open daily.

CAMELOT POTTERY & CRAFT CENTRE, Roger Irving Little, The Old Bakery, Boscastle. Tel. Boscastle 291
Hand-thrown traditional Cornish pottery, individual slipware, and the only makers of unique Mochaware. Craft section displaying for sale a wide selection of good hand-made craft items from Cornwall and the world.
Open all day, every day.

CELTIC POTTERY, The Old Schoolhouse, Wesley Place, Newlyn, Penzance. Showroom: 6 The Strand, Newlyn. Tel. Penzance 4375
Hand-thrown and cast individually decorated earthenware and stoneware by Maggie Fisher and Ev Stevens. Coffee-sets, mugs, dishes, etc.
Showrooms open daily—6 The Strand, Newlyn. Sloop Craft Market, St Ives.

CLOCKHOUSE POTTERY (Virginia Bamford), Fore Street, Tregony. Tel Tregony 666
Decorative and domestic earthenware hand-thrown on the premises.
Open daily Monday–Saturday 10 am–6 pm. Other times by appointment.

JOHN DAVIDSON, New Mills Pottery, Ladock Truro, situated eight miles east of Truro on A39 between Ladock and Fraddon. Tel Grampound Road 209 (0726-88209)
Hand-made stoneware for kitchen and table.
9 am–9 pm summer, otherwise 9 am–6 pm.

PETER E. DYKES, 'The Brooklets Cottage Pottery', Bossiney Road, Tintagel, Cornwall. Tel. 247

Specialising in hand-thrown stoneware pottery.

THE FOSTER'S POTTERY COMPANY, Tolgus Hill, Redruth. Tel Redruth 5754

Earthenware pottery, coffee-sets, novelty gift-ware, also selection of hand-made domestic and decorative pottery.

Showroom open daily 9 am–5 pm. Conducted tours 9 am–3.45 pm. Closed Bank Holidays.

PAULA HUMPHRIS POTTERY WORKSHOP, Mill Hill, Polperro. Tel Polperro 439

Coiled stoneware pots, earthenware animal figures, decorative fish tiles.

Call at workshop door or Rose Cottage or telephone for appointment.

LAMB SWANN POTTERY, Adit House, Tresowas Hill, Ashton, nr Helston. Tel Germoe 2393

A wide variety of hand-made vessels in earthenware, stoneware and porcelain.

Visitors welcome.

LAMORNA POTTERY (Peter & Shirley Brown), Lamorna, nr Penzance. Tel. St Buryan 330. Situated on B3315 out of Penzance

Large selection of tableware, lamp-bases, vases and individual pieces in earthenware and terra-cotta. Glazes reflect the colours of this beautiful valley.

Open daily 9 am–9 pm. Ample car-parking.

LEACH POTTERY, St Ives. Tel. St Ives 6398

Domestic ware, oven-proof stoneware and porcelain. Also individual pots by Bernard Leach, Janet Leach and others.

Showroom open daily 9 am–5 pm, Saturday 9.30 am–12 noon. Also on sale in London at Liberty's, Marjorie Parr Gallery, Chelsea and Leach Pottery Showroom, Turret Book Shop at Kensington Church Walk, W8, David Mellor, 4 Sloane Square, London SW1.

E. T. LEAPER, Chapel Euny Farm, Brane, Sancreed, Penzance. Adjacent to Carn Euny Ancient Monument. Tel St Buryan 346

Coffee-sets, mugs, dishes, decorative glazes a speciality.

Normal business hours. Visitors welcome.

THE MARAZION POTTERY, Marazion. Tel Marazion 565

Hand-made domestic and decorative pottery.

Showroom open 9 am–9 pm June to September, 9 am–5 pm October to May.

MOSS POTTERY (Bernard & Maureen Moss),

Castle Gate, Ludgvan, Penzance. Tel. Penzance 2936

Hand-decorated earthenware. Designed, made and decorated on the premises.

PAUL MURRAY, Pottery Workshop, Praze-an-Beeble, Camborne. Tel. Praze 325

Hand-thrown domestic and table earthenware.

Open all day, every day.

NEWLYN HARBOUR POTTERY, Newlyn, Penzance (opposite Fish Market). Tel. Mousehole 508

Domestic pottery and individual pieces, ceramic tiles and jewellery by Dennis Lane.

THE ORIGINAL CORNISH POTTERY, Chapel Hill, Truro. Tel. Truro 2928

This hand-craft pottery on the site of which is a seventeenth-century kiln base, is one of the last five in Great Britain who were in production before the days of mass-production.

Visitors welcomed, 9 am–5 pm. Processes may be seen 10 am–12 noon and 2 pm–4 pm Monday to Friday.

PENDERLEATH POTTERY (Anthony & Christiane Richards), Cripples Ease (opposite Engine Inn), Nancledra, Penzance. Tel. Cockwells 462

Hand-made pottery coffee-sets, tankards, tea-pots. These are all made on the premises.

Open all day, every day.

PENTEWAN POTTERY, Pentewan.

Pottery can be seen in course of production on the premises. Also a fine selection of crafts including tapestry bedspreads and clothing.

9 am–5.30 pm (10 pm in Summer).

POLPERRO POTTERY, Crumplehorn, Polperro. Tel. Polperro 567

Hand-made stoneware, domestic and individual pieces.

Open all day.

MARY A. RICH, Penwerris Pottery, Cowlands Creek, Olk Kea, nr Truro. Tel. Truro 6926

A wide range of thrown stoneware and porcelain pots. Domestic ware and individual pieces. The workshop is situated at the head of Cowlands Creak, two miles from King Harry Ferry.

Please telephone for appointment.

SANCREED STUDIOS, Sancreed House, Sancreed, Penzance. Tel. St Bunyan 419

Hand-made domestic pottery and individual pieces by Michael Truscott. Pine and allied crafts.

Showrooms open 10 am–5 pm daily.

STUDIO CERAMICS, 'The Barbican', Battery

Road, Penzance Harbour. Tel. Penzance 5610

Art and domestic tiles, some slab pottery, including lamps. Individual tiles or in sets for walls, fireplaces or other decorative features.

Open most of the year (closed October). Out of season suggest telephoning first.

TOLCARNE POTTERY, The Coombe, Newlyn. Tel. Penzance 2884

Domestic and architectural ceramics in stoneware and porcelain.

Commissions for ceramic panels and murals accepted. Visitors by appointment.

TREGURNOW POTTERY, Newtown, St Buryan. Tel. St Buryan 469

Hand-thrown tableware (including coffee-sets and tea-sets). Traditional frog-mugs, animal figures and chess-sets by George and Margaret Smith.

Visitors by appointment only.

TREMAEN POTTERY LTD, Newlyn Slip, Penzance. Tel. Penzance 4364

Pottery designed and hand-built by Cornishmen in Cornwall. The style of this pottery is taken from the weathered natural stone which surrounds the Cornish Coast.

Showroom open all year round 9 am–5.30 pm.

TREMAR POTTERIES LTD, Trecarne, nr Liskeard. Tel. Liskeard 42771

Oven to table stoneware, complete range of tableware, slip casting and jolleying production techniques.

Workshops and showroom open daily to visitors 10 am–10 pm.

TROIKA POTTERY, Fradgan Place, Newlyn, Penzance. Tel. Penzance 5425

Hand-decorated semi-porcelain pottery.

JOHN VASEY POTTERY, Griggs Forge, Hayle.

Varied range of high-fired domestic stoneware, coffee-sets, casseroles, cider-jars, wine-sets and many individual pieces. Colourings 'Oxides' dug from local tin-mines.

Summer 9 am–dusk, Winter 9.30 am–5.30 pm.

WEST CORNWALL POTTERY, Pendeen, on B3306 between St Ives and Land's End. Tel. St Just 461

Oil-fired, hand-thrown stoneware. Mainly tableware and useful pots.

Summer 6 days, 9 am–7 pm. Winter 6 days, 9.30 am–5.30 pm.

DAVID WESTON, David Weston Pottery, West Wharf, Mevagissey. Also David Weston Gallery, Pentewan.

Hand-thrown stoneware, sculpture and lamp-bases of thrown and slab construction. Ceramic figures.

Easter to October.

WEST CORNWALL POTTERY, 'Trepedn', Treen, Logan Rock, nr Porthcurno, on B3315 between Land's End and Penzance.

Oil-fired hand-thrown stoneware. Tableware, large vases, pitchers, etc.

Summer 11 am–9.30 pm every day. Winter—knock on the door.

Cumberland

ALLISON POTTERY AND STUDIO, 32–34 Main Street, Brampton. Tel Brampton 2685

Range of thrown and hand-built stoneware.

9 am–6 pm.

Derbyshire

ATLOW MILL POTTERY, Colin & Jenny Carr, Atlow, nr Ashbourne. Tel. Hulland Ward 279

Thrown and cast stoneware. Range of tableware, kitchenware and ovenware.

Almost always open. Please telephone.

L. & M. MOUNT, 10 Commercial Road, Grindleford, Sheffield S30 1HA. Tel. Grindleford 30455

Stoneware pottery. No cast-ware. Individual pieces. Hand-thrown and slab-built work.

Devonshire

BRANSCOMBE POTTERY, Branscombe, Seaton. Tel. Branscombe 248. Partners: Eric Golding, Michael Vaughan-Jones.

Hand-thrown reduction-fired stoneware. There is a standard range of table- and ovenware in a variety of glazes as well as individual bowls and vases, some of which are hand-decorated. Orders can be accepted for special items.

Visitors are welcome at any reasonable time.

BERNARD FORRESTER, Bramblemoor Studio Pottery, Broadhempston, nr Totnes, South Devon. Tel. Ipplepen 214

Individual stoneware, porcelain, earthenware pots decorated with iron, copper, manganese, cobalt and gold and silver lustre. Member of Devon Guild of Craftsmen, Fellow of the Society of Designer Craftsmen.

Visitors always welcome.

ALAN GRANT, Budleigh Pottery, Shandford Cottage, Station Road, Budleigh Salterton.

A wide range of hand-thrown stoneware pottery. Oven-proof domestic ware, large cider-jars, tiles, stoneware jewellery and individual pieces.

Visitors welcome.

MICHAEL HATFIELD, Seckington Pottery Models, Winkleigh. Tel. Winkleigh 478

Ceramic sculptures of figures, portrait heads and animal studies. Detailed models of breeds of animals in clay or life-size in cement fondu for outside display.

Visitors welcome, advisable to telephone.

LIONEL HEATH, Old Forge Pottery, Shaldon, nr Teignmouth. Tel. Shaldon 2415

Hand-thrown stoneware pottery. Domestic ware and individual pots, coffee-sets, etc.

Showroom and workshop open daily all year round.

DAVID LEACH, Lowerdown Pottery, Bovey Tracey. Tel. Bovey Tracey 3408

A wide range of stoneware and porcelain as well as individual pieces, together with other crafts of a high standard.

9 am–6 pm Monday to Friday, 9 am–1 pm Saturday.

MICHAEL LEACH, Yelland Pottery, Fremington, Barnstaple. Tel. Instow 300

Decorative hand-made stoneware in catalogued shapes as well as individual pieces.

9 am–5 pm, Saturday 9 am–1 pm.

OLIVER MOSS, Riverside Studio, Axmouth, Seaton. Tel. Seaton 2625

Cast, jollied and thrown pottery. Decorated in coloured glazes. Good selection of other West Country pottery and handcraft.

9 am–10 pm Summer.

NEWPORT POTTERY (Denis & Wendy Fowler), 72 Newport Road, Barnstable (A361). Tel. Barnstaple 72103

Decorative and functional hand-made pottery.

Open 10 am–8 pm Monday–Saturday and by appointment.

THE OLD POUND POTTERY (Aubrey Coote), Membury, Axminster. Tel. Stockland 431

Pottery made here and by Wessex craftsmen on display. Full range of earthenware and stoneware.

Open Tuesday to Saturday 11 am–5.30 pm during season, other times please phone.

NICOLA RAFFAN, Lockhouse, Dunsford, Exeter. Tel. Christow 237

Wide range of domestic stoneware pottery.

Usually there, week-ends advisable to phone.

M. C. SKIPWITH, Lotus Pottery, Stoke Gabriel, Totnes. Tel. Totnes 303

Hand-made earthenware, stoneware and porcelain, domestic and individual pieces and occasional furniture and toys.

9 am–1 pm, 2 pm–6.30 pm.

WELCOMBE POTTERY, The Old Smithy Inn, Welcombe, nr Bideford, North Devon. Tel. Morwenstow 305. Clive C. Pearson.

A one-man pottery producing a wide range of domestic ware which includes oven- to tableware, coffee-, wine-, water- and tea-sets. Also many individual pieces, lamp-bases, etc, in stoneware and earthenware.

Open Winter Monday–Saturday. Summer 7 days 9 am–9 pm.

Dorset

ANSTY POTTERY, Little Ansty, Dorchester. Tel. Milton Abbas 568

K. and I. Gregory produce hand-made wood-fired ceramic urns, conservatory jardinières, large and small flower planters, tableware and ceramic sculpture. Specialised pieces done on commission.

Visitors phone for appointment.

CHARMOUTH POTTERY (Michael Hendrick), Charmouth, Dorset. Tel 594

Hand-made stoneware, high-fired earthenware, producing domestic items, mugs, jugs, bowls, coffee- and tea-sets, casseroles, large and small individual pieces.

Pottery and Showroom open Monday–Saturday 9 am–6 pm.

DAVID EELES, The Shepherd's Well Pottery, Mosterton, Beaminster. Tel. Broadwindsor 257 (Showroom on premises), Crewkerne–Bridport Road, A3066.

Pottery, stoneware, slipware and porcelain, ovenware, tableware, lamps, cider- and wine-jars, platters, small and large individual pieces.

10 am–8 pm all days.

THE GARDEN STUDIO, Church Knowle, nr Corfe Castle, Wareham. Tel Corfe Castle 633. Simon & Tanya Dobbs.

Artist pottery, contemporary paintings and sketches.

Open at all times.

LESLIE GIBBONS, ATD, 'The Owl Pottery', 108

High Street, Swanage, Dorset.

Highly decorated hand-made earthenware (thrown and moulded), ceramic jewellery, hand-decorated tiles. Individual dishes with bold graphic designs and pictorial motifs in slip and majolica.

Resident. Open all year round, except Sunday and Thursday afternoons.

JO & GERRY HARVEY, The Creative Workshops, Middle Piccadilly Farm, Holwell, Sherborne.

Hand-thrown stoneware, wide variety of domestic ware and individual pieces, commissions undertaken. Craftwork including dolls, leather goods, embroidered smocks.

Studio open Saturday and Sunday morning or by appointment.

Weekly pottery Summer courses, S.A.E. brochure.

ADRIAN LEWIS-EVANS, Stoney Down Pottery, Rushall Lane, Lytchett Matravers (100 yards east of the A350 Blandford–Poole road at Stoney Down Cross). Tel. Lytchett Minster 2392

Stoneware and porcelain. Ash glazed vases, pitchers, tankards. Dorset 'Owl' cider flagons, etc.

Nearly always open.

ROBIN & LESLIE LORD, Manor Close Pottery, St James's, Shaftesbury. Tel. Shaftesbury 2764

Stoneware and porcelain. Domestic and individual pieces. Garden pots, including Dorset Cress Hogs, Parsley Pots and Patio Planters. Electric ceramic table and night-lights.

Resident on premises so nearly always open. Visitors welcome.

TERESA MASTERS (Addison), Toller Pots, Manor Farm, Toller Porcorum, Dorchester. Tel. Maiden Newton 476

Individual thrown and hand-built pottery stoneware and earthenware. Many hand-painted or hand-decorated. Also paintings and drawings.

At home most days, but please phone if possible.

TICKNER POTTERY (Yetminster) Ltd, nr Sherborne. Tel. Yetminster 303

Earthenware, pottery, thrown and decorated by hand in a 300-year-old thatched cottage. Animal, bird and country sports themes, designed by John Tickner, a speciality.

10 am–6 pm Monday to Saturday.

Essex

MASHAY HALL POTTERY, Little Yeldham, nr Halstead. Tel Great Yeldham 284

Hand-made pottery, slip decorated earthenware, stoneware. Speciality: traditional salt-jars.

9 am–5 pm Monday to Friday. Week-ends by appointment.

THE NEWPORT POTTERY (Stephanie Kalan), London Road, Newport, nr Saffron Walden. Tel. Newport 358

Hand-made pottery: red ware, stoneware, porcelain, sculpture.

9.30 am–5.30 pm including Saturday and Sunday.

Gloucestershire

CAMPDEN POTTERY & CRAFT SHOP, Leasbourne, Chipping Campden

Hand-thrown pottery made on the premises. Other crafts available including weaving, wood- and stone-carving, corn-dollies, baskets and costume jewellery. Wooden toys a speciality.

Open 9.30 am–6 pm.

EVENLODE POTTERY (D. & D. Kunzemann), Evenlode, nr Moreton-in-Marsh

Domestic pottery in slipware, hand-thrown on premises. Potter resides on premises—open at any reasonable time.

THE FOREST OF DEAN POTTERY (Peter Saysell), Bream, nr Lydney, Mon–Glos border, 5 miles from Wye Valley. Tel. Whitecroft 414

All types of thrown and built pottery, stoneware and earthenware, specialising in architectural relief murals (external and internal). Oil-paintings, drawings, sculpture also produced on premises and displayed in gallery.

Living on premises, visitors welcome to gallery and studio.

JUDY LAWS, Sheep Street Studio, Sheep Street, Stow-on-the-Wold. Tel 0451 30220

Porcelain and terracotta jewellery—ceramics, wall panels designed and hand-made by Judy Laws. Permanent exhibition of wild-life paintings by A. Oxenham. Contemporary paintings by Michael Oxenham. Hand-weaving and pottery by artist craftsmen.

JENNY POOLE, Delves Cottage, Wigpool Common, nr Mitcheldean. Tel Drybrook 788

Small pottery in the Forest of Dean producing domestic slip decorated earthenware mugs, bowls, jugs and general ovenware. Brush decorated

stoneware goblets, bowls and individual items. Hand-painted majolica tiles.

Visitors welcome any time, but it is advisable to telephone first.

MARJORIE SMITH, 66 Prestbury Road, Cheltenham, Glos GL52 2DA. Tel. Cheltenham 52782

Original hand-modelled small sculptures in terracotta, etc, of children and other figures. Unique pottery character Owls—various designs and sizes. Tiles and tile panels—original designs —brilliant colours—also unusual 3D tiles. Member of the Craftsmen of Gloucestershire.

Visitors by appointment.

THE SNAKE POTTERY (Peter C. Brown), Green Street Cottage, Cam Green, Dursley. Tel. Dursley 3260

Range of unusual English traditional earthenware, hand-thrown from local clay: frog-mugs, puzzle-jugs, figure-mugs and jugs; slipware platters, decorated beer-mugs, etc. Inscribed and commemorative ware a speciality. Figure chess-sets made. Member of the Craftsmen of Gloucestershire.

Advisable to phone.

WINCHCOMBE POTTERY LTD, Winchcombe. Tel. Winchcombe 602462

Wide range of hand-made and domestic and individual stoneware.

Workshop and showroom open to visitors. Monday to Friday 9 am–5 pm, Saturday 9 am–1 pm. Closed Sunday. Situated on A46 1 mile from Winchcombe towards Broadway.

Hampshire

GRINDON POTTERY (Julian Grindon-Welch), White Cottage, Penwood, Burghclere, Newbury, Berkshire RG15 9ER. Tel. Highclere 253277

A small studio producing hand-made domestic stoneware, ceramic sculpture and garden pottery.

Closed Sunday and Friday.

THE OLD FORGE POTTERY (Harry Clark & Clive Nethercott), 37 Durrants Road, Rowlands Castle. Tel. Rowlands Castle 2632

High-fired stoneware pottery; original designs; complete dinner-services made to order; commissions undertaken in ceramics and in wood—relief panels—sculpture, etc.

Open daily 9.30 am–6 pm including Saturday and Sunday.

ST MARYBOURNE POTTERY (David Maynard &

John Holden), Baptist Hill, St Mary Bourne, Andover. Tel. St Mary Bourne 384
Studio pottery, stoneware, specialising in kitchen-ware, work to order. Also assorted scented candles. The workshop is an old Baptist chapel situated in one of Hampshire's prettiest villages near the River Bourne.
9 am–6.30 pm October to April, 9 am–8 pm May to September.
SURREY CERAMIC CO. LTD, Kingwood Pottery, School Road, Grayshott, Hindhead (½ mile off A3 in Hampshire). Tel. Hindhead 4404
Earthenware and hand-made stoneware. Comprehensive range of containers for all flower arrangements. Ware for kitchen and informal use.
Open to visitors: Works and Gift Shop Monday to Friday, 9 am–5 pm. Gift Shop only, Saturday 9 am–1 pm.
SHEILA & DENIS WILLISON, Overstone Pottery, 260 Brook Lane, Sarisbury, Southampton SO3 6DR. Tel. Locks Heath 84474
Domestic and decorative ware. Tin glazed wax-resist earthenware.
Visitors welcome. Open Tuesday–Sunday 9 am–6 pm C/D.

Herefordshire
WELLINGTON MILL (formerly Ross-on-Wye Pottery), Wellington Mill, Westhope Road, Wellington HR4 8AR. Tel. Canon Pyon 391
Decorative, pierced pottery, lamp-bases, dishes, candle-holders and plant pot-holders.
Workshop only.
URSULA & TONY BENHAM, Mill Pottery, Mill Lane, Wateringbury, nr Maidstone. Tel. Maidstone 812363
All hand-thrown stoneware. Wide variety domestic ware and individual pieces and large range of lamps. Displayed in eighteenth-century water-mill.
Living on premises, visitors welcome.
VALERIE & RONALD JOHNSTONE, Dene Court, Woodchurch, nr Ashford, Kent. Tel. Woodchurch 274. 3 miles Tenterden.
Hand-thrown and hand-modelled pottery and ceramic sculpture. Lamp-bases of original design. Also vases, tankards, casseroles, etc.
Closed Mondays. Visiting any hour. Situation 1 mile on Tenterden side of Woodchurch.
LANGTON POTTERY, by the Green, Langton, nr Tunbridge Wells. Tel Langton 2014
Hand-made stoneware by Gordon Plahn. Oven- and tableware; water-, coffee- and tea-sets, plates, mugs, jugs, bowls, casseroles and individual pieces.
Week-days 9 am–6 pm.
COLIN & LESLIE PEARSON, The Quay Pottery, Wickham Lodge, 73 High Street, Aylesford, Maidstone. Tel. Maidstone 77916
Range of domestic stoneware, plates, cups and saucers, stewpots, coffee-sets, punch-sets, wine-goblets, bowls, etc. Also hand-built and thrown individual vases.
Visiting at most times including week-ends, but telephone call appreciated as this could avoid disappointment.
JOHN SOLLY POTTERY, 36 London Road, Maidstone. Tel. Maidstone 54623
Hand-made domestic and studio pots in slipware and high-fired earthenware. Also runs a Summer school, July to September. Brochure by request.
Hours of business 9 am–5.30 pm Monday to Friday, 9 am–mid-day Saturday.
DAPHNE & CHRISTOPHER WREN, Wye Pottery, Wye, nr Ashford. Tel. Wye 812251
Pottery and craft goods for sale. Pottery made on the premises.
Summer season, usually open 10 am–5.30 pm. Closed Sunday, Monday and pm Wednesday. Restricted hours during winter.

Lancashire
KATHY CARTLEDGE, Cobblestones, Raikes Road, Little Thornton, nr Blackpool. Tel. Thornton 2035
Small studio pottery producing tableware and architectural mosaics and murals.
Living on premises. Visitors welcome by appointment.
BARRY & AUDREY GREGSON, The Lunesdale Pottery, Farrier's Yard, Caton, nr Lancaster (barely 2 miles off M6 exit road No. 34 on A683 behind Ship Inn, centre of village. Ample car-park). Tel Caton 770284
Full range of earthenware and stoneware, hand-made on the premises for domestic and decorative use. Ceramic sculptures. Pottery figures.
Visitors always welcome. Resident.
KNEEN THORNTON POTTERY, Potters Barn, 2 Fleetwood Road North, Thornton Cleveleys, nr Blackpool. Tel. Cleveleys 5045
Individual hand-thrown pottery, in high fired earthenware, stoneware and porcelain. Domestic and decorative items. Large range of ceramic jewellery.
Open from June until Christmas 2 pm–5 pm daily. Resident. Visitors welcome any other time by appointment.
PILLING POTTERY, School Lane, Pilling, nr Preston, Lancs. Tel. Pilling 307
Craftsmen in ceramics. Very extensive range of hand-made pottery. Large retail craft shop. Wholesale enquiries welcome. Manufacturers of pottery equipment, kilns, wheels, etc. Wholesale price lists and equipment catalogue available. Private tuition on the premises. Resident.

Leicestershire
MARION ALDIS, Zion House Pottery, South Croxton, Leicester LE7 8RL. Tel. Gaddesby 363
Hand-made stoneware with mainly wood-ash glazes. Tableware lamp-bases, animal sculpture, especially owls and bulls, wall decorations. Individual pieces. Named mugs and plates for children.
All day Saturday and Sunday. Advisable to telephone in week but open most of the time.
C. J. & J. CARTER (DipAD), 'The Studio', Highfields Farm, Grendon Road, Pinwall, nr Atherstone, Warwickshire.
We offer a selection of hand-made, high-quality items in semi-porcelain creamware. Tableware and individual pieces. Teapots and coffee-pots are a speciality.
Open Tuesday to Saturday (inclusive) during normal business hours.
MUGGINS, DAN MOOR & RAY DAVIES, Burton Bandalls, Cotes, Loughborough. Tel. 66582
Master-craftsmen producing a range of decorative wares including bottles, mugs, punch-bowl sets, etc, hand-thrown stoneware with modelled coloured clays and wide range of glazes.

Lincolnshire
ROBERT BLATHERWICK, The Old Bakery, Reepham, Lincoln.
Slipware and tin-glazed domestic pottery, tiles, ceramic jewellery and sculpture.
Open almost any time (resident).
PRU GREEN, Alvingham Pottery, Alvingham, Louth. Tel. South Cockerington 230

Hand-thrown pottery, earthenware, coffee-sets, decorated jars, beakers, dishes and jewellery. Gallery for local artists and craftsmen to exhibit work.
9.30 am–5.30 pm daily, including Sunday.

Norfolk
KEN & JENNY ALLEN, 1 Grammar School Road, North Walsham.
Large life-like pottery cats of most common breeds.
Open normal hours.
PIPPA CLOWES, The China Cottage, The Street, Coltishall, Norwich NOR 67Y.
Pottery and porcelain restoration.
Tuesday–Friday 9.30 am–5 pm.
BLO' NORTON POTTERY, Tony Apps, Corner Farmhouse, Blo' Norton, Diss. Tel. Garboldisham 420.
Hand-made stoneware, table and kitchenware. Individual pieces.
Living on premises. Visitors welcome.
MARY & TERRY CUTLER, Sheringham Studio Pottery and Workshops, 17 High Street, Sheringham. Tel. Sheringham 3403
Hand-thrown stoneware pottery and individual pieces.
Monday–Saturday 9.30 am–5.30 pm. July and August evenings and Sundays also.
CLIVE DAVIES POTTERY, Thorpe Hall Cottage, Withersdale, Harleston, Norfolk. Tel. Fressingfield 407
Reduced stoneware. Wide selection table and ovenware.
Visitors welcome.
EDGEFIELD POTTERY, Dawn & Terry Hulbert, Old Hall Cottage, Rectory Lane, Edgefield (on Holt–Norwich road). Tel. Saxthorpe 379
Stoneware pottery made on the premises. Hand-thrown tableware, also individual hand-built pots and sculptures of a distinctive nature.
Open all year round.
LUCINDA JEPHSON, Field Barn Cottage, Gt Dunham, King's Lynn. Tel. Litcham 283
Small studio pottery producing hand-made stoneware, earthenware, domestic and individual pieces.
Visitors welcome.
JETTY'S POTTERY (Jetty & Adrian Farncombe), 30 Church Street, Sheringham. Tel. Sheringham 3552

Hand-made earthenware. Wide range of functional tableware, lamps, mirrors, flower-holders, birds and sculptured and carved forms. All pieces individually made without the use of a wheel or slip-moulds.
Resident. Visitors welcome almost any time or phone.
JOHN JOYNER, The Loddon Pottery, Bugdon House, 5 Bridge Street, Loddon, Norwich. Tel. Luddon 647
Stoneware pottery displayed in the ancient kitchen of the eighteenth-century house.
Loddon, an old Broadland town on the River Chet, is 10 miles from Norwich on the A146.
Resident. Visitors welcome. Demonstrations by appointment.
WEST MARSHALL, Whittington Pottery, Church Lane, Whittington, Stoke Ferry. Tel. Stoke Ferry 491
Hand-made stoneware pottery, domestic and individual pots, including tea- and coffee-sets, ovenware, mugs, jugs, vases, all sizes of bowls, and clay pipes.
Visitors welcome. Appointment advisable.
MILLHOUSE POTTERY (Alan Frewin), 1 Station Road, Harleston. Tel. Harleston 852556
A large range of hand-made traditional English slipware for kitchen and table use. Cider-jars, casseroles, pie-dishes, coffee-sets, store-jars, plates, cruets, salt-kilns, large decorated platters.
Monday–Saturday 9 am–6 pm, early closing Thursday. Open most Sundays.
STALHAM POTTERY, High Street, Stalham. Tel. Stalham 614
A wide selection of hand-made stoneware pottery, oven and tableware. Individual pieces.
Open Monday to Saturday (inclusive), 9.30 am–5.30 pm.
PRISCILLA THOMS, Magpie, Fersfield, nr Diss. Tel. Bressingham 396
Domestic stoneware thrown on continental kick-wheel, also large hand-built pots.
Resident. Visitors welcome.
JOHN & KATE TURNER, The Cottage (next door to the Ship Inn), Narborough, King's Lynn. Tel. Narborough 208
Hand-made stoneware, some porcelain, domestic ware and individual pieces.
Visitors always welcome. Always open.

Northumberland

PAT GINKS, Ford Pottery, Ford (7 miles north of Wooler)
Oven-proof stoneware, domestic ware, hand-thrown on the premises. Ash glazes.
Almost any time (resident).

Nottinghamshire
CHRISTOPHER S. ASTON, Yew Tree Cottage, High Street, Elkesley, nr Retford. Tel. Gamston 391 (on A1, 4 miles north of Tuxford on route between Lincoln and York)
Hand-made stoneware, domestic and individual pots.
Any day 10 am–6 pm.
WOOD END POTTERY (K. A. O'Donovan), nr Cuckney, Mansfield (on A616 between Cuckney and Creswell). Tel. Warsop 2599
Residential pottery courses. A wide range of domestic stoneware, ovenware and individual pieces, with an occasional selection of reproduction Roman pottery.
Any day 9 am–6 pm.

Oxfordshire
RUSSELL COLLINS, Netting Cottage, Netting Street, Hook Norton, nr Banbury, Oxon.
Domestic stoneware, some porcelain, individual pots.
Monday–Friday 9 am–6 pm. Saturday 9 am–1 pm. Sunday—phone first.
DEDDINGTON POTTERY (Jo Carson), The Tchure, Deddington
Hand-thrown domestic pottery, slipware made on premises.
Monday to Friday and Saturday morning. Saturday afternoon and Sunday by chance.
YELLOW POTTERY, Fawler (5 miles W. Woodstock)
High-fired stoneware—hand-thrown reduction-fired tableware—plates, bowls, coffee-sets, mugs and casseroles, etc. Free-standing non-functional slabwork forms with glaze and engobe surface treatment.
Callers are very welcome. The village of Fawler is situated midway between Stonesfield and Charlbury, approximately 5 miles west of Woodstock. Enquiries for orders and tuition welcome.

Shropshire
SEVERN GORGE POTTERY (Roy Evans), Blist Hill,

off Coalport Road, Coalport
*Hand-made tableware, kitchenware, lamp-bases.
Cider-flagons in earthenware and stoneware.
Large pots a speciality. Printed bone-china plates
and tiles of local views.*
The Pottery is situated on the Ironbridge
Gorge Museum Trust site at Blists Hill, in old
brick-kilns. The site is extensive and affords an
interesting exhibit of the Industrial Revolu-
tion together with good walks and interesting
scenery.
Open 10 am–6 pm week-days, 10 am–7 pm
week-ends. Closed Mondays.
JOHN TEMPLE, Bridgnorth Pottery, St Leonard's
Close, Bridgnorth
*Hand-thrown stoneware pottery, mostly domestic
ware, some individual decorative pieces. There is
a showroom open to the public.*
Open Tuesday, Wednesday, Thursday, Friday, Saturday 9.30 am–5 pm.

Somerset
WAISTEL & JOAN COOPER, Studio Pottery,
Culbone Lodge, Porlock (on public footpath
to Culbone Church from Porlock Weir or
Silcombe Farm). Tel. Porlock 539
*Stoneware. All individual pieces, bowls, mugs,
jugs, lamps, vases and special pieces, decorated
with metal oxides or woodash glazes.*
Studio usually open to public 10 am–7 pm.
ANNE & DAVID HISCOCK, Wedmore Pottery,
Wedmore
*Small studio pottery in rural Somerset producing
tin-glazed earthenware; stoneware twig-vases,
candle-sconces, and lamp-bases.*
Display open 9 am–9 pm every day, and Wells
Market every Saturday.
FISHLEY HOLLAND, The Pottery, Clevedon.
Tel. Clevedon 2952
*Glazed earthenware vases, jugs, tankards, coffee-
sets, bowls, dishes and other ornamental work.*
9 am–5.15 pm Monday to Friday, 10 am–12
noon Saturday.
BRYAN & JULIA NEWMAN, The Pottery, Aller,
Langport. Tel. Langport 250244
*Stoneware pottery. Domestic ware and ceramic
sculpture.*
9 am–8 pm daily.
NORTH STREET POTTERY, Ilminster. Tel. Ilmin-
ster 3175
Decorative and domestic pottery made here by

*Connie Crampton. Also work by other Somerset
potters.*
Open June to September (inclusive) and at
other times by arrangement. Tuesday to
Saturday inclusive 11 am–5 pm.
QUANTOCK DESIGN, West Bagborough, Taun-
ton. Tel. Bishop's Lydeard 429
*Hand-made stoneware kitchenware, vases, indi-
vidual pieces and general pottery with imprinted
designs.*
9 am–5 pm.
SANDFORD POTTERY (June Woods), Sandford
House, Perry Green Lane, Wembdon, Bridg-
water. Tel. Bridgwater 3222
*High-fired earthenware and oxidised stoneware.
Domestic ware and individual pieces.*
Studio and showroom open most of the year;
week-days 10.30 am–6.30 pm, half-day Wed-
nesday.
LES SHARPE, The Pottery, Hinton St George,
Crewkerne, Somerset. Tel Crewkerne 3630
*Wide range of oven-, kitchen- and table-pots in
stoneware.*
Visitors welcome any day, any time.
NORMAN UNDERHILL, 5 Church Square, Mid-
somer-Norton, nr Bath and Wells. Tel.
Midsomer-Norton 2520
*Unique hand-made figurines in earthenware,
mostly old English characters but some moderns.*
Resident. Open every day but advisable to ring
before visiting.
THE WELLS POTTERY, 72 St Thomas's Street,
Wells.
*High-fired decorated earthenware. Hand-thrown
bowls, jugs, mugs, etc. Some individual pieces.*
Resident.
WHITNELL CRAFT POTTERY, John Harlow, Fid-
dington, Bridgwater. Tel. Nether Stowey 663
*Hand-made ovenware, tableware and individual
pieces. Whole range matching in form and
decoration. Other crafts for sale in large show-
room on premises.*
Resident. Open 9 am to 6 pm every day except
Monday.
DAVID WINKLEY, Vellow Pottery, Vellow, nr
Stogumber, Williton, Taunton. Tel. Stogum-
ber 458
*A very wide range of stoneware for domestic use—
mugs, jugs, bowls, cooking-pots, coffee-sets, teapots, etc—together with individual pieces in
stoneware and porcelain.*

8.30 am–6 pm Monday to Saturday.

Staffordshire
SALLIE ROBINSON STUDIO POTTERY, 13 Boon
Hill, Bignall End. Tel. Stoke-on-Trent 720523
Hand-made studio pottery and ceramic jewellery.
8.30 am–5 pm.

Suffolk
ALDRINGHAM CRAFT MARKET, nr Leiston. Tel.
Leiston 830397
Studio pottery, garden and domestic ware.
BRETTENHAM POTTERY, The Forge, Brettenham,
Suffolk IP7 7QP (nr Lavenham). Tel. Rattles-
den 620
*Formerly 'Intaglio Designs', this new workshop
will be producing ceramic tiles and pottery.*
Showroom open normal business hours.
BULMER BRICK & TILE CO. LTD, The Brickfields,
Bulmer, Sudbury. Tel Twinstead 232
*Hand-made bricks, roofing tiles, brickettes,
moulded ware, terracotta, etc. Specialists in
period restoration work.*
All hours.
JAMES HART, Mudlen End Studio, Felsham,
Bury St Edmunds (4 miles from Lavenham).
Tel. Cockfield Green 470
*Traditional potter and modeller. Hand-made
models of old houses and buildings, heavy working
horses, pastoral figures and pew groups.*
Resident. Advisable to telephone.
NEEDHAM POTTERY, Wood Farm, Linstead
Magna, Halesworth. Tel Linstead 301
*Stoneware. A wide range of domestic ware is
thrown, including mugs, plates, jugs, bowls, large
cups and saucers, butter- and cheese-dishes, salt-
jars, casseroles, etc.*
Open any time for all enquiries.
ROBERT TARLING, Kersey Pottery, River House,
Kersey, nr Ipswich. Tel. Hadleigh (Sfk) 2092
Hand-thrown domestic and decorative stoneware.
Resident.
JOAN WARNER, The Old Rectory, Westhall,
Halesworth
*Unique hand-built ceramics. Stoneware con-
tainers for 'Ikebana', sculpture and paintings.*
By appointment please.
HENRY WATSON'S POTTERIES LTD, Wattisfield.
Tel. Walsham-le-Willows 239
*A wide range of domestic studio pottery in matt
colours, a new kitchen brown glaze and also*

brilliant red and orange glazes. This pottery is extremely functional and attractive.

8.30 am–4.30 pm Monday to Saturday. Closed Sunday.

ROBIN WELCH POTTERY. Tel Stradbroke 416
Range of domestic ash glazed stoneware as selected by the Design Centre. Individual pieces, sculpture and ceramic panels.

Showroom open 10 am–5.30 pm, by appointment, to see around workshop. Trade customers any time.

Surrey

CRANLEIGH POTTERY, The Old School, High Street, Cranleigh. Donald Marsh, NDD
Oxidised stoneware thrown to order.
Pottery shop open Monday to Friday.

GEOFFREY MAUND POTTERY, 13 Whytecliffe Road, Purley. Tel. 01-6683802
Hand-painted pottery.
Monday to Saturday, 9 am–5.30 pm.

THE POTTERY STUDIO, 37 Church Street, Leatherhead. Tel. Leatherhead 75127
Hand-made pottery, domestic and individual pieces, made on the premises by Eileen Stevens, also work by local potters. Stoneware and earthenware.

Sussex

BRICKHURST POTTERY (Keith & Fiona Richardson), Laughton, nr Lewes. Tel. Ripe 305
Traditional Sussex black metallic pottery (hand-made) and various coloured earthenware.
Open Monday, Wednesday, Friday, 9.30 am–5 pm, week-ends by appointment.

BRIDGEFOOT POTTERY, Stedham, nr Midhurst. Tel. Midhurst 2626
Individual pieces; repetition work by Ray Marshall.
Visitors welcome. Open Monday to Friday 10 am–5.30 pm, week-ends by chance.

MILLAND POTTERY AND GALLERY, Milland, Liphook
Hand-thrown tableware, mugs, jugs, bowls, etc. Individual pieces.
Visitors welcome. 9.30 am–5 pm, Saturday 9.30 am–1 pm. Bank Holiday Mondays.

EMMA PHILPS (Potter), Sharrods, Upper Dicker, Hailsham. Tel. Hellingly 451
Hand-made stoneware and earthenware; bowls, plates, dishes and other tableware; lamps; hand-

made tile tables.
Visitors welcome most week-days 2 pm–5.30 pm (closed Saturday) or any other time by appointment. Phone call advisable.

RYE POTTERY, Ferry Road, Rye. Tel. Rye 3363
Earthenware and stoneware made and decorated by hand. Tableware, vases, lamp-bases, cruets, coffee-sets, mugs, jugs, etc.
8.30 am–12.30 pm, 1.30 pm–5.30 pm. Saturday 9.30 am–12.30 pm, 2.30 pm–5 pm. Closed Sunday.

IDEN POTTERY, The Strand, Rye. Showroom: Conduit Hill, Rye. Tel. Rye 3413
Iden Pottery. Hand-made coffee-sets, tea-sets, lamp-bases, individual studio vases and bowls, ovenware.
9 am–12 noon, 1 pm–5 pm, 6-day week. Sunday afternoon.

Warwickshire

ELIZABETH BLUNDELL, Pumphouse Pottery, Avon Dassett, nr Leamington Spa. Tel. Farnborough (Warwicks) 317
Slipware casseroles and oven-pots, tea-sets, coffee-sets, plant-pots, mugs, jugs, bowls, etc.
8.30 am–6 pm Monday to Friday. 9.30 am–12.30 pm, Saturday and Sunday.

BARBARA CASS, The Arden Pottery, 31 Henley Street, Stratford upon Avon. Tel. Stratford upon Avon 4638
This workshop produces moderately priced hand-thrown stoneware of high artistic quality. Barbara Cass mixes all her own clays, colours and glazes which gives her work a personal distinction.
Workshop open for sales throughout the year, Monday to Saturday.

KENILWORTH POTTERY, 186 Warwick Road, opposite St John's Church, Kenilworth. Tel. Kenilworth 52725
Stoneware pottery by Sylvia Hardaker, for kitchens and table use, teapots, coffee-sets, casseroles, individual pots, etc.
Showroom open 10 am–5 pm Monday to Saturday.

RON MORGAN (Potter), Whitefriars Gate, Much Park Street, Coventry. Tel. Coventry 27560
Hand-made stoneware pottery.
Resident.

FRITZ & SONYA STELLER, Square One Design Workshop, The Myrtles, Smiths Lane, Snitterfield. Tell. Snitterfield 352

Sculpture, ceramics, stoneware pottery, ceramic murals.
Visitors to workshops and showroom welcome any time.

Westmorland

CERAMICS & GLASS, The Institute, Hawkshead, nr Ambleside
Domestic pottery and ceramic sculpture made in the workshop by Frank Singleton.
Open daily 10 am–6 pm. Sundays Whitsun to September.

AVIS & BERNARD LOSHAK, Esthwaite Pottery, Hawkshead, Ambleside. Tel. Hawkshead 241
Hand-made stoneware pottery. Pots for plants and flowers. Tableware.
Summer: 10.30 am–6.30 pm most days. Winter: by appointment or by chance.

Wiltshire

JOHN COLLETT, Townsend Farm, Littleton Drew, Chippenham. Tel. Castle Combe 782441
Wide variety of hand-thrown saltware and earthenware pottery by John Collett.
Workshop and showroom always on view.

ROBERT & SHEILA FOURNIER, The Fournier Pottery, Tanyard, Lacock, nr Chippenham. Tel. Lacock 266
Thrown and built stoneware. Tableware, kitchenware and individual pots.
Visitors welcome but please phone or write for appointment.

HARNHAM MILL POTTERY, West Harnham, Salisbury. Tel. Salisbury 22364
Hand-made stoneware by Beresford Pealing. The pottery and showroom in this twelfth-century mill are easily accessible by the Town Path over the water meadows from Crane Street in the centre of Salisbury, or by road through Harnham.
10.30 am–7 pm (including Sunday in Summer).

IVAN & KAY MARTIN, Cricklade Pottery, Cricklade, nr Swindon. Tel Cricklade 436
Hand-made domestic pottery in slipware and stoneware. Members of the Craftsmen of Gloucestershire.
9 am–6 pm Monday to Saturday.

ROSE VILLA POTTERY, 4–5 Water Lane, Salisbury. Tel. Salisbury 29317
Hand-thrown and hand-decorated stoneware by Josephine Chamberlain and Peter Revby. Wide variety of individual pots and pieces as well as

domestic ware.

Worcestershire

VICTORIA MULLINS, Avoncroft Pottery, Hampton Lovett, nr Droitwich
Hand-thrown and built stoneware and terracotta for domestic, decorative and garden use. Ceramic jewellery also produced.
Open 9 am–6 pm Monday to Friday and most Saturdays.

Yorkshire

'CLEVE POTTERY', Skipsea, nr Driffield (on Hornsea–Bridlington road). Tel. Skipsea 351
Cruets, preserves, beakers, tankards, vases, ashtrays, animal figures.
Shop open daily all year.
PETER DICK, Coxwold Pottery, Coxwold, York. Tel. Coxwold 344
Coxwold Pottery produces a range of hand-made pots for most uses; kitchen and tableware are a speciality. Impressed patterns and slip-trailing are used for decoration but wood-firing gives Coxwold pottery its special quality.
Visitors welcome to the shop 10 am–5 pm week-days. Phone in advance of week-end visits.
CURLEW POTTERY, 11 Crossgate, Otley. Tel. Otley 4188
Hand-made stoneware and earthenware. Domestic and individual pieces thrown in the showroom.
Tuesday to Saturday inclusive, 10 am–1 pm and 2 pm–4.30 pm.
E. A. & G. R. CURTIS, Littlethorpe Potteries, Ripon. Tel. Ripon 3011
Horticultural pottery manufacturers, specialising in hand-thrown terrace pots, etc.
9 am–6 pm. Appointments preferred.
HAWORTH POTTERY (Anne & Robert Shaw), 27 Main Street, Haworth, nr Keighley
Domestic pottery and ceramic sculpture, hand-made in eighteenth-century weavers' cottage in romantic moorland Brontë village.
Visitors to workshop—showroom always welcome (including Sunday).
MOLLIE HILLAM, The Pottery, Paradise, The Moravian Settlement, Fulneck, Pudsey. Tel. Pudsey 71440
Hand-made stoneware pottery for the table, for the kitchen, and individual pieces.

10 am–6 pm. Open daily except Sunday.
WOLD POTTERY, Routh, Beverley. Tel. Leven 236
Hand-thrown pottery, coffee-cups, etc. Bowls and dishes impressed by real leaves or embossed with school, college, trade-mark or any other crest.
Pottery and shop open daily 10 am–mid-day. 1 pm–5 pm. Sunday by appointment. 4½ miles from Beverley.

WALES

Caernarvonshire

CONWAY POTTERY, Castle Street, Conway. Tel. Conway 3487
Hand-made stoneware pottery: coffee-sets, beakers, beer-mugs, casseroles, decorative bowls and dishes, jugs, oil- and vinegar-bottles, goblets and candle-holders.
Open Summer 9.30 am–9 pm. Winter 10 am–5 pm.
JOHN DAVIES, Gwynedd Pottery, nr Fourcrosses, Pwllheli. Tel. Pwllheli 2932
Hand-made pots for use in the kitchen and on the table. Stoneware, reduction fired. Price list sent on request. Member of the Guild of North Wales Potters.
The pottery is remotely situated ¾ mile off the A499 road, 2½ miles NE of Pwllheli.
BERWYN JONES, Tucwmmwd Ceramics, Llanbedrog, Pwllheli. Tel. Llanbedrog 296
A new studio producing oil-fired reduced stoneware, specialising in hand-made tableware, pressed dishes and individually decorated pieces.
Open week-days 10 am–8 pm during season.
BILL & OLGA KINSMAN (Artist Potters), Bryn Coch Pottery, Nebo, Penygroes. Tel. Penygroes 367
Unusual wheel work and hand-modelled pottery, including animal and other studies in earthenware and stoneware. Specialising in individual pieces, most of which are not repeated. Glazes made from local materials give finishes not produced in other areas.
11 am–9 pm Monday to Friday and Sunday. Saturday 3.30 pm–9 pm.
LLANFAIR YM MAULLT STUDIO POTTERY, Penrhyn Castle, Bangor
Llanfair ym Maullt Pottery is situated in Penrhyn Castle and is open all the year. A wide range of useful and decorative pottery.

Always open.
PORTMADOC POTTERY, Snowdon Mill, Portmadoc. Tel. Portmadoc 2785
Dishes, plates, bowls, mugs, teapots, coffee-pots, vases, etc. Each piece individually hand-decorated in jewel colours.
Trade only, by appointment (9 am–4.30 pm). Retail sales from all Craftcentre Cymru shops.

Cardiganshire

ABATY POTTERY, Pontrhydfendigaid, Ystrad Meurig. Tel. Pontrhydfendigaid 667
Hand-thrown domestic stoneware.
Open all the year. Closed on Saturday and Sunday.
BARDON POTTERY, Constant Farm, Tregaron
Oil-fired stoneware. Hand-thrown tableware and individual pieces.
Resident.
TREGARON POTTERY LTD, Castell Flemish, Bronant, nr Tregaron. Tel. Bronant 639
A wide selection of hand-made stoneware pottery.
Open all year round.

Denbighshire

ACER LAS POTTERY, Saron, Denbigh LL16 4SN. Tel. Llanynys 320
Ceramic Welsh hand-craft by Gottfried. Specialising in fine hand-thrown earthenware. A large range of artistic ware of every description. This pottery is situated in one of Wales's most scenic areas and although isolated can be easily reached by car. Appointments are advisable so that directions can be given.
Home-made teas are available on fine days in the garden.
COPPERS YARD POTTERY (Alan Brunsdon & Maggie Humphry), Cerrigydrudion. Tel. Cerrigydrudion 422
Hand-made stoneware. Individual figurative pieces, table- and ovenware.
Resident. Almost any time.
DAVID FRITH POTTERY, Ruthin Road, Denbigh. Tel. Denbigh 2805
Hand-thrown tableware, pressed dishes, earthenware and stoneware.
Showroom 9 am–5.30 pm. Sunday in season.
LLANGOLLEN POTTERY, Regent Street, Llangollen. Tel. Llangollen 2249 and Chirk 2543
Wide variety of thrown and cast earthenware.
9.30 am–6 pm Monday to Friday. Indefinite

hours, Saturday and Sunday.

Flintshire
RA STUDIO AFON POTTERY, Afonwen Mill, Afonwen, nr Mold. Tel Caerwys 459
Makers of reproduction antique pottery, figurines and decorative silk-screen tiles.
8.30 am–5.30 pm (excluding Sunday).

Glamorganshire
HELYG POTTERY, Claypits, Ewenny, nr Bridgend
Tableware, individual pieces, slab-built pots (stoneware only).
Open every day 9 am–6 pm.
JOHN HUGHES GALLERY & POTTERY, The Broadway, Pontypridd. Tel 404859
Specialising in ceramic figures of Welsh mythological and native characters, coracle men, miners, kings and warriors. Also small amusing animal figures and highly glazed earthenware pottery.
Open daily and week-ends. Visitors always welcome.
G. SOUTHCLIFFE, Creigiau Pottery, Creigiau, 8 miles from Cardiff, off A4119. Tel. Pentyrch 207
Hand-made tableware, coffee-sets, etc, in various colours, and Welsh copper lustre traditional to Wales.
Monday to Friday 9 am–5 pm, Sunday 2.30 pm–5 pm, Saturday 10.30 am–5 pm. Closed for lunch daily 1 pm–2 pm.

Merionethshire
MAWDDACH POTTERY, Fairbourne
Unusual hand-made pottery, ceramic sculpture, mugs, dishes, flower-containers in stoneware and earthenware. Lamp-bases and individual pieces. Traditional Welsh slipware.
THE SEREN CENTRE, Berwyn Street, Bala. Tel Bala 385
Mel Mars Pottery—hand-made stoneware pottery and decorated tiles. Individual pieces as well as standard domestic lines. Member of Guild of North Wales Potters. Judy Keeling—silver and gold jewellery. Sheila Kerr—hand-loom weaving. Also shop/showroom, coffee-bar and art gallery. Visiting craftsmen during the summer. Craftsmen who would like workshop facilities for short periods should contact the Centre.
VIVIEN SHRIMPTON, Prysgau Pottery, Llwyn-

gwril. Tel Fairbourne 386
Hand-made, individual pottery, wall-plaques, tiles. Hand-painted tiles or designs in relief. Variety of designs and sizes. Resident. Visitors welcome.

Pembrokeshire
BONCATH POTTERY LIMITED, Felin Wen, Boncath. Tel. Boncath 473
Earthenware with screen-printed decoration.
HAVEN CRAFT POTTERY, Commercial Row, Pembroke Dock
Specialising in commissioned work, sculpture and ceramic jewellery. Manufacturers of hand-thrown earthenware in unique glazes.
Open to public all year round 9.30 am–6.30 pm.
CENTRE 68 GALLERY AND WORKSHOP, Penmynydd, Dinas, Newport. Tel Dinas Cross 203
Earthenware pottery. Stone and enamelled copper, jewellery, paintings, drawings and prints (lino and screen). Ceramic sculpture.
Week-days 10 am–1 pm and 2 pm–7 pm. Easter and Spring weeks, June, July, August and September. By appointment other times.
CROCHENWAITH A CERAMEG CEMAES. Cemaes Pottery & Ceramics, Leonard Rees, Parc-y-Gilwen, Brynhenllan, Dinas. Tel 376
Domestic and decorative stoneware, ceramic panels and tiles.
Resident.
HAVERFORDWEST POTTERY (T. J. & A. P. Whalley), Haroldston House, Clay Lane, Haverfordwest. Tel. Haverfordwest 2611
Manufacturers of hand-thrown stoneware in unique glazes. Wide range of standard lines of tableware (coffee-services, tea-sets, casseroles, bowls, etc).
Business hours: Monday–Friday 9 am–1 pm, 2 pm–6 pm. Saturday only 9 am–1 pm. Closed Sunday.
JONES THE POTTER LTD, Cwm Ebrill, Moreton Saundersfoot. Tel. Saundersfoot 2267
Bill Jones produces a colourful range of earthenware, with the individuality of the hand-made pot, but also with the fine finish of a good craftsman. Visitors are always welcome at the pottery, which is delightfully situated on a hillside just off the main Tenby–Carmarthen road.
Accommodation available.
LANDSHIPPING POTTERY (John Vergette), Landshipping, Narberth (4½ miles off A4075 Haver-

fordwest–Pembroke road). Tel. Martletwy 225
Earthenware pottery in original colours in traditional and modern designs. Also farm guest house accommodation available.
Resident. Any time.
'RICK FLETCHER POTTERY', Willesdon House, St Thomas's Green, Haverfordwest
A full range of domestic stoneware, oven to tableware pottery in a unique swirl brush glaze. All pieces are individually hand-made and shown in the Design Centre, London, and Craft Centre of GB.
Visitors welcome to our showroom display.
Open Monday to Friday 10 am–7 pm.
SAUNDERSFOOT POTTERY, Wogan Terrace, Saundersfoot. Tel. 2406
A wide range of hand-thrown earthenware pottery by Carol Brinton with unique glazes in both modern and traditional designs.
Resident. Any time.
TENBY POTTERY, Upper Frog Street, Tenby. Tel. Tenby 2890
Hand-made pottery.
Summer: 10.15 am–1 pm, 2.15 pm–5.30 pm, 7.45 pm–9 pm. Closed Wednesday, Saturday evening, Saturday afternoon, and all day Sunday.
Winter: 10 am–1 pm, 2.15 pm–5.30 pm.

Radnorshire
DRAGON POTTERY, East Street, Rhayader. Tel. Rhayader 318
Hand-decorated pottery.
Open 1st June to 30th September—daily including Sunday, 9 am–6 pm 1st October to 31st May—Monday to Friday, 9 am–5 pm.
WYE STUDIO POTTERY (Adam Dworski), Clyro, Hay-on-Wye. Tel Hay-on-Wye 510
Hand-thrown pottery, plaques, sculpture and tiles.

SCOTLAND
Fireshire
CRAIL POTTERY, Crail. Tel Crail 413
Hand-made domestic pottery, ceramic sculpture and murals: mostly stoneware, wood-fired.
Monday to Friday 9 am–5 pm Summer.

Inverness-shire
CASTLEWYND STUDIOS LTD, Inverdruie, Avie-

more. Tel. Aviemore 645
Earthenware and stoneware, made and decorated by hand. Figures, animals and a range of pots (saut-buckets, mugs, jugs, plates, etc).
Open daily Monday to Saturday 9 am–5.30 pm. Extended during season.

Kirkcudbrightshire
JOHN DAVEY, Old Bridge Pottery, Bridge of Dee, Castle Douglas. Tel. Bridge of Dee 239
Domestic stoneware, lamp-bases, jugs, bowls, dishes and platters in brown and coloured glazes, decorated with wax resist. Individual pieces and ceramic sculpture.
8.30 am–6 pm daily Monday to Friday. Weekend visits by appointment.

Midlothian
GRAHAM MCVITIE CERAMICS, Tynehead Cottages, Tynehead, by Pathhead. Tel. Heriot 235
Small cottage pottery producing varied domestic and decorative stoneware, including sculpture, all of individual design.

Perthshire
JEAN C. HOWDEN, The Pottery, Muthill
Hand-thrown stoneware pottery. Finely finished bowls, mugs, coffee-sets, etc, in five beautiful colours.
Open from 9.30 am–5.30 pm all year round except Sunday.

Roxburghshire
IAN & ELIZABETH HIRD, The Kelso Pottery, The knowes, Kelso. Tel. Kelso 2027
Hand-made stoneware pottery—domestic and individual pieces, piggy-banks and 'feelies', candlesticks and decorated plates.
Studio open 9 am–6 pm Monday to Saturday.

Stirlingshire
BARBARA DAVIDSON POTTERY, 18 Main Street, Larbert. Tel. 4430
Hand-thrown pottery. All types of functional ware, including dinner-services. Also hand-made open textured lamps from local clay.
Showroom open Monday–Friday 9 am–5.30 pm, Saturday and Sunday 2.30 pm–5.30 pm. Commissions accepted for murals and special items.

NORTHERN IRELAND

Antrim
PORTRUSH POTTERY, 93–95 Main Street, Portrush. Tel. Portrush 3739
Earthenware pottery—functional, decorative.

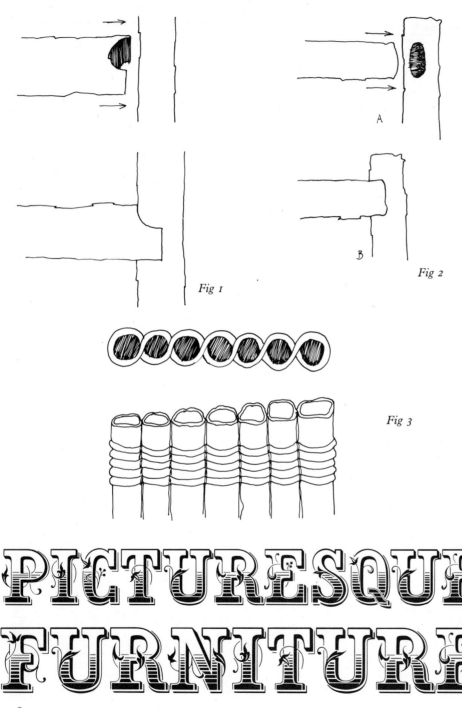

Fig 1

Fig 2

Fig 3

PICTURESQUE FURNITURE

RUSTIC WORK

This craft has sharply declined, probably because of the shift in taste away from wooden garden furniture to that made of tubular aluminium, stretched with plastic or canvas. There are signs, however, that the need for rustic work is now increasing once more, so that a knowledge of how to produce chairs and tables might be beneficial, either for a commercial venture or purely for the joy of making this delightful furniture oneself.

THE MATERIALS

The pleasure of this craft is that the material can be obtained in almost any county for the taking, or certainly very cheaply. Unhewn timber in the form of oak is preferable, but any of the hardwoods such as chestnut, beech or hornbeam are suitable. Even larch wood or Scots pine can be utilised, but most softwoods are unsuitable. As to obtaining the wood, there are a number of ways to do this. One way is to come to an agreement with a local forester or farmer who is growing copse on his land so that a steady supply of timber will be available. There are other sources where wood of the required size will be available for the taking (or with permission as the case may be), such as areas where tree-felling is taking place, or land is being cleared for farm or building use. As only thick branches of about 2 inches to 3 inches in diameter are needed for the main structure work, it will be found that this is rejected by timber merchants, farmers and foresters etc. and is normally burnt—so keep your eyes open.

TREATMENT

Opinions will differ as to whether the bark should be left on the poles or branches, or whether it should be stripped off so that the underlying wood can be stained and polished. If stripping the bark is preferred, then the timber must be allowed to dry or season for a number of weeks before working, otherwise the stain and polish will not take.

If copse wood is available, then there will probably be no clearing up of the poles such as removing any small side branches, twigs or growths. Always try and get straight branches but if there are side growths, then remove them right up to the main stem. Sometimes roots or unusually-shaped branches can be utilised in the construction of a piece of furniture. Look out for unusual graining in the different parts of a piece of timber so that it can be utilised and afterwards enhanced with polishing.

JOINTS AND CONSTRUCTION

There are a couple of ways to join pieces of rustic timber together. The simplest way is to nail the pieces together using wrought-iron nails, wire pattern or flathead nails. To ensure a good join between each piece it is necessary to carve a flat surface at the joints, using either an axe or a wood chopper (fig 1).

A more sophisticated method of joining is obtained by cutting a mortice in one piece of the timber, (normally the vertical pieces) and using the cross piece as tenon which is thus inserted into the mortice, glued (fig 2) and then nailed.

Use the mortice and tenon joining method for constructing the parts of a piece of furniture where stress will occur, e.g. the back to the vertical uprights and the cross supports to the legs. Remember to drive home all nails thoroughly to avoid the danger of tearing clothing. Another good tip to remember when nailing pieces together is to support them behind, which will help the nails to be hammered in easily. When constructing the seat of a chair, or the top of a table, it is normal to lash together a number of logs as one would do in building a raft. The logs can be either nailed together, or just hammered on to a back support (fig 3).

DECORATION

Finished pieces of furniture can be decorated with pieces of bark or small pieces of branches if need be but try and keep the design as simple as possible. The whole essence of rustic work is that it is a simple, sturdy and long-lasting method of making furniture, so bear this in mind.

SOURCES OF MATERIALS

Rustic poles:

We have already shown how to obtain timber, but if you have money to burn, or want a steady supply of good, but expensive (we think) rustic poles, then the company below sells it in various sizes:

COUNTRYCRAFT, Roberts Bridge, Sussex.
Nails of all sizes and types can be obtained from your nearest hardware shop, as well as varnishes and stains etc.

BIBLIOGRAPHY

Many old home encyclopedias show methods of producing rustic furniture, so keep your eyes open at jumble sales and second-hand bookshops.

COURSES

A knowledge of basic joinery or carpentry will obviously be helpful. This can be learnt in the evening at a number of Adult Evening Institutes so check out your nearest branch.

WESTDEAN COLLEGE, Chichester, Sussex, does courses on cottage and rustic furniture.

RUSTIC-WORK CRAFTSHOPS TO VISIT

OLD FORGE COUNTRYCRAFTS (B. & A. Watkins), The Old Forge, Pimperne, Blandford Forum. Tel. Blandford 2288
Thatched bird-tables, rustic furniture. Carved coffee-tables, stools, plaques, house-name plates by skilled Dorset craftsmen. All types of fencing and hand-forged wrought ironwork of all kinds.
8 am–6 pm all days. Resident.
'RIDGEWELL CRAFTS', the Village Green, Ridgewell, Halstead (A604, 6 miles Haverhill). Tel. Ridgewell 272
Craftsmen in hand-made English elm furniture. 'Essex' oyster stools and reproduction spinning-chairs, farmhouse-type furniture and bar furniture for the licensed trade. Garden furniture.
J. A. TAYLOR, T/A COUNTRY WOODCRAFTS, Folly Farm, Gt Dunmow. Tel. Gt Dunmow 2547 (evenings only)
Hand-made oak and elm furniture a speciality— to order only.
Monday to Saturday 10 am–5 pm.

ASTON WOODWARE, Aston Hill (A40), Lewknor. Tel. Kingston Blount 51500
Designers and makers of garden and indoor furniture.
Week-days 9 am–6 pm. Week-ends by appointment.
RUSTIC CRAFTS LTD, Bixley Lane, Beckley, Rye. Tel. Beckley 275
Rustic and roundwood outdoor furniture, structures and requisites for gardens, parks and picnic areas. Special features include a stronger and improved mortise-and-tenon joint (Patent No. 1,240,980) with a stress-relieving angled shoulder cut and matching recessed shoulder housing. A high standard of preservative treatment, including impregnation by means of vacuum-pressure plant.
Visitors welcome any time, but advisable to phone first.
MICHAEL THUT, Howe Lane, Nafferton, Driffield. Tel. Nafferton 361
Wooden garden furniture. 'Cottage'-type domestic furniture, Welsh dressers in oak and elm, monk benches and tables for patio and garden, flower-troughs and tubs in assorted hard-woods, bird-tables, nesting-boxes, etc.
Normal working hours. Visitors by appointment preferably.

AN INTRODUCTION TO SPINNING

SPINNING is one of the most fundamental processes ever discovered by man, so old that it almost has spiritual connections. Certainly it is one of the loveliest of all the crafts for it is the basis and starting point of many others, i.e. dyeing, weaving, printing. Spinning with a spindle is very easy to learn and once the knack of it has been acquired, a lot of yarn can be produced in a relatively short time. Using a spinning wheel is more complicated and as they are so very expensive and difficult even to make, we will not bother with it in this book.

Until a fleece has been obtained, there is nothing to stop you practicing and experimenting with other materials:

(a) TRAVELLERS' JOY (*Clematis Vitalba*) Old Man's Beard.

A common climbing perennial found widespread in the country which in the Autumn produces its unmistakeable greyish-white woolly plumes of hairy fruit. Try spinning the hairs.

(b) COTTON GRASS (*Eriophorum angustifolium*) Bog Cotton.

A widespread and common perennial grass found in bogs and swamps, mostly on acid soils in the north. The grass produces small, brownish green flowers which later form very conspicuous long white cottony seed 'bols'. Try spinning the fluffy bols.

(c) GLASS FIBRE.

(d) COTTON WOOL.

(e) HUMAN AND ANIMAL HAIR.

When walking through the country it is often possible to collect pieces of sheep wool that have become entangled in bushes or barbed wire. The best results, however will always be with the real wool (fleece), silk or flax, and of the three materials, wool is the easiest to spin for a beginner.

SPINNING WOOL

The basic principle of any spinning process is that of twisting together relatively weak fibres so that the resultant yarn has considerably more strength. The way the fibres are twisted together will determine the nature of the yarn. Tweed, for instance, is made up of yarn which has had its fibres all mixed up in a criss-cross fashion giving it a rough feel (*fig 1*). On the other hand, most wool knitting yarns have their fibres drawn out together which gives it a soft feel (*fig 2*).

Terminology

Certain terms will be used during this chapter which apply to the wool fleece and the spinning of that fleece. The following are simple descriptions which ought to be learnt.

STAPLE: Wool grows on sheep in locks, that hang in varying lengths according to (a) the region of the body of the sheep, (b) the breed of the sheep, and (c) the habitat of the sheep. Each lock is called a staple.

FIBRE: Each staple is made up of numerous hairs or fibres.

SCALE: Each fibre is made up of tiny scales which overlap each other from the root to the tip and this enables any foreign matter that may have got caught in the sheep's coat to gradually work its way out instead of remaining embedded.

CRIMP: Each staple is more or less 'crimped' which means that it contains a number of natural waves. The more crimps per inch in a staple, the finer the wool is judged for spinning and most of the best kinds have as many as 20 crimps per inch.

KEMP: This is the hair that grows usually on the legs and hind of the sheep and is not really appreciated for spinning because it is very coarse. It can be spun, but the resultant yarn will not be soft and it will be difficult to spin anyway. The wetter the sheeps habitat, the more kemp it will grow as rain runs off hair more easily than soft wool.

Fleeces

Britain offers a great number of sheep breeds, of which there are three basic types:

(a) DOWN BREEDS: These are sheep that inhabit the lower hills and down and normally give fleeces with short, fine staples.

(b) MOUNTAIN BREEDS: These are sheep that inhabit the hilly and mountainous districts and normally produce a long, coarse wool with plenty of kemp.

(c) LONG WOOLS: These are sheep native to the grass lowlands and coastal plains and normally produce a long, coarse wool.

Although there may not be the chance of choosing a particular fleece from a particular breed, the following will be more suitable for the hand spinner:

(a) SOUTH DOWN: A breed that inhabits the chalk hills around Lewes, Sussex. The fleece normally has short, very crimped staples with an average weight per fleece of $3\frac{1}{2}$–$4\frac{1}{2}$ lb.

(b) DEVON CLOSEWOOL: A breed native to Exmoor, with a fleece containing close, fine staples and an average weight per fleece of $4\frac{1}{2}$–6 lb. This wool is recommended for tweed.

(c) CHEVIOT: A descendant breed from the

Fig 1

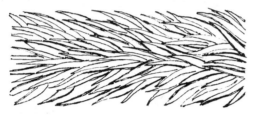

Fig 2

Fig 3a

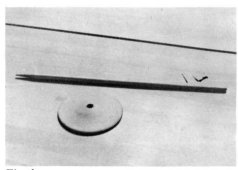

Fig 3b

ancient tan-faced sheep crossed with South-down and Merino breeds. It is a native of the Cheviot hills and the green southern hills of Scotland. Fleeces are compact with crisp staples of about 4 inches and an average weight per fleece of 4–4½ lb.

(d) SHETLAND: This breed produces an exceptional wool and if it is at all possible, try and get hold of fleeces from this breed which is a native of the Shetland and Orkney Isles. The fleece is made up of very fine wool with an outer coating of air. This breed does not have its coat shorn but 'rooed' or plucked.

(e) EXMOOR HORN: A breed that inhabits North Devon and parts of Somerset. The fleece is made up of soft lustrous wool with an average weight per fleece of 3½–4 lb.

(f) KENT: A native breed found on the marshes of Romney. A highly crimped staple of fine wool grows on this sheep with an average weight of 6–8 lb. Fleeces from this breed are highly recommended as they are plentiful, of high quality, and easy to spin.

Preparing the Fleece

Environmental conditions which may vary from season to season and from area to area have a considerable effect on the formation of the fleece. Wind, snow, dirt and the continual rubbing of a sheep's coat against rocks and vegetation all affect the quality of the various parts of a fleece and generally it will be found that the best wool comes from the shoulders and the most coarse from the lower back and belly.

Having obtained a fleece it must then be graded into the best, second best, third best, and so on. As already said, the best wool comes from the shoulders which normally produce the longest, and more crimped staples. The grading will begin with this wool and will end up with the coarse kemp. To do the grading, a large area like a room or shed should be cleared and clean paper laid on the floor. The fleece, which has probably been folded and tied in a particular way for transit purposes, must then be carefully unfolded and spread out on the floor. Experience will determine the best way to sort a fleece, but I have found that having five, large polythene bags (dustbin-liner size) ready and breaking down the

quality into five grades is a good form to stick to. Label the bags 1, 2, 3, 4 and 5 and put the best fleece in bag No. 1, the second best in bag No. 2 and so on. Reject any lumpy, body-soiled wool completely as this will save time later. Don't however, wash the fleece at this stage as it will remove the lanoline oil found naturally on the fibres, and this oil is an aid in the spinning process.

Spindles

Spindles can be bought in most craftshops, but considering what they are, it seems needless to waste money on them, as they are so easy to make. Basically, a spindle consists of two parts, a tapered stick jammed into a circular disc *(figs 3a, b)*. Both parts can be separated simply by pulling apart. The tapered stick can have a notch at the top but this is not necessary and I prefer to have a notchless spindle. Although sizes have been given in the diagram above, it must be said that spindles come in various sizes throughout the world so that by experimenting, a personal size may be found to fit your own spinning style.

The circular base can be cut out of 3 or 5 ply wood or something of a similar thickness and the spindle stem can be made from dowelling rod. Drill a ⅜-inch hole in the middle of the disc. The thickest part of the tapered stick should be slightly larger than this hole so that it will jam firmly into it. No spindle should be heavy in weight because this will break the yarn in the spinning process. On the other hand, a spindle that is too light will not spin properly.

TEASING & CARDING

Before the staples of wool can be spun, they must first be fluffed out into a light, airy mass and all dirt or foreign bodies removed. There are two ways to do this: teasing, which is purely a hand process, and carding, which uses two bat-like tools called carders. Of the two methods, carding is the more thorough and carded fibres will produce long, luscious soft yarn of the knitting wool quality. Teasing will produce a rough yarn suitable for tweed.

Teasing

Take one or two staples (use a 4th- or 5th-grade

Fig 4

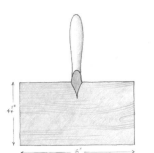
Fig 5

Fig 7a

Fig 7c

Fig 6

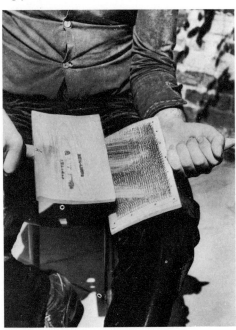
Fig 7b

Fig 8

Fig 9

53

wool to practice with) and gently ease the fibres apart, picking out any bits and pieces in the process. The ideal consistency should be a light, fluffy ball, not unlike cotton wool. This will now be ready for spinning.

Carding

Carding is the hardest and most important part of any spinning process because it determines the quality of the yarn. It is difficult to correctly describe carding in a book because it is a very subtle process dependent on delicate hand movement and the way the wool is manipulated between the tools. For this reason, only a brief description will be given, as well as diagrams on how to make a pair of carders.

The tools used for this process are known as carders and consist of two bat-shaped pieces of wood, backed on one side with a piece of 'scratch card' *(fig 4)*. Scratch card is used in the textile industry for industrial carding and can be purchased in some ironmongers or do-it-yourself shops. It is often sold as a medium to iron velvet on and consists of material embedded with metal thongs. The wood for the base of the carders should be strong, either ash or a thick plywood. The sizes can be seen in *(fig 5)*. The scratch card can be fixed on to the wooden base by a strong glue and a row of staples around the outside.

Mark each carder 'left' and 'right' respectively and always remember to use the left hand carder in the left hand and the right hand carder in the right hand because the scratch card thongs gradually get worn in a certain direction with use.

To actually card, a few staples must first be stretched out over the surface of the left hand carder *(fig 6)* and with the other carder in the right hand, they should both be brushed over each other until the fibres are drawn out evenly *(fig 7a, b, c)*. This process should be repeated from one carder to the other for a few minutes until all the fibres are evenly distributed through the thongs *(fig 8)*. The fibres are then carefully removed in one layer using the thongs of the carder not carrying the wool fibres and gently rolled into a loose roll ready for spinning. This roll is often called a 'rove' *(fig 9)*.

PRODUCING A CONTINUOUS YARN

(a) Starting

Get hold of a yard of coarse wool yarn and tie onto the spindle as shown in *(fig 10)*. This is used to guide the fibres around itself into a yarn. Then, using your left hand, take a small handful of the carded wool (rove), and, with the spindle in the right hand, held between the finger and thumb, allow 9 inches of the coarse wool yarn to lie over the wool in the left hand and draw out some of the fibres and wrap them round the yarn as in *(fig 11)*.

(b) Twisting

Press your finger and thumb firmly on the carded wool and coarse wool yarn (left hand) a small way above the drawn out fibres. Then twist the spindle round in a clockwise fashion with your right finger and thumb *(fig 12)*. In doing this, the yarn and the wool fibres will begin to twist together, being prevented from running up into the rest of the wool because of the grip you are exerting with your left thumb and finger.

(c) Drawing out

As the spindle revolves in the clock-wise direction, move your right hand finger and thumb up to about ¾ inch of your left and grip the yarn. Then, let go a little of the left hand grip of finger and thumb and allow about 2–3 inches of yarn and fibres to pass down as you pull the left hand up *(fig 13)*.

(d) Releasing

Again exert pressure between your left hand finger and thumb on the fibres and then release pressure with the right so that the twist from the revolving spindle can run up the new stretch of fibres and yarn *(fig 14)*. Keep repeating these last two operations, the drawing out and the releasing until the fibres have begun to form a yarn. At all times the spindle must be kept turning in the same direction, do not let it reverse. This is quite a difficult art, not an operation that can be mastered in one go. The art of it is in drawing out with one hand, enough fibres from the handful of wool to make the yarn and in judging when, and how much, to release twist from the other hand so that a

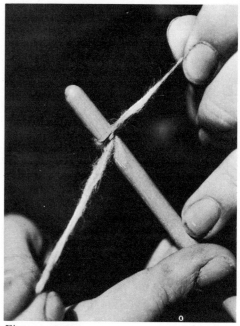
Fig 10

Fig 11

Fig 12

Fig 14

Fig 13

Fig 15

strong and even yarn is produced. Quite often in beginning to spin, you will find that the spindle will stop and start to spin the other way and so unwind all your effort. Don't be put off, just start again and you will eventually get the hang of it. Also, don't be discouraged by the lumpiness of your yarn at the beginning, experience will remedy this.

Winding on

In order to wind on the newly-spun yarn, remove it from the notch at the top of the spindle and also remove it from under the whorl and then wind it up and down crosswise on the spindle *(fig 15)*, allowing each successive layer to reach a little higher so that when full, it resembles a tight cone. Leave enough yarn undone so that it can be hitched as before. Keep repeating all the sequences and keep adding fleece until it has all gone.

Emptying the Spindle

Don't allow too much yarn to accumulate on the spindle as the heavy weight may break it. When it is reasonably full, push up the whorl which, in doing so, will eject the neatly wound cone. When winding from the cone, put it on a stand which you can make consisting of a stick held on to a wooden base, i.e. dowling rod about $\frac{1}{8}$ inch in diameter.

SOURCES OF MATERIALS

Small quantities of coloured, plucked Angora rabbit wool are available from:
MRS HICKSON, Cauldron Barn Farm, Swanage, Dorset BH1G 1QQ.

Fleece may be obtained from the following people, subject to demand. It is best to order fleece well in advance as it sells very quickly:
KEITH & VERONICA BROADBENT, Potash Farm, Tutlington, Aylsham, Norfolk.
CRAFTSMAN'S MARK LTD, Broodlands, Short Heath, Farnham, Surrey.
GUERNSEY WEAVERCRAFT, Juniper Cottage, Belmont Road, St Peter Port, Guernsey.
MCTAGGERT BROS. (FLEECE) LTD, Wilton Mills, Harwick, Scotland.
GREGORY J. PRENTICE (Wool Dealers) Ltd, Ashford, Kent.

EBENEZER PRIOR LTD, Dyson Street, Bradford, Yorkshire.

MR ERNEST STAFFORD, St Mary on the Marsh, nr Romney, Kent.

Any further enquiries regarding the purchase of fleece should be sent to MRS J. MACDONALD, Craigard, Drinnishadder, Harris, Isle of Harris, Scotland, *or to the following major organisations :*
THE BRITISH WOOL MARKETING BOARD, Kew Bridge House, Kew Bridge Road, Brentford, Middlesex.
THE NATIONAL SHEEP ASSOCIATION, Groves, Jenkins Lane, St Leonards, Tring, Hertfordshire.
WOOL FEDERATION, Commerce House, Bradford 1.

There are, however, a number of societies which deal specifically with a certain breed of sheep and which, we are sure, will be very helpful to anyone wishing to purchase fleece. A complete list is given on this page.

Spindles, carders, wool cards and spinning wheels can be obtained as follows :
BODDY'S BOOKSHOP, 165 Linthorpe Road, Middlesborough, Teeside. *Sells spinning wheels.*
JOE CARDIFF, Tycanol, Crymych. Tel. Crymych 243 (1½ miles south of Crymych village on the main Cardigan to Tenby road). *Mr Cardiff is a spinning-wheel maker and woodturner.*
RICHARD DELL, Craft Centre, Teignmouth, Devon.
MISS K. R. DRUMMOND, 30 Hart Grove, Ealing Common, London W5.
FRANK HERRING & SONS, 27 High West Street, Dorchester, Dorset. *Sells spinning wheels.*
ELIZABETH LEADBETTER, 7 Owley Wood Road, Weaverham, Northwich, Cheshire. *This lady sells an imported spinning wheel from New Zealand, complete with bobbins and other necessary equipment and instructions. The spinning wheel can be bought in assembled or kit form. Spindles, carders and wool cards are also available.*
PETER TEAL, Spinning-Wheel Maker, Mill House Studios, Parracombe. Tel. Parracombe 347. *For spinning-wheels, distaffs and bobbin-holders. Mr Teal is closed all day Thursday.*

SOURCES OF MATERIALS IN THE USA

Fleeces, handspinning equipment, spinning wheels and other sundries can be obtained from :
CRANE STATION, 3025 N. Campbell, Tucson, Arizona, 85719.
HALCYON, 'THE WEAVER'S FRIEND', 1121 California Street, Denver, Colorado 80204.
HANDWEAVES COUNTRY-STYLE, Northfield, Vermont 05663.
RAVEN HOCKETT, Box 116, Lagunitas, N. California, 94938.
THE MAKINGS, 2001 University Avenue, Berkeley, N. California 94704.
LAS PAJARITAS STUDIO, 6901 Guadalupe Trail N.W. Albuquerque, New Mexico 87107.
STRAW INTO GOLD, 5550 College Avenue, P.O. Box 2904, Oakland, N. California 94618.
SUNLIT YARNS, Mount Vernon, Maine.
THE WEAVING DEPOT, 818 Manhattan Beach Boulevard, Manhattan Beach, California 90266.
THE YARN LOFT, 1442 Camino Del Mar, Del Mar, California 92014.

SOCIETIES

MIDLAND HAND WEAVERS ASSOCIATION, 51 Westridge Road, Birmingham 15.
Fosters enthusiasm for handspinning and is a very helpful organisation.

Sheep-breeding societies :
BLACKFACE SHEEP BREEDERS ASSOCIATION, 15 Rutland Street, Edinburgh EH1 2AG.
CHEVIOT SHEEP SOCIETY, 5 Tower Knowe, Hawick, Roxburgh.
CLUN FOREST SHEEP BREEDERS ASSOCIATION, 11 Blackfriars Street, Hereford.
DALESBREAD SHEEP BREEDERS ASSOCIATION, The Rock, Underbarrow, Kendal, Westmorland.
DERBYSHIRE GRITSTONE SHEEP BREEDERS ASSOCIATION, Carr Crest, Carr Hill Road, Upper Cumberworth, Huddersfield.
DEVON CLOSE-WOOL SHEEP BREEDERS SOCIETY, c/o Vic & Partners, Okehampton, Devon.
DORSET DOWN SHEEP BREEDERS ASSOCIATION, 40 South Street, Dorchester.

DORSET HORN SHEEP BREEDERS ASSOCIATION, Bank Chambers, Dorchester.
EPPYNT HILL & BEULAH SPECKLED FACE SHEEP SOCIETY, c/o Campbell & Edwards, Market Street, Builth Wells, Wales.
EXMOOR HORN SHEEP BREEDERS ASSOCIATION, 32 The Avenue, Minehead, Somerset.
HAMPSHIRE DOWN SHEEP BREEDERS ASSOCIATION, 38 Endless Street, Salisbury, Wiltshire.
HERDWICK SHEEP BREEDERS ASSOCIATION, c/o G. T. Hartley, Turner Hall, Seathwaite, Broughton-in-Furness, Lancashire.
JACOB SHEEP SOCIETY, c/o National Sheep Association, Groves, Jenkins Lane, St Leonards, Tring, Hertfordshire.
LEICESTER LONG-WOOL SHEEP BREEDERS ASSOCIATION, The Exchange, Driffield, Yorkshire.
LINCOLN LONG-WOOL SHEEP BREEDERS ASSOCIATION, 8 Guildhall Street, Lincoln.
LONK SHEEP BREEDERS ASSOCIATION, c/o W. H. Gastall, Daisy Hill, Waddington, Clitheroe, Lancashire.
OXFORD DOWN SHEEP BREEDERS ASSOCIATION, c/o Boulton & Cooper Ltd, Market Place, Malton, Yorkshire.
SCOTCH BLACKFACED SHEEP BREEDERS ASSOCIATION, 2 Church Lane, Tavistock, Devon.
SHROPSHIRE SHEEP BREEDERS ASSOCIATION, Offa House, St Peter's Square, Hereford.
SOUTH DOWN SHEEP SOCIETY, 5 Grove Place, Bedford.
SUFFOLK SHEEP SOCIETY, Showground, Bucklesham Road, Ipswich, Suffolk.
SWALEDALE SHEEP BREEDERS ASSOCIATION, Edengate, Warcrop, Appleby, Westmorland.
TEESWATER SHEEP BREEDERS ASSOCIATION, 20 Galgate, Barnard Castle, County Durham.
WELSH MOUNTAIN SHEEP SOCIETY, c/o The Royal Welsh Agricultural Society, Llanelwedd, Builth Wells, Wales.
WELSH HALF-BRED SHEEP BREEDERS ASSOCIATION, c/o WAOS, Brynawel, Aberystwyth, Wales.
WENSLEYDALE LONG-WOOL SHEEP BREEDERS ASSOCIATION, Cartmel, Church Walk, Ulverston, Lancashire.
WHITE FACE DARTMOOR SHEEP BREEDERS ASSOCIATION, 12 High Week Street, Newton Abbot, Devon.
WILTSHIRE HORN SHEEP SOCIETY, c/o Misses M. & G. Elliot, The Homestead, Kislingbury, Northamptonshire.

SERVICES

For any special information concerning spinning contact the following who are experts in this field.

HILDA BREED, Flansham Cottage, Cootham, Pulborough, Sussex.

RUTH HURLE, 47 East Street, Saffron Walden, Essex.

MISS MORFUDD ROBERTS, Bronberllen, Trefnant, Denbigh, North Wales.

BIBLIOGRAPHY

GUIDE TO HANDSPINNING, by Grasett.

SPIN YOUR OWN WOOL & DYE IT & WEAVE IT, by Molly Duncan Bell & Sons Ltd.

SPINNING WHEELS available from the Ulster Museum, Stranmillis, Belfast, Northern Ireland.

SPINNING WOOL Dryad Press.

YOUR HANDSPINNING, by Elsie Davenport Sylvan Press Ltd.

Check also the publications available from the following organisations.

INTERNATIONAL WOOL SECRETARIAT PUBLICATIONS, Dorland House, 18–20 Regent Street, London SW1.

COURSES

ADULT EDUCATION CENTRES, Check FLOODLIGHT Magazine for courses in London.

CRAFTSMAN'S MARK YARNS, Trefnant, Denbigh, Wales. *Tuition given in handspinning.*

THE HANDWEAVERS STUDIO & GALLERY LTD, 29 Haroldstone Road, London E17.

Westdean College, Chichester, Sussex.

SPINNING STUDIOS TO VISIT

H. POUNCEY, The Stables, Craigdarroch Estate, Moniaive. Tel. Moniaive 236

A woodcraft workshop set in the grounds of Annie Laurie's old home, specialising in spinning wheels, particularly Shetland, Hebridean and Scandinavian types. Full-size working wheels and half-size models. Matching chairs, stools and tables, etc. Customers' special orders for furniture undertaken.

WHITE HORSE SPINNERS AND WEAVERS (AUDREY & CLEMENT CHARLES), Beech Bank, Bratton, nr Westbury. Tel. Bratton 382

Floor-rugs (mostly from hand-spun yarn), tweeds, etc. Hand-spun/hand-knitted sweaters. Open normal business hours (prior notice of arrival appreciated). Week-ends by appointment.

QUANTOCK WEAVERS, The Old Forge, Plainsfield, Over Stowey, nr Bridgwater. Tel. Spaxton 239. Established 1930

Hand-spun natural dyed wool a speciality in tweeds, wraps, knee-rugs, scarves, etc. Open most days from Easter to October, from 10.30 am–1 pm, 2.30 pm–5 pm. Advisable to telephone. Winter months by appointment only.

MUSEUMS

ULSTER MUSEUM, Stranmillis, Belfast, Northern Ireland. Full of wonderful exhibits for those interested in spinning.

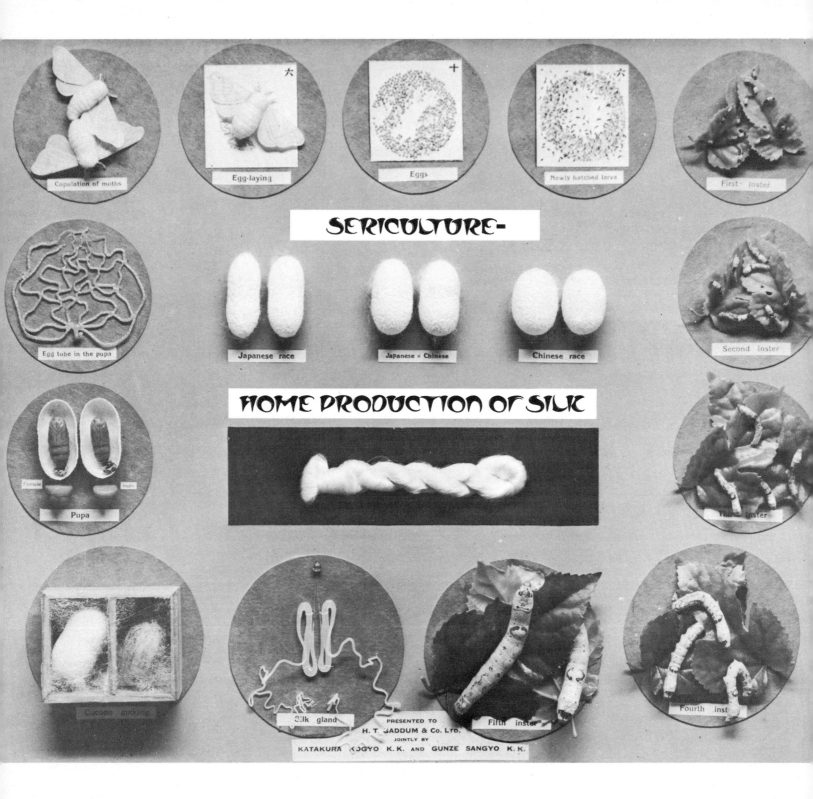

SERICULTURE-

HOME PRODUCTION OF SILK

Copulation of moths
Egg-laying
Eggs
Newly hatched larva
First inster
Egg tube in the pupa
Japanese race
Japanese × Chinese
Chinese race
Second inster
Pupa
Female
Male
Third inster
Cocoon making
Silk gland
Fifth inster
Fourth inst

PRESENTED TO
H. T. GADDUM & Co. Ltd.
JOINTLY BY
KATAKURA KOGYO K.K. AND GUNZE SANGYO K.K.

SILK IS PERHAPS THE WORLD'S LOVELIEST NATURAL FIBRE. IT HAS MANY EXCELLENT PROPERTIES THAT ENSURE A CONSTANT DEMAND FOR BOTH THE SPUN THREAD AND THE WOVEN FABRIC. THE PROPERTIES OF SILK WHICH PLACE IT SO HIGH IN VALUE ARE:

FINENESS : *A single strand from a cocoon is finer than human hair.*

LUSTRE : *No other natural fibre compares with the glossiness of silk.*

STRENGTH : *Silk has great strength in relation to its fineness and it retains its strength in use.*

SOFTNESS : *Nothing compares with a silk garment next to the skin.*

ELASTICITY : *The spun thread has remarkable 'give and take' and will stand up to hard wear without breaking or fraying.*

NON-FLAMMABLE: *Silk is the only natural fibre that is flame proof which makes it ideal when made up into fabric for children's or old people's nightdresses etc.*

PRODUCING SILK AT HOME

All things considered, it seems a worthwhile proposition to produce spun silk at home by rearing the silk worms from the egg stage and spinning the fibres from the cocoons into silk thread. Although producing silk on a small scale can never become a commercial venture (it takes 1,400 cocoons to make 1 lb of raw silk), enough thread can be produced over a period of time which should satisfy one's own personal needs. In any case, the whole process from egg to thread is an amazing one. The only objection to producing silk is the obvious distaste held by some to destroying the cocoon-bound silkworm in order to remove the silk fibres. The decision is therefore purely personal as to whether it is valid to produce silk at all.

Rearing the Silk Worms

Both eggs and caterpillars (silkworms) of the Silk Moth (Bombyx Mori) can be obtained from a number of butterfly farms and other specialists in this country (see the end of this chapter for addresses). Silk Moth eggs are very tiny, each one being about the size of a pinhead, but once the eggs have hatched, the silkworms eat voraciously and grow up to 3 inches in length in five weeks. The ideal food for them to feed on is the leaves of the White Mulberry tree, but other material such as lettuce and mallow leaves are just as good, the only difference being in the quality of silk that is ultimately produced.

Silkworms must have a warm climate to live in and thought will be needed to ensure they have ideal conditions. High-sided boxes, such as empty cardboard packing-cases are ideal if the tops are cut off, making the sides about 1 foot high. Dry twigs can be placed in each box which gives the silkworms somewhere to climb on when not eating.

As the silkworms have enormous appetites, it is essential that they have a continual supply of fresh leaves each day during their five weeks of growth. After this, the silkworms will begin to spin themselves cocoons. This is done by secreting fluid silk mixed with a gummy saliva produced from two large glands called sericteria, through tiny openings in their throats. The fluid silk immediately hardens when it comes in contact with the air, and being sticky in nature, it readily adheres to itself which makes it a relatively easy matter for the silkworms to produce their silky tombs. Each cocoon normally takes from 3–4 days to complete and contains about 3,500 yards of fibre.

Preparing the Cocoon

In order to 'stifle' the cocoons, they must be dropped into boiling water for a few minutes. This immediately kills the silkworms and also softens the fibres. After removing the cocoons from the boiling water, they must then be left to soak for a couple of hours in warm water in order to thoroughly soften the fibres. This facilitates an easy removal of them in the winding-off process.

Winding Off

Each cocoon is made up of three layers of fibre. The outer layer is coarse and is the least lustrous so can be discarded for spinning purposes. Immediately underneath the outer layer is the best fibre, which is even, glossy and less confused in the way it has been wound by the silkworm. The inner layer is rather confused and generally useless for spinning purposes.

The photograph opposite, illustrating the life-cycle of the silkworm, shows specimens at each stage of development. Starting from the top left-hand corner and proceeding in a clockwise direction, we see (1) the mating of the moths, (2) the egg-laying, (3) the eggs, and (4) the tiny caterpillars hatching. Figs. (5–9) show silkworms in their five distinct ages, culminating in the two full-grown specimens (9). Within each silkworm are glands of silk (10). (11) illustrates the building of the cocoon, and (12) the pupa or chrysalis found by cutting the cocoon open; the egg tubes are shown in (13). In the centre are specimens of different types of cocoons, and below them a skein of raw silk.

Winding off is in itself a difficult process and only practice and experience will make it easier. The first thing is to lift up the outer fibre and for this a pointed wooden stick or some other suitable tool is used. The outer layer of fibre is wound off until the next layer is exposed. This middle layer of fibre is quite often the most difficult to lift off and to help things along, a little brush made of birch twigs is used which will lift off the fibres. The real skill comes when the fibres from a number of cocoons have to be wound off and at the same time spun together. As a general rule, a decent thread will need five fibres twisted together, so one thread from five cocoons, or two threads from two cocoons and one from another etc. are spun. The ideal thing for the silk thread to be wound on to is a cardboard tube of smallish dimensions (the tubes in the middle of toilet rolls are ideal). Obviously, one is going to get into a mess at first with winding off, but don't despair for it comes right in the end.

Preparing the Thread for Use

Before any of the spun silk can be used for dyeing, weaving or sewing purposes it must first be thoroughly washed in a soapy solution in order to remove the sticky gum on the spun fibres. The easiest way to do this without making a mess of the yarn is to wind the thread into a skein and tie the skein securely at one end with a piece of strong thread. In this way, the yarn can be thoroughly washed without any fear of knotting.

SOURCES OF MATERIALS

Silk-moth eggs, larvae and pupae can be obtained from:
R. N. BAXTER, 16 Bective Road, London E7.
T. A. FOX, 28 Boxwell Road, Berkhamstead, Hertfordshire.
LULLINGSTONE SILK FARM LTD, Ayot House, Ayot St Lawrence, Hertfordshire.
L. HUGH NEWMAN, The Butterfly Farm Ltd, Bexley, Kent.
WORLDWIDE BUTTERFLIES LTD, Seafields House, Charmouth, Bridport, Dorset.

White Mulberry trees can be obtained from:
HILLIER & SONS, Winchester, Hampshire.
GEORGE JACKMAN & SON (Woking Nurseries) LTD, Woking, Surrey.
KNIGHTS NURSERIES LTD, Hailsham, Sussex.
LULLINGSTONE SILK FARM LTD, Ayot House, Ayot St Lawrence, Hertfordshire.

SOCIETIES

COTTON, SILK & MAN-MADE FIBRES RESEARCH ASSOCIATION, Shirley Institute, Manchester M20 8RX.
THE SILK CENTRE, Dorland House, 18–20 Regent Street, London SW1.

SILK EDUCATIONAL SERVICE, 10 Cliffe Road, Barton-on-Sea, Hampshire BH25 7PB.
This organisation is run by a lady called Mrs Love who is something of a world authority on silk. It produces lots of leaflets and books on all matters relating to silk, as well as some lovely educational 'sets' which contain samples of raw silk, cocoons and fabrics etc.
SILK AND MAN-MADE FIBRES LIBRARY, c/o Westminster Central Reference Library, St Martin's Street, London WC2. *For information on all aspects of silk.*

BIBLIOGRAPHY

SILK, by P. W. Gaddum/available from THE SILK EDUCATIONAL SERVICE, 10 Cliffe Road, Barton-on-Sea, Hampshire BH25 7PB. Price: 50p.
SO SPINS THE SILKWORM, by Lady Hart Dyke.

PLACES TO VISIT

LULLINGSTONE SILK FARM, Ayot House, Ayot St Lawrence, Hertfordshire.
Provides a live exhibition of the production of raw silk from the silkworm egg to the reeled hank. The farm has provided raw silk for two Coronations, the Investiture of the Prince of Wales, four royal weddings and other royal occasions. Facilities can be arranged for evening and school parties.

*Silkworm clambering a furry leaf to take
the sun :
spin and reel and weave in a hurry
till her thread is spun.
The wind blows,
the silkworm slows,
her body marking time,
gently lays a silky trail
along the leaves of lime.*

BRIDGET ST JOHN

NATURAL AND CHEMICAL DYEING

With the increase of interest in spinning and weaving and the production of garments and accessories, there is a need for a comprehensive knowledge of dyeing techniques for the whole range of yarns, threads and fabrics, whether they be made from natural or synthetic fibres. We have therefore divided this chapter into two principle areas: (a) dyeing with natural dyestuffs that will include vegetables, flowers, lichens, barks, berries and minerals, and (b) dyeing with synthetic dyestuffs, manufactured from chemicals.

Before actually getting down to details, it may be worthwhile to explain why, when, and where to use the two types of dyestuffs. The most important point to remember is that natural dyes will only 'take' on natural fibres such as cotton, silk, wool and jute etc., and will be of no use to the man-made fabric range of polyesters, rayons, tricels and terylenes etc. Secondly, it is a totally false notion that the colours obtained from natural dyestuffs are better, brighter and more vibrant than those obtained from the synthetic dye range. Any and every colour from any natural material can be matched easily and perfectly with a dye from a tin. If it is bright, vibrant colours you need, then use a synthetic dye. In general, natural dyes give warm, delicate colours, especially from the plants and minerals available in Britain. The third point to remember is that natural dyeing processes are involved, uneconomical and wasteful, incorporating the use of vast quantities of natural dyestuffs and water. Great skill must be used in getting lengths of material to dye evenly with natural dyes and for this reason, it is advisable to dye only threads and yarns because these take the dye far more readily and evenly. So only dye yarns and threads with natural dyes unless you are prepared to spend a great deal of time in the process. Finally, we must also come down to cost and economics. Synthetic dyes are far more economical in both the amount of dye needed per 1 lb of material, as well as cost per tin. Natural dyestuffs, though free for the taking, will need time in collecting and invariably involve cost in travelling to the various parts of the country to pick up particular minerals and flora. Synthetic dyestuffs, though needing far less water, are not bio-degradable, whereas the opposite is the case with natural dyes. The final choice must be yours.

NATURAL DYESTUFFS

Use these dyestuffs only for cottons, calico, canvas, hessian, linen, jute, wool and silk. They are also suitable for yarns containing a mixture of synthetic and natural fibres, but remember that only the natural fibres will take the dye.

What to use
Any plant will give some colour, whether it be from the roots, stems, leaves, flowers or fruit. Sometimes, a different colour can be obtained from the various parts of a single plant, and these colours will not only vary with the district it is found growing in, but also vary according to the time of year it is harvested. Go out into the garden or the nearest bit of countryside and bring indoors as many samples of flowers, fruit, nuts, berries, moss, lichens, fungi etc. as you can, but be discreet in what is picked (never pick rare plants). Culinary vegetables and fruits are also a good source of colour.

The following is a comprehensive list of the sorts of plants to look out for, though others will be found in the course of experience. (It is a good idea to keep a dye book and to keep notes on the plants etc., picked, the time of year, the habitat and how the colour was extracted.)

BLACKS
Blackberry *(fruit)*	Flag Iris *(root)*
Elder *(fruit)*	Dock *(root)*
Meadowsweet	Oak Galls
Walnut *(bark)*	

BROWNS
Buckthorn *(fruit)*	Birch *(bark)*
Oak *(bark)*	Blackberry *(fruit)*
Various Lichens	Bird Cherry *(fruit)*
Walnut *(bark)*	Hop *(leaves)*
Sloe *(fruit)*	Larch
Onion Skins	Pine Cones *(fruit)*
Elm *(leaves)*	Horse Chestnuts
Juniper *(fruit)*	*(skins)*

GREYS
Hawthorn *(berries)*	Dogrose *(hips)*
Blackberry	Hypericum
French Marigold	Willow Leaves
(flower)	Yew Bark
Blackberry *(leaves)*	Red Cabbage
Privet	Broad Beans
Woody Nightshade	

REDS
Begonia *(red flower)*	Madder
Blackberry	Sorrel
St John's Wort	Bedstraw
Various Lichens	Alkanet

YELLOWS
Plum Leaves	Gorse
Alder	Bog Ashodel
Broom	Bracken
Dog's Mercury	Ash

BLUES
Blackberry *(fruit)*	Cornflower *(flower)*
Buckthorn *(fruit)*	Carrot *(root)*
Sloe *(fruit)*	Bear Berry *(fruit)*
Whortleberry *(fruit)*	Woad *(leaves, stems)*
Dogs Mercury	

GREENS
Cow Parsley *(leaves and stem)*	Apple *(skins)*
	Lily-of-the-Valley
Privet	Sorrel
Elder	Tansy
Ling	Reeds
Bracken	Horse Tail
Buckthorn	Ageratum *(flower)*
Alder	

ORANGES
Dahlia *(orange flower)*	Weld
	Canna *(red flower)*
Various Lichens	Beetroot *(root)*
Onion skins	

PURPLES
Elderberries	Birch Bark
Damson	Bryony

YELLOWS
Blackmustard	Apple Skins
Red Clover	Beech Nuts

Plane Leaves	Heather
Chamomile	Golden Rod
Yellow-Wort	Dyer's Greenwood
Pear	Weld
Weld	Calendular *(flower)*
Pine Cones	Dock *(leaves and*
Marigold	*stems)*
Various Lichens	Nettles *(leaves and*
Ling	*stems)*
Ragwort	Broad Beans
Poplar	Beetroot
Privet	

MORDANTS

Some natural dyestuffs will need nothing added to make the colour adhere to the cloth. Oak galls, lichens and walnut bark are three such dyestuffs and they are called SUBSTANTIVE. However, almost all vegetable dyes will need what is known as a 'MORDANT', a mineral which helps to adhere the colour to the yarn or fabric fibres by making a ground. The colour particles then adhere to the mineral ground instead of the fibres themselves. The most commonly used mordants of mineral origin are: Alum *(potassium aluminium sulphate)*; Chrome *(bichromate of Potash)* and Tin *(Ferrous sulphate or Copperas)*.

PRE-WASHING PROCESSES

To obtain good colours of even distribution, the yarn or fabric must be thoroughly washed and rinsed before being added to the dyebath. This washing process is known as 'SCOURING', and it should remove all dirt, oil, starch or sizing from the fibres.

Washing Wool

Use only natural soap and soft water. All skeins of yarn must be tied securely before washing (and dyeing) otherwise the resulting tangle will be a great headache afterwards. Tie the skeins in a figure of eight and don't tie them too tightly as this will prevent the water from penetrating thoroughly into the wool. It's often a good idea to tie the skeins with a different-coloured piece of wool, or in the case of dyeing, to use black wool or some medium such as string so that it is easily found and

removed after the dyeing process.

Wash the wool in lukewarm water (95°F) and squeeze out the suds. Repeat the washing procedure again and then thoroughly rinse three or four times until the rinsing water is perfectly clear. Always handle the wool gently but wash speedily as this prevents the fibres from 'FELTING', i.e. going hard and fibrous. Always wash and rinse wool in the same temperature water and never wring it dry.

Washing Cotton

Dissolve the soap in hot, soft water (140°F). Wash as for wool and rinse thoroughly once. With the second rinse, have the water hotter and leave the material to soak for $\frac{1}{2}$ hour. Give it two final rinses in lukewarm water.

Washing Silk

Raw silk is normally covered with a sticky gum which must be completely removed. Use $\frac{1}{2}$ lb soap flakes for each 1 lb of silk. Tie the skeins of silk in a muslin bag and add to the hot soapy water. Bring to the boil and simmer for 1 hour, after which the silk should be given three rinses in hot water.

MORDANTING

Always use a separate bucket for each mordant and never mix them. Never use a tin mordant in a galvanished bucket as it will seriously corrode the surface. Each mordant must be thoroughly dissolved in the water solution before adding the material or yarn.

(1) ALUM *(potassium aluminium sulphate)*

To mordant wool with ALUM **use the following recipe.** (Heavy wool will need double the amount of alum):
1 lb wool, 4 oz alum, 1 oz cream of tartar and 4 gallons of water.

Dissolve the alum and cream of tartar in all the water. Thoroughly wet the wool before putting it in the mordant bath and squeeze out all excess water. Bring the solution with the wool to the boil, letting it simmer for 1 hour. Every now and then, turn the wool gently in the solution to ensure even penetration. Remove it from the heat and allow it to cool

naturally, leaving the wool in the solution overnight. Next day, remove the wool, squeeze out all excess water and store, rolled in a dry towel until it is needed for dyeing. Do not rinse before dyeing.

To mordant cotton with ALUM **use the following recipe.**
1 lb cotton, 4 oz alum, 1 oz washing soda (sodium carbonate) and 4 gallons of water.

Dissolve the alum and soda in all the water. Thoroughly wet the cotton and squeeze out excess water. Add the cotton to the solution and bring to the soil, simmering for 1 hour. Remove from the heat and allow to cool naturally, leaving the cotton in the solution overnight. Next day remove the cotton and store as for wool.

Sometimes alum is used with tannin which has the effect of enhancing the dye colour. It is only really suitable for cotton and the process takes three days to prepare.

To mordant cotton with ALUM **and** TANNIN **use the following recipe.**
1 lb cotton, 8 oz alum, 2 oz washing soda and 1 oz tannic acid (or 1 oz powdered oak galls). Dissolve half the alum and half the soda in 4 gallons of water. Thoroughly wet the cotton in water, squeeze out all excess water and add it to the solution. Slowly heat the mixture to boiling point, simmering for 1 hour. Allow the cotton to remain overnight in the solution. Next day, remove the cotton, squeeze out all excess water and add to a solution of all the tannic acid in 4 gallons of water. Heat the solution to 140°–160°F and keep it at this temperature for 1 hour. Allow it to cool naturally after removing from the heat and allow the cotton to stand overnight in the solution. Next day, dissolve the remaining alum and soda in 4 gallons of water and repeat the heating and cooling process, allowing the cotton once again to stand overnight. Finally store as described above.

(2) CHROME *(Bichromate of Potash, Potassium Bichromate)*

To mordant wool with CHROME, **use the following recipe:**

1 lb wool, ½ oz chrome and 4 gallons of water.

Thoroughly dissolve the chrome in all the water and follow as for alum, except that added care is needed to keep the light away from the wool, not only while it is in the mordant solution, but also afterwards until it is needed. To prevent the light entering the mordant bath, cover it with a lid of some description. Store in complete darkness.

To chrome cotton, follow the same method as for cotton using the same recipe as for wool (above).

(3) TIN (*Stannous Chloride, Muriate of Tin*)

TIN **is not suited to mordanting cotton on its own and so the following recipe is for wool:**

½ oz tin, 2 oz cream of tartar and 4 gallons of water.

Follow the same method as described for mordanting with alum. Tin can be used in conjunction with alum, to give bright colours especially bright reds and yellows. Never over-do the use of tin as it can make wool fibres brittle.

(4) IRON (*Ferrous Sulphate, Copperas*)

This mordant is used after the fabric or yarn has been part-dyed. Use the following recipe:

1 lb wool/cotton, ½ oz iron, 2 oz cream of tartar and 4 gallons of water.

Add the material to the dye bath and bring it to the boil, simmering for ½ hour. Remove the material and add the iron and cream of tartar to the dye solution, thoroughly dissolving them in the dye bath. Return the wool to the dye bath and continue to simmer it for another ½ hour. This process is known as 'SADDENING'.

EXTRACTING THE DYE AND DYEING

There are a number of ways to remove the colour from the various plants, barks, fruit etc. We have described the three easiest ways. A mortar and pestle, or some other crushing device is helpful, e.g. a hammer and bread board.

1ST METHOD   Thoroughly bruise or crush the dyestuff and place it in a stainless-steel saucepan, bucket or pot. (As a general rule use about 1 lb of dyestuff to every 1 lb of yarn or fabric.) Pour boiling water over the dyestuff until everything in the pot is well covered. Allow the dyestuff to steep in the water for three days, giving it a good stir each day. At the end of the three days, strain the contents of the pot through a piece of muslin into the dye bath. Before entering the yarn or fabric to the dye bath, thoroughly wet it and squeeze out all excess water. Bring the dye bath to the boil and simmer for 1 hour. (If there is not enough water/dye solution to cover the material completely, top up with clean water until it does so.) Never overboil yellow dyes as this tends to dull the colours. On the other hand, some colours may need longer boiling than ½ hour. Remember that the colour of the material in the dye bath will always be darker than when the material is dry, so always dye to a slightly darker colour than that which is desired.

2ND METHOD   Place the bruised or crushed dyestuffs in a large stainless-steel pot and cover it adequately with cold water. Bring the pot to the boil and simmer for ½ hour. Allow to cool and then strain through muslin into the dyebath. For actual dyeing, follow the method described above.

3RD METHOD   Place the bruised or crushed dyestuffs in a stainless steel or glass pot and cover with household ammonia. Steep for three days as described in the first method. Strain the contents of the pot through muslin into the dye bath and after thoroughly wetting the fabric or yarn, and squeezing out all excess water, add it to the ammonia solution. Leave the contents of the pot in a warm place for three days, or heat it to a temperature of (140°F) and keep at that heat for 1 hour.

The colours obtained from using ammonia will be extremely vibrant, but the set-back is the awful smell. If you can stomach the stench of ammonia, then go ahead and try it. Remember to thoroughly rinse the dyed material after it has been removed from the dye bath.

SYNTHETIC DYEING

There is a vast range of chemical dyes available these days for with the ever-increasing production of new man-made fibres, dyes are made especially to suit them. However, not only can synthetic dyestuffs be used to dye man-made fibres, but also for natural fibres such as wool, silk and cotton. Because of the complexity of the synthetic range, we have chosen the major groups of dyes which will be more than adequate for the average needs.

Acid Dyes (*For dyeing wool, silk, rayon and nylon*)

The trade names of some acid dyes are: COOMASSIE (SKILBECK) (ICI), AZO (ICI), TARTARINE (ICI), CARBOLAN (ICI), LISSAMINE (ICI), DISSULPHINE (ICI).

METHOD

As with most synthetic dyes, acids are extremely concentrated and the tiniest amount of dye will produce a good strong colour. If synthetic dyes are going to be used quite regularly it will be extremely advisable to get hold of gram-weight scales, with weights from 1 gram up to 100 grams. Another very necessary item is the colour card index, available from ICI which is a book of colours with the colour percentage next to each one. For instance a particular yellow may have 0·5% next to it. This percentage is used in the following formula to determine the exact weight of dye needed to dye a particular weight of cloth or yarn to the exact colour in the colour card index.

$$\frac{\text{Weight of Wool}}{1} \times \frac{\text{Colour percentage}}{100}$$

$$= \textbf{Weight of dye needed.}$$

Having worked out how much dye will be needed for a given weight of wool, dissolve it in a tiny amount of water and add it to the dye bath which should contain enough water to completely cover the material. Add a few drops of ACETIC acid to the solution. If this reasonably mild acid cannot be got hold of, add a cupful of strong vinegar instead. After thoroughly wetting the material and squeezing out the excess water, add it to the dye bath and bring it to the boil. Once boiling, keep it simmering until the material being dyed has absorbed all the colour in the dye bath, so that the water is clear. When, and only when, the water is clear will the colour be that which was intended in the colour card index.

Remove the material from the dye bath and thoroughly rinse it in warm water. With wool, rinse it in hot water.

Direct Dyes *(For dyeing cotton, linen, viscose rayon and some wool)*
These are dyestuffs that need no mordant where vegetable or animal fibres are concerned, i.e. cotton, silk, etc.

Some trade names of direct dyes are:
SOLAMINE (SKILBECK), CHLORAZOL (ICI), DURAZOL (ICI).

METHOD
Exactly the same formula and method is used with these dyes as was described for acid dyes.

Reactive Dyes *(For dyeing cotton, wool, viscose)*
This range of dyes includes the famed 'Procion M' which is widely used for 'Tie-dye' and 'Batik'. The formula is split into two parts, being mixed separately, and then the two solutions added to each other. The formula is as follows:

Procion M. Part (a) Urea + water + dye
Part (b) Bicarbonate of soda + soda ash + water.

This is a cold water dyeing process and the solution is only good for two hours, after which it becomes ineffective.

METHOD
The material is first thoroughly wetted and all excess water removed. It should be then put in the dye solution and left there until the colour absorbed is the one required. Remember though, that any material in the dye bath will be darker wet than dry, so allow for this by dyeing to a slightly darker colour than the one desired.

SOURCES OF MATERIALS

Mordants can be obtained from:
COMAK CHEMICALS LTD, Swinton Works, Moon Street, London W1.
ELIZA LEADBEATER, Granville House, 6 Granville Street, Winsford, Cheshire: *sells most mordants as well as dyeing equipment (stainless-steel buckets, tongs and scales etc.). Also available are some vegetable dyes, sold by the ounce and woad seeds.*
SKILBECK BROTHERS LTD, 55 & 57 Glengall Road, London SE15. *Urea and soda ash are also available from this company.*

Synthetic Dyes are available from:
COMAK CHEMICALS LTD, Swinton Works, Moon Street, London N1. *Also vegetable and chemical dyes.*
DYLON INTERNATIONAL LTD, 139–151 Sydenham Road, London SE26.
I.C.I. DYESTUFFS DIVISION, P.O. Box 42, Hexagon House, Blackley, Manchester M9 3DA.
SKILBECK BROTHERS LTD, 55 & 57 Glengall Road, London SE15.
UNI-DYE, Rear Castle Yard, Church Street, Ilkley, Yorkshire: *these people specialise in small quantities of dyestuffs.*

SOURCES OF MATERIALS IN THE USA

APPLE ROOM, 5101½ Hoover, Los Angeles, S. California.
GLEN BLACK/LOCAL COLOR, 1414 Grant Avenue, San Francisco, California: *Procion dyes only.*
STEPHEN BLUMRICH, 3223 Hyde Street, Rear Oakland 94601, California.
CIBA CHEMICAL & DYE CO., Fairlawn, New Jersey. *Synthetic dyes.*
FAB DEC, Box 3062, Lubbock 79410, Texas.
FEZANDIE & SPERRLE INC., 103 Lafayette Street, New York. *Synthetic dyes.*
FLOWERS, SEEDS & LEAVES, ROOTS & BARKS OF TREES, Box 794 Redway 95560, N. California.
HALYCYON 'THE WEAVER'S FRIEND', 1121 California Street, Denver, Colorado 80204.
ARNOLD HOFFMAN & CO. LTD, 55 Canal Street, Providence, Rhode Island. *Procion dyes only.*
THE MAKINGS, 2001 University Avenue, Berkeley, N. California 94704.
NATURE'S HERB COMPANY, 281 Ellis Street, San Francisco, California. *Vegetable dyes.*
PUTNAM FADELESS DYES INC., 301 Oak Street, Quincy, Illinois 62301. *Vegetable dyes.*
THE YARN LOFT, 1442 Camino Del Mar, California 92014.

SOCIETIES

BRITISH CHEMICAL AND DYESTUFFS ASSOCIATION, 126 Westminster Palace Gardens, Artillery Row, London SW1.
SOCIETY OF DYERS AND COLOURISTS, P.O. Box 244, Grattan Road, Bradford 1, Yorkshire. *Founded in 1884 to promote technical advance in the tinctorial arts.*

SERVICES

If you have a special problem concerning the use of natural dyes contact:
GWEN MULLINS, Shuttles, Graffham, Petworth, Sussex: *Mrs Mullins is an expert on the use of natural dyes.*

BIBLIOGRAPHY

JOURNAL OF THE SOCIETY OF DYERS AND COLOURISTS/available as above (Monthly).
SCOURING AND DYEING WITH VEGETABLE DYE RECIPES, by K. Grasset/The London School of Weaving.
SPIN YOUR OWN WOOL, DYE IT & WEAVE IT, by Molly Duncan/Bell & Sons Ltd.
THE USE OF VEGETABLE DYES, by Violetta Thurstan/Dryad Press.
VEGETABLE DYES, by E. Mairet/Faber & Faber Ltd.

The following books are available from Eliza Leadbeater, Granville House, 6 Granville Street, Winsford, Cheshire:
DYES & DYEING.
DYE PLANTS & DYEING: A HANDBOOK.
DYE PLANTS II.
YOUR YARN DYEING.

COURSES

WEST DEAN COLLEGE, Chichester, Sussex. Provides short courses on vegetable dyeing.
ADULT EDUCATION CENTRES often provide courses on tie and dye and other processes. Check FLOODLIGHT MAGAZINE for courses in London.

Man's life is laid in the loom of time
To a pattern he does not see,
While the Weaver works and the shuttles fly
Till the doom of Eternity.

ANONYMOUS

WE WOULD have liked to devote a good deal more time to weaving than has actually happened as this is an important craft, not just because it is a logical end to the processes of spinning and dyeing wool or other fibres, but because it has such enormous possibilities in terms of what can be done creatively with threads and yarns. In the end, it was decided that just the basic process of what is called 'weaving' should be illustrated and that as much information as possible on further education and sources of materials, etc. would be more useful in such a limited space as this book.

Materials

Literally almost anything can be woven: wool, cotton, silk and linen threads and yarns, raffia, straw, paper, metal threads, strips of felt, old cloth, string, rope, nylon and much else.

The Basic Process

The six diagrams shown here illustrate th most basic of all looms. *(Figs 2–5)* show simpl looms made from card with the warp threade through. Here one would use a large darnin

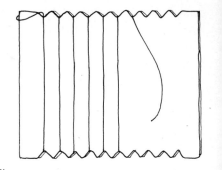

Fig 2

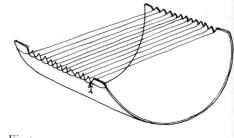

Fig 3

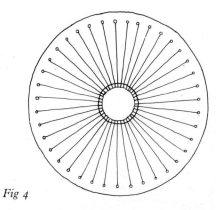

Fig 1

Fig 4

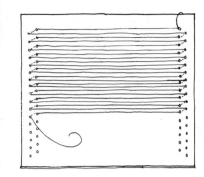

Fig 5

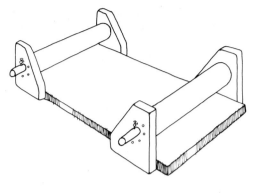

Fig 7

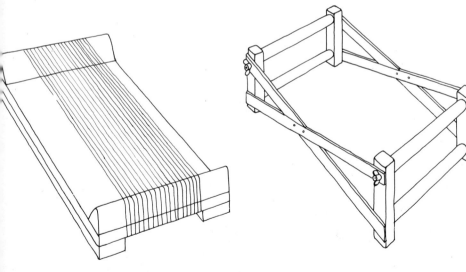 _[Fig 9 loom illustration top right]_

Fig 9

…eedle to thread through the warp. *(Figs 6 and …)* show two simple looms constructed from …ood. *(Fig 7)* is a box loom and the threads of …e warp are wrapped round the outside. With …ese two looms, a ruler with the weft wrapped …und is ideal for passing the yarn back and …rth, although a shuttle is the proper piece of …quipment to use *(fig 1)*.

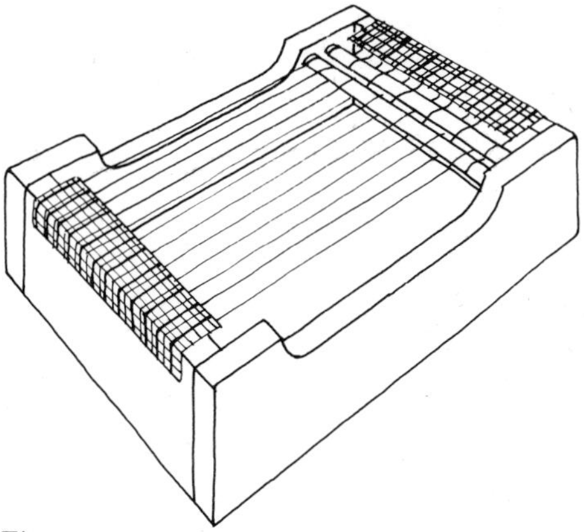

In *(figs 8 and 9)* two roller looms are shown. The rollers have the warp threads wrapped round at each end and the weft thread would be passed through in the same way as mentioned above.

With the looms illustrated, although they are extremely simple, a good deal of creative weaving can be achieved. The important thing is to experiment with different threads and patterns and to enjoy what is basically a very simple process.

Terminology

BEAM. The bar or roller stretching across a loom.
BEAMING. The process whereby the warp threads are wound on to the back roller or beam.
BEATER. The piece of a loom which presses down the rows of weft threads.
BEATING. The process of pressing down the weft thread while weaving.
BREAST ROLL. The front beam of a loom.
CANE. A new warp.
CANE ROLL. The back beam of a loom.
CANE STICKS. Sticks used for fastening the warp in a beam.
CARD LOOM. The simplest of all looms; notched cardboard with warp threads wound to and fro over the notches *(see illustrations 2–5)*.
CROSS. A collection of warp threads crossed in the form of a figure of eight to keep them tidy.
CROSS STICKS. Smooth rods for keeping the cross in order.
DAMASK. A style of weaving introduced from Damascus.
DENT. One space between two wires on a reed.

Fig 6

Fig 8

DIAPER. A system of weaving small patterns.

DOUBLING. The winding of two or more threads together.

DRESSING THE LOOM. Setting up the looming in readiness for weaving.

ENTERING HOOK. A thin hook for drawing the warp threads through the eyes in a rigid heddle.

END. A warp thread.

ENDS PER INCH. A standard unit or measure in weaving of warp threads per inch.

EYES. The openings in a rigid heddle through which the warp threads are passed.

GATING. Adjusting a loom.

HAND SHUTTLE. A smooth slat of wood, notched at both ends, for holding the weft thread in order to pass it backwards and forwards between the warp threads (fig 1).

HARNESS. A collection of heddles.

HEDDLE. The metal loop containing the eye through which the warp threads are threaded and by which these threads are raised or lowered in order to pass through the weft thread. One of the simplest arrangements on a loom is with one heddle, where every other warp thread is passed through it. When the heddle is raised, it also lifts up thread numbers 1, 3, 5, 7, 9, 11, etc. and separates them from thread numbers 2, 4, 6, 8, 10 etc. Once raised, the weft thread can be passed through the gap between the two layers of threads. Having passed through the weft thread, the heddle is then lowered and the weft thread passed back through the layers of warp threads. In this way a simple 'under and over' woven fabric is made, commonly known as a 'tabby weave'.

JACQUARD. A loom invented by M. Jacquard and used in pattern weaving.

LOOM. Any device whereby a warp is supported and kept in order for weaving.

LOOP. A doubled over length of thread.

PATTERN DRAFTING. A plan in diagram form for warp threading.

PICK. A single row of weft.

REED. A comb-shaped device for keeping the warp ends in order and for beating the weft threads together.

REED HOOK. A thin hook for drawing the warp ends through the reed.

SELVAGE. The edge of the woven cloth.

SHAFT. The frame upon which the heddle or heddles are threaded.

SHED. An opening between the two layers of warp ends through which the weft thread is passed.

SLITS. Alternating openings in a heddle between the eyes through which the warp ends are passed.

SPACING. Arranging threads in groups.

SPREADING. The process of laying out the warp threads to a set pattern for weaving.

TABBY. A plain weave, i.e. under and over.

TAKE UP. The process of gradually winding on the woven cloth to the breast beam.

TAPESTRY. Tabby weaving, in mosaic using a loose weft.

TARTAN. A material striped in warp and weft.

TIE UP. The process whereby the warp ends are tied to the front roller or breast beam.

TWILL. A material which has a diagonal effect produced by the movement of the weft threads during weaving.

WARP. The longitudinal threads tied taut on to a loom.

WARP HOOK. See Entering Hook.

WARP STICKS. Smooth wooden pieces of wood, slat shaped which are placed between the warp threads during the process of tying the warp on to the cane roll or back beam of the loom.

WARPING. Preparing a warp.

WARPING-MILL. A device for warping large warps.

WARPING BOARD. A device, namely a frame or board with pegs inserted around which the warp threads are wound.

WEB. A piece of finished weaving.

WEAVE. The end result of interlacing ends and picks, i.e. warp and weft.

WEFT. The crossing thread of a warp.

YARN. Thread of any description. There are several basic yarns of which seven have been illustrated below.

(a) SPIRAL or CORKSCREW. Consists of a fine thread interfolded with a coarse thread.

(b) GIMP. Consists of a single tightly twisted core over which a loosely twisted thread has been folded.

(c) KNOT. Consists of a single twisted thread.

(d) SLUB. A thread spun tight and loose at regular intervals which produces 'bumps' in the yarn.

(e) SPIRAL SLUB. A twisted slub yarn.

(f) GIMP SLUB. A single twisted core over which a slub yarn has been folded.

(g) LOOP. An intertwining of a single fine thread and a loose thicker thread, played out at regular intervals to produce loops.

SOURCES OF MATERIALS

Looms can be obtained from :

E. J. ARNALD & SON LTD, Butterfly Street Leeds 10.

BODDYS BOOKSHOP, 165 Linthorpe Road, Middlesborough, Teesside. *Swedish handlooms and accessories.*

BRADLEYS, 82 North Lane, East Preston Sussex. *Hand-made Inkle looms.*

HARRIS LOOMS, Northgrove Road, Hawkhurst Kent. *Recommended for quality.*

ELIZA LEADBEATER, 7 Owley Wood Road Weaverham, Northwich, Cheshire. *Looms of various types.*

LERVARD (UK) LTD, 18 Vernon Buildings Westbourne Street, High Wycombe, Buckinghamshire.

LILLSTINA, 7 Owley Wood Road, Weaverham Northwich, Cheshire. *Suppliers of the high-quality Swedish loom in both table and floor models.*

LONDON SCHOOL OF WEAVING, 136 Kensington Church Street, London W8.

GEO. & JOHN B. MAXWELL, Foldersham, Burgess

Hill, Sussex.
WEAVEMASTER, G. R. Wood & Co., 206 Kensington Church Street, London W8.
ARROL YOUNG, Netherdale, Galashiels, Scotland.

Looms for producing beadwork, complete with instructions, can be purchased from the following people :
FRED ALDOUS, P.O. Box 135, 37 Lever Street, Manchester M60 1UX.
ELLS & FARRIER, 5 Princess Street, Hanover Square, London W1R 8PH.
THOMAS HOME, St Philips Drive, Royton, Lancashire.
THE NEEDLEWOMAN SHOP, 146–148 Regent Street, London W1R 6BA.

Weaving yarns can be obtained from :
RAIE BARNETT, 7 Ralston Street, London SW3 4DT. *Woollen knop, worsted, cottons and fancy yarns.*
BORGS OF LUND, P.O. Box 1096, Lund 1, Sweden. *Linen samples.*
CAMBRIAN WOOL SUPPLIERS, Llanwrytd Wells, Breconshire. *Welsh yarn.*
R. CARDEW, Summer-dyne, Forest Side, Rowlands Castle, Hampshire. *Slubby flax and other weaving yarns.*
HILARY CHETWYND, Spindle Hoo, Itchen Stoke, nr Alresford, Hampshire. *Silk—send S.A.E. for samples.*
CHICHESTER HANDWEAVERS, Oakbank, Fordwater Road, Chichester, Sussex. *Send foolscap S.A.E. for lists.*
MR A. K. GRAUPNER, Corner House, Valley Road, Bradford, Yorkshire. *Wools and some cottons.*
WILLIAM HALL & CO. (MONSALL) LTD, 177 Stanley Road, Cheadle Hulme, Cheshire SK8 6RS. *Fancy yarns and Swedish linen.*
THE HANDLOOM WEAVERS, Fourways, Rockford, Ringwood, Hampshire. *Cottons, silk, man-made fibres and other yarns.*
J. HISLOP BATHGATE & CO., Victoria Mill, Galashiels, Scotland. *Tapestry and rug wools.*
ROBERT LAIDLAW & SONS LTD, Seafield Mill, Keith, Scotland. *Shade cards and prices on request.*
MACTAGGERT BROS. (FLEECE) LTD, Wilton Mills, Hawick, Scotland.

MERSEY YARNS, Mrs Margaret Seagroatt, 2 Staplands Road, Liverpool L14 3LL. *Jute, hemp, cottons.*
TEXERE YARN LTD, 9 Peckover Street, Bradford 1, Yorkshire. *Cotton.*
THE WEAVERS WORKSHOP, Monteith House, 61 The Royal Mile, Edinburgh. *For small quantities of jute, silk, mohair and wools.*
YARNS, 28 Upper East Hayes, Bath BA1 6LD.

SOURCES OF SUPPLY IN THE USA

PHYLLIS COHEN—WEAVER'S STUDIO, 233 Glen Road, Weston, Massachusetts 02493.
CONTESSA YARNS, P.O. Box 37, Lebanon, Connecticut 06249.
CRAFT YARNS OF RHODE ISLAND INC., 603 Mineral Springs Avenue, Pawtucket, Rhode Island 02862.
CRANE STATION, 3025 N. Campbell, Tucson, Arizona 85719.
THE CRAFT PATCH, Box 493, Temple 04984, Maine.
CREATIVE HANDWEAVERS, 3824 Sunset Boulevard, Los Angeles, S. California.
CUSTOM HANDWEAVERS & GALLERY ALLIED ARTS GUILD, Arbor Road & Creek Drive, Menlo Park, California 94025.
SANDY DELOZIER, 300 Augusta Street, San Antonio, Texas.
DHARMA TRADING CO., 1952 University Avenue, Berkeley, California 94701.
DUCK WITH AN UDDER, 1108 14th Street, Arcata, N. California 95521.
FLOWERS, SEEDS & LEAVES, ROOTS & BARKS OF TREES, Box 794, Redway, N. California 95560.
FOLKLORICO YARN CO., 522 Ramona Street, Palo Alto, N. California.
IDA GRAE, WEAVER, 424 La Verne Avenue, Mill Valley, N. California.
GREEN MOUNTAIN CREATIVE CRAFTS, Hinesburg, Vermont 05461.
HALYCON, 'THE WEAVER'S FRIEND', 1121 California Street, Denver, Colorado 80204.
HANDLOOMS, 15149 River Road, Box 858, Guerneville, N. California.
HANDWEAVERS COUNTRY-STYLE, Northfield, Vermont 05663.
HARRISVILLE DESIGNS, Harrisville, New Hampshire 03450.

HEDDLECRAFT, 713 Grant Street, Denver, Colorado 80203.
RAVEN HOCKETT, Box 116, Lagunitas, N. California 94938.
K.M. YARN CO., 18695 Wyoming, Detroit, Michigan 48221.
LOOM ROOM, 30 Pleasant Street, Forge Village, Massachusetts 01828.
MACRAME & WEAVING SUPPLY CO., 63 E. Adams Street, Chicago, Illinois 60603.
THE MAKINGS, 2001 University Avenue, Berkeley, N. California 94704.
BETTY MEADOR WEAVING STUDIO, 9600 Euclid N.E. Albuquerque 87112.
MEXISKEINS, P.O. Box 1624, Missoula, Montana 59801.
ROBERT C. NELSON, P.O. Box 1212, Concord, Massachusetts 01742.
NORWOOD LOOM CO., Box 272, Baldwin, Michigan 49304.
LAS PAJARITAS STUDIO, 6901 Guadalupe Trail N.W. Albuquerque, New Mexico 87107.
PENDLETON SHOP, HANDWEAVING STUDIO, Jordan Road-box 233, Sedona, Arizona 86336.
SCHACHT SPINDLE CO., 180 Walnut Street, Boulder, Colorado 80302.
SCHOOL PRODUCTS CO. INC., 312 E. 23rd Street, New York, N.Y. 10010.
SHEEP VILLAGE, 352 Miller Avenue, Mill Valley, N. California.
THE SHOP, Highway 49, P.O. Box 133, Amador City, N. California 95601.
PAULA SIMMONS, Box 12, Suquamish, Washington 98392.
STRAW INTO GOLD, 5550 College Avenue, P.O. Box 2904, Oakland, N. California 94618.
SUNLIT YARNS, Mount Vernon, Maine.
TAHKI IMPORTS, 336 West End Avenue, New York, N.Y. 10023.
TEXTILE CRAFT CENTER, 703 Lighthouse Avenue, Pacific Grove, N. California 93950.
TEXTILE CRAFTS, 856 N. Genesee Avenue, Los Angeles, S. California 90046.
THREADBARE SHOP, Heritage Square, Golden, Colorado 80401.
THREE BAGS FULL, 1035 Guerrero Street, San Francisco, N. California.
THREE BLACK SHEEP, 3115 Washington Boulevard, Marina Del Rey, S. California.
VILLAGE WEAVING STUDIO, 207 Elm Street, P.O. Box 365, Alto, Texas 75925.

THE VERSATILE SPINNER, Robert Yelland, Wilderness Road, Branscomb, N. California 95417.
THE WANDERING EYE, 108 Beacon Street, Somerville, Massachusetts.
WARP & WOOF POTPOURRI, 514 N. Lake Avenue, Pasadena, S. California 91101.
THE WEAVING DEPOT, 818 Manhattan Beach Boulevard, Manhattan Beach, S. California 90266.
WEAVING SHOP, 1708 Walnut Boulder, Colorado 80302.
WEAVING WORKSHOP, 3324 N. Halsted, Chicago, Illinois 60657.
WILD & WOOLLY WEAVING SUPPLIES & GALLERY, 125 15th Street, San Jose, N. California 95112.
YARN DEPOT, 545 Sutter Street, San Francisco, N. California.
THE YARN LOFT, 1442 Camino Del Mar, Del Mar, S. California 92014.

Looms and weaving equipment can be obtained from the following people :

AYOTTE'S DESIGNERY, Centre Sandwich, New Haven, Connecticut 03227.
BEXEL HANDLOOMS, 2470 Dixie Highway, Pontiac, Michigan.
EDWARD BOSWORTH, 132 Indian Creek Road, Ithaca, New York.
COUNTRYSIDE HANDWEAVERS, Box 1225, Mission, Kansas 66222.
CRAFTOOL COMPANY, Industrial Road, Woodridge, New Jersey 07075.
GILMORE LOOMS, 1032 North Broadway Avenue, Stockton, California 95205.
HERALD LOOMS, Bailey Manufacturing Co., 118 Lee Street, Lodi, Ohio 44205.
LECLERC INDUSTRIES, P.O. Box 267, Champlain, New York.
L. W. MACOMBER, 166 Essex Street, Saugus, Massachusetts.
MAGNOLIA WEAVING, 2635, 29th Avenue, W. Seattle, Washington 98199.
NEW VALLEY HANDWEAVING SERVICE, P.O. Box 76, Pinedale, California 93650.
ROBIN & RUSS HANDWEAVERS, 102 West Court Street, Ithaca, New York, 14850.
SCHOOL PRODUCTS COMPANY, 312 East 23rd Street, New York.
THE SILVER SHUTTLE, 1301, 35th N.W., Washington D.C.

Yarns of all description, including flax, wool and silk threads are available from the following people :
BRIGGS & LITTLE WOOLLEN MILLS, Harvey Station, New Brunswick, Canada.
COUNTRYSIDE HANDWEAVERS, Box 1225, Mission, Kansas, 66222.
FREDERIC J. FAWCETT INC., 129 South Street, Boston, Massachusetts.
GARY JONES SHEEP FARM, RR3, Peabody, Kansas.
MAGNOLIA WEAVING, 2635, 29th Avenue, W., Seattle, Washington 98199.
OLD MILL YARN, P.O. Box 115, Eaton Rapids, Michigan 48827.
PATERNAYAN BROS INC., 312 East 95 Street, New York.
SHUTTLE CRAFT, P.O. Box 6041, Providence, Rhode Island.

SOCIETIES

AMALGAMATED WEAVERS ASSOCIATION, 1st Floor, 74 Corporation Street, Manchester M4 2BX.
THE GUILDS OF WEAVERS, SPINNERS & DYERS, 84 Lordship Park, London N16 5UA.
This is an organisation made up of an amalgamation of several guilds which aim to :
(a) Encourage and maintain integrity and excellence of craftsmanship
(b) Foster a sense of beauty of material, texture, colour and design
(c) Provide opportunities for interchange of information, for enlarging knowledge at holiday schools, for demonstrations, lectures and library facilities
(d) To co-operate with other guilds having like aims.

A full list of these guilds now follows :
Berkshire
Mrs S. L. Batley, 20 Croft Lane, Speen, Newbury RG14 1RR.
Birmingham and District
Mrs L. F. Stringfellow, 680 Evesham Road, Crabbs Cross, Redditch, Worcestershire.
Buckinghamshire
Mr F. J. Ruck, The Meads, Millshot Drive, Chequers Hill, Amersham.
Cheshire
Mrs Louise Littleton, 26 Glebelands Road, Knutsford, Wal 6 9DZ.

Cornwall
Mrs Lyne, 52 Falmouth Road, Truro.
Coventry and District
Mrs A. Ludgate, 3 Babbacombe Road, Coventry, Warwickshire.
Devon
Mrs H. M. Lee, 16 Whiteway Road, Kingsteignton, Newton Abbot.
Dorset
Mrs M. Richmond, 16 Parkstone Avenue, Poole.
Edinburgh
Miss Elizabeth Mackay, 37 Mountcastle Drive South, Portobello, Edinburgh 15.
Gloucestershire
Mrs B. G. Martin, Victoria Villa, Cotswold Close, Brimscombe, Stroud GL5 2UA.
Hallamshire and District
Miss O. M. Brown, 115 Stubley Lane, Dronfield-Woodhouse, Sheffield S18 5YL.
Hampshire
Miss Nancy Goschen, Broadlands, Shortheath, Farnham, Surrey.
Kent
Mrs J. E. Church, Kent Bridge Lodge, Kingsdown, deal.
Lancashire and the Lakes
Miss M. Scragg, 69 Brookhouse Road, Caton, Lancaster.
London and Home Counties
Hon. Registrar: Miss Raie Barnett, 7 Ralston Street, London SW3. Tel: 01-352 8740.
Secretary: Mrs A. M. Kennedy, 80 Scotts Lane, Bromley, Kent BR2 0LX.
Midland Hand-weavers Association
Mr P. B. Chawner, 51 Westridge Road, King's Heath, Birmingham 13.
Monmouthshire
Mrs Isabel F. McGraghan, A.T.D., 30 Alltyryn Court, Newport.
Norfolk and Suffolk
Miss I. M. Sturgeon, 21 Cotmer Road, Oulton Broad, Lowestoft.
Oxford
Mrs Patricia Baines, 23 St Margarets Road, Oxford OX2 6RX.
Somerset
Mrs Joan Williamson, 120 West Street, Bridgwater.
Sussex
Miss Dorothy M. Ablett, 76 Dean Court Road, Rottingdean.
West Hertfordshire
Mrs R. F. George, 38 Orchard Drive, Watford, Hertfordshire.
Worcestershire
Miss V. L. Lockyer, 41 Howsell Road, Malvern Link.

Wiltshire
Mrs P. M. Haines, Witches Wood, The Firs, Kingsdown, Chippenham.
York and District
Col. H. R. Barton, M.B.E., 25 Grosvenor Terrace, York.

HARRIS TWEED ASSOCIATION LTD, 92 Academy Street, Inverness, Scotland. *Gives information on the production of Harris Tweed and helps protect its name.*
LONDON JUTE ASSOCIATION, 69 Cannon Street, London EC4. *For all information concerning the purchase of jute in this country.*
MIDLAND HAND WEAVERS ASSOCIATION, 51 Westridge Road, Birmingham 15. *Fosters interest in hand spinning, dyeing and weaving.*

SERVICES

For any special information concerning weaving contact the following people who are experts in this field:
TADEK BEUTLICH, Gospels, Beacon Road, Ditchling, Sussex. *For information relating to man-made fibres.*
HILDA BREED, Flansham Cottage, Cootham, Pulborough, Sussex.
RUTH HURLE, 47 East Street, Saffron Walden, Essex.
MARIANNE STRAUB, c/o The Textile Department, Royal College of Art, Kensington Gore, London.

BIBLIOGRAPHY

TEXTILE HISTORY/David & Charles Ltd, P.O. Box 4, South Devon House, Railway Station, Newton Abbot, Devon. (Annually in December.) Price: £1.05.
THE WEAVERS, SPINNERS AND DYERS ASSOCIATION QUARTERLY JOURNAL/available from 84 Lordship Park, London N16 5UA. *This magazine is full of interest and extremely useful.*
BEAD LOOMS/Crafts Unlimited, The Old Mill, Nannerch, nr Mold, Flintshire.
CARD LOOM WEAVING/Dryad Press.
CREATIVE DESIGN IN WALL HANGINGS, by Lili Blumenau/Allen & Unwin Ltd.
HAND WEAVING ON TWO-WAY LOOMS/Dryad Press.

PRACTICAL FOUR-SHAFT WEAVING, by Vera Miles/Dryad Press.
SIMPLE WEAVING, by Hilary Chetioynd/Studio Vista.
TABLET WEAVING/Dryad Press.
THE TECHNIQUES OF RUG WEAVING, by Peter Collingwood/Faber & Faber Ltd.
THE TECHNIQUE OF WEAVING, by John Tovey/B. T. Batsford Ltd.
THE TECHNIQUE OF WOVEN TAPESTRY, by Tadek Beutlich/B. T. Batsford Ltd.
THE WEAVER'S CRAFT, by Simpson/Dryad Press.
WEAVING, by Nell Znamierowski/Pan Books Ltd.
WEAVING ON FOUR-WAY TABLE LOOMS/Dryad Press.

Weaving Pattern Books

A HANDWEAVER'S PATTERN BOOK, by M. Davidson/Spencer International Press Inc., New York.
HANDWEAVING PATTERNS FROM FINLAND, by Pyssalo and Merisato/Blandford Press Ltd.
KEY TO WEAVING, by M. Black/Spencer International Press Inc., New York.
SWEDISH HANDWEAVING, by M. Selander/Studio Vista.
WEAVES AND PATTERN DRAFTING, by John Tovey/B. T. Batsford Ltd.
WEAVING PATTERNS, by M. Selander/Werzäta Forlag, Goteburg.
WEAVING PATTERNS FOR THE TWO-WAY LOOM, by Vera Miles/Dryad Press.

COURSES

ADULT EDUCATION CENTRES. *Check* FLOODLIGHT MAGAZINE *for your nearest centre in London.*
BRADFORD TECHNICAL COLLEGE in conjunction with BRADFORD REGIONAL COLLEGE OF ART, Great Horton Road, Bradford BD7 1AX. *A 13-month course which includes practical knowledge of handspinning, dyeing, materials, hand loom, weaving and cloth finishing. The culmination of the course is the Bradford Certificate in Hand Loom Weaving, replacing the now defunct City & Guilds of London Institute Hand Loom Weaving Certificate. Course fees are £42 and accommodation is available during the summer schools in the Halls of Residence at Bradford*

University.
THE HAND WEAVERS STUDIO & GALLERY, 29 Haroldstone Road, London E17.
LONDON SCHOOL OF WEAVING, 136 Kensington Church Street, London W8. *Full and part-time courses. Send for details.*
THE WEAVERS WORKSHOP SUMMER SCHOOL, The Secretary, 'Foundations', The Weavers Workshop, Monteith House, The Royal Mile, Edinburgh EH1 1SR.
WEST DEAN COLLEGE, Chichester, Sussex. *Provides courses at various levels.*

Vocational, Degree and Post-Graduate Courses
CITY OF BIRMINGHAM POLYTECHNIC, Art and Design Centre, Corporation Street, Birmingham B4 7DX. Tel. 021 359 3611.
CAMBERWELL SCHOOL OF ARTS AND CRAFTS, Peckham Road, London SE5 8UF. Tel. 01 703 7485.
CENTRAL SCHOOL OF ART AND DESIGN, Southampton Row, London WC1B 4AP. Tel. 01 405 1825.
DYFED SCHOOL OF ART, Picton Place, Carmarthen.
GOLDSMITHS' COLLEGE, SCHOOL OF ART, New Cross, London SE14 6NW. Tel. 01 692 7171.
HORNSEY COLLEGE OF ART, Crouch End Hill, London N8 8DG. Tel. 01 348 1761.
CITY OF LEICESTER POLYTECHNIC, P.O. Box 143, Leicester LE1 9BH. Tel. 0533 50181.
LOUGHBOROUGH COLLEGE OF ART AND DESIGN, Radmoor, Loughborough, Leicestershire. Tel. 050 93 61515.
LOWESTOFT COLLEGE OF FURTHER EDUCATION, School of Art, St Peter's Street, Lowestoft.
MANCHESTER POLYTECHNIC, Faculty of Art and Design, Cavendish Street, All Saints, Manchester M15 6BR. Tel. 061 273 2715.
MALVERN COLLEGE OF FURTHER EDUCATION SCHOOL OF ART, Albert Road North, Malvern.
NUNEATON SCHOOL OF ART, Coton Road, Nuneaton.
NORTH STAFFORDSHIRE POLYTECHNIC, Faculty of Art and Design, College Road, Stoke-on-Trent ST4 2DE. Tel. 0782 45531.
ROYAL COLLEGE OF ART, Kensington Gore, London SW7.
WEST SURREY COLLEGE OF ART AND DESIGN, Farnham Centre, West Street, Farnham,

Surrey. Tel. 025 13 22441.
WINCHESTER SCHOOL OF ART, Park Avenue, Winchester, Hampshire. Tel. 0962 61891.
ULSTER COLLEGE, The Northern Ireland Polytechnic, Jordanstown, Newtownabbey, Co. Antrim. Tel. 023 124 5131.
WEST SURREY COLLEGE OF ART AND DESIGN, Farnham Centre, 24 West Street, Farnham.
THE POLYTECHNIC WOLVERHAMPTON, Faculty of Art and Design, North Street, Wolverhampton WV1 1DT. Tel. 0902 29911.

WEAVING STUDIOS TO VISIT
ENGLAND
Cambridgeshire
SPEEN WEAVERS & SPINNERS, Speen, Aylesbury. Tel. Hampden Row 303. Nearest towns, High Wycombe, Great Missenden, Princes Risborough
Hand-woven rugs, silks, linens, wools and cottons. Cot and full-sized blankets. Tapestries and tweeds.
Open daily, Saturday and Sunday inclusive, but please telephone before morning visit.
FENWEAVE, 37 & 39 Main Street, Witchford, nr Ely. Tel. Ely 2150.
Country workshop, looms working producing a variety of woollen, silk, linen, and cotton articles.
Resident—almost any time.

Cornwall
MOUNT HAWKE WEAVERS, Mount Hawke, Truro. Tel. Porthowan 501. Also at Sloop Craft Market, St Ives and Barbican, Penzance
All articles hand-woven. Comprehensive range in modern colours includes floor-rugs, bedspreads, tweeds, evening-dress materials.
Weavers can be seen at work. Open every day.
VANESSA ROBERTSON, Chy-an-gwyador, Bojewyan Stennack, Pendeen, Penzance.
Hand-loom weaver, natural fibres and vegetable dyes.
Visitors by appointment only.
TWEENSTREAM WEAVERS, Tweenstream, Lowerton, nr Helston. Tel. Helston 2411 (03-265 2411).
Tweeds in exclusive colour blends, suit and skirt lengths, stoles and scarves, etc. Woven on the premises by the owners from yarn spun and/or dyed in Scotland.
Always open. Local road plan supplied on request to prospective visitors.

Cumberland
F. B. MERCER, Eastern Cottage, Hallbankgate, Brampton. Tel. Hallbankgate 309.
A craft producer of hand-woven tweeds suitable for ladies' skirts and costumes. Every process from weaving to finishing carried out entirely by hand.
Visitors welcome any time but advisable to ring as this is a one-man cottage industry.

Devonshire
THE BOVEY HANDLOOM WEAVERS (Angus Litster), 1 Station Road, Bovey Tracey. Tel. Bovey Tracey 3424.
Tweeds, ties, scarves, rugs and stoles, all in pure, new wool.
9 am–5.30 pm. Early closing 1 pm Wednesday.
AUNE VALLEY WEAVERS, Aveton Gifford, Kingsbridge. Tel. Loddiswell 240. On the main road from Kingsbridge to Plymouth.
A large selection of local and other tweeds, knitwear, sheepskin rugs, gloves, slippers.

Dorset
J. & N. WHITAKER HALL, Thursley, 26 High Park Road, Broadstone. Tel. Broadstone 3522.
Hand-weaving: ties, scarves, stoles, shawls, rugs, trolley-cloths, table-mats, cushion-covers, etc.
Visitors welcome 10 am–1 pm and 2.30 pm–5.30 pm most days, but please phone for appointment.

Essex
URSULA BROCK, Tolleshunt D'Arcy Hall, Maldon. Tel. Tolleshunt D'Arcy 225.
Hand-woven Jacquard silks.
By appointment.

Lincolnshire
NOELLE M. BOSE, 'Westoby', West End, Winteringham, nr Scunthorpe DN15 9NS. Tel. Winterton 729.
Hand-woven floor-rugs, knee-rugs, shoulderbags, cushion-covers, table-mats and pramcovers. Curtain material tweed.
Visitors welcome any time.

Oxfordshire
JEAN ROBERTS, 110 Newland, Witney. Tel. Witney 5218.
Hand-woven floor rugs.
Resident, but best phone first.

VARDOC FABRICS LTD, Church Lane, Old Marston, Oxford. Tel. Oxford 42515.
Hand-loom and power-loom weavers. Pure wool neckties and head-squares.
9 am–5 pm Monday to Friday.

Suffolk
PETER COLLINGWOOD, Old School, Nayland, nr Colchester. Tel. Nayland 401.
Hand-woven floor-rugs, wall-hangings.
Any time, any day.
MARY JANE TOULSON, The Cottage, Old Street, Haughley, Stowmarket. Tel. Haughley 391.
Hand-woven floor-rugs and wall-hangings.
Resident.

Westmorland
FABRICATIONS, Design & Weaving Studio (Mr Neil Galloway), Grasmere.
Exclusive range of cloth designed and power woven in Grasmere by Neil Galloway. The latest range includes a selection of designs produced in the undyed natural colours of the Herdwick Sheep, native to the Lake District. A new workshop will be in production early in 1973.
HAND-LOOM WEAVER, Old Coach House, Grasmere (Chris Reekie & Sons). Tel. Grasmere 221.
Hand-weaving done on premises. Exclusive colours and designs. Mohair rugs, scarves, stoles a speciality.
Open every day.

Wiltshire
BEROWALD INNES, Pinkney Pound, nr Sherston, Malmesbury. Tel. Sherston 373.
Specialists in the hand-weaving of floor-rugs and wall-hangings, and also the working of heraldic embroidery (wool on canvas).
Resident (except from Christmas till Easter). Almost always in but advisable to telephone if possible.
WHITE HORSE SPINNERS AND WEAVERS (AUDREY & CLEMENT CHARLES), Beech Bank, Bratton, nr Westbury. Tel. Bratton 382.
Floor-rugs (mostly from hand-spun yarn), tweeds, etc. Hand-spun/hand-knitted sweaters. Tie-dyed pure silk squares and scarves, also handmade buttons from local woods. Potpourri made from old English recipes.
Open normal business hours (prior notice of arrival appreciated). Week-ends by appointment.

Yorkshire

BRONTE TAPESTRIES, Storr Heights, Thornton, Bradford. Tel. Thornton 2409. STD 027484 2409.

A group of hand-loom weavers working in the village of Thornton, making a wide selection of hand-woven articles ranging from ties to tapestries, all kinds of clothing available in rich subtle colours and the most attractive range of rugs you have ever seen.

Open all days, telephone if possible week-ends. Colour brochure available on request, send S.A.E.

GREWELTHORPE HANDWEAVERS, Grewelthorpe, Ripon. Tel. Kirkby Malzeard 209.

A true country workshop in a 200-year-old barn. Fine worsted cloth hand-woven on the premises by Janie and Malcolm McDougall on their specially designed hand-loom. Browse round the craft-shop which contains the selected work of over 50 accredited craftsmen in all fields.

Open from 9 am to 6 pm or until dusk, whichever is later, all year including Sunday (closed Monday).

LOTTE PHILLIPS, 3 Cliffe Ash, Golcar, nr Huddersfield. Tel. Huddersfield 54321.

Individually designed, well-made, hand-woven articles: ties, belts, scarves, shoulder-bags, cushions, tabards, tonags, etc.

Any time, including evenings and week-ends, but please telephone first.

WALES

Breconshire

CAMBRIAN FACTORY LTD, Llanwrtyd Wells. Tel. Llanwrtyd Wells 211.

Welsh tweeds, rugs, head-scarves, ready-made skirts, skirts and gents' suits to measure, scarves, knitting-wool, socks, ties, tweed purses and hand-bags, blankets, quilts.

Monday to Friday, 8 am–5.30 pm, Saturday, 9 am–12 noon, 9 am–4.30 pm July to Sept.

Caernarvonshire

BRYNKIR WOOLLEN MILL, Golan, Garndolbenmaen, North Wales LL51 9YU. Tel. Garndolbenmaen 236.

Pure wool tapestry and honeycomb bed-covers, tweeds, flannels and tapestry cloth, small woollen gifts and knitting wool carded, spun and woven on the premises.

9 am–5 pm Monday to Friday. 9 am–noon Saturday in Summer.

HANNAH JONES LTD, Welsh Woollen Mills, Penmachno, Betws-y-Coed. Tel. Betws-y-Coed 352.

Pure wool tweeds, tapestry cloth, tapestry quilts, tailored garments, craft goods.

Mill open to the public all year round Monday to Friday, 9 am–4.30 pm.

Mill Shop open all year round Monday to Friday, 9 am–6 pm. Also on Saturday and Sunday during the Summer months.

TREFRIW WOOLLEN MILLS LTD, Vale of Conway Woollen Mills, Trefriw. Tel. Llanrwst 640462.

Manufactures from the raw wool of hand-knitting wools, travelling-rugs, tapestry and honeycomb quilts, plain and cellular blankets, tapestry and tweed by the yard.

Mill and Shop Monday–Friday 8 am–4.45 pm. Shop only Saturday 10 am–4 pm. Sundays in July and August 2.30 pm–5 pm.

Cardiganshire

CURLEW WEAVERS (GIL & KAY POULSON), Troedyraur Old Rectory, nr Rhydlewis. Tel. Rhydlewis 357.

Individual tweed, lightweight evening and wedding-dress fabrics; lightweight travel-rugs and bedspreads; ties and men's jackets; Curlew Tweedster clothes; puppets and numerous small articles; co-ordinated curtain and upholstery materials.

Visitors welcomed 8 am–5 pm Monday to Friday.

LERRY TWEED MILLS, Lerry Mills, Talybont. Tel. Talybont 235.

Manufacturers of hand-woven and home-spun tweeds. Stockists of tapestry quilts, tapestry cloth, rugs, blankets, small gifts and tapestry clothes.

Shop: 9 am–6 pm Monday to Saturday, Afterwards by appointment. Mill: 9 am–12.30 pm, 1.30 pm–5 pm Monday to Friday.

JOHN MORGAN & SON, Woollen Manufacturers, etc, Rock Mills, Capel Dewi, Llandysul. Tel. Llandysul 2356.

Blankets, tapestry quilts, table-mats, cushion-covers, tea-cosies, men's socks and stockings and other Welsh crafts.

Carmarthenshire

CAMBRIAN MILLS (FELINDRE) LTD, Drefach, Felindre, Llandyssul. Tel. Felindre 209.

Blankets, quilts, honeycomb quilts, tapestry quilts, tapestry coats, gents' tweed ties, flannels, shirtings and traditional designs, ladies' and gents' shirts (made on premises), motor-rugs, head-squares, scarves and aprons.

Showrooms are open from Monday to Friday 8 am–5 pm and by appointment.

CORGI HOSIERY LTD, Ammanford. Tel. Ammanford 2104.

Hand-framed Intarsia botany, shetland, lambswool and cashmere knitwear and hosiery. Welsh tapestry, tweed or flannel hand-tailored garments, made to measure.

Visitors welcomed 8 am–4.15 pm.

CWMDUAD WOOLLEN MILLS, Cwmduad. Tel. Conwil Elfet 337.

Wide range of tapestry clothing, including capes, skirts and anoraks. Tapestry handbags and purses, sheepskin rugs, hats, gloves and slippers.

9 am–6 pm including Sunday.

JOHN JONES (DERW) LTD, Derw Mills, Pentrecourt, Llandysul. Tel Llandysul 3361.

Pure new wool tapestry quilts, tapestry cloth, lightweight worsted flannels and tapestry clothes, car-rugs, floor-rugs, blankets.

9 am–5 pm Monday–Friday.

D. LEWIS & SONS LTD, Rhydybont Mills (Est 1830), Llanbyther. Tel. 97/285.

Tapestry garments, quilts, blankets, tweeds, flannels, floor-rugs, gifts.

Merionethshire

THE WEAVER'S LOFT, Jubilee Road, Barmouth.

Weavers of pure new wool tapestry cloth. Stockists of tweed and flannel by the yard; clothing, tapestry bed-covers.

Weaving from 9 am–5 pm. Shop open 9 am–9 pm (7 days in Summer).

Harris loom

Pembrokeshire

WALLIS WOOLLEN MILL, Ambleston, nr Haverfordwest. Tel. Clarbeston 297.

Traditional fabrics, wide range of colours and designs, to International Woolmark standards. Tapestry bedspreads approved by Design Centre. High-class dressmaking at mill. Coats, capes, dresses, handbags and purses, etc. Shop at mill.
Monday to Friday 10 am–6 pm.

SCOTLAND

Aberdeenshire

RUSSELL GURNEY WEAVERS, Brae Croft, Muiresk, Turriff AB5 7HE. Tel. Turriff 3544.

Exclusively designed hand-woven tweeds, dress materials and suitings in traditional and modern colour ranges. Estate checks designed. Hostess skirts in brushed worsted, lambswool, etc. Scarves and rugs, cushion covers in overshot patterns.
Visitors welcome any time but telephone to avoid disappointment.

Dumfriesshire

MOFFAT WEAVERS, Mill, Ladyknowe, Moffat. Shop: High Street, Moffat. Tel. Moffat 20134.

Tweed, tartan, scarves, ties, knitwear, woollen and mohair rugs.
Mill: 7 days per week, 9 am–5 pm.
Shop: 6 days per week, 9 am–6 pm, Sunday 10.30 am–6 pm.

Renfrewshire

AGNES HAMILTON, Monica Hardie (Handloom Weavers), Pilmuir Farm, Newton Mearns. Tel. 041-639 1845.

Interesting and unusual designs of soft and floor-rugs, scarves, stoles, shawls and table-mats. Specialising in exclusive hand-woven christening-shawls.
10 am–6 pm (week-ends if requested).

NORTHERN IRELAND

Down

GERD-HAY-EDIE, FSIA, Mourne Textiles Ltd, Old Killowen Road, Rostrevor, Newry. Tel. Rostrevor 373.

Hand-woven tweeds; top-grade fashion for dresses, suits and coats. A few rugs, bedspreads and tweed curtains.
9 am–5.30 pm. Looms working five days a week. Saturday by appointment only, by phone.

MAKING RUGS

We are going to describe five methods of producing a rug and the method chosen must be determined on the economical factors involved. For instance, if a rug is needed quickly, without any loss of creativity in the design, then the woven technique or machine tufting technique may be the answer, even more so if rugs are to be produced commercially. Handmade rugs always tend to take rather a long time to make so bear this in mind, unless a number of people can get together communally and work on the same rug. There is no reason why the various techniques shouldn't be mixed together, e.g. machine tufting and embroidered rugs.

Handworked Pile Rug

There are various methods of working a wool pile rug but the common way is to hook the wool pieces through the rug canvas or hessian to give a series of small tufts which collectively form a pile. The canvas or hessian takes the place of the warp and weft threads in a woven carpet. Special rug canvas can be purchased which is usually marked up in squares every 8 ridges so that the design to be worked can easily be translated from the design sheet to the canvas, rather like the way one uses graph paper. Special rug wool can be obtained already cut to the required length (about 2 inches) from craftshops, but it is a very expensive way to buy wool and bulk buying from a mill or wool supplier is far more economical. Also, by obtaining unbleached wool in bulk, it can be dyed any colour your design requires.

Method

Assuming bulk wool has been purchased, the first job is to cut it into 2 inch lengths. This can simply be done by binding the wool round a long slat of 1 inch wood and then cutting down the middle *(fig 1)*.

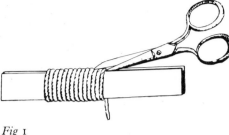

Fig 1

The pieces of wool are worked into the canvas or hessian with a special rug hook which pulls the wool through and knots it in one process. There are a number of different types of hook on the market. One type is like an ordinary crochet hook with a movable latch which prevents the hook from catching when drawn back through the canvas. Another type

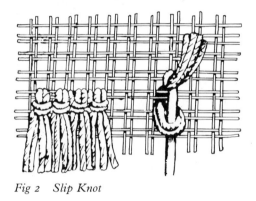

Fig 2   *Slip Knot*

is similar in action to a pair of pliers incorporating a simple device which knots the wool on the canvas in one go. Both are easy ways of producing what is simply a slip knot *(fig 2)*.

If a fine wool is being used then every hole in the canvas should be worked but if the normal 2 ply—cable wool is used, it may be knotted every alternate hole, depending on the thickness of pile desired. Try experimenting with different thicknesses of wool together in one rug, even string and other material can be knotted. After drawing out the design of the rug on the canvas (ink is best to mark the canvas) begin to work the wool. (If the canvas has any raw edges it may be best to turn in the

ends $1\frac{1}{2}$ inches and work through the two thicknesses.) Work systematically from one end of the rug to the other. The following diagrams show how the wool is knotted on the canvas.

It will be found easier to work on a flat surface like a table and knot in rows from left to right so this leaves the finished part nearest yourself. When the rug is finished, back it with a close woven hessian. This can be done by either glueing with a P.V.A. medium, or sewing. In either case, the hessian must be turned in at the edges for 2 inches to form a clean edge.

Embroidered Rug

A heavy jute canvas is used here and worked with tapestry stitches. The finished product is a hard-wearing rug and uses about $\frac{1}{4}$ lb of wool per square foot. Some good stitches to use are: cross stitch, knotted stitch and chain stitch *(figs 3, 4 and 5)* but there are others worth experimenting with.

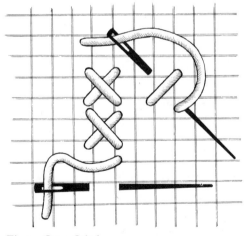

Fig 3   Cross Stitch

The rug can be backed in the same way as for hand-worked pile rugs, or left as it is and edged with blanket stitch *(fig 6)*.

Needlewoven Rug

These are quick and easy to make and are

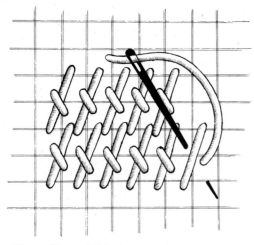

Fig 4   Knotted Stitch

Fig 5   Chain Stitch

strongly recommended for economic reasons. The work is normally done on heavy woollen material or jute. Basically, some of the warp or weft threads are removed and replaced by new ones using rug wool. If threads are removed at even distances then rather a fine geometric pattern can be built up. A canvas needle is all that is needed for this technique. Back the rug in the normal way or edge with blanket stitch.

Machine Tufted Rug

For those who want to concentrate more on design and who don't fancy long hours of knotting or stitching, then machine tufting may be the answer *(fig 7)*. Although new machines are expensive (about £148), second-hand ones can be got hold of and they are easily repaid in terms of output. Once the knack of using the machine has been mastered, and they are amazingly simple to use, then a 6-foot square carpet can be made in a day from start to finish.

Method

The machine uses wool at a phenomenal rate so that wool must first be wound on to bobbins either bought from a mill, or made at home (toilet rolls are a good thing to use). Always practice first on a scrap of material before attempting an actual rug as the distances between the rows of tufts must be even and of a uniform distance. Experience has shown that about $\frac{1}{8}$ inch is an optimum measurement. Making the rows of tufts too far apart will produce bare patches so watch out for this. Incidently, the machine will not take thick rug wool, knitting wool being about the best sort to use, nor will it take a large area of cloth because of the limited distance between the needle and the machine body. The best material to work on is strong, thick cotton or calico—don't use canvas.

Keep the design as simple and geometric as possible as manoeuvering the cloth is difficult when attempting to break away from straight lines. When the whole rug has been tufted (larger rugs can be made by sewing pieces together) it must be backed with a close-woven hessian or canvas because the machine does not knot, it only pushes the wool through and back again. The backing must be thoroughly glued with P.V.A. medium so be careful to do this part of the operation absolutely thoroughly. Turn in the edges of the backing material before glueing so as to make a clean, even edge.

The Machine Stitched Rug

A special tool that is used to machine-stitch material for rug use can be bought from The Singer Sewing Machine Company. It's called

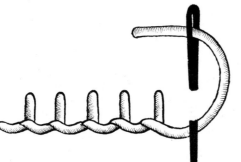

Fig 6   Blanket Stitch

Fig 7   Tufting Machine

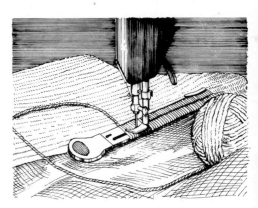

Fig 8   Singer Guide

a 'Singercraft Guide' and is basically a two-pronged piece of metal on which the wool is wound evenly, thus enabling a line of machine stitching down to the centre of the two prongs *(see fig 8)*. This binds the wool to the backing material (normally thick cotton or calico for this method) and after machining, the guide is slipped out and the remaining wool loops are cut with a pair of scissors to produce two rows of tufts. This process is repeated over the whole area of the backing material until a solid pile of tufts has been achieved. The rug is then finished off in the normal way, by backing with hessian.

Rag Rug

There are two principle methods of producing a rag rug: in one the rags are pulled through the canvas with a large crochet hook, and knotted with a slip knot as in a handworked pile rug. In the other, the rags are twisted and sewn together or braided. Rag rugs are immensely cheap to make and are beautiful when finished. All sorts of rags can be used and are O.K. left the colours they are or dyed. Some good effects can be obtained by either mixing dyed and undyed rags together in one rug, or by part-dyeing the rags in a dark colour, i.e dark blue or dark brown, so that a whole range of beautiful muted colours are produced by the action of the dye on the existing colours of the rags.

1ST METHOD

Strong, open meshed hessian or sacking is best for a hooked rag rug. After determining the actual size of the rug, allow another 2 inches all round when cutting out the piece of hessian to allow for turning in and hemming. It may be found easier to work the hessian stretched over a wooden frame, but it is not essential. The rags should be cut into $\frac{1}{2}$-inch strips, the length being determined by the depth of pile required (about 2–3 inches).

Have a pile of rag strips on your lap and using a coarse crochet hook, simply hook the strips through, one at a time, to form loops in the hessian. The loops can either be knotted with a simple slip knot, or left as they are (as in a machine tuft) whereby the whole rug must then be firmly glued with P.V.A. medium to a

Fig 9   Plaiting

close-woven hessian or canvas so as to prevent the rags from working their way loose.

It may be a good idea to work the rags with a longer length than the required pile, so that the finished rug can be trimmed with scissors to give an even surface—it all depends on the nature of the pile required.

2ND METHOD

Cut the rags into 2-inch widths. Turn each side of each piece in $\frac{1}{2}$ inch and iron flat; then fold over and hem on a machine so that about 1 inch width strips are formed. This is important as all the frayed edges are then concealed inside. Next, join the strips together end to end so that a number of lengths about $1\frac{1}{2}$ yards long are formed. Until these lengths are used it will be found helpful to wrap them round a cardboard tube to keep them nice and flat.

Take three lengths and begin plaiting them together as one would plait hair *(fig 9)*. It is a good idea to produce a good number of plaits in one go otherwise it becomes a bore breaking off from braiding to produce more plaits. To make the finished rug, simply sew the plaits together in a circle, starting from the middle and working outwards. Use strong waxed thread for sewing. Any size of circular rug can be made by simply working in more and more plaits. Lovely effects can be obtained by playing with colour: for instance, making the centre a dark colour and working out to a bright colour, or by making bands of separate colours. This kind of rug needs no backing.

SOURCES OF MATERIALS

Canvas and hessian can be obtained from:
JOHN LEWIS, Oxford Street, London W1.
THE NEEDLEWOMAN, Regent Street, London W1. *Also most department stores and local craft shops.*
Cottons and calico can be obtained from the following people:
EMIL ADLER, 46 Mortimer Street, London W1.
BRADLEY TEXTILES LTD, 15 Stott Street, Nelson, Lancashire.
JOSHUA HOYLE & SONS (MANCHESTER) LTD, 12 Bowland, London EC4.
JOHN LEWIS, Oxford Street, London W1.

LIMERICKS, 89 Hamlet Court Road, Westcliffe-on-Sea, Essex.

MCCULLOCH & WALLIS, Dearin Street (off Oxford Street), London W1.

TOOTAL, BROADHURST & LEE & CO. LTD, 56 Oxford Street, Manchester 1.

WOOLFINS, Great Tichfield Street, London W1.

P.V.A. medium can be obtained from your local hardware shop or builders' merchant.

Rughooks, threads, crochet hooks and other sundries are available from your local shop or from:

MACE & MAIRN, 89 Crane Street, Salisbury.

THE NEEDLEWOMAN, Regent Street, London W1.

Special rug yarns are available from:

MISS R. BARNETT, 7 Ralstone Street, London SW3.

ARTHUR BELL LTD, Langholm, Scotland.

L. GATHIER & CO. LTD, 6/9 Charterhouse Square, London EC1. *Monofil.*

CRAFTSMENS MARK, Freshank, Denbeigh, North Wales. *Handspun yarns.*

HUGH GRIFFITHS, Brookdale, Beckington, Bath. *Yarns of all kinds.*

J. HISLOP BATHGATE & CO., Victoria Mill, Galashiels, Scotland.

T. M. HUNTER, Brora, Sutherland, Scotland. *Cheviot and other tweed yarns.*

JOHN KEENEN & CO. LTD, 64 Little Horton Lane, Bradford 5. *Worsted in oil 2 ply.*

HUGH MACHAY & CO. LTD, Durham Carpets, P.O. Box No. 1, Durham City. *Rug Wools. No samples, just a price list: cheap and very good.*

MULTIPLE FABRIC CO. LTD, Dudley Hill, Bradford BD4 9PV. *Horse, hair, human hair, camel hair, mohair, white and grey wool yarns.*

THE RUG-CRAFT CENTRE, Dept W, Croft Mill, Hebden Bridge, Yorkshire HX7 8AP. *Send for free samples and price list.*

MRS M. SEAGROATT, 2 Staplands Road, Liverpool L14 3LL. *String and jutes.*

SOUTHWOCK AND CASE LTD, 38 Canning Place, Liverpool 1. *Warp string.*

STODDARTS (HALIFAX) LTD, Empire Works, Halifax. *2 and 6 ply rug wool.*

J. & W. STUART LTD, Esk Mills, Musselburgh, Scotland. *Netting twine.*

TEXERE YARNS, 9 Peckover Street, Bradford 1, Yorkshire.

THE WEAVERS' SHOP, Dept 50, King Street, Wilton, Salisbury. *Wilton rugwool in many colours.*

JACOBS, YOUNG & WESTBURY LTD, 199 Borough High Street, London SE1. *Rushes and loom cord.*

Wool in bulk can be obtained from A. K. GRAUPNER, Corner House, Valley Road Bradford BD1 4AA. *This firm, believe us, is often the cheapest and the service is good.*

Tufting Machines manufactured and supplied by DAVID ALMOND LTD, Union Works, Bacup Road, Waterfoot, Rossendale, Lancashire. The machines come in two parts; the Venor single needle tufting machine, with spares, price £104 and the Unit Stand and Motor for the above machine, price £48. Delivery 6 to 8 weeks.

SOURCES OF MATERIALS IN THE USA

Rugwool can be obtained from the following people:

BRIGGS & LITTLE WOOLLEN MILLS, Harvey Station, New Brunswick, Canada.

CONTESSA YARNS, P.O. Box 37, Lebenon, Connecticut 06249.

OLD MILL YARN, P.O. Box 115, Eaton Rapids, Michigan, 48827.

PATERNAYAN BROS INC., 312 East 95th Street, New York.

Yarns can be obtained from the addresses listed at the end of the weaving chapter (see p. 71), but more specialised rug yarns, as well as rug hooks, canvas and other equipment can be obtained from:

THE BLACK SHEEP, The Cannery, San Fransisco, N. California.

JOAN MOSHIMER, North Street, Kennebunkport, Maine.

TERRY'S RUG SHOP, 95 Pleasant Street, Waterville, Maine.

BIBLIOGRAPHY

RUG MAKING/Crafts Unlimited.
RUG MAKING, by I. P. Roseaman/Dryad Press.
RUGMAKING, by Joan Droop/Bell & Sons Ltd.
RUGMAKING, by Nell Znamierowski/Pan Books Ltd.
RUG WEAVING/Dryad Press.
WOVEN RUGS, by Ronald Grierson/Dryad Press.

COURSES

Most ADULT EDUCATION CENTRES have classes where instruction on rugmaking is given, so check your local school.

KIDDERMINSTER COLLEGE OF FURTHER EDUCATION, Hoo Road, Kidderminster, Worcestershire. *Provides 2-year vocational courses in carpet design.*

WEST DEAN COLLEGE, Chichester, Sussex. *Runs short courses on rugmaking.*

SMOCKS and SMOCKING

THE TRADITIONAL English smock was popular for the very reason that it was a simple garment, easily made, economical in terms of the amount of material needed and above all, very hard-wearing. Since those early days, the smock has always made some sort of a come-back in popularity and has been altered and adapted according to contemporary taste. It is this flexibility and adaptability of the smock to current fashion that makes it so unique, and also the fact that there are a whole range of stitches to personalise each garment so that each one can be completely individual.

SMOCKING

The need of securing and, at the same time, ornamenting gathers in heavy materials (e.g. linen) gave rise to the special form of fancy gathering called 'smocking'. Smock is an old English word for shift or chemise, hence the term 'smocking' came to be applied to the ornamental gathering of the necks of these garments and also of the elaborate, beautifully-embroidered linen 'Smock-Frock' of the field labourers. A great variety of patterns exist, but they are all executed in the same way so one explanation will suffice for all.

Gathering

By 'gathering' the material, i.e. for the neck and sleeves of a smock, is meant the forming of small pleats by drawing up rows of stitching (*fig 1*). The gathers are made by a series of running stitches done very regularly in a straight line, always along the weft of the material. To make it a relatively easy matter in gathering the material, rows of transfer dots can be bought which are ironed on, thus giving a clear guide where to pass the needle and thread. Pick up only a small portion of material at each dot and be very careful to make each gather exactly the same. For each line of dots use one thread which must be knotted at one end to stop it slipping out. The threads once passed through the dots must then be drawn in to produce pleats which are set by placing the material on an ironing board, wrong side

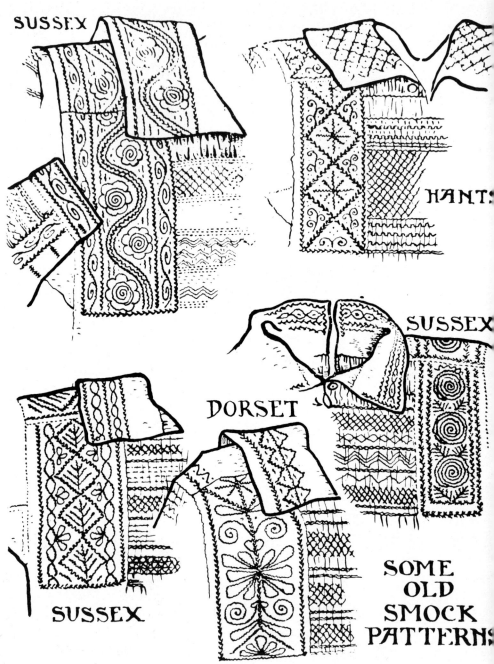

SUSSEX

HANTS

DORSET

SUSSEX

SUSSEX

SOME OLD SMOCK PATTERNS

82

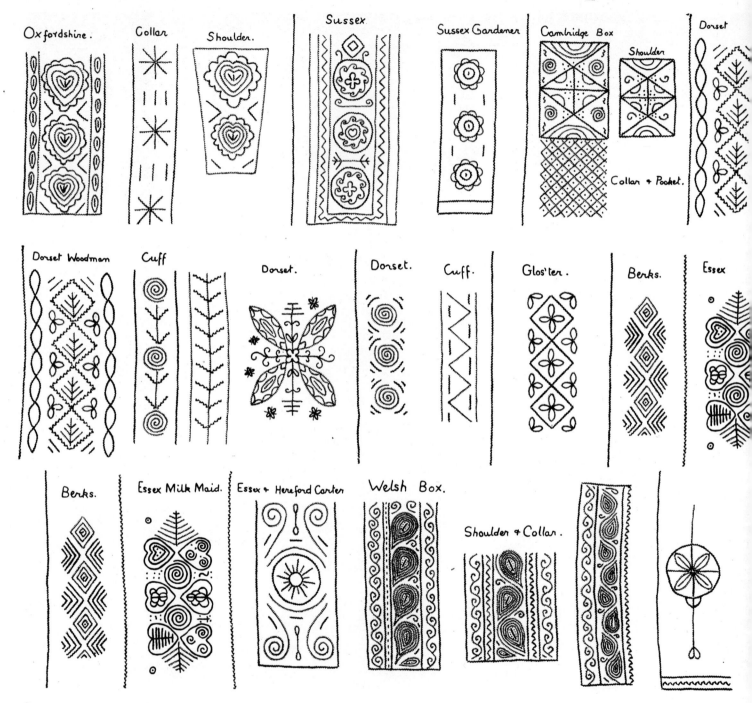

Oxfordshire.

Collar

Shoulder.

Sussex.

Sussex Gardener

Cambridge Box

Shoulder

Collar & Pocket.

Dorset

Dorset Woodman

Cuff

Dorset.

Dorset.

Cuff.

Glos'ter.

Berks.

Essex

Berks.

Essex Milk Maid.

Essex & Hereford Carter

Welsh Box.

Shoulder & Collar.

84

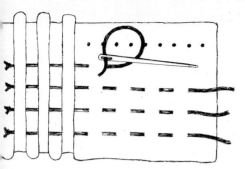

Gathering the Pleats
Fig 1

...up, putting a damp cloth over the smocking and passing a hot iron lightly over it. Do not press. The gathering threads are then removed and the material is now ready for the decoration of the gathers, or 'smocking'. Incidentally, a contrasting coloured thread is helpful for gathering, as it makes it easy to see on the material.

Smocking (Design)

It is a good idea to plan out the design of the smocking on paper beforehand to get it nicely proportioned and the colours right. There are lots of pattern variations within the choice of stitches so a little experimentation on a spare piece of material may be helpful. The basic idea is to contrast straight stitches with diagonal stitches for visual interest. Colour combinations are very important too and will be a matter of personal taste, but try to get a good blending harmony of colour which will go well with the background material.

Materials

There are many materials which are suitable for smocking. Traditionally, linen was used but this is an expensive and somewhat heavy fabric. Cottons, poplin, lawn, organdie, silk, shantung, wool and voile are just some of the alternative materials. Avoid textured fabrics as these are difficult to gather.

Thread

Stranded cotton is the standard thread for smocking and is used in different strand thick-nesses according to the weight of the backing material. For heavy materials such as linen, use four strands together; for standard materials such as cotton use three strands together and for light weight materials such as organdie use 2 strands.

Stitches

Outline Stitch

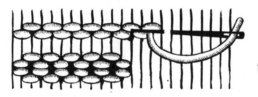

Cable and Double Cable Stitch

Feather Stitch

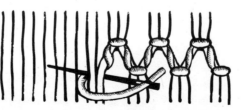

Vandyke Stitch

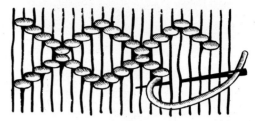

Trellis and Wave Stitch

Diamond Stitch

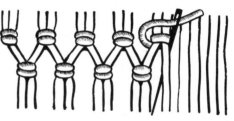

Honeycomb Stitch

SOCIETIES

THE EMBROIDERERS GUILD, 73 Wimpole Street, London W1M 8AX.

BIBLIOGRAPHY

ENGLISH SMOCKS, by Alice Armes/Dryad Press.
FUNDAMENTALS OF SMOCKING, by Dorothy Wenbourne/Hertfordshire Federation of Women's Institutes.
SMOCKING, Leaflet No. 131/Dryad Press. Price: 10p.
SMOCKING BOOK, by Chella Thornton/McClelland and Stewart Ltd, Toronto, Canada.
SMOCKING IN EMBROIDERY, by Margaret Thomson/B. T. Batsford Ltd.

85

CREATIVE KNOTTING or macramé as it is now commonly known, is another craft that has greatly increased in popularity in the last few years. The basic materials used in this craft are cheap and easy to obtain and as there are only two basic knots to learn, it can be an easy matter to produce, quickly and easily, all sorts of bags, belts, chokers, bracelets and other accessories, as well as wall hangings and three dimensional work. Attractive fringes and braids can also be made for curtains, fabrics and garments.

Materials
All the following are suitable yarns that will hold a knot without slipping:

Twines
Parcel strings
Rug wool
Cords (nylon & plastic)
Crochet cotton
Piping cord
Embroidery cottons
Synthetic metal yarns
Rope
Cellophane string.

Beads, shells and sequins etc. can be worked into the design.

Obviously, the particular piece of work being knotted will determine the size and nature of the material to be used, i.e. large for large objects and small for small objects. As a general rule, a piece of work will use up $3\frac{1}{2}$–4 times the length of finished work to length of yarn (i.e. 4 inches of knotted material needs 16 inches of yarn). Always work out a sampler first before starting an actual piece of work to see just how much yarn will be needed.

Equipment
All knotting is worked from a foundation thread which can be either tied to the back of a

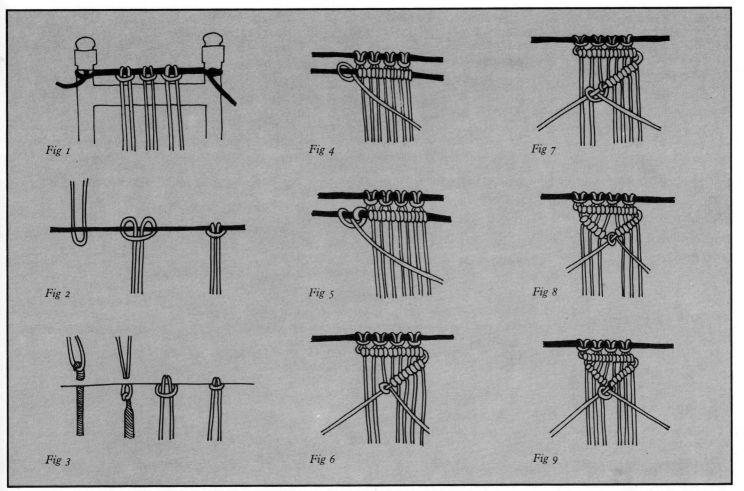

Fig 1

Fig 2

Fig 3

Fig 4

Fig 5

Fig 6

Fig 7

Fig 8

Fig 9

chair *(fig 1)*, or pinned down on to a board with drawing pins. Apart from this, only the string or whatever is to be knotted, a pair of scissors and such things as beads and other embellishments will be required.

Setting on

(Fig 2) shows how the threads are first attached to the foundation string. *(Fig 3)* shows how this same method is used to attach threads to a piece of fabric for the beginning of a fringe or braid. The knot used is a reverse double half-hitch knot.

Basic Knots: (a) SIMPLE OR DOUBLE HALF-HITCH

This knot is the knot used for cording, useful to finish or start of a piece of work, or for the production of strong belts.

HORIZONTAL CORDING

Take four pieces of string and set on to the foundation string. This will now produce 8 pieces of hanging string. Take an end one and lay it across all the others. Take the string next to it and knot it as in *(fig 4)*. Take each string in turn and knot them in the same way until the end of the line has been reached *(fig 5)*.

The same process is now repeated only this time using string no. 1 as the string bearer that is laid across. Repeat this left-to-right, right-to-left knotting process until you have the required length of work.

DIAGONAL CORDING

(Figs 6 and *7)* show how, by laying the cord bearer at 45°, a diagonal line can be knotted.

CROSSED DIAGONAL CORDING

(Fig 8) shows how two cord bearers are used to form two diagonals that meet in the middle. The two bearers should then be knotted and

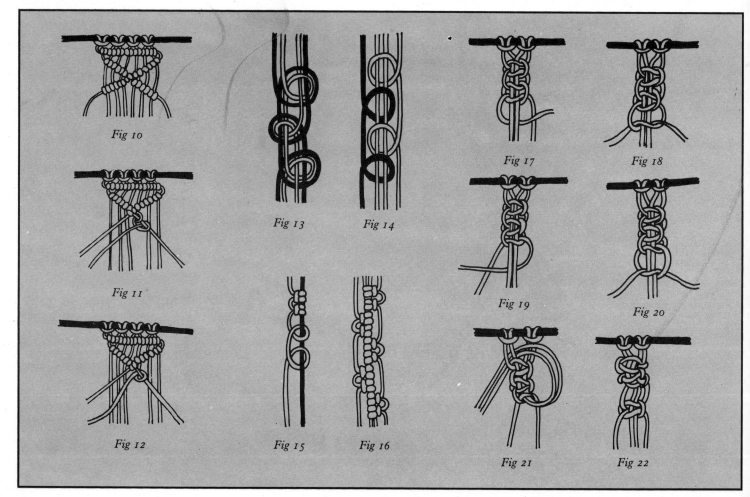

Fig 10

Fig 11

Fig 12

Fig 13

Fig 14

Fig 15

Fig 16

Fig 17

Fig 18

Fig 19

Fig 20

Fig 21

Fig 22

carried on outwards as in *(figs 9, 10, 11 and 12)*.

BRAIDS USING THE HALF HITCH *(figs 13, 14, 15 and 16)*

THE FLAT KNOT
This is worked with four strings and is built up as shown below:

(a)	(b)	(c)	(d)
(fig 17)	*(fig 18)*	*(fig 19)*	*(fig 20)*
left under middle and over right	right over middle and through left	right under middle and over left	left over middle and under right

THE FLAT KNOT BUTTON
By threading the two centre threads up into the finished knotting every now and then, attractive knot balls can be made *(figs 21 and 22)*.

PLAITING
Plaiting can be very effective when used in conjunction with other knots.

JOSEPHINE KNOT
This is best worked on a flat surface like a wooden board as each knot can then be pinned to make working easier *(figs 23, 24, 25 and 26)*.

INCREASING
To add a new thread to a piece of work, it is simply attached by a reverse double half-hitch knot as used to get on threads to the foundation cord.

EDGINGS
Attractive edgings or 'picots' can be worked into a design. The diagrams below show some of them *(figs 27, 28, 29 and 30)*.

Beads and other decorative materials can be worked into the design and also strings or threads of different colours can be used to create a pattern, determined by the knot being used. By experimenting with the knots and various coloured strings and threads, some very beautiful results can be produced.

SOURCES OF MATERIALS

Beads can be obtained from:
ELLS & FARRIER Ltd, 5 Princes Street, London W1.
THE BEAD SHOP, 53 South Molton Street, London W1.

The following people sell twines, ropes and cords in bulk or in small amounts:
ARTHUR BEALE, 194 Shaftesbury Avenue, London WC2.
BRITISH TWINES LTD, 112 Green Lanes, London N16.

CUYAHOGA STUDIO, 10 Wheatlands Farm Road, Kilbarchan, Renfrewshire. *Sells unusual yarns for macramé.*
M. MALLOCK & SONS, 44 Vauxhall Bridge Road, London SW1.
MCCULLOCH & WALLIS LTD, 25–26 Dering Street, London W1. *(Sells piping cord only.)*

Many hardware shops and garden shops sell string and twine, and needlework shops will sell threads and yarns of various sorts. Marine centres are a good source of materials as cords and twines can be purchased there in large quantities.

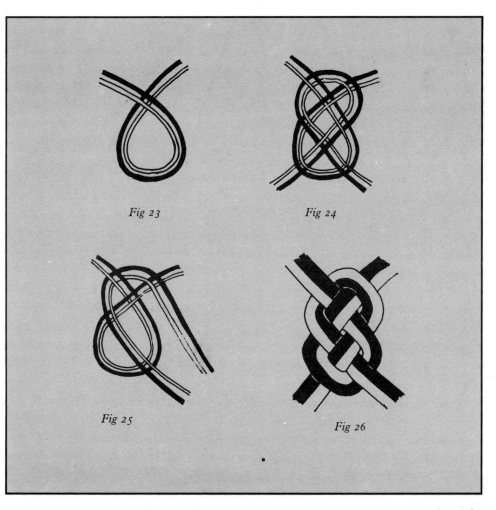

Fig 23

Fig 24

Fig 25

Fig 26

SOURCES OF MATERIALS IN THE USA

J. I. COCHRAN, 717 West Avenue, A Kingsville, Texas 78363.
PHYLLIS COHEN WEAVERS STUDIO, 233 Glen Road, Weston, Massachusetts 02493.
CRANE STATION, 3024 N. Cambell, Tucson, Arizona 85719.
MACRAMÉ AND WEAVING SUPPLY CO., 63 East Adam Street, Chicago, Illinois 60603.
MACRAMÉ BY ROBERS ORIGINALS, 1934 Prism, Houston, Texas 77043.
REEVES KNOTIQUE, Box 5011, Riverside, California 92507.
SHEEP VILLAGE, 352 Miller Avenue, Mill Valley, N. California.
THE SHOP, Highway 49, P.O. Box 133, Amador City, N. California 95601.
THREE BLACK SHEEP, 3115 Washington Boulevard, Marina Del Rey, S. California.
TROMP & TREADLE, 41901 Woodbrook Drive, Wayne, Michigan.
WARP & WOOF POTPOURRI, 514 N. Lake Avenue, Pasadena, California 91101.
THE WEAVING SHOP, 1708 Walnut Boulder, Colorado 80302.
WEAVING WORKSHOP, 3324 N. Halsted, Chicago, Illinois 60657.
YARN BARN, 1364 S. Mary Avenue, Sunnyvale, N. California, 94087.

SOCIETIES

THE EMBROIDERER'S GUILD, 73 Wimpole Street, London W1M 8AX.

BIBLIOGRAPHY

THE ART OF MACRAMÉ—MODERN DESIGN IN KNOTTING, by Joan Fisher/Hamlyn Ltd.
CORD KNOTTING, by E. M. MacDonald/Dryad Press.
CORD KNOTTING—Leaflet No. 127/Dryad Press. Price: 10p.
DECORATIVE KNOTTING, by K. M. Woods/Dryad Press.
DESIGNING WITH STRING, by Mary Sneyd/B. T. Batsford Ltd.
INTRODUCING MACRAMÉ, by Eirian Short/B. T. Batsford Ltd.
KNOTS: USEFUL & ORNAMENTAL, by George Russel Shaw/Ward Lock Ltd.
MACRAMÉ, by Imelda Manalo Pesch/Oak Tree Press Ltd.
MACRAMÉ, by Nell Znamierowski/Pan Books Ltd.
MACRAMÉ THE ART OF CREATIVE KNOTTING, by Virginia I. Harvey/Van Nostrand Reinhold Co., New York.
MACRAMÉ, A PRACTICAL INTRODUCTION, by Ann Mary Pilchner/Bell & Sons Ltd.
NETMAKING FOR ALL, by Charles Hodgate/Mills & Boon Ltd.
NETS & KNOTS FOR FISHERMEN & OTHERS, by Quinton Winch/Dryad Press.
NETTING, by P. Cumming/Dryad Press.

COURSES

ADULT EDUCATION CENTRES. Check FLOODLIGHT magazine for courses in London.

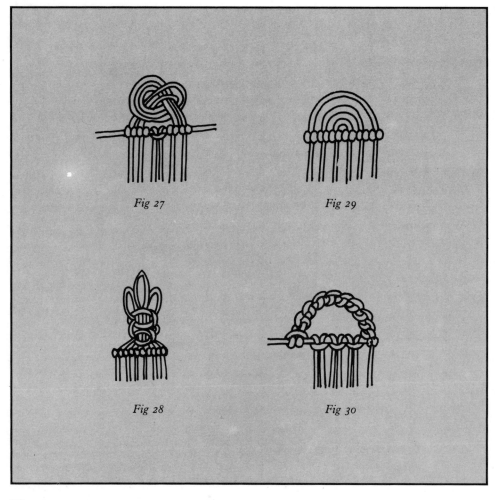

Fig 27

Fig 29

Fig 28

Fig 30

It seems strange that the only places ever entrusted with the graceful design of a sundial are always some dark corners of a village square or park or the pompous and extravagant grounds of a private estate. Even when the dial does reach the ordinary urban gardens it is invariably hidden next to the potting shed and always covered by brambles and bird droppings.

Surely this ancient monument to the passage of time needs to be preserved and with its lost charms and mystique given a purpose in today's society.

From the comfort of your own garden a really nice sun-clock can be assembled, but if by lousy council planning you have no garden, a ceiling in your home will do just as well. In this case, time is not recorded by a moving shadow but by a moving point of light, and a very bizarre effect it has too.

The idea of using a ceiling for a sundial may seem crazy at first but as you see it taking shape above your head you will be pleasantly surprised.

EQUIPMENT

The only equipment needed is very simple and can be all bought from Woolworths for a few shillings (apart from the wrist-watch which you can borrow for a day from somebody if you don't already have one). The rest of the list includes plenty of thin string; a pencil; a pleasing variety of coloured paints; one small paint brush; one small hand mirror; a piece of paper (the same size as the mirror); a coloured chalk; a box of drawing pins and a small tube of glue.

METHOD

Fix the mirror horizontally on to the bottom part of the window ledge and after making a hole about the size of a sixpenny piece in the paper, paste it to the mirror. If you now cast your eyes to the ceiling you will see (as long as the sun is shining) a small point of light. Now at five, ten or fifteen minute intervals, mark off in pencil the different positions of this spot. The way to do this is to check the time against the sun-dot and at 12.00 for example, you mark off that point, at 12.05 you do it again and so on. Keep this up all the time that sunlight can enter the room. Once the sun has moved round your house and the dot has disappeared, you will have a series of pencil marks stretching across the ceiling.

Now this is the tricky part. From the centre of your window, imagine a vertical line leading to the ceiling: where this imaginary line touches the ceiling draw a small X.

From this fixed position (X) with the aid of drawing pins, fasten a piece of string and allow it to pass through one of the pencil dots until it reaches the far wall, making sure it's well secured and taut. With a second piece of string, using the X as a starting point again, go through the motions once again, this time of course choosing a different dot. Do this again and again until all the dots have been married to the X by the strings.

Now run your block of coloured chalk (a light blue will be best because this will not alter the colour of your paints) along each string and pluck them separately as you would a guitar string. This action transfers the chalk on to the ceiling in nice clean lines. Once this has been done all the strings can then be taken down.

With extreme care, paint along each chalk line; there's no quick and easy method for doing this so just take things easy and it will turn out nicely.

You might like to choose different colours for different time sections. For example, red for hours, dark blue for half-hours and green for quarters, but that's a matter of personal judgement. It is very important that you paint these lines right across the ceiling to the far walls because in June, when the sun is high, the light spot will be near the window, in August, out in the middle of the ceiling and in Winter, with the sun low in the sky, far away towards the opposite wall.

If you still have some excess energy after all that, why not paint in the Zodiac Signs or the different stars that are visible all year round. But most important of all, don't forget to number the painted lines with the required times. These can either cut the lines at the different sections or be placed at the sides in the form of a semi-circle across the ceiling.

You might be lucky and have a room with two windows, one facing East and the other West. If that's the case then you can expect continual sunshine, but if you have only one window, say facing East the sunlight will only be limited to the morning or facing West, the afternoon.

If you've got an uncooperative landlord who wouldn't appreciate a sundial on his ceiling, the next best thing is to do everything as written, but instead of painting the hourly lines directly on to the ceiling, simply paint the strings in the chosen colours and gently tack them in to position.

Even if the sun refuses to shine this year, at least you'll have an incredible ceiling to gaze at.

A SUNDIAL WORKSHOP TO VISIT

GERALD DUNN, SUNCLOCK SPECIALIST, Great Downs, Tollesbury, Maldon CM9 8RD. Tel. Tollesbury 280

It's quite amazing how this craft has blossomed over the last few years for it is by far the most popularly practised craft around; with perhaps the exception of tie-dye and batik. Candles can now be made in all shapes, sizes, colours, with or without perfume and they are dead easy to make after a bit of practice. Materials are cheap and the outlets for candles are plenty, and the demand steady.

MATERIALS NEEDED

Candles are made from wax, and there are various types of wax available, including beeswax, bay-berry wax, paraffin wax and tallow. Of all these, paraffin wax is the cheapest and the most easily available. Refined paraffin wax must be used with stearic acid which then becomes 'candlewax': the basis of most manufactured candles. The list of materials needed is as follows:

Paraffin wax, Stearic acid (or Stearin), a sturdy kitchen thermometer, a double pan boiler, various saucepans, oil essences (*for perfumed candles*), beeswax, or beeswax sheets (*for beeswax candles*), moulds (*these will be discussed later*), wax dyes and a sharp knife.

MIXING AND PREPARING THE WAX (PARAFFIN)

The correct proportion of stearic acid to paraffin wax is 10% stearic acid to wax, i.e. 1 lb stearic acid to 10 lb paraffin wax. As the wax normally comes in blocks, it must be broken down with a hammer into small pieces to enable it to be put in the double boiler for melting. Stearin, or stearic acid must be melted in a separate pan and if any wax dyes are going to be used, they should be added to this same pan. Wax dyes are normally extremely concentrated so that only a tiny pinch will be needed to give quite a strong colour. If too much dye is used, the resulting candles will be very dark and will not 'glow' when lit. If a perfumed candle is to be made the oil essence (just a few drops) must also be added to the melted stearin.

The wax should be melted in the double boiler (easily made by putting one saucepan on to the top of another the same size, the one beneath being filled with water) and heated to a temperature of 180 F (or 82 C). The melted stearin (with or without dye and perfume) are added to the melted wax and thoroughly mixed. The resultant mixture is then poured into a warm jug which makes it easy to pour into the mould. It is very important that pouring temperature should be 180 F (82 C) at all times.

WICKS

The size of wick in relation to the size of the candle is very important, and the rule is: the larger the candle, the larger the wick. A small wick in a large candle will produce a pool of molten wax at the burning point and this will result in extinguishing the flame. On the other hand, too large a wick will produce a large smoky flame and the candle will burn itself out quickly. Experience alone will provide the right wick to use for each candle made.

Wicks can either be purchased from a reputable candle supplier or be made by soaking lengths of bleached stranded cotton in boracic acid.

Methods

There are three ways of actually making a candle: by dipping, by using moulds, and by rolling with beeswax sheets.

Dipped Candles Fill a jar with the already-prepared candle-wax mixture, making sure that the jar is a bit taller than the intended length of the candle. Tie the wick to a stick and dip it in the wax mixture and remove it (*fig 1*) when the wax adhering to the wick is dry, repeat the process until the thickness of the candle is what you need and allow it to cool. When the candle is completely cold, trim the bottom with a sharp knife.

Interesting effects can be obtained by dipping the wick into, and out of, jars containing different coloured wax. By finally dipping the finished candle in cold water immediately after the last dip in wax, a shiny surface can be achieved. Another way to use the dipping method is to mould the wax on the wick in your hands whilst it is still warm. By doing this, shapes can be worked, such as a pear shape, especially if with each dip, progressively less of the candle is dipped in the molten wax.

Moulded Candles This method involves pouring molten wax into some container of a particular shape, so that when the wax is cold, the mould can be removed, leaving the desired shape. There are a number of ways to make moulds, apart from those ready-made metal or

have molten wax running everywhere.

Take the mould (an empty 'squeezy' bottle, for example) and cut the tip off the top with a pair of scissors. Make a small hole in the centre of the bottom and thread the wick through it and tie a knot to prevent it coming back through *(fig 2)*. Tie the other end of the wick, which comes out the open top of the mould, tightly round a stick so that there is no slack, and fit it into two notches which can be cut at the top of the mould *(fig 2)*. Any slack can be taken up at the base of the mould where the knot is by tying another knot. Next, pour the wax into the mould, saving some to top up with because the cooling wax will contract in the mould. After thirty seconds, cool the mould in a bowl of cold water, but make sure that no water enters the mould. After an hour, a well will appear at the top, so break the skin and top up with the spare mixture. Now leave the candle for three or four hours, by which time it should be hard enough to remove from the mould.

As a general rule, rapid cooling in cold water will produce a hard, even, shiny surface whereas a slow cooling will result in a surface containing air bubbles which is also quite pleasing. To prevent the mould from toppling over in the cooling bath, a weight of some description may be necessary on top. When the candle has been removed from the mould, level the base with a sharp knife and trim the wick.

BEESWAX CANDLES

Beeswax can be purchased in sheets so that the

Fig 1

Fig 2

pouring process can be eliminated. Take a sheet of wax and cut it to the required height of the candle. Lay the sheet on a flat surface and place the wick at one end, making sure that the wick is longer at both ends than the width of beeswax sheeting. Next, begin rolling the wick in the sheet, very carefully, until the required thickness of candle has been reached. Press the end of the sheet into the body of the candle, warming it with the warmth from your hands and smoothing the ends in until the candle is a perfect cylindrical shape. Finally trim the wick and level the bottom, if needs be, with a sharp knife.

THE BASIC, PRIMITIVE CANDLE

In the old days, candles were made by dipping rushes into tallow, lard or wax and these were called rushlights. The rush commonly used was the Soft Rush (Juncus Effusus) *the most common rush in Britain.*

Method

The rind must be stripped from the cylindrical pithy stalks, leaving just two longitudinal pieces on either side of the pith to hold it together. This pith wick is then dipped into

BALLOON CANDLES

Fill a balloon with water until it is of the required dimension needed for the candle. It should be then dipped into the molten wax and allowed to cool. This process should be repeated until a shell of good thickness has been reached whereupon the balloon can carefully be pulled away. When dipping, make sure that only about three-quarters of the balloon goes into the molten wax otherwise it will be impossible to pull it away from the wax shell. Next, pour a little molten wax into the shell and revolve it around the inside of the wax mould as one does with brandy in a brandy glass and allow it to cool. Repeat this process until the shell is really thick. Top the shell up with wax until it is half full and allow it to cool in the cooling bath. When it is rock hard, drill a hole through the middle, insert the wick and finally fill the wax shell to the top, allowing it to cool in the cooling bath. The bottom will need levelling off flat with a knife to allow the candle to stand upright. At all times, make sure no water gets into the top of the shell when cooling.

CAVITY CANDLES

To make a candle rather like gruyère cheese, chunks of ice are put in the mould and the molten wax poured over them. When the ice melts away, there will be cavities left and this produces some very interesting effects. It is important to remember with this technique that the wick must first be dipped a few times in wax before securing it in the mould, otherwise the water will get in and soak it, thus making burning impossible.

Finishes and textures A number of textures and finishes can be added to the surface of candles to increase their beauty. Molten coloured wax can be dripped or painted on to the surface, either in a rigid pattern or ad hoc. A hot knife or some other tool can be pressed into the surface so that indentations are made which will give nice textures. Alternatively, the surface can be cut into with a knife and either left as it is, or molten coloured wax poured in to the holes. Bits of coloured wax can be stuck on the outside by welding with a hot knife.

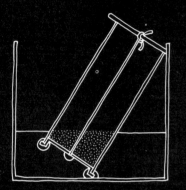
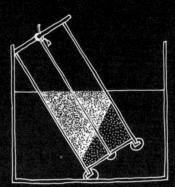

Fig 3

molten wax or tallow in exactly the same way as described on page 95 and when of a required thickness, the bottom should be levelled and the wick trimmed.

VARIATIONS

By improvising with various coloured wax, as well as using hard and melted wax, a number of interesting candles can be produced :

CHUNKY CANDLES

Fill the mould with small chunks of hard, coloured wax after having first inserted the wick in the way described above. Pour into the mould some molten wax, either white or of another colour and cool in the cooling bath.

MULTI-COLOURED CANDLES

Pour in some molten wax of one colour into a mould and allow it to cool until the surface is spongy. Pour in another coloured wax and repeat the operation until the mould has been filled. To give an interesting effect, the mould can be inclined at an angle to provide diagonal layers *(fig 3)*.

97

What is so exciting about making candles is the fact that there is so much room for experimentation. Try out as many techniques as you can, make up your own and get hold of as many different moulds as possible. If there are a few disasters, it doesn't matter because the wax can always be melted down and used again.

SOURCES OF MATERIALS

All materials for candle making can be obtained in bulk from:
BAIRD & TATLOCK LTD, P.O. Box 1 Romford RM1 1HA.
CAMPBELL TECHNICAL WAXES, Thames Road, Crayford, Kent.
CANDLES, 89 Parkway, London NW1.
CANDLE MAKERS' SUPPLIES LTD, 4 Beaconsfield Terrace, London W14.
CORONET TRADING CO. LTD, 44 Station Lane, Hornchurch, Essex RM12 6NB.
CRAFTCO, 30 Prince of Wales Crescent, London NW1.
W. H. HOWSON LTD, 49–60 Borough Road, London SE1.
KANDELL DESIGNS, Dept 35, 4b Lonsdale Road, London NW6. *(Good for bulk quantities of paraffin and stearin wax.)*
KIM & CYNTHIA WAXCRAFT, 58/76 Willow Vale, Uxbridge Road, London W12.
MARGARET'S, 18 Gateway Parade, Whinfell Way, Gravesend, Kent.
POTH HILLE, 37 High Street, Stratford, London E15. *(Sells a wide range of waxes.)*
WILLIAMS CAMPBELL & CO. LTD, Brittania Works, West Drayton, Middlesex.
Essential oils can be obtained from many herbal stores such as:
BALDWINS, Walworth Road, Kennington, London.
Stranded Cotton for wicks can be bought at most needlework shops, or from:
THE NEEDLEWOMAN, Regent Street, London W1.

SOURCES OF MATERIALS IN THE USA

THE CANDLESTICK, Village Fair, 777 Bridgeway, Sausalito, California.
CELEBRATION, Box 28, Pentwater, Michigan.
GREEN MOUNTAIN CANDLE CO., Crafton Road, Townsend, Vermont.
HEARTHSIDE CANDLESHOP, Woodrow H. Dill, Main Street, Fairlee, Vermont.
'K' THE CANDLER, Coast Gallery, Highway 1, Big Sur, California.
JAYNE KELLY, 116 South 20th, Philadelphia, Pennsylvania.
MELTING POT, 225 W. Champlost Avenue, Philadelphia, Pennsylvania.
MI-WUK CANDLE WORKS, INC., 808 R Street, Sacramento, California.
POURETTE MFFG. CO., 6818 Roosevelt Way N.E., Seattle, Washington.
THURBSTER GURBELLS CANDLES, 21 Edgewood Avenue, Mill Valley, California.
UNIQUE CANDLES, 301 Windermere Avenue, Drexel Hill, Pennsylvania.

SOCIETIES

SOAP, CANDLE & EDIBLE FAT TRADES EMPLOYERS' FEDERATION, 2 Kingscote Street, London EC4.

BIBLIOGRAPHY

CANDLE MAKING/Crafts Unlimited, The Old Mill, Nannetch, nr Mold, Flintshire.
CANDLE MAKING/Search Press Ltd.
CANDLEMAKING & DECORATIONS, by Valerie Janitch/Hamlyn Ltd.
AN INTRODUCTION TO THE ART OF CANDLE-MAKING/Candle Makers' Supplies Ltd, 4 Beaconsfield Terrace, London W14.

COURSES

ADULT EDUCATION CENTRES, *Check Floodlight Magazine for courses in London.*
CRAFT O'HANS, The Old Mill, Nannetch, nr Mold, Flintshire. *Afternoon, evening, weekend or whole week courses available.*

CANDLE-CRAFT STUDIOS TO VISIT

England
CORNWALL
ART CANDLES, 7 Walker Lines, Bodmin, Cornwall. Tel Bodmin 3258
Hand-made candles by Bob and Jill Bishop. Various shapes; special orders taken.
Open all week. Please telephone first.

Wales
DENBIGHSHIRE
'CANDLES IN THE RAIN' (Bill & Val Norrington), The Old Smithy, Nantglyn, nr Denbigh. Tel. Nantglyn 389
Specialist in unique, hand-made candles, leather-work (handbags, belts, etc, made from hide), macramé and silk-screening.
Visitors welcome.

MERIONETHSHIRE
CELMI CANDLES, Cynfal House, Ffestiniog. Tel Ffestiniog 675
Hand-made candles in paraffin wax and beeswax, also wax sculptures. Permanent exhibition of pottery, slate and metal craft.
10.30 am–6 pm Monday to Saturday.
2 pm–5 pm Sunday (Summer only).

Jack be nimble, Jack be quick,
Jack Jump over the candle-stick.

Hard and Soft Country Baskets

IT IS MOST LIKELY that there will always be a steady need for baskets of all shapes and sizes so that by taking up this craft, a decent living can always be assured. Most of the materials needed can be had for the taking from the countryside, thus making the cost of producing work on an economical basis a surety. We have split the definition of the sorts of basketwork into two main fields; hard basketry and soft basketry. With most of the 'soft' materials, other work can be made like mats, chair seatings etc, but this will have to be covered in perhaps another book, more fully than has been here.

HARD BASKETRY

This includes the use of cane, willows, dogwood and other twiggy material, a detailed list of which will shortly follow. As a general rule, select straight, one-year-old twigs with no side shoots which must be pliable enough to bend round the fist. The best time to collect material is between November and March and it should be stored in the dark until needed. Never hack any one tree or bush to bits, but rather select a few twigs from a number of plants so as not to despoil them. Use a pair of secateurs or a pruning knife to cut the twigs and make as clean a cut as possible. Never make a hole in a hedge by indiscriminate cutting as it may let out animals enclosed in a field.

Suitable material to collect

BRAMBLE *(Rubus Fruticosus)* Blackberry
Widespread and abundant in woods, hedges, and bushy and waste places and on heaths and cliffs. Can be picked when either green or red as in the Autumn. The prickles can be removed by rubbing the stems with a handful of rags. Stems have a uniform thickness.

CLEMATIS *(Wild or garden varieties)*
The joints of these plants will give a pleasant texture to a basket. Twigs have a uniform thickness.

DOGWOOD *(Thelycrania Sanguinea)*
Widespread and common in woods, thickets and hedges, especially on chalk and limestone. Use the wild variety which is fine but firm to handle, and the garden variety which is infinitely more pliable. Twigs tend to taper in thickness.

ELM *(Ulmus)*
The best parts to use will be found growing from the base of the trunk as side shoots. Twigs tend to taper in thickness.

HONEY-SUCKLE *(Lonicera Periclymenum)*
Widespread, common in woods, hedges and bushy places. Use both the wild and cultivated varieties. The bark should be peeled off as it tends to crack when worked. Twigs tend to taper in thickness.

IVY *(Hedera Helix)*
Widespread and abundant in woods, often carpeting the ground, in hedgerows and on walls and rocks. A versatile medium of varying beauty. Twigs have a uniform thickness.

HAZEL *(Corylus Avellana)*
Widespread and common in woods, hedgerows and bushy places. A fine material to work, with either the bark left on or peeled. Twigs tend to taper in thickness.

LARCH *(Larix Decidua)*
Select the straightest twigs and those that bend well—discard the rest. Twigs tend to taper in thickness.

LIME *(Tilia Europaea)*
Produces lovely black twigs which tend to taper in thickness.

PRIVET *(Ligustrum Vulgare)*
Twigs can be used although they tend to be short in length. Twigs tend to taper in thickness.

ROSE *(Rosa)*
Both the Dogrose and Guelder rose can be used as well as most of the cultivated varieties. Remove the thorns in the same way as for Brambles. Twigs have a uniform thickness.

SLOE *(Prunus Spinosa)* Blackthorn, Quickthorn.
Widespread and abundant in woods, scrub and hedgerows. Produces pleasant bright green shoots which are highly pliable. Twigs have a tendency to taper.

SNOWBERRY *(Symphoricarpos Rivularis)*
Fairly frequently naturalised in hedges, by

streams and in bushy places. Produces lovely silver green shoots which need care in handling. Twigs tend to taper in thickness.

WILD BROOM *(Sarothamnus Scoparius)*
Produces vivid green shoots which darken with age. Use both the wild and cultivated varieties. Twigs tend to taper in thickness.

WILLOW *(Salix)* Osier, Sallow
The most popular material to use in basketry (apart from cane) because of its flexibility and endurance to rough handling. There are three types commonly used: (1) *Salix Friandra* (ALMOND WILLOW) which is generally widespread and often found by fresh water. This willow produces high quality lengths. (2) *Salix Viminalis* (OSIER) which is widespread and common in moist places. This willow produces stout lengths more suited to large-sized baskets. (3) *Salix Purpurea* (PURPLE WILLOW) which is widespread and locally frequent near fresh water, especially in fens. This willow produces small slender lengths of great strength and are used for very best sorts of baskets. Strangely enough, although these willows grow wild, they give better quality lengths when cultivated in special 'Osier beds'. The main willow growing area is now to be found in Somerset in an area drained by the rivers Tone, Yeo and Parret. The best time to purchase these cultivated rods is in the Autumn when the annual willow auctions are held. When obtaining rods in this way, a great saving is made compared to buying material from craft shops.

Preparation

Almost all collected material with the exception of Bramble, Elm and peeled rods will need preparation known as 'fading' before it can be used. This is a drying process which renders the rods pliable. Bundles of rods of each specific variety should be tied and left out in the open, preferably under a bush or hedge for a specific time that will range from about two weeks to three months, depending on the thickness of the rods and the weather. The rods must not be allowed to dry out completely otherwise they will become brittle and will be then useless for working. When ready, the rods should feel 'leathery'. Should, however, they become too dry, soak them for a couple of days in a bucket of water, leave for

one day, and then keep wrapped in a damp cloth until needed for use.

Terminology

BASE or BOTTOM STICKS Short lengths forming the foundation of a basket lid or base.

BORDER The finishing edge of a basket side or lid, formed by pulling the side stakes down and weaving them into an ordered pattern.

BOW ROD A bent rod of stout dimensions used to form the heart of a handle.

PAIRING Two rods worked alternately under and over each other to form a twist.

PRICKING UP To insert side stakes to a base and bend up for the weaving of the sides of the basket.

RAND A single rod worked in front of one stake and behind another—basic basket weaving.

ROUND One complete movement made round the circumference of a basket or lid.

SLATH The interwoven sticks which form the bottom of a basket.

STAKES Rods used to form the foundation for weaving the sides of a basket. Side stakes should be thinner than the base or bottom sticks and are, as a general rule, about 8 inches longer than the intended height of the finished basket.

WALING The process by which three or more rods are worked (woven) in sequence in front of two, three or more side stakes and one behind.

WEAVERS Lengths used in the weaving of a basket being woven round the side stakes.

Sorting

Some degree of sorting is necessary as the various parts worked into the making of a basket must be of various lengths and thicknesses in relation to each other. Bottom sticks must be made from the thickest rods, then side stakes, and finally weavers, which should be the thinnest. Weavers should be as long as possible, at least long enough to form one round. All material must be worked damp so soak for an hour or so in water before use.

Method

This is for a simple, round basket. Take 6 bottom sticks, slit 3 in the middle and insert

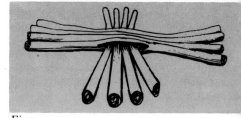

Fig 1

the other 3 through the slits *(fig 1)*. Take a good long weaver and make a loop tie in the middle *(fig 2)*. Next, open out the bottom

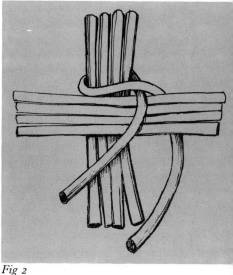

Fig 2

sticks like the spokes of a wheel and start weaving in and out with the two ends of the weaver. This is known as '*pairing*' *(fig 3)*. When the required diameter of the base has been reached, cut off what is left of the bottom sticks and, taking a side stick for every end of bottom stick, sharpen their ends with a knife and insert each one by the side of the bottom stick ends *(fig 4)*.

Remember to make the height of each side stake 8 inches longer than the intended height of the finished basket. Once inserted, turn up (prick up) the side stakes and keep in place with a loop of string or cord *(fig 5)*.

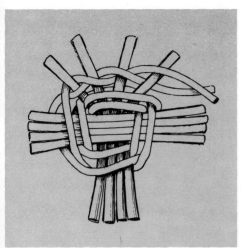

Fig 3

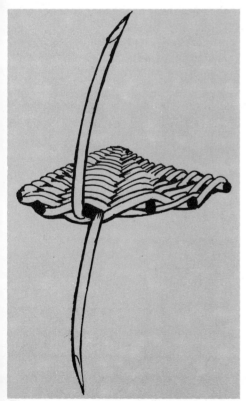

Fig 4

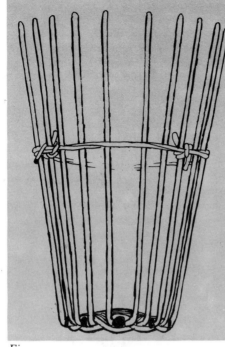

Fig 5

Waling

A basket is normally started off with 2 or 3 rounds of waling. Take three rods about side stake thickness and place each one behind three successive side stakes. Weave each rod as for the pairing on the base except that each must be worked in front of two stakes instead of one *(fig 6)*. Work 2 or 3 rounds in this way.

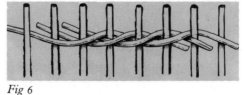

Fig 6

Weaving or Randing

Each weaver must be long enough to go round the whole circumference of the basket plus about 1 inch. Take the thickest end of the weaver *(butt)* and insert behind a side stake

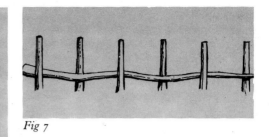

Fig 7

(fig 7). Begin weaving in front and behind each side stake until the end is reached which should end behind a side stake.

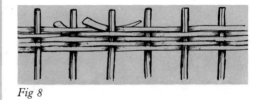

Fig 8

To join a new weaver to the basket, simply insert the same stake *(fig 8)* and continue weaving in the same way.

As a guide to how many weavers should be used on a basket, use as many as you have side stakes. When all the weavers have been worked, finish off with 2 or 3 rounds of waling.

Borders

Figures 9, 10, 11 and *12* show ways of nicely finishing the top of a basket, or the side of a lid. With borders 9, 10 and 11, known as scallop borders, a good length of side stake

Fig 9

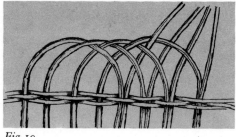

Fig 10

will be needed for bending over and working well into the weave. With border *12*, a trac border, only a couple of inches of side stakes will be needed.

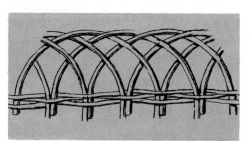

Fig 11

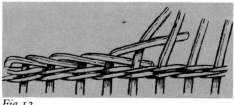

Fig 12

Handles

Take a good thick base rod, long enough to form a decent bow and sharpen both ends. Insert each end well down into the top waling each side of the basket. Next, take three thin weavers and insert through the top waling and plait over the handle rod to the other side, finishing off by inserting the ends into the top waling *(fig 13)*.

Fig 13

SOFT BASKETRY

Here we will discuss the use of rushes, reeds, sedges, grasses and rafia.

Grasses

There are many grasses which can be cut, dried and used for soft basketry. Look out for the following:

PURPLE MOOR-GRASS (*Molinia Caerulea*) Grows 1–3 feet high in marshes, fens and wet heaths and moors.

FLOTE GRASS (*Glyceria Fruitans*) Grows 2–3 feet high in and by slow-moving water.

GREAT WATER GRASS (*Glyceria Maxima*) Grows 3–8 feet high at the margins of fresh and brackish water.

MEADOW FESCUE (*Festuca Pratensis*) Grows 2–4 feet high in woods and on shady banks.

HAIRY BROME (*Bromus Ramosus*) Grows 3–5 feet high in woods and hedge banks.

MEADOW OAT (*Helictotrichon Pratense*) Grows 1–2 feet high in established grassland, especially on chalk and limestone.

FALSE OAT (*Arrhenatherum Elatius*) Grows 2–4 feet high in waste places and by roads.

MEADOW FOXTAIL (*Alopecurus Pratensis*) Grows 1–4 feet high on cultivated ground.

Rafia

Rafia is imported and is therefore an expensive medium to purchase. Nowadays, however, there are synthetic substitutes which can be used, as well as a medium called *Seagrass*, both sold in craft shops. We do not recommend using either, because of the price, but felt it right to mention them.

Reeds

The best reed in Britain is *Phragmites Communis*, which is our tallest grass growing 5–8 feet high in swamps. There are, however, other types of reeds found within two families: the BUR-REED family and the REEDMACE family. The only one worth mentioning is the BRANCHED BUR-REED (*Sparganium Erectum*), growing 1–2 feet high by fresh water.

Rushes

There are a number of species of rushes suitable for all sorts of rushwork. Look out for the following:

SOFTRUSH (*Juncus Effusus*) Flowering rush. Grows 1–4 feet high in damp grassy and marshy places. This rush is cultivated in the shallows of the Great Ouse, near St Ives in Huntingdonshire especially for the rush industry.

BULRUSH (*Scirpus Lacustris*) Great Green Rush. Grows 3–8 feet high in rivers and round lakes.

FALSE BULRUSH (*Typha Latifolia*) Great Reedmace, Catstail. Grows 3–8 feet high in swamps and by fresh water.

LESSER BULRUSH (*Typha Angustifolia*) Lesser Reedmace. Grows in swamps and by fresh water.

SEA CLUBRUSH (*Scirpus Maritimus*). Grows by the banks of estuaries and inlets near the sea.

Sedges

SEDGE (*Cladium Mariscus*). Grows 6 feet high in fens in East Anglia only.

MOOR SEDGE (*Carex Binervis*). Grows 1–2 feet high in marshes and boggy woods on acid soil, as well as on moorland and rough grassy places.
BOTTLE SEDGE (*Carex Rostrata*). Grows 1–2 feet high in all kinds of wet peaty marshes.
POND SEDGE (*Carex Acutiformis*). Grows 3–5 feet high in swamps.
DROOPING SEDGE (*Carex Pendula*). Grows 3–5 feet high in damp clayey woods.
COMMON SEDGE (*Carex Nigra*). Grows 1–3 feet high in all kinds of wet peaty places.

Harvesting & Storing

Rushes and reeds are cut in mid-summer, about mid June through to August according to the weather. They are cut as low as possible with a fagging hook or sickle. When harvesting, it is important to keep them as flat as possible and a boat is usually needed to get access to the rushes and reeds. It is helpful if it is a flat boat like a punt which will facilitate the material being laid across flat. It is necessary to allow the rushes and reeds to dry out after harvesting and this can be done by either leaving them flat on the banks of the river, or by leaving them against wooden racks. Never allow the full sun to bleach them white. The drying process normally takes about three weeks when the material should then be stored in a cool dark out-house or loft. Another way is to lay the material in wire baskets fitted by a bracket to a wall in a shed or garage. It is always important to remember that rushes should only be cut from the same stock every other year, otherwise they will become thin and straggly in growth. The same goes for sedges and these should be dried and stored in the same way.

Terminology

BOLT A bundle of rushes, bound by a strap 45 inches in length.
BUTT The thick end of the rush nearest the root.
PARING WEAVE Two rushes worked under and over each other.
SPOKE Pieces cut from the 'butt' of a rush to form the beginning of a base for a basket.
TIP The top and thin end of a rush.
A bolt of rushes will normally be enough to make one fair-sized shopping basket.

106

Preparation

Once the rushes have dried, they must be gathered together into a sheaf and tied by a strap or length of thick string to form a bolt. As each rush is needed for use, it can be drawn out from the butt end of the bolt and the strap tightened as the bolt decreases in size. In this way, breakages are eliminated.

Just before use, the rushes should be laid out in the open and sprinkled with water from either a hose sprinkler or watering can, turning them over now and again. They must now be laid in a well damped blanket or felt, wrapped up tightly and then left for four hours out of sun and wind. Having done this, the rushes will be nicely softened for working and if no more than one or two are removed from the bundle at a time for working, they will remain in this soft, supple state for about two days. If any of the rushes become too dry and sticky, they must then be dried out completely and re-watered again.

Method

With rushes and reeds, there are so many ways of using them, whether for baskets, mats, furniture or accessories that we cannot possibly do any justice to a subject that would need a whole book to cover in any depth. We will, however, describe a very simple way of making mats and baskets. Further reading will be referred to in the bibliography, as well as information on courses and education.

To make simple use of rushes, reeds, grasses and sedges in 'soft' work, there are two principle ways of doing so; plaiting and tying. In the first case rushes and reeds are more suitable for here three lengths are plaited, using the three plait method, to form lengths ready to make up into the finished piece of work. In the second instance, sedges and grasses are taken in small handfuls and tied securely at 1-inch intervals with a strong waxed thread. By working new handfuls in as the first handful finishes, a continuous length can be made.

With either the plaited rushes (*fig 14*) or the tied sedges and grasses (*fig 15*) a mat can be simply made by curling the lengths round in a circle, working outwards and adding new lengths where needed (*fig 16*), using wax

Fig 14

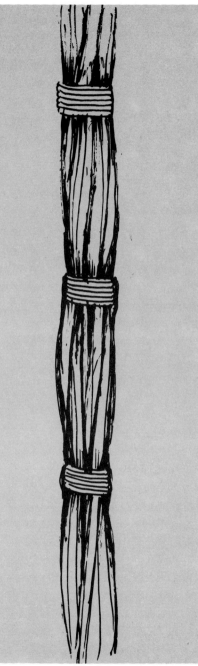

Fig 15

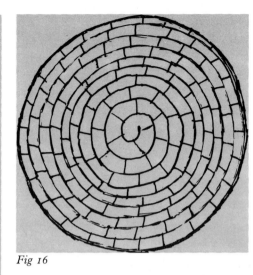

Fig 16

should be started in the same way as for a mat, i.e. from the middle and working outwards. But when the ultimate size of the base has been reached, the lengths must then be sewn upwards to form the sides, and finished off with a double row of lengths at the top. A handle can be made by plaiting three or more rushes together and sewing into the top *(fig 20)*.

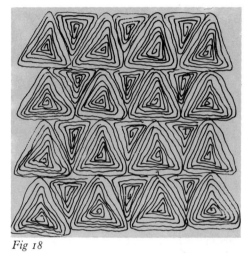

Fig 18

thread to hold it all together (a canvas needle is best to sew the thread in this type of work). From this beginning, intricate patterns can be produced by bending the lengths to the required design. The following are some patterns to follow, but, you can easily make up your own. The essence of this method is to tie securely with the waxed thread *(figs 17, 18, 19)*.

To make a simple basket *(fig 18)* the base

Fig 17

Fig 19

Fig 20

Dyeing

Rushes, reeds, rafia and the family of grasses and sedges can be dyed various colours. Willow can also be dyed with a little more care. All these materials must be thoroughly soaked in water before plunging into the dye bath. The following dyes are recommended:

METHYLENE BLUE 2B150
AURAMINE ON150 (yellow)
CHRYSOIDINE T160 (orange)
METHYL VIOLET 2B200
MALACHIFE GREEN CRYSTALS
RHODANIME B500 (crimson)

If you wish to dye with vegetable dyes, the rushes, sedges, grasses or raffia should first be steeped in a mordant made of alum water. An ounce and a half of alum is dissolved in a pint of boiling water (large quantities of material will need more alum in proportion to water) and then the material must soak in this solution for at least twelve hours. Then while it is still damp, it must be put into the dye. See the chapter on vegetable dyes (p. 62) for details of dye colours.

SOURCES OF MATERIALS

Dyes:

Available from SKILBECK BROS LTD, 55 Glengall Road, London SE15.

Raffia:

For information concerning the whereabouts of retail raffia stockists contact: TURABAST COMPANY, Red Lion Wharf, 4 Bankside, London SE1.

Rushes:

Rushes available from TOM METCALFE ARNOLD, 'Wildcroft', Holywell, St Ives, Huntingdonshire.
DEBDEN RUSH WEAVERS, Debenham, Suffolk.
JACOBS YOUNG & WESTBURY LTD, 199 Borough High Street, London SE1.
M. J. TELEKI, 20 Compton Road, London NW10.
WAVENEY APPLEGROWERS LTD, Common Road, Aldeby, Beccles, Norfolk.

Willow suppliers:

Any further information concerning the whereabouts of willow suppliers can be obtained from: W. GADSBY & SON (BURROWBRIDGE) LTD, Burrowbridge Basket Works, Burrowbridge, Bridgwater, Somerset.

SOURCES OF MATERIALS IN THE USA

NEWELL WORKSHOP, 19 Blaine Avenue, Hinsdale, Illinois.
H. H. PERKINS COMPANY, 10 South Bradley Road, Woodbridge, Connecticut.

SOCIETIES

NATIONAL FEDERATION OF MANUFACTURERS FROM CANE, WILLOW & WOVEN FIBRE, c/o R. V. Morris, 632 Radford Road, Nottingham NG7 7EY.

BIBLIOGRAPHY

BASIC BASKETRY, by Leonard G. Allbon/Max Parish.
BASKETS AND BASKETRY, by Dorothy Wright/B. T. Batsford Ltd.
BASKETRY THE EASY WAY, by O. R. Scott/Central Press.
BASKETRY THROUGH THE AGES, by H. H. Bobart/Oxford University Press.
CANEWORK, by Charles Crampton/Dryad Press.
CANEWORK FOR THE DOLLS' HOUSE, by Winifred Garrett & Mary Thornton/Dryad Press.
A CANEWORKER'S BOOK—FOR THE SENIOR BASKET MAKER, by Dorothy Wright/Dryad Press.
INTRODUCING RUSHCRAFT, by K. Whitburn/B. T. Batsford Ltd.
THE JUNIOR BASKETMAKER, by Charles Crampton/Dryad Press.
PLAITED RAFFIA WORK, by Constance Ward/Dryad Press.
PRACTICAL RUSHWORK, by Norah Florance/Dryad Press.
RAFFIA FIGURES AND ANIMALS/Dryad Press.
RAFFIA WORK/Dryad Press.
RUSH BASKETS AND MATS, Leaflet No. 112/Dryad Press. Price: 10p.
THREE CANEWORK BORDERS/Dryad Press.
WILLOW BASKET WORK, by A. G. Knock/Dryad Press.
WILLOW BASKETRY, by Mabel Roffey/Pitman & Sons Ltd.

COURSES

ADULT EDUCATION INSTITUTES. *See a current copy of 'FLOODLIGHT' magazine for courses in London.*
HENRY GIBBS, Wycombe Cane and Rush Works, High Wycombe, Buckinghamshire. *The Gibbs' are anxious to get young people interested in learning the craft of cane and rushwork. Write to them for details.*
WEST DEAN COLLEGE, Chichester, Sussex. *Short courses on Raffia work, Rush weaving, Strawcrafts, Willow work and Basketry.*

WILLOW, CANE AND RUSHWORK STUDIOS TO VISIT

England

BEDFORDSHIRE

MRS P. M. MORGAN, Mill Lane, Pavenham, Bedford. Tel. Oakley 2393
Table-mats, rush baskets, assorted shapes and sizes. Rush-covered containers for bulbs, pot plants or flower arrangements. Rush chair seats renewed.
Any time by appointment.

DEVONSHIRE

DESMOND SAWYER, LSIA, The Key, Ferry Road,

Topsham. Tel. Topsham 4615
Basketware and other gifts.
9 am–5.30pm.

GLOUCESTERSHIRE
BERNARD COTTON, 'Trout House', Warren's
Cross, Lechlade. Tel. Lechlade 496
*Rush-seating of chairs. Sets of early country
chairs for sale.*
BERTRAM JELFS, 'Goose Grout', Wraxall Road,
Warmley, Bristol BS15 BDW. Tel. Bristol
673849
*Only best quality English basketry in cane,
willow and rush supplied. Cane furniture a
speciality. Seating in cane, rush, seagrass, cord
and willow skeining.*
9 am–5 pm Monday to Friday.

NORFOLK
STANLEY BIRD (BASKETWARE) LTD, Seabird
Works, 28 Southgates Road, Great Yarmouth.
Tel. Great Yarmouth 3392
*Manufacturers of baskets, hampers and willow
and cane furniture.*

SOMERSET
WILLIAM GADSBY & SON (BURROWBRIDGE) LTD,
Burrowbridge, nr Bridgwater. Tel. Burrow-
bridge 259
Baskets and hampers, rustic willow furniture.
9 am–5 pm, except Sunday.

SUFFOLK
DEBEN RUSH WEAVERS, High Street, Debenham,
Stowmarket. Tel. Debenham 349
*Rush table-mats, place-mats, log-baskets, mat-
ting and carpets, shopping-baskets and other
items. Osier baskets and chairs. Antiques restored
and polished. Upholstery.*
Workrooms open Monday to Friday 9 am–5
pm. Shop open Monday to Friday 9 am–5 pm.

SUSSEX
THOMAS SMITH (HERSTMONCEUX) LTD, Trug
Factory, Herstmonceux. Tel. Herstmonceux
2137
*Willow baskets with chestnut rim and handle for
garden and floral décor.*
9 am–5 pm; Saturday 9 am–12 noon.

WILTSHIRE
TOOLCRAFT, 2 Canon Square, Melksham (pro-
prietress C. Holt-Wilson). Tel. Melksham
703041 or 708709 (STD 0225)
*Stools and chairs woven to order. Range of styles
and colours. Rocking-chairs for children a
speciality. Also old rush chairs and cane chairs
reseated.*
Visitors welcome, but advisable to phone first.

YORKSHIRE
J. W. TAYLOR & SON (BASKET MAKERS AND
WILLOW GROWERS), Ulleskelf, nr Tadcaster.
Tel. Tadcaster 2138
*All types of cane and wicker furniture for house
and garden. Rustic fencing, chair caning, rush
seating, Moses-baskets, log-baskets, stools made
in rush, cane and willow. Also food-hampers,
fishing-hampers, pigeon-hampers, pet-baskets,
flower-baskets, linen- and blanket-boxes, etc.*
9 am–9 pm daily.
BRIARDENE CRAFTS (MR M. WILKINSON), Moor
Lane, Sherburn-in-Elmet. Tel. South Milford
2086
*Craftsmen-made cane and rustic furniture. Any
type of basket-work.*
Open 7 days a week.
J. BURDEKIN, BASKET WORKS, Flushdyke, Ossett.
*Over 100 years' experience in the making of all
types of baskets, rush chairs and furniture.*
Open Monday–Sunday, 8 am–7 pm.

Wales
FLINTSHIRE
JAMES JOHNSON & SON, Station Road, Bangor-
on-Dee, nr Wrexham. Tel. Bangor-on-Dee
417
*All kinds of baskets made to order and specifica-
tion. Repairs undertaken. Also willow growing.
Large selection of sun lounge furniture in cane,
willow, bamboo.*
9 am–9 pm, including Saturday and Sunday.
ROBYN & BETI ELLIS JONES, Oak Trees, Nant
Patrick, nr St Asaph LL17 0BN, County of
Clwyd. Tel. Trefnant 608
*Rushwork: small rush articles for the table,
flower arrangers' baskets a speciality.*
Any time—best to telephone first.

Hand-Made Paper

Paper can be prepared from all fibrous substances, in particular those in the form of vegetation.

Wood is the most widely used in commercial paper making but tends to have rather limited possibilities when a variety of hand-made papers are sought. Plants on the other hand are very versatile, especially those species that are abundant on road verges or in meadows and woods throughout the country. Each species will produce a paper different in quality and texture from another; therefore a wide range of papers can be made for varying purposes.

EQUIPMENT

You will need a large saucepan (or pressure cooker), caustic soda, a bucket, bleaching powder, an earthenware jar (or large mixing jug), some scissors (or shears), a mallet, a large pestle and mortar (or a stone slab), a large plastic bin, a small tank, 2 yards of copper wire, some old blankets, a press (or large stones), a large dish, a wooden board and a thermometer.

Relevant items in the above list of equipment should not be made of naked iron as this metal is susceptible to rust and must be kept away from all pulp and paper.

METHOD

Collect your plants in late Summer or early Autumn and store on a stone floor, keeping them wet until they begin to decompose. In this way it will be easier for you to obtain the skeleton fibres essential for making paper.

When the material has sufficiently rotted, chop it into $\frac{1}{2}$-inch lengths and put into a large saucepan or pressure cooker filled with water. Add a good measure of caustic soda and boil for at least 3 hours making sure it doesn't boil dry. To test whether you have put in enough soda, the water should have a greasy feel to it when rubbed between the fingers. (Caustic soda is a strong alkaline and can cause burns if not washed off immediately after testing.)

Empty the boiled material into a bucket and wash thoroughly till the water becomes clear. At the same time squeeze and pound the pulp with your hands so that the fleshy parts are removed in readiness for bleaching. Place the bleaching powder in an earthenware jar, fill with cold water and leave it to settle after stirring. Pour the bleach over the fibres and leave the mixture for at least 12 hours occasionally stirring with a stick. As the fibres will be damaged if they are too strongly bleached, it is best to test a small quantity first. In actual fact, a light fawn is the ideal colour to achieve when bleaching and should conditions allow, the final bleaching can take place outside in the sunlight.

Once again, wash the fibres thoroughly and after wringing out the surplus water, cut them into small pieces of no more than $\frac{1}{2}$ inch (a pair of shears will be ideal for this task). Crush the pulp with the pestle and mortar so that the fibres split lengthways (similar to bamboo) and continue crushing until the right consistency is obtained (the longer you crush the smoother will be the paper).

If a pestle and mortar isn't available a similar effect can be obtained by beating the pulp with a mallet on a stone slab, but the result will be a more uneven paper.

Should you require to store the pulp, a large plastic bin will be adequate. For periods of up to 4 months a preservative such as Santobrite can be added.

Before you actually begin making sheets of paper it may be best to produce a couple of sample sheets primarily to obtain information on texture, weight etc. Simply place a nylon kitchen sieve of about 8–10 inches in diameter into a tray filled with warm water and into this heap 2 or 3 cupfuls of pulp. Allow the pulp to move freely on the sieve and distribute it evenly with your hand. Lift the sieve away from the tray and after the excess water has drained away, place it in the sunlight or a warm room and allow it to dry. To peel off the sheet of paper, simply run the tip of a sharp knife around the edge to break contact with the frame. The thickness of course can be controlled by the amount of pulp put into the frame.

A more specialised frame is needed for the making of quality paper and here we suggest you construct a frame on to which a piece of perforated zinc has been nailed. Fabric can in fact be substituted for the zinc but both the paper and cloth need to be completely dry before being separated in the paper-making process. Zinc, on the other hand, is rigid enough to enable you to turn the frame upside down and press it on to a wet blanket for drying.

This method, of course, allows the frame to be in continuous use. For good-quality paper stack the alternate blankets and sheets of paper on top of each other and squeeze out the water by means of heavy weights or in a press. After pressing, separate the pile and allow the individual sheets to dry together with its blanket. This method is for the making of rather thin paper. For much thicker stock it is essential to keep more pulp on the mould and therefore a second frame has to be constructed.

This frame, known as the deckle, sits loosely upon the main frame and is a kind of lid which overlaps the sides slightly. This too should have perforated zinc nailed to it and the frame can be prevented from buckling if a number of thin wooden supports are fitted. The zinc too must be supported and this should be done by tacking parallel lengths of brass wire to the frame at 1 inch intervals.

Paper made from this process is known as 'wort' and possesses no watermark. Should you require your own insignia or decoration in the form of a watermark, a design can be fitted on to the upper surface of the mould. As the design is in relief, it prevents the same amount of pulp lying under it than on the rest of the mould and where this occurs the paper becomes thinner—hence the transparency when held up to the light. Good watermarks, by the way, can only be produced on paper made from finely-beaten pulp.

The method for making heavier paper with the use of the deckle is as follows:

At the side of your tank filled with pulp, place a large dish in which is a wooden board slightly larger than your mould. To the rear of this there should be a pile of saturated blankets one of which is laid in readiness on the board.

Fit the deckle in position over the mould and slowly lower the two vertically into the pulp at the far side of the tank. With a firm grip, continue lowering and slowly bring it into the horizontal position about an inch or two below the surface of the pulp. Now lift the mould so that it sits on the surface and shake slightly sideways and then forward to enable the fibres to matt together. Lift the mould away from the tank, tilt it on to one corner to drain for a few moments and then remove the deckle. Turn the mould upside down and press it on to the wet blanket. Now carefully raise the mould leaving the sheet of paper transferred to the blanket. This process can then be repeated after covering the paper with another saturated blanket and adding a cupful or so of fresh pulp to the tank.

After a number of sheets have been produced, place a wooden board on top of the pile and press to remove the excess water. Separate the individual sheets and blankets and leave to dry either in the sunlight or in a warm room. Once dry, the sheets of paper can be removed from their blankets and pressed again for a short period of time.

Paper made in this manner is slightly absorbent and although it is therefore unsuitable for use as writing paper it is well suited for various printing processes. Should you require paper for writing or painting on, then it will need to be sized with gelatine. This can be done in two ways.

Firstly by heating the pulp slowly till it reaches 98°F and then adding the gelatine or by allowing the sheets of paper to mature for a week or so and then dipping them in a bath of size and pressing for a second time.

If you want sized paper quickly the first method is best as it cuts out an additional delaying process.

BIBLIOGRAPHY

SHELL BOOK OF THE COUNTRYSIDE/Phoenix Rainbird.

COURSES

WESTDEAN COLLEGE, Chichester, Sussex. *Short courses on papermaking.*

"just Strollin' along"

We had a pleasant walk today,
Over the meadows and far away,
Across the bridge by the water-mill,
By the woodside, and up the hill;
And if you listen to what I say,
I'll tell you what we saw to-day.

Amid a hedge, where the first leaves
    Were peeping from their sheaths so shy,
We saw four eggs within a nest,
    And they were blue as the summer's sky.

An elder-branch dipp'd in the brook,
    We wondered why it moved and found
A silken-hair'd, smooth water-rat
    Nibbling and swimming round and round.

Where daisies open'd to the sun,
    In a broad meadow, green and white,
The lambs were racing eagerly—
    We never saw a prettier sight.

We saw upon the shady banks
    Long rows of golden flowers shine,
And first mistook for buttercups
    The star-shaped yellow celandine.

Anemones and primroses,
    And the blue violets of spring,
We found whilst listening by a hedge
    To hear a merry ploughman sing.

And from the earth the plough turn'd up
    There came a sweet Refreshing smell,
Such as the lily of the vale
    Sends forth from many a woodland dell.

We saw the yellow wallflower wave
    Upon a mouldering castle wall,
And then we watched the busy rooks
    Among the ancient elm-trees tall.

And leaning from the old stone bridge,
    Below we saw our shadows lie,
And through the gloomy arches watch'd
    The swift and fearless swallows fly.

We heard the speckle-breasted lark
    As it sang somewhere out of sight,
And we tried to find it, but the sky
    Was filled with clouds of dazzling light.

We saw young rabbits near the wood,
    And heard a pheasant's wing go 'whir',
And then we saw a squirrel leap
    From an old oak-tree to a fir.

We came back by the village fields,
    A pleasant walk it was across them,
For all across the houses lay
    The orchards red and white with blossom.

Were I to tell you all we saw
    I'm sure that it would take me hours,
For the whole landscape was alive
    With bees, and birds, and buds, and
        flowers.
'THE SPRING WALK' BY THOMAS MILLER

RAMBLER'S RIGHTS[1]

THE DELIGHTS of walking the hills and dales, the moors and fens, the meadows and downs of Britain are manifold, but to most of those who set out to discover ancient footpaths and bridleways, a knowledge of the laws concerning rambling may be obscure or non-existent. What follows is a brief guide to the laws on footpaths, and further information may be obtained from The Ramblers' Association which has been working and fighting for many years to protect the 100,000 miles of public paths in the countryside of England and Wales.

WHAT IS A PUBLIC PATH?
A public path in the countryside is either a footpath or a bridleway. On footpaths the public have the right of passage on foot only. On bridleways they have the right of passage on horseback and on bicycle as well. Most paths in the countryside are unsurfaced tracks across fields, through woods or over uncultivated land. But legally they are no different from the metal-surfaced paths you may find in the built-up parts of towns and villages. Indeed,

[1] We are indebted to The Ramblers' Association for all the information supplied in this chapter.

legally, a public path in the country is part of the Queen's highway and subject to the same protection in law as a trunk road.

HOW DO I KNOW WHETHER A PATH IS A PUBLIC RIGHT OF WAY OR NOT?
The safest evidence is the definitive map of paths which all county councils were required to prepare by the National Parks and Access to the Countryside Act of 1949. Most counties in England and Wales now have such maps and you have the right to inspect them at the county and county district offices. Some counties sell copies of the definitive map. As the definitive maps are completed, the rights of way are marked in red on the latest edition of the Ordnance Survey one inch to the mile map for the area. But note: a path can be public even if it is not on the definitive map.

HOW DOES A PATH BECOME PUBLIC? MUST IT BE WALKED FOR 20 YEARS?
In legal theory, paths become rights of way because the owner 'dedicates' them to public use. In fact this rarely happens, but the law assumes that if people are allowed to use a path freely for upwards of 20 years then the owner intends dedication. Most public paths came about in this way. The converse is not true. A path does *not* cease to be public because it is unused for 20 years. The legal maxim is: 'Once a highway, always a highway.'

Paths can also be created by agreement between highway authorities and owners or by compulsory order, subject, in the case of objection, to the Secretary of State for the Environment's consent. Creation orders are very rare and hard to obtain. (Highways Act, 1959, Sections 27 and 28 and Countryside Act, 1968, Schedule 3, Part 1.)

WHO OWNS THE PATHS?
The owner of the property over which the path passes. The soil is his, but there is a right of passage over that particular strip of soil.

HOW WIDE SHOULD A PATH BE?
The theory is that the path should be whatever width was dedicated to the public. This width may be mentioned in the local enclosure award or in the statement accompanying the definitive

map. But in many cases the proper width will be a matter of what has been past practice on that particular path.

ARE HORSES ALLOWED ON PUBLIC PATHS?
Riders have a right to use bridleways, as the name implies. Fences and gates on these paths must be such that a rider can easily negotiate them without dismounting. Thus a locked gate on a bridleway is an obstruction. Riders have no right to use footpaths, but they often do and are not usually breaking the law in so doing. If use of a footpath by riders becomes a nuisance (e.g. by destroying the surface) the highway authority can make a byelaw forbidding riders to use that particular path. Alternatively riders can be physically prevented from using it by gateing the path and locking the gates (but then proper provision must be made for walkers). The owner of the land could also sue riders for trespass if they rode on a footpath without his permission.

IS IT ILLEGAL TO DRIVE CARS OR MOTORBIKES ON PUBLIC PATHS?
Anyone who drives a vehicle on to a footpath or bridleway is liable to a fine of up to £5 under section 18(1) of the Road Traffic Act, 1960.

WHEN IS A ROAD USED AS A PUBLIC PATH?
*RUPP*s as they are commonly known, are usually green lanes or unsurfaced tracks which have never carried enough traffic to merit maintenance. The great majority are unsurfaced and have never been much used by traffic except for packhorses in the old days and farm and access vehicles today. The classification of these ways as RUPPs was an invention of the National Parks Act of 1949 designed to ensure that they were recorded on the definitive maps and not lost completely. The classification is now in process of abolition and all RUPPs will eventually be reclassified as either footpaths, bridleways or byeways (Countryside Act, 1968, Schedule 3, Part III).

WHAT ARE THE HIGHWAY AUTHORITIES?
In rural areas they are usually the county councils. In urban areas they are the borough or urban district councils.

IS IT ILLEGAL TO PLOUGH UP A PATH?
There is no general rule. A few paths are held to have been 'dedicated subject to the right to plough'. On others there is a statutory right to plough provided the farmer gives at least a week's notice of his intention to the highway authority. But failure to restore the path to a reasonably usable condition is illegal. The farmer must restore the path within six weeks of giving notice, or within three weeks of starting to plough if he fails to give notice. If he thinks he cannot restore the path within the time limit he may apply for a temporary change of route (diversion) of the path to the highway authority. Such diversions are limited to three months and must be prominently advertised at either end of the diverted section. The statutory right to plough never applies to paths along the edge of fields. (Section 29, Countryside Act, 1968.)

CAN A FARMER KEEP A BULL IN A FIELD CROSSED BY A PUBLIC PATH?
In most counties it is forbidden by byelaw to keep a bull more than twelve months old at large in a field crossed by a right of way. Some counties permit bulls if accompanied by cows. Check with your county council. If there is no byelaw the farmer is within his rights.

WHAT IS TRESPASS?
The civil tort of trespass arises from the bare fact of unauthorised entry. However, unless he could prove injury to his property, a landowner could probably only recover nominal damages by suing in such a case. But of course you might have to meet his legal costs. Thus a notice saying Trespassers Will be Prosecuted, aimed for instance at keeping you off a private drive, may be effective but is pretty meaningless. Prosecution could only arise if you trespass *and* do damage, which forms the crime of malicious damage to property.

WHAT IS A MISLEADING NOTICE?
A misleading notice is one calculated to deter you from using a public right of way. For example a notice saying PRIVATE at the point where a public footpath enters a park. Such notices should be reported immediately to the highway authority. They are illegal (Section 57 of the National Parks and Access to the Countryside Act) on paths shown on the definitive map.

WHO IS SUPPOSED TO LOOK AFTER THE STILES AND GATES ON A PATH?
Maintaining these is primarily the owner's responsibility, but the highway authority must contribute a quarter of the cost and more if it wishes. If the landowner fails to keep his stiles and gates in proper repair the authority can, after 14 days notice, do the job themselves and send the bill to the owner. (Section 28, Countryside Act, 1968.)

WHAT IS WAYMARKING?
Waymarking is a means of indicating the line or direction of a path at points where it may be difficult to follow. There are a variety of systems in use, ranging from splashes of coloured paint on walls and gates, through wooden arrows, stencilled paint arrows and metal discs to cairns of stones set up at intervals along moorland and mountain paths.

IF A PATH HAS BEEN PLOUGHED AND CROPS HAVE GROWN OVER IT, CAN I WALK THROUGH THE CROPS?
Yes. But be careful to do no damage. Stick as close as you can to the line of the path and go in single file. (But forgetting all legalities, I think it would benefit everyone concerned if you follow the edge of the crops round to the point where you meet the path.)

CAN I WALK WHERE I LIKE ON UNCULTIVATED LAND?
No. You can generally go as you please on uncultivated *common* land. But that is by custom, not of right. On privately owned mountains, moors and downs the situation is very different. Most of such land is preserved for sport or is used for grazing sheep. In some areas you will find nobody minds your walking over land of this kind. In others it is a different story. In a few areas, mostly in the Peak District National Park, sizeable stretches of such country have been opened to the public by access agreements between the planning authority and the landowner under the 1949 National Parks and Access to the Countryside Act.

WHAT IS AN OBSTRUCTION ON A PATH?
Anything which interferes with your right to proceed along it, e.g. barbed wire fence across the path or a heap of manure dumped on it. Overgrowing vegetation is not normally treated as an obstruction but is dealt with under path maintenance.

ARE ALL THE PATHS SUPPOSED TO BE SIGNPOSTED?
No. Under the Countryside Act (Section 27(2)) the highway authorities have a duty to put up a signpost at all junctions of footpaths and bridleways with metalled roads. But few counties have much signposting at the moment and the Act lays down no time limit within which this sizeable job must be done. Also parish councils can relieve the highway authorities of the obligation for particular paths in a parish.

WHICH LOCAL AUTHORITIES ARE RESPONSIBLE FOR KEEPING PATHS CLEAR?
In the countryside the rural district councils have a general duty under the Highways Act of 1959 'to assert and protect the rights of the public to use and enjoy all the highways in their district and to prevent, as far as possible, the stopping up or obstruction of those highways'. The highway authority (the county council usually) are statutorily responsible for maintaining the path. They also deal with ploughing problems, stiles and gates and footbridges. Parish councils have a useful power to maintain paths but no statutory obligation. Highway Authorities have the power under Section 134 of the Highways Act of 1959 to require owners to cut back overgrowth.

PUBLIC PATH CLEARING BY VOLUNTEERS[2]

As more and more people want to use the public paths and as more and more local authorities get around to signposting them, the sense of frustration on the part of individuals who try to walk the paths and find them overgrown or otherwise impenetrable grows.

In many districts today groups of the

[2] *Information taken from a Fact Sheet issued by The Ramblers' Association, with its kind permission.*

Ramblers' Association members, local amenity and footpath societies, parish councils and other bodies have decided that the answer to this problem is self-help. If the path is blocked take your coat off and go and clear it. That sounds simple and in essence it is, but there can be snags. There are easy ways and difficult ways of doing it. You need the right tools. You need the necessary permissions. This tells you what you need to know.

Value
The value of path clearance is obvious. It keeps paths open and gets them used. This in turn discourages any future attempts at extinguishment of the paths on grounds of lack of use. Path clearance is good publicity for the organisation undertaking it, which is thus seen to be doing a constructive job. Finally, a vigorous path clearance programme often serves to stimulate local authorities into stepping up their signposting programme and tackling problems such as ploughed and illegally obstructed paths. It is sometimes argued that volunteers who clear paths are doing the landowner's or local authority's work for them. Our experience is that voluntary effort of this kind stimulates those with legal responsibilities to discharge them more effectively.

Permission
Any individual may remove so much of an obstruction on a public path as may be necessary to enable him to pass. That does not entitle an organised party of people to go out for the specific purpose of clearing, e.g. an overgrown path. **You need permission.**

There are three sources of permission:

1 The *owner or tenant* of the land crossed by the path.
2 The *parish council*. Parish Councils are empowered (Section 46 of the Highways Act of 1959) to maintain public paths and they can allow individuals or organisations to act as their agents.
3 The *county councils* (or other highway authorities). They have ultimate responsibility for maintaining the path and again may give you permission to do so.

We advise getting permission from the owner or tenant in the first place. You will be surprised how often this is possible. Check the exact line of the path with the owner/tenant (or his representative). A walk along the path to be cleared with the estate agent, farm manager, gamekeeper or the owner or farmer himself is invaluable. You will learn a lot about how the land is managed and you will probably find yourself launched on a period of co-operation with an owner who previously seemed hostile to path-users.

Remember: farmers and landowners naturally fear trespass and vandalism. A system of clearly marked and easy-to-follow paths ensures that people know where they have a **right** to go and prevents unwitting trespass.

If the owner or tenant does refuse permission, then is the time to go to the parish council or county council.

Organising the Party
The first essential is for the working party to have a clearly nominated leader. His responsibilities are:

1 To see that everyone is using the proper tools and using them safely.
2 To see that the path is cleared to same width and standard throughout its length.
3 To see that the working party sticks to the correct line of the path.
4 To see that the path is left tidy and litter-free when the job is completed.

Tools
Beginners at the clearance game naturally tend to use the tools most readily available: the secateurs, sickles and shears which most gardeners have around. Of course you must use the tools which best fit the job in hand, but two weapons in particular have been found useful:

1 THE 'EVERSHARP SCYTHETTE': This tool is shaped like a golf club with a serrated edge on the business end and it works wonders on undergrowth. (See p. 119 for details.)
2 THE 'TOGGLE LOPPER'. In effect these are king-size secateurs. These are invaluable for the heavier cutting jobs on overgrown hedges. They are also very serviceable on saplings and branches up to about $1\frac{1}{4}$ inches in diameter. (See p. 119 for details.)

With these two weapons you are well equipped to deal with the main kinds of overgrowth both up in the air and down on the ground. The most serious obstacles which these tools will not cope with are tree stumps and branches thicker than $1\frac{1}{4}$ inches. These should be sawn back to ground level so as not to leave a stumbling block in the path. For these use a Rolcut folding pruning-saw convenient for carrying in a rucksack. This measures 11 inches when folded and costs £1.10. For heavier work a Sandvik 24-inch bow saw works wonders. To uproot difficult tree stumps a mattock is the ideal tool. It is like a pick axe with a 4-inch blade at right angles to the handle and a 2-inch blade parallel with the handle. It costs approximately £2. These are two specialist tools for more advanced clearing work but they are not essential to start with. The great advantage of 'Toggle Loppers' and 'Scythettes' is that they do not have blades as sharp as the normal sickle and are therefore much safer to use when parties of people are involved.

The leader of a clearance party has an important safety role. He should see that all members of the team are working far enough apart not to get in each other's way and he should also ensure that leather or gardening gloves are being worn to deal with hawthorn, brambles and nettles etc.

Width

How wide should your path be? A good working minimum, if you can achieve it, is 4 feet wide for a footpath and 6 for a bridleway. But there is no general legal requirement that a path should be of a certain width. There may be a note in the statement accompanying the definitive map, but this is unusual. In other cases the width will be governed by the local custom. In any case make sure you agree the width with the landowner or highway authority before starting work.

Bear in mind that on a bridleway, overhanging vegetation should be cut back to a height of 9 feet to allow riders through.

How Many People?

This is very difficult to estimate. It depends on the nature of the path, the experience of the leader and his team and the weather. It is the leader's job to estimate how many people he needs, but here is a rough guide. It will take 8 workers a day to clear 300 yards of really dense growth (e.g. when two hedges have grown together and intermeshed) to a width of 6 feet. A day's work is from say 10.00 am to 5.00 pm with a lunch break.

Clearing up

Arrangements must be made for disposing of the overgrowth, brushwood, etc., which has been cleared. The simplest method is a bonfire. Don't make the common beginner's error of siting your bonfire at one end of the path. It means a long walk for those clearing the other end to bring material to it. Put it in the middle and make sure that the fire is burnt out or safely damped down before leaving.

Which Paths?

If you are doing a pilot scheme or a one-off job, i.e. not part of a continuing programme of clearance over a given area, do a path which will give maximum return on the time and labour expended. Choose a path about which people have complained or one which will open the way to other linking walks. Often a few hundred yards of clearance opens up several miles of paths.

Relate the paths you choose for clearance to the highway authority's signposting programme. Many county councils are now putting up path signs on a significant scale for the first time ever. Often these signs advertise paths which have become completely impenetrable. A good idea is to choose newly signposted paths in this category.

If you clear a path which is not signposted, ask the highway authority to follow up your work by putting up a sign. After all you have been doing the authority's job for it (Section 38, Highways Act, 1959) and it is reasonable to expect a quid pro quo. The highway authority can also authorise you to waymark the path if this is appropriate. But they must consult the landowner first [*Countryside Act, Section 27(1) and (5)*]. You can always help things along by asking the landowner when you first approach him about clearance.

From the landowner's point of view the argument for waymarking is the same as that for clearance. Clear, well-marked paths prevent people straying.

Birds' Nests

Path clearance can damage bird life if undertaken at the wrong time of the year or without proper care.

Many species of birds nest in hedgerows and the nesting season runs roughly from the beginning of April to the end of August. Avoid clearance operations which involve drastic cutting back of hedgerows or heavy clearance of undergrowth during this period. Your main clearance season should be the Autumn and Winter. It is easier then anyway because the foliage is less. But public paths are not nature reserves and the clearance of light growth (nettles, brambles and the odd overhanging frond) is a legimate Summer activity. There are plenty of other things for path workers to do in the Summer, e.g. bridge-building, waymarking and stile repairs. Summer too is the time to start negotiating with landowners and local authorities for next winter's clearance programme.

Insurance

Some country councils require volunteer parties clearing paths as their agents to be insured against claims for damage, e.g. the lopping of a tree off the line of the path. And some volunteer groups feel happier if their own members are insured against injury. Consult an insurance broker about cover. It is not expensive. A typical rate to insure an organisation running regular clearance parties with a total membership of 150 is about £5 per annum.

Publicity

Work on clearing a path is never work wasted, but maximise its value by making sure you get what you are doing into the newspapers. Constructive volunteer work of this kind is a natural news story for your local press and can sometimes fill an odd spot on a regional TV magazine programme as well. Invite the news media at least a week in advance so that they can send a photographer and/or reporter to cover the operation. When inviting the press

'The Old Mill' by John Shelley.

indicate points of interest about the path, e.g. an archaeological site or a good view point. When the path has been cleared send the local papers a press release telling them the job has been done, how long it took and how many took part. Make sure you provide an address and (if possible) a telephone number to which the newspaper can refer for further queries.

SOURCES OF MATERIALS

Map-reading aid:
The Ramblers' Association has produced a handy device for obtaining grid references quickly and accurately. Called 'The Romer', it is printed on clear plastic and is available from the Association at 10p (including postage).

Path-clearing tools:
The 'Eversharp Scythette' costs £1 (including postage) and may be obtained from the manufacturer: T. & J. Hutton & Co. Ltd, Phoenix Works, Ridgeway, Sheffield. For orders of 1 dozen (send £8), the price of each 'Scythette' is reduced to 67p.

The 'Toggle Lopper' costs £3.85 and is manufactured by Rolcut, Blatchford Road, Horsham, Sussex.

SOCIETIES

CENTRAL RIGHTS OF WAY COMMITTEE, Suite 4, 166 Shaftesbury Avenue, London WC2.
COMMONS, OPEN SPACES AND FOOTPATHS PRESERVATION SOCIETY, Suite 4, 166 Shaftesbury Avenue, London WC2.
EASTBOURNE RAMBLING CLUB, c/o 28 Kinfauns Avenue, Eastbourne.
LINTON DISTRICT AMENITY SOCIETY'S RIGHT OF WAY GROUP, The Village College, Linton, Cambridgeshire.
MEOPHAM FOOTPATHS GROUP, c/o 'Wrenbury', Wrotham Road, Hook Green, Meopham, Kent DA13 0HX.
THE MID-HERTFORDSHIRE FOOTPATH SOCIETY, 9 Handside Green, Welwyn Garden City, Hertfordshire.
THE NORWICH DISTRICT FOOTPATH SOCIETY, c/o 1 Bridle Road, Keswick Norwich NOR 60D.
THE OFFA'S DYKE ASSOCIATION, March House, Wylewm Street, Knighton, Radnorshire. *Gives details of the Offa's Dyke Path and provides an accommodation list for the area.*
THE OXFORD FIELDPATHS SOCIETY, 325a Woodstock Road, Oxford.
POTTERS BAR SOCIETY FOOTPATHS GROUP, 12 Oakroyd Close, Potters Bar, Hertfordshire.
THE RAMBLERS' ASSOCIATION, 1–4 Crawford Mews, York Street, London W1M 1PT. *The R.A. is an association for all who enjoy walking in the countryside and wish to see its paths and beauty protected. Membership costs £1 per annum with concessionary rates for married couples, retired people, students and young people. Its 28,000 members receive the quarterly journal RUCKSACK free and this contains regular advertising by reputable equipment and clothing suppliers.*
ST ALBANS & DISTRICT FOOTPATH SOCIETY, 38 Carlisle Avenue, St Albans, Hertfordshire.
SCOTTISH RIGHTS OF WAY SOCIETY, 32 Rutland Square, Edinburgh 1.
THE SWALE FOOTPATH GROUP, 'Scilloria', Lawson Street, Teynham, Sittingbourne, Kent.

SERVICES

The Ramblers' Association operates a library of 1-inch maps for its members. These may be hired for a nominal charge. Many public libraries also lend O.S. 1-inch sheets.

BIBLIOGRAPHY

Rambling is fine, but not in a bibliography, so we have divided this subject in the following way:

Footpath Law and Maintenance

FOOTPATH WORKER/available from The R.A., 1–4 Crawford Mews, London W1M 1PT. Subscription: 25p per annum.
A quarterly bulletin of footpath news containing information on the latest legal cases, inquiry decisions and progress with county path surveys etc.
PARISH COUNCILS AND PUBLIC PATHS: Fact Sheet No. 5/The R.A. (as above). Free.
PATH-CLEARING FOR PLEASURE, by Don Gresswell/available from the author at Baker's Barn, Cadmore End Common, High Wycombe, Buckinghamshire. Free (but send postage).
This publication is a reprint of an article which first appeared in the Summer 1969 issue of THE COUNTRYMAN. Don Gresswell is a member of The R.A. Southern Area Footpaths Committee and Secretary of the Rights of Way Group of The Chiltern Society: his article details the experience gained in an extended path clearance programme.
A PRACTICAL GUIDE TO THE LAW OF FOOTPATHS, by Ian Campbell LL.B., / available from The Commons, Open Spaces and Footpaths Preservation Society, Suite 4, 166 Shaftesbury Avenue, London WC2H 8JH. Price: 25p (plus postage).
Deals thoroughly with all aspects of footpath law.
PUBLIC PATH CLEARING BY VOLUNTEERS: Fact Sheet No. 6/The R.A., 1–4 Crawford Mews, London W1M 1PT. Free.
RIGHT OF WAY: A 'CHILD'S GUIDE' TO THE LAW OF FOOTPATHS IN QUESTION AND ANSWER FORM/available from The R.A. (as above). Price: 5p. (plus postage).

Forest Guides

ARGYLE FOREST PARK/The Forestry Commission, 25 Savile Row, London W1X 2AY. Price: 35p.
DEAN FOREST AND WYE VALLEY/The Forestry Commission. Price 32½p.
FORESTS OF CENTRAL & SOUTHERN SCOTLAND/The Forestry Commission. Price: 62½p.
FORESTS OF NORTH EAST SCOTLAND/The Forestry Commission. Price: 25p.
GLAMORGAN FORESTS/The Forestry Commission. Price 25p.
GLEN MORE FOREST PARK/The Forestry Commission. Price 42½p.

NEW FOREST/The Forestry Commission. Price: 35p.

NEW FOREST OF DARTMOOR/The Forestry Commission. Price: 21p.

NORTH YORKSHIRE FORESTS/The Forestry Commission. Price: 65p.

EAST ANGLIAN FORESTS/The Forestry Commission. Price: 50p.

LOCAL GUIDES FOR WALKERS

England: The Eastern Counties

CIRCULAR WALKS AROUND SCUNTHORPE/Scunthorpe Civic Trust. Free.

THE FOOTPATHS OF LINTON DISTRICT, by Linton District Amenity Society's Rights of Way Group/available from the Society at: The Village College, Linton, Cambridgeshire. Price: 2½p (5p by post).

RAMBLES IN NORFOLK, by Mrs J. le Surf/available from the author at: 6 Atthill Road, Norwich NOR 8OJ. Price: 25p (28p by post).

RAMBLES IN RUTLAND, by Michael Fisher/available from The Uppingham Bookshop, High Street, Uppingham, Rutland. Price: 5p (plus a foolscap S.A.E.).

RAMBLING IN LINCOLNSHIRE, by J. N. Cole/available from the author at: 18 New Road, Waltham, Grimsby, Lincolnshire. Price: 25p.

THIRTY MORE NORFOLK WALKS, by The Norwich District Footpath Society/available from A. R. Cartwright, 1 Bridle Road, Keswick, Norwich NOR 6OD. Price: 25p.

WALKS AND RIDES AROUND CAMBRIDGE/Cambridgeshire & Isle of Ely County Council. Available from G. Smith, 5 Garlic Row, Cambridge CB5 8HW. Price: 40p.

England: The Midlands and the Welsh Border

CHURCH STRETTON RAMBLES, by Robert Smart/available from the author at: Church Stretton, Shropshire. Price: 21p.

DOVEDALE GUIDE/Derbyshire Countryside Ltd, Lodge Lane, Derby. Price: 90p.

DOVEDALE GUIDE/available from the 'Come to Derbyshire' Association, 1 Uttoxeter New Road, Derby. Price: 12½p.

EDALE, LATHKILL, PADLEY VALLEYS, Nature Trail Booklets/The Peak Park Planning Board, Aldern House, Bakewell, Derbyshire. Price: 5p each.

GOYT VALLEY STORY/available from Clifford Rathbone, 'The Hollies', Bollington Road, Bollington, Macclesfield, Cheshire. Price: 25p.

INTER-HOSTEL WALKING ROUTES: COTSWOLDS/available from Mr A. J. Drake, 2 Beech Lodge, The Park, Cheltenham, Gloucestershire GL50 2RX. Price: 14½p (including postage) (*Complete set of leaflets.*)

CLEEVE HILL TO DUNTISBOURNE ABBOTTS. Price: 4p (including postage).

DUNTISBOURNE ABBOTTS TO CLEEVE HILL. Price: 4p (including postage).

CLEEVE HILL TO STOW-ON-THE-WOLD. Price: 4p (including postage).

DUNTISBOURNE ABBOTS TO CHEDWORTH ROMAN VILLA WITH CONNECTIONS TO STOW-ON-THE-WOLD. Price 3½p (including postage).

CHEDWORTH ROMAN VILLA TO DUNTISBOURNE ABBOTS. Price: 3½p (including postage).

STOW-ON-THE-WOLD TO CHARLBURY. Price: 4p (including postage).

CHARLBURY TO STOW-ON-THE-WOLD. Price: 4p (including postage).

INTER-HOSTEL WALKING ROUTES: FOREST OF DEAN AND WYE VALLEY/available as above.

MITCHELDEAN TO WELSH BICKNOR. Price: 3½p (including postage).

WELSH BICKNOR TO MITCHELDEAN. Price: 3½p (including postage).

ST BRIAVELS TO WELSH BICKNOR. Price: 3½p (including postage).

WELSH BICKNOR TO ST BRIAVELS. Price: 3½p (including postage).

NOTTINGHAMSHIRE WALKS, by John Brock/BBC Radio Nottingham. Available from BBC, 35 Marylebone High Street, London W1M 4AA. Price: 50p.

THE PENNINE WAY AND WALKING IN DERBYSHIRE/available from The Peak Park Planning Board, Aldern House, Bakewell, Derbyshire.

TWENTY WALKS IN MID-CHESHIRE/available from Phillip, Son & Nephew Ltd, 7 Whitechapel, Liverpool L69 1AN. Price: 27½p.

TWENTY WALKS IN S.W. LANCASHIRE/available as above. Price: 12½p.

TWENTY WALKS IN WIRRAL/available as above. Price: 25p.

WALKING AROUND CHIPPING CAMPDEN, by The North Cotswold Group of the Voluntary Warden Service/available from local shops or by post from: F. A. Holland, Latymer, Chipping Campden. Price: 10p (including postage).

WALKING IN DERBYSHIRE/available from The Peak Park Planning Board, Aldern House, Bakewell, Derbyshire. Price: 22½p.

WALKS AROUND EDALE, by F. Heardman/available as above. Price: 4p.

WALKS AROUND DOVEDALE, by A. Bates/available as above. Price: 4p.

WALKS AROUND LONGDENDALE, by A. Bridge/available as above. Price: 4p.

WALKS IN LEICESTERSHIRE, by Leicestershire Footpaths Association/City of Leicester Publicity Department, Bishop Street, Leicester. Price: 33p.

WALKS IN THE DERBYSHIRE DALES/Derbyshire Countryside Ltd. Available from Clifford Rathbone, 'The Hollies', Bollington Road, Bollington, Macclesfield, Cheshire. Price: 25p.

WAYMARKED FOREST PATHS IN THE FOREST OF DEAN/available from Mr A. J. Drake, 2 Beech Lodge, The Park, Cheltenham, Gloucestershire GL50 2RX. Price: 4½p (including postage).

WAYMARKED FOREST PATHS IN HIGHMEADOW WOODS/available as above. Price: 4p (including postage).

ENGLAND:

The North and the Border

AN INTRODUCTION TO NATURE TRAILS & WALKS/available from The Lake District National Park Information Centre, Brockhole, Windermere, Westmorland. Free (but send postage).

ARNSIDE AND SILVERDALE/Dalesman Publishing Co. Ltd, Clapham (via Lancaster), Yorkshire. Price 15p (plus postage).

AROUND INGLETON AND CLAPHAM, by Ron and Lucie Pearson/Dalesman Publishing Co. Ltd, as above. Price: 20p (plus postage).

AROUND ULLSWATER AND PENRITH/Dalesman Publishing Co. Ltd, as above. Price: 12½p (plus postage).

A SHORT GUIDE TO THE ROMAN WALL, by R. G. Collingwood/Harold Hill and Son, Killingworth Place, Gallowgate, Newcastle-upon-Tyne. Price: 12½p.

A SHORT WALK FROM AMBLESIDE/available from The Lake District National Park Information

Centre, Brockhole, Windermere, Westmorland. Free (but send postage).

BORDER & DALES HOSTEL GUIDE, by The Border & Dales Regional Y.H.A. Group/available from the Group at: 30 Baliol Square, Lower Barn, Durham. (Price: 25p (including postage).

BOWNESS AND HAWKSHEAD/available from The Lake District National Park Information Centre, Brockhole, Windermere, Westmorland. Free (but send postage).

BUTTERMERE/The R.A. Lake District Area. Available from bookshops in the Lake District or from Mr R. Taylor, 62 Loop Road North, Whitehaven, Cumberland. Price: 10p (plus postage).

CENTRAL LAKELAND/Dalesman Publishing Co. Ltd, Clapham (via Lancaster), Yorkshire. Price: 12½p (plus postage).

CONISTON, by D. Cameron/The R.A. Lake District Area. Available from bookshops in the Lake District or from Mr R. Taylor, 62 Loop Road, North, Whitehaven, Cumberland. Price: 10p (plus postage).

THE COWN EDGE WAY, by The R.A. Manchester Area/available from The Area Sales Secretary: Mr S. McNab, 41 Slateacre Road, Gee Cross, Hyde, Cheshire. Price: 12½p (including postage).

EAST YORKSHIRE RAMBLES/available from A. Brown & Sons Ltd, Perch Street West, Hull, HU5 3UA. Price: 42p (including postage).

THE EASTERN FELLS, by A. Wainwright/The Westmorland Gazette, 22 Stricklandgate, Kendal. Price: 75p (plus postage).

ENNERDALE, by Roland Taylor/The R.A. Lake District Area. Available from bookshops in the Lake District or from Mr R. Taylor, 62 Loop Road North, Whitehaven, Cumberland. Price: 10p (plus postage).

ESKDALE, by Douglas Ramsden/The R.A. Lake District Area. Available as above. Price: 12½p (plus postage).

ESKDALE, by Roland Taylor/The R.A. Lake District Area. Available as above. Price: 10p (plus postage).

THE ENCHANTED HILLS/The Chorley Guardian, 32a Market Street, Chorley, Lancashire. Price: 37½p.

EXPLORING THE NORTH EAST AROUND ALNWICK/ H. O. Wade, 5 East View, Highfield, Rowlands Gill. Price: 15p (including postage).

EXPLORING THE NORTH EAST AROUND HEXHAM/ available as above. Price: 15p (including postage).

EXPLORING THE NORTH EAST AROUND MORPETH/ available as above. Price: 15p (including postage).

EXPLORING THE NORTH EAST AROUND SOUTH NORTHUMBERLAND/available as above. Price: 15p (including postage).

EXPLORING THE NORTH EAST AROUND THE COASTAL AREA OF OUTSTANDING NATURAL BEAUTY available as above. Price: 15p (including postage).

EXPLORING THE NORTH EAST AROUND THE NORTHUMBERLAND NATIONAL PARK/available as above. Price: 15p (including postage).

THE FAR EASTERN FELLS, by A. Wainwright/The Westmorland Gazette, 22 Stricklandgate, Kendal. Price: 75p (plus postage).

FOLLOW ANY STREAM/The Chorley Guardian, 32a Market Street, Chorley, Lancashire. Price: 37½p.

FORTY RAMBLES, by Ian Brodie/The Lancashire Evening Post, 127 Fishergate, Preston. (Gives detailed walks around Preston.) Price: 25p.

GRANGE AND CARTMEL/Dalesman Publishing Co. Ltd, Clapham (via Lancaster), Yorkshire. Price: 12½p (plus postage).

GRASMERE, by Roland Taylor/The R.A. Lake District Area. Available from bookshops in the Lake District or from Mr R. Taylor, 62 Loop Road North, Whitehaven, Cumberland. Price: 10p (plus postage).

GREEN PASTURES/The Chorley Guardian, 32a Market Street, Chorley, Lancashire. Price: 37½p.

GUIDE TO THE DERWENT VALLEY, by Roland Taylor/The R.A. Lake District Area. Available from bookshops in the Lake District or from Mr R. Taylor, 12 Loop Road North, Whitehaven, Cumberland. Price: 10p (plus postage).

HEATHER IN MY HAT/The Chorley Guardian, 32a Market Street, Chorley, Lancashire. Price: 37½p.

HIGH PEAK, by Eric Byne and Geoffrey Sutton/ Secker and Warburg Ltd. Price: £2.50.

KESWICK AND NORTHERN LAKELAND/Dalesman Publishing Co. Ltd, Clapham (via Lancaster), Yorkshire. Price: 12½p (plus postage).

FURTHER WALKS FOR MOTORISTS IN THE DALES, by The R.A. West Riding Area/Gerrard

Publications, 6 Edge End Avenue, Brierfield, Nelson, Lancashire. Price: 42½p (plus postage).

LAKE DISTRICT WALKS FOR MOTORISTS, by J. Parker/Gerrard Publications (as above):

Central Area: Grasmere, Ambleside, Windermere, Coniston. Price: 50p (plus postage).

Northern Area: Keswick, Borrowdale, Ullswater. Price: 50p (plus postage).

Western Area: Buttermere, Wastwater, Eskdale west of Coniston and to the Coast. Price: 50p (plus postage).

THE LAKELAND PEAKS, by W. A. Poucher/ Constable & Co. Ltd. Price: £1.50.

LANGDALE, by Roland Taylor/The R.A. Lake District Area. Available from bookshops in the Lake District or from Mr R. Taylor, 62 Loop Road North, Whitehaven, Cumberland. Price: 10p (plus postage).

LET'S GO FOR A RAMBLE/The Manchester Evening News, 164 Deansgate, Manchester M60 2RD. Price: 12½p.

LET'S TAKE A WALK/The Chorley Guardian, 32a Market Street, Chorley, Lancashire. Price: 37½p.

MALHAMDALE/Dalesman Publishing Co. Ltd, Clapham (via Lancaster), Yorkshire. Price: 20p (plus postage).

MANX HILL WALKS, by The Manx Conservation Council Footpaths Group/available from 'Landsworth', Beach Road, Port St Mary, Isle of Man. Price: 25p (plus postage).

NIDDERDALE/Dalesman Publishing Co. Ltd, Clapham (via Lancaster), Yorkshire. Price: 12½p (plus postage).

NEWLANDS, by Roland Taylor/The R.A. Lake District Area. Available from bookshops in the Lake District or from Mr R. Taylor, 62 Loop Road North, Whitehaven, Cumberland. Price: 10p (plus postage).

NORTH YORK MOORS WALKS FOR MOTORISTS, by Geoffrey White/Gerrard Publications, 6 Edge End Avenue, Brierfield, Nelson, Lancashire. Price: 50p.

THE NORTHERN FELLS, by A. Wainwright/The Westmorland Gazette, 22 Stricklandgate, Kendal. Price: 75p (plus postage).

THE NORTH-WESTERN FELLS, by A. Wainwright/ The Westmorland Gazette (as above). Price: 75p (plus postage).

OVER THE FIVE-BARRED GATE/The Chorley Guardian, 32a Market Street, Chorley, Lan-

cashire. Price: 37½p.

THE PEAK AND THE PENNINES, by W. A. Poucher/
Constable & Co. Ltd. Price: £1.50.

PEAK DISTRICT WALKS FOR MOTORISTS, by
Clifford Thompson/Gerrard Publications, 6
Edge End Avenue, Brierfield, Nelson, Lanca-
shire. Price: 50p.

PENNINE WALKS AROUND HEBDEN BRIDGE, by
The Calder Civic Trust/available from D.
Bond, 82 Cragg Road, Mytholmroyd, Hebden
Bridge, Yorkshire. Price: 75p (plus postage).

RAMBLERS' CHEVIOT/Harold Hill & Son, Killingworth Place, Gallowgate, Newcastle-upon-
Tyne NE1 4SL. Price: 30p.

RAMBLERS' TYNEDALE/Harold Hill & Son (as
above). Price: 17½p.

RAMBLES FROM BOLTON, by Harry T. Hampson/
John Head. Price: 12½p.

RAMBLES IN THE DALES, by The R.A. West
Riding Area/Gerrard Publications, 6 Edge End
Avenue, Brierfield, Nelson, Lancashire. Price:
40p (plus postage).

RAMBLERS' WAY, by P. Walshaw/Gerrard Publications (as above). (In two volumes.) Price:
17½p each.

ROUND PRESTON WALK/The R.A. Preston &
Fylde Group. Available from Mr R. Taylor,
62 Loop Road North, Whitehaven, Cumberland. Price: 13p (including postage).

RYEDALE AND THE VALE OF PICKERING, by J. H.
Ruston/Dalesman Publishing Co. Ltd, Clapham (via Lancaster), Yorkshire. Price: 12½p
(plus postage).

SELECTED WALKS IN THE LAKE DISTRICT, by
Roland Taylor/The R.A. Lake District Area.
Available from bookshops in the area or from
Mr R. Taylor, 62 Loop Road North, White-
haven, Cumberland. Price: 12½p (plus postage).

SIDETRACKS IN TEESDALE, by A. Falconer/
available from S. Cardwell, 11a Lynton
Gardens, Darlington, Co. Durham. Price: 17½p.

THE SOUTH-EASTERN FELLS, by A. Wainwright/
The Westmorland Gazette, 22 Stricklandgate,
Kendal. Price: 75p (plus postage).

THE SOUTHERN FELLS, by A. Wainwright/The
Westmorland Gazette (as above). Price: 75p
(plus postage).

SWALEDALE, by Ron and Lucie Pearson/
Dalesman Publishing Co. Ltd, Clapham (via
Lancaster), Yorkshire. Price: 20p (plus post-
age).

TEN WALKS FOR MOTORISTS IN THE WIRRAL, by 'Greenways'/available from The Belvedere Press (Publications), 22 Rake Lane, Wallasey, Cheshire. Price: 25p (plus postage).

THE TOWPATH TROD (Along the Leeds and Liverpool Canal), by The West Riding Area and the North-Eastern Branch of the Inland Waterways Association/available from Mr C. Speakman, 32 Ayresome Avenue, Roundhay, Leeds 8, Yorkshire. Price: 17½p (including postage).

TWO WALKS FROM GLENRIDDING(available from The Lake District National Park Information Centre, Brockhole, Windermere, Westmorland. Free (but send postage).

ULLSWATER, by Harry Appleyard/The R.A. Lake District Area. Available from bookshops in the Lake District or from Mr R. Taylor, 62 Loop Road North, Whitehaven, Cumberland. Price: 10p.

UPPER EDEN VALLEY, by Gordon Wood/Dalesman Publishing Co. Ltd, Clapham (via Lancaster), Yorkshire. Price: 12½p (plus postage).

WALKER'S MAP OF THE ISLE OF MAN/available from Manxtracks, Dhoon Platt, Maughold, Ramsey, Isle of Man. Price: 25p (including postage).

WALKING IN AIREDALE, by The R.A. Bradford Group/Dalesman Publishing Co. Ltd, Clapham (via Lancaster), Yorkshire. Price: 35p (plus postage).

WALKING IN CLEVELAND, by A. Falconer/available from S. Cardwell, 11a Lynton Gardens, Darlington, Co. Durham. Price: 25p.

WALKING IN HISTORIC YORKSHIRE, by Colin Speakman/Dalesman Publishing Co. Ltd, Clapham (via Lancaster), Yorkshire. Price: 40p (plus postage).

WALKING IN SOUTH YORKSHIRE, by J. L. Ferns/Dalesman Publishing Co. Ltd (as above). Price: 35p (plus postage).

WALKING IN THE CRAVEN DALES, by Colin Speakman/Dalesman Publishing Co. Ltd (as above). Price: 35p (plus postage).

WALKING IN THE DALES, by Col P. T. Straubenzee/available from the author at: Spennithorne House, Spennithorne, Leyburn, Yorkshire. Price: 19p.

WALKING IN THE ISLE OF MAN/available from The Island Tourist Board.

WALKING ON THE NORTH YORK MOORS, by The

R.A. N. Yorks and S. Durham Area/Dalesman Publishing Co. Ltd, Clapham (via Lancaster), Yorkshire. Price: 35p (plus postage).

WALKS AROUND HARROGATE, by The R.A. Harrogate Group/available from P. L. Goldsmith, 20 Pannal Ashgrove, Harrogate, Yorkshire. Price: 45½p (including postage).

WALKS AROUND LANCASTER, by The R.A. Lancaster and Morecambe Group/available from 22 Endsleigh Grove, Lancaster. Price: 23p (including postage).

WALKS AROUND RYLSTONE/available from C. Speakman, 32 Ayresome Avenue, Roundhay, Leeds LS8 1BE. Price: 5p.

WALKS FOR MOTORISTS IN THE DALES, by The R.A. West Riding Area/Gerrard Publications, 6 Edge End Avenue, Brierfield, Nelson, Lancashire. Price: 40p (plus postage).

WALKS FROM KENDAL, by The R.A. Kendal Group/obtainable from Mr M. Leak, 4 Woodgate, Kendal. Price: 15p (send S.A.E.).

WALKS IN BRONTË COUNTRY, by Alan Lawson/Gerrard Publications, 6 Edge End Avenue, Brierfield, Nelson, Lancashire. Price: 20p (plus postage).

WALKS IN HODDER COUNTRY, by Alan Lawson/Gerrard Publications (as above). Price: 22½p (plus postage).

WALKS IN LIMESTONE COUNTRY, by A. Wainwright/The Westmorland Gazette, 22 Stricklandgate, Kendal.

WALKS IN PENDLE COUNTRY, by Alan Lawson/Gerrard Publications, 6 Edge End Avenue, Brierfield, Nelson, Lancashire. Price: 20p (plus postage).

WASDALE, by Roland Taylor/The R.A. Lake District Area. Available from bookshops in the Lake District or from Mr R. Taylor, 62 Loop Road North, Whitehaven, Cumberland. Price: 10p (plus postage).

WEARDALE, by Douglas Ramsden/Dalesman Publishing Co. Ltd, Clapham (via Lancaster), Yorkshire. Price: 12½p (plus postage).

WENSLEYDALE/Dalesman Publishing Co. (as above). Price: 15p (plus 6p postage).

THE WESTERN FELLS, by A. Wainwright/The Westmorland Gazette, 22 Stricklandgate, Kendal. Price: 75p (plus postage).

THE WHITE ROSE WALK, by Geoffrey White/Dalesman Publishing Co. Ltd, Clapham (via Lancaster), Yorkshire. Price: 20p (plus postage).

WINDERMERE, by Joy Greenwood/The R.A. Lake District Area. Available from bookshops in the Lake District or from Mr R. Taylor, 62 Loop Road North, Whitehaven, Cumberland. Price: 10p (plus postage).

YORKSHIRE'S THREE PEAKS (Dalesman Publishing Co. Ltd, Clapham (via Lancaster), Yorkshire. Price: 20p (plus postage).

ENGLAND:

The South-East

ADUR TO ARUN, by H. L. Reeves/ Sheepdown Publications. Price: 50p.

AFOOT IN ESSEX, by Frank Dawes/Letchworth Printers Ltd, Norton Way, North Letchworth SG6 1BH, Hertfordshire. Price: 50p.

AFOOT IN HERTFORDSHIRE, by Frank Dawes/Letchworth Printers Ltd (as above). Price: 40p.

BERKHAMSTED, ASHRIDGE AND DISTRICT FIELD-PATH MAP, by The Berkhamsted Citizens Association/available from 7 Oxfield Close, Berkhamsted, Hertfordshire. Price: 35p.

BETWEEN KENNET & THAMES/The Parish Councils of Englefield, Pangbourne, Purley, Theale, Tidmarsh with Sulham and Tilehurst. Available from the Clerk to the Tilehurst Parish Council, 26 Bath Road, Reading, Berkshire. Price: 13p (including postage).

CENTRAL HAMPSHIRE, by P. H. Carne/Winchester Information Office. (Several leaflets.) Price: 1½p each.

A CIRCULAR WALK FROM KEMSING HOSTEL/The Y.H.A. Southern Regional Group, 58 Streatham High Road, London SW16. Free (but send S.A.E.).

COOKHAM FOOTPATH MAP/The R.A. East Berkshire Group. Available from Peter Nevell, 'Donnybrook', Altwood Road, Maidenhead, Berkshire SL6 4BP. Price: 13p (including postage).

COUNTRY WALKS, BOOK 1/London Transport, 55 Broadway, London SW1. Price: 30p.

COUNTRY WALKS, BOOK 2/London Transport (as above). Price: 30p.

CUCKFIELD WALKS, by The Cuckfield Society/available from 22 South Street, Cuckfield, Sussex. (Seven leaflets.) Price: 2½p each (including postage).

DISCOVERING WALKS IN THE CHILTERNS, by R. J.

Pigram/available from Shire Publications, 12B Temple Square, Aylesbury, Buckinghamshire. Price: 30p.

FIFTEEN WALKS AROUND FOLKESTONE, by Marjorie Walton/available from Cross's, 91 Sandgate Road, Folkestone, Kent. Price unknown.

FIVE COUNTRY WALKS AROUND SUNNINGHILL, by P. Hathaway/available from the author at: 41 Victoria Road, South Ascot. Price: 9p (including postage).

FOOTPATH MAP OF HENLEY-ON-THAMES N.W., by The Chiltern Society/available from Shire Publications, 12B Temple Square, Aylesbury, Buckinghamshire. Price: 12½p (including postage).

FOOTPATH MAP OF HENLEY-ON-THAMES S.W., by The Chiltern Society/available from Shire Publications (as above). Price: 12½p (including postage).

FOOTPATH MAP OF MARLOW, by The Chiltern Society/available from Shire Publications (as above). Price: 12½p (including postage).

FOOTPATH MAP OF SARRATT AND CHIPPERFIELD, by The Chiltern Society/available from Shire Publications (as above). Price: 12½p (including postage).

FOOTPATH MAP OF THE COUNTRYSIDE EAST OF OXFORD/The Oxford Fieldpaths Society, 325a Woodstock Road, Oxford. Price: 12½p (including postage).

FOOTPATH MAP OF WENDOVER & DISTRICT, by The Chiltern Society/available from Shire Publications, 12B Temple Square, Aylesbury, Buckinghamshire. Price: 12½p (including postage).

FOOTPATH WALKS AROUND POTTERS BAR, by Helen and Dick Baker for the Potters Bar Society Footpaths Group/available by post from 12 Oakroyd Close, Potters Bar, Hertfordshire. Price: 18p (including postage).

FOOTPATH WALKS AROUND ST ALBANS, by St Albans & District Footpath Society/available from 38 Carlisle Avenue, St Albans, Hertfordshire. Price: 23p (including postage).

FOOTPATH WALKS AROUND WELWYN GARDEN CITY, by The Mid-Hertfordshire Footpath Society/available from the Society's Secretary, Mr E. M. Bavin, 9 Handside Green, Welwyn Garden City, Hertfordshire. Price: 20p.

FOOTPATH WALKS IN MID-HERTFORDSHIRE FOR MOTORISTS, by The Mid-Hertfordshire Foot-

path Society/available from 24 Fearnley Road, Welwyn Garden City, Hertfordshire. Price: 30p (plus postage).

THE FOREST WAY, by Essex County Council/available from the County Council at County Hall, Chelmsford. Free.

FOURTEEN WALKS IN AND AROUND TONBRIDGE, by Tonbridge Civic Society/available from G. Hook, 56 Dry Hill Park Road, Tonbridge, Kent. Price: 35p (including postage).

A GUIDE TO THE PILGRIMS' WAY AND NORTH DOWNS WAY, by Christopher J. Wright/Constable & Co. Ltd. Price: £1.90.

HURLEY FOOTPATH MAP/The R.A. East Berkshire Group. Available from Peter Nevell, 'Donnybrook', Altwood Road, Maidenhead, Berkshire SL6 4BP. Price: 10p (plus postage).

Isle of Wight County Council Long-Distance Trail Leaflets:

BEMBRIDGE TRAIL

HAMSTEAD TRAIL

NUNWELL TRAIL

SHEPHERDS TRAIL

STENBURY TRAIL

TENNYSON TRAIL

WORSLEY TRAIL

A wallet, containing a leaflet on each trail, is available from County Hall, Newport, Isle of Wight. Free (but send postage).

THE LOST ROADS OF MEOPHAM, by James Cawley/Meopham Publications Committee, 'Wrenbury', Hook Green, Meopham, Kent. Price: 25p.

MAP OF FOOTPATHS AND BRIDLEWAYS AROUND HORSHAM/The West Sussex Gazette. Obtainable from Miss J. Edward, The Horsham Consumer Group, 109 Depot Road, Horsham, Sussex. Price: 20p.

MILFORD HOSTEL TO EWHURST GREEN HOSTEL (Footpath Route)/The Y.H.A. Southern Regional Group, 58 Streatham High Road, London SW16. Free (but send S.A.E.).

NINE CIRCULAR WALKS FROM KEMSING HOSTEL/The Y.H.A. Southern Regional Group (as above). Free (but send S.A.E.).

ON FOOT IN EAST SUSSEX/The Eastbourne Rambling Club. Available from 28 Kinfauns Avenue, Eastbourne. Price: 30p.

THE PENN COUNTRY, by The Chiltern Society/available from Shire Publications, 12B Temple Square, Aylesbury, Buckinghamshire. Price:

12½p (including postage).

THE PILGRIMS' WAY FROM WINCHESTER TO CANTERBURY, by Sean Jennett/Cassell & Co. Ltd. Price: £3.15.

PUBLIC FOOTPATHS, BRIDLEWAYS & BYWAYS IN BENENDEN PARISH (Maps & list of paths)/available from The Parish Clerk, Two Ponds, Benenden, Cranbrook, Kent. Price: 5p (plus postage).

PUBLIC RIGHTS OF WAY IN THE TATSFIELD/LIMPSFIELD AREA, by The Bromley & District Consumers' Group/available from the Group at 20 Abbotsbury Road, Bromley, Kent. Price: 10p (including postage).

RAMBLES IN HAMPSHIRE & SUSSEX, by Dennis Haggard/available from the author at Stroudbridge Cottage, Stroud, Petersfield, Hampshire. Price: 30p.

RAMBLING THROUGH KENT, by V. W. Morecroft/The Kentish Times. Available from the R.A. Southern Area, 1–4 Crawford Mews, London W1H 1PT. Price: 40p (plus postage).

RIGHTS OF WAY MAP FOR MAYFIELD PARISH/available from The Clerk to the Parish Council, 104 Stanmer Villas, Brighton, Sussex. Price: 40p.

ROMAN WAYS IN THE WEALD, by Ivan D. Margery/J. M. Dent & Sons Ltd. Price: £2.00.

SAFFRON WALDEN HOSTEL TO HARLOW HOSTEL FOOTPATH ROUTE/The Y.H.A. South-Eastern Countryside Committee, 58 Streatham High Road, London SW16. Free (but send S.A.E.).

SEVENOAKS RURAL DISTRICT RIGHTS OF WAY MAPS (Northern & Southern sections)/available from C. Ferguson, 19 Cyclamen Road, Swanley, Kent BR8 8HH. Price: 25p per section (including postage).

SEVENTEEN DOWNLAND WALKS FROM SHOREHAM, LANCING, SOUTHWICK AND PORTSLADE/available from Shoreham Urban District Council, The Town Hall, Shoreham BN4 5EJ. Price: 5p.

SHOREHAM WALKS, by Colin Ulph/available from Shoreham Urban District Council (as above). Price: 5p.

SIX WALKS FROM COBHAM/Meopham Footpaths Group. Available from J. Cawley, 'Wrenbury', Wrotham Road, Hook Green, Meopham, Kent DA13 0HX. Price: 5p (send foolscap S.A.E.).

SIX WALKS FROM HARVEL/Meopham Footpaths Group. Available as above. Price: 5p (send foolscap S.A.E.).

SIX WALKS FROM HODSELL STREET/Meopham Footpaths Group. Available as above. Price: 5p (send foolscap S.A.E.).

SIX WALKS FROM MEOPHAM GREEN/Meopham Footpath Group. Available as above. Price: 5p. (send foolscap S.A.E.).

SIX WALKS FROM NURSTEAD & ISTEAD RISE/Meopham Footpaths Group. Available as above. Price: 5p (send foolscap S.A.E.).

SOUTH SUSSEX WALKS, by Lord Teviot and M. B. Quinion/BBC Radio Brighton. Price: 30p.

TEN WALKS AROUND BREDHURST/The Faversham Society. Available from The Swale Footpath Group, 'Scillonia', Lawson Street, Teynham, Sittingbourne, Kent. Price: 25p (including postage).

TEN WALKS AROUND FAVERSHAM/The Faversham Society. Available as above. Price: 25p (including postage).

TEN WALKS AROUND SITTINGBOURNE/The Faversham Society. Available as above. Price: 25p (including postage).

THAME FOOTPATH MAP/available from The Town Hall, Thame, Oxfordshire. Price unknown.

WALKING ALONG THE BASINGSTOKE CANAL, by D. Gerry/available from P. Walker, 6 Carlyon Close, Farnborough, Hampshire. Price: 15p.

WALKING AROUND HAWKHURST, CRANBROOK AND GOUDHURST, by the S.E. London & Kent R.A. Group/available from the Group at 1 Braeside Close, Sevenoaks, Kent. Price: $17\frac{1}{2}$p (including postage).

WALKING AROUND OXFORD, by The Oxford Fieldpaths Society/The Oxford Illustrated Press, Shelley Close, Kiln Lane, Risinghurst, Oxford. Price: 30p.

WALKING WITH THE WEST ESSEX, by The West Essex R.A. Group/available from Fred Mathews, Glen View, London Road, Abridge, Essex. Price: 25p.

WALKS AROUND BINFIELD/available from The Clerk, Binfield Parish Council, Binfield, Berkshire. Price: 13p (including postage).

WALKS IN THE THAMES-SIDE CHILTERNS, by The Chiltern Society's Rights of Way Group/available from Spurbrooks, Station Road, Bourne End, Buckinghamshire. Price: 50p.

WALKS ON ASHDOWN FOREST AND AROUND TUNBRIDGE WELLS, by H. Longley-Cook/available from The Waterdown Press, Winter Hill,

Frant, Tunbridge Wells. Price: 75p (including postage).

WALTHAM ST LAWRENCE AND DISTRICT FOOTPATH MAP/The East Berkshire R.A. Group. Available from Peter Nevell, 'Donnybrook', Altwood Road, Maidenhead, Berkshire SL6 4BP. Price: 10p (plus postage).

WESTERHAM OFFICIAL GUIDE (includes a map showing all footpaths in the parish)/available from Forward Publicity Ltd, Bell House, 36–38 High Street, Carshalton, Surrey. Price: 15p.

WINSLOW FOOTPATHS, by Joseph Lowrey/ available from the author at: 23 Station Road, Winslow, Buckinghamshire. Price: 8p (including postage).

WYCOMBE N.W., by The Chiltern Society/ available from Shire Publications, 12B Temple Square, Aylesbury, Buckinghamshire. Price: 12½p (including postage).

ENGLAND:

The South West

BRIDPORT AND WEST BAY—WALKS AND PICNIC SPOTS/available from John Hobson, c/o Carl Lentall & Co., Lyme Regis. Price: 7½p.

BRIEF GUIDE TO DARTMOOR, by Brian Le Messurier/David & Charles Ltd. Price: 12½p.

COASTAL PATHS OF THE SOUTH WEST, by Edward G. Pyatt/David & Charles Ltd. Price: £2.75.

COME WALKING IN DEVON/Devon County Council, County Hall, Exeter, Devon. Price unknown.

COUNTRYSIDE TRAILS BY CAR/available from The County Planning Officer, County Hall, Taunton, Somerset. Price: 5p.

EXMOOR COASTAL WALKS, by Tim Abbott/The Cider Press, Weymans, Gunswell Lane, South Molton, Devon. Price: 10p.

EXMOOR WALKS/The Cider Press (as above). Price: 13p (including postage).

FOOTPATH AND GENERAL GUIDE TO WEMBURY/ available from The Clerk, Wembury Parish Council, Channel View, Andurn Estate, Down Thomas, Plymouth. Price: 10p (including postage).

FOOTPATHS IN BRIXHAM, by Mr H. L. Hamling/ available from the author at: Brixham County Secondary School, Brixham, Devon. Price: 15p.

LYME REGIS—WALKS AND PICNIC SPOTS/available from John Hobson, c/o Carl Lentall & Co., Lyme Regis. Price: 7½p.

MOTORING AND WALKING IN AND AROUND EXETER, PLYMOUTH, TORQUAY, THE SOUTH HAMS (four separate guides) by Arthur Clamp/ Westaway Guides, 159 St Margaret's Road, Plympton, Plymouth, Devon. Price: 12½p each.

MOTORING AND WALKING ON EASTERN DARTMOOR, by Arthur Clamp/ Westaway Guides (as above). Price: 12½p.

MOTORING AND WALKING ON NORTHERN DARTMOOR, by Arthur Clamp/Westaway Guides (as above). Price: 12½p.

MOTORING AND WALKING ON SOUTHERN DARTMOOR, by Arthur Clamp/Westaway Guides (as above). Price: 12½p.

ANCIENT TRACKWAYS OF WESSEX, by H. W. Timperley and Edith Brill/J. M. Dent & Sons Ltd. Price: £2.75.

NATURE TRAIL NORTH HILL, MINEHEAD/available from The County Planning Officer, Somerset County Council, Bedford House, Park Street, Taunton. Price: 5p.

THE NEW FORESTS OF DARTMOOR/The Forestry Commission, 25 Savile Row, London W1X 2AY. Price: 12½p.

RAMBLES IN DORSET/available from The Southern National and Western National Omnibus Co. Ltd, Queen Street, Exeter, Devon. Free (but send foolscap S.A.E.).

RAMBLES IN WEST SOMERSET AND ON EXMOOR FROM MINEHEAD/available as above. Free (but send foolscap S.A.E.).

SEATON AND BEER—WALKS AND PICNIC SPOTS/ available from John Hobson, c/o Carl Lentall & Co., Lyme Regis. Price: 7½p.

SHAFTESBURY: WALKS AROUND THE TOWN/available from Shaftesbury Tourist Board. Price unknown.

SHORT DORSET WALKS, by G. M. Robertson/ Sherbourne Press. Price: 15p.

SOME DORSET WALKS, by G. M. Robertson/ Sherbourne Press. Price: 15p.

STROLLS AROUND SIDMOUTH/The Sid Vale Association. Price: 12½p.

WALKS AROUND LYNTON AND LYNMOUTH/The Lyn Publicity Association, Lynton, Devon. Price: 4p.

WALKS IN WEST CORNWALL/The West Cornwall Footpaths Preservation Society. Obtain-

able from Mrs Graham White, Croft Hooper, Ludgvan, Penzance. Price: 28p (including postage).

WALKS ON NORTH HILL, MINEHEAD/available from The County Planning Officer, Somerset County Council, Bedford House, Park Street, Taunton. Price: 2½p.

WAYMARKED WALKS IN EXMOOR NATIONAL PARK (Nos. 1 and 2)/available as above. Price: 7½p and 12½p respectively.

WHERE TO WALK IN WESSEX, by The R.A. South-East Wiltshire Group/available from Wessex Tourist Services, 68 Endlass Street, Salisbury. Price: 20p (plus postage).

The following leaflets give detailed descriptions of the footpaths in the following areas and are available free of charge from The County Planning Officer, County Hall, Exeter: LUSTLEIGH, POSTBRIDGE, MANATON, DARTMEET, HOLNE, TWO BRIDGES.

SCOTLAND

ARRAN/The Scottish Youth Hostels Association, 7 Glebe Crescent, Stirling. Price: 6p (plus postage).

CAIRNGORMS/The Scottish Youth Hostels Association (as above). Price: 10p (plus 3p postage).

THE CAIRNGORMS, by Henry Alexander/The Scottish Mountaineering Club Trust. Price: £2.00.

CENTRAL HIGHLANDS, by C. R. Steven/The Scottish Mountaineering Club Trust. Price: £1.90.

EDINBURGH AND THE BORDER/The Scottish Youth Hostels Association, 7 Glebe Crescent, Stirling. Price: 7½p (plus postage).

GARTH AND GLEN LYON/The Scottish Youth Hostels Association (as above). Price: 6p (plus postage).

GLENCOE AND GLEN NEVIS/The Scottish Youth Hostels Association (as above). Price: 7½p (plus postage).

A GUIDE TO MELROSE AND THE SCOTT COUNTRY (includes a section of walks)/available from The Clerk to the Town Council, Melrose, Roxburghshire. Free.

GUIDE TO THE WESTERN HIGHLANDS, by W. H. Murray/Collins, Sons & Co. Ltd. Price: £1.80.

HILL WALKING IN ARRAN, by R. Meek/W. & R. Chambers Ltd, 11 Thistle Street, Edinburgh. Price: 22½p.

SLANDS OF SCOTLAND, by Norman Tennant/
The Scottish Mountaineering Club Trust.
Price: £2.25.

SLAND OF SKYE, by Malcolm Slesser/The
Scottish Mountaineering Club Trust. Price:
£2.25.

LOCH LOMOND AND TROSSACHS/The Scottish
Youth Hostels Association, 7 Glebe Crescent,
Stirling. Price: 10p (plus postage).

NORTHERN HIGHLANDS, by Thomas Strang/The
Scottish Mountaineering Club Trust. Price:
£2.25.

NORTHERN HIGHLANDS/The Scottish Youth
Hostels Association, 7 Glebe Crescent, Stirl-
ng. Price: 7½p (plus postage).

PITLOCHRY WALKS AND STROLLS/available from
The Secretary and Information Officer, Pit-
lochry Tourist Association, 28 Atholl Road,
Pitlochry. Free.

RAMBLES IN THE HEBRIDES, by Roger Redfern/
Robert Hale & Co. Price: £1.05.

THE ROMANS IN ROXBURGH (Leaflet)/available
from Roxburgh County Planning Department,
Newtown Street, Boswells, Roxburgh. Free.

THE SCOTTISH LOCHS, by Tom Weir/Constable
& Co. Ltd. Price: £1.25.

THE SCOTTISH PEAKS, by W. A. Poucher/
Constable. Price: £1.25.

SKYE/The Scottish Youth Hostels Association,
7 Glebe Crescent, Stirling. Price: 7½p (plus
postage).

SUGGESTED TOURS AND WALKS TO PLACES OF
INTEREST ON THE ISLAND OF SKYE/The Isle of
Skye Tourist Association, Portree, Isle of Skye.

Price: 7½p (including postage).

SOUTHERN HIGHLANDS, by J. D. B. Wilson/The
Scottish Mountaineering Club Trust. Price:
£1.25.

TORRIDON HIGHLANDS, by Brenda G. Macrow/
Robert Hale & Co. Price: £1.25.

WALKS IN AND AROUND PEEBLES/available from
The Secretary, Peebleshire Tourist Association, High Street, Peebles. Price: 5p.

WALKING IN SCOTLAND—YOUR QUESTIONS AN-
SWERED, by The Scottish Area of the R.A./
available from Mr A. J. Graham, 173 Braid-
craft Road, Glasgow SW3. Free (but send
postage).

WESTERN HIGHLANDS, by J. A. Parker/The
Scottish Mountaineering Club Trust. Price:
£1.50.

WALES

THE ASCENT OF SNOWDON, by E. G. Rowland/ available from Vector Production, Hafodty, Dinorwic, Deiniolen, Caernarvonshire. Price: 12½p (plus postage).

COLWYN BAY YOUTH HOSTEL—WALKS AND PLACES OF INTEREST IN COLWYN BAY AND DISTRICT/available from The Youth Hostels Association, North Wales and Isle of Man Regional Group, 40 Hamilton Square, Birkenhead, Cheshire L41 5BA. Free (but send postage).

ELENITH, by Timothy Porter/The Youth Hostels Association (South Wales Region). Available from The Y.H.A., 25 Park Place, Cardiff. (Describes walking routes in the 300 square miles of mountains S.E. from Plynlimmon.) Price: 18p (including postage).

FROM OFFA'S DYKE TO THE SEA THROUGH PICTURESQUE MID WALES, by Carl D. Ehrenzeller/available from St Christopher's Youth Hostel, Llandrindod Wells, Radnorshire. Price: 25p (plus postage).

HILL WALKING IN SNOWDONIA, by E. G. Rowland/available from Vector Production Hafodty, Dinorwic, Deiniolen, Caernarvonshire. Price: 20p (plus postage).

LLANBERIS AREA GUIDE (including valley and mountain walking routes)/Vector Productions Hafodty (as above). Price: 25p.

LOOKING AROUND NEWPORT (PEMBROKESHIRE)/ available from Newport Primary School, Newport, Pembrokeshire. Price: 30p.

NORTH WALES FOR THE COUNTRYGOER, by Jessica Lofthouse/Robert Hale & Co. Price: £1.75.

PEMBROKESHIRE COUNTRYSIDE/available from The Pembrokeshire Countryside Unit, Broad Haven, Haverfordwest (set of five leaflets). Price: 15p.

RAMBLES IN GLAMORGAN AND MONMOUTHSHIRE/ available from The R.A. South Wales Area, c/o Mr M. E. Trimble, 5 Meads Close, Newport, Monmouthshire. Price unknown.

RAMBLES IN NORTH WALES, by Roger Redfern/ Robert Hale & Co. Price: £1.25.

RAMBLING ROUND RADNORSHIRE, by Carl D. Ehrenzeller/available from St Christopher's Youth Hostel, Llandrindod Wells, Radnorshire. Price: 15p (plus postage).

SNOWDONIA NATIONAL PARK/available from The National Park Information Officer, Plas Tanybwlch, Maentwrog, Blaenau, Ffestiniog, Merioneth (leaflet detailing all Trail Guides). Free.

TEN WALKS IN GOWER, by S. Lee/The Gower Society.

THIRTY WALKS (MONMOUTH SECTION OF BRECONS NATIONAL PARK)/available from The National Park Information Centre, Monk Street, Abergavenny. Price: 5p (plus postage).

TWENTY WALKS IN NORTH WALES/Philip, Son & Nephew Ltd, 7 Whitechapel, Liverpool L69 1AN. Price: 25p.

WALKS IN AND AROUND MONMOUTH AND THE WYE VALLEY/The Monmouth Chamber of Commerce. Price: 2½p.

THE WELSH PEAKS, by W. A. Poucher/Constable & Co. Ltd. Price: £1.25.

WELSH WALKS AND LEGENDS, by Showell Styles/ John Jones Cardiff Ltd, 21 Duffryn Close, Cardiff. Price: 60p.

LONG-DISTANCE FOOTPATHS

Of the official long-distance footpaths sponsored by the Countryside Commission only five: the Pennine Way, the Cleveland Way, the Pembrokeshire Coast Path, the Offa's Dyke Path and the South Downs Way, are officially open. The other official routes are still in the process of development. Details of the latest progress appear regularly in the R.A.'s quarterly journal, RUCKSACK, which is free to members. The Dales Way, Cotswold Way and the North Buckinghamshire Way are 'unofficial' long-distance paths, i.e. not sponsored by the Countryside Commission.

After listing the main long-distance footpaths and suggesting suitable Ordnance Survey maps for each, there follows a bibliography of useful long-distance footpath publications.

Cleveland Way

This was opened on 24th May, 1969. It stretches 93 miles in a horseshoe-shaped route around the North York Moors National Park from Helmsley to Filey. The following 12-inch O.S. maps are required: 86, 91, 92, and 93.

Cotswold Way

This route, stretching for approximately 100 miles from Chipping Campden to Bath, was originally put forward by the R.A. and since adopted by Gloucestershire County Council. The following 1-inch O.S. maps will be required: 144 and 156.

Basic details of the route may be obtained from Mr A. J. Drake, 2 Beech Lodge, The Park, Cheltenham, GL50 2RX. Price: 7p (please send S.A.E.).

Dales Way

This is a 73-mile route from Ilkley near Leeds through the Yorkshire Dales National Park to Bowness on Windermere in the Lake District. This path has been devised by the West Riding Area of The R.A. and is open for walking through the greater part of its length. The following 1-inch O.S. maps will be required: 89, 90 and 96.

North Buckinghamshire Way

This 30-mile route was developed by the R.A. Southern Area from existing public paths between Chequers Knap (near Princes Risborough in the south) and Wolverton in the north. At the southern end the Way makes a junction with the Ridgeway (see below). The following 1-inch O.S. maps are required: 146 and 159.

North Downs Way

This 141-mile route stretches from Farnham in Surrey to Dover and was approved by the Minister of Housing and Local Government in July 1969, but 36 miles of rights of way are still to be negotiated. The eastern end of the path forks, providing a choice of routes to Dover, one looping northward to pass through Canterbury. Forty-three miles of the Way were officially opened between Hollingbourne, near Maidstone, and Canterbury and Dover on 29th May, 1972, and most of this section is in fact the Canterbury loop. The following 1-inch O.S. maps will be required: 169, 170, 172 and 173.

Offa's Dyke Path

This 168-mile, ancient boundary between England and Wales, stretches from Chepstow to Prestatyn and was opened in July 1971. Some few small sections may still be under negotiation. The following 1-inch O.S. maps will be required: 108, 117, 118, 128, 129, 141, 142 and 155.

Details of completed sections and strip maps etc. may be obtained by writing to the OFFA'S DYKE ASSOCIATION, March House, Wylewm Street, Knighton, Radnorshire. Price: 5p (please send a foolscap S.A.E.).

Pembrokeshire Coast Path

Opened on 16th May, 1970, this 167-mile route stretches from Cardigan, round the coast of Pembrokeshire to Amroth. The following 1-inch O.S. maps will be required: 138, 139/151 and 152.

Pennine Way

This was opened on 24th April, 1965. It stretches 250 miles from Edale in the Peak District to the Cheviots and Kirk Yetholm. The following 1-inch O.S. maps are required: 102, 101, 95, 84, 83, 76, 77, 71 and 70.

Ridgeway

This route stretches from Ivinghoe Beacon, Buckinghamshire, to Avebury, Wiltshire, following the line of the Chiltern escarpment and the Ridgeway along the top of the Berkshire and Wiltshire Downs. This route has now been opened by the Countryside Commission. The following 1-inch O.S. maps are required: 157, 158 and 159.

There are no publications available at present, but a guide will be published shortly by The R.A. and The Chiltern Society.

South Downs Way

This 80-mile bridleway between Eastbourne and the Hampshire border is now virtually complete. It was officially opened on 15th February, 1972. The following 1-inch O.S. maps will be required: 181, 182, 183.

South-West Peninsula Coast Path

This consists of five separate schemes, approved between 1952 and 1963, which will eventually form a continuous route 515 miles long from Dorset to Somerset. Many sections are still under negotiation, but the Cornish

part was formally opened in May 1973. The following 1-inch O.S. maps will be required: 163, 164, 174, 176, 177, 178, 185, 186, 187, 188, 189 and 190.

Wolds Way

This route has been approved in principle by the Countryside Commission and the East Riding County Council. It is a 66-mile path from Filey (linking with Cleveland Way) to North Ferriby and most of the route is open for walkers. The following 1-inch O.S. maps are required: 92, 93, 98 and 99.

LONG DISTANCE FOOTPATHS

THE CLEVELAND WAY, by Bill Cowley/Dalesman Publishing Co. Ltd, Clapham (via Lancaster), Yorkshire. Price: 42½p.

THE CLEVELAND WAY/The Countryside Commission (leaflet). Free.

THE CLEVELAND WAY, by Alan Falconer/H.M.S.O. Price: £1.80.

THE PEMBROKESHIRE COAST PATH, by E. & T. Roberts: *Cemeas to St Davids; Whitesand Bay to Neyland; Pembroke Dock to Amroth*/available from Garm, Llasnychaer, Fishguard, Pembrokeshire. Price: 5p each (plus postage).

CORNISH COASTAL FOOTPATHS/The Tor Mark Press, Trethellon House, St Aubyns Road, Truro, Cornwall. Price unknown.

THE CORNISH COASTAL PATH/The R.A. Available from the Association at 1–4 Crawford Mews, York Street, London W1H 1PT. Price: 10p (including postage).

CORNWALL COAST PATH, by The Cornwall Tourist Board/available from the Board at County Hall, Truro. Price: 25p (including postage).

THE COTSWOLD WAY: A WALKER'S GUIDE, by Mark B. Richards/Thornhill Press, 7 Russell Street, Gloucester. Price: 85p.

ALONG THE SOUTH DOWNS WAY, by Eastbourne Rambling Club/available from 28 Kinfauns Avenue, Eastbourne. Price: 25p (plus postage).

THE DALES WAY, by The R.A. West Riding Area/Dalesman Publishing Co. Ltd, Clapham (via Lancaster), Yorkshire. Price: 42½p (plus postage).

LYKE WAKE WALK, by Bill Cowley/Dalesman Publishing Co. Ltd (as above). Price 37½p.

OFFA'S DYKE PATH/The Countryside Commission (leaflet). Free.

OFFA'S DYKE PATH, ed. by Arthur Roberts/The R.A., 1–4 Crawford Mews, York Street, London W1H 1PT. Price: 10p (plus postage).

OFFA'S DYKE STRIP MAP NO. 1: CHEPSTOW—ST BRIAVELS/available from Mr A. J. Drake, 2 Beech Lodge, The Park, Cheltenham, Gloucestershire GL50 XRX. Price: 7½p (including postage).

THE NORTH BUCKINGHAMSHIRE WAY, by The R.A./available from The Association at 1–4 Crawford Mews, York Street, London W1H 1PT. Price: 10p (including postage).

THE NORTH DOWNS WAY/The Countryside Commission (leaflet). Free.

THE PEMBROKESHIRE COAST PATH/The Countryside Commission (leaflet). Free.

PENNINE WAY COMPANION, by A. Wainwright/The Westmorland Gazette, 22 Stricklandgate, Kendal. Price: 90p.

THE PENNINE WAY/The Countryside Commission (leaflet). Free.

THE PENNINE WAY/The R.A./available from The Association at 1–4 Crawford Mews, York Street, London W1H 1PT. Price: 10p (including postage).

THE PENNINE WAY, by Tom Stephenson/H.M.S.O. Price: £1.50.

THE PENNINE WAY IN NORTHUMBERLAND, by Mr L. Herbert/available from the author at 18 King George Road, Newcastle-upon-Tyne NE3 2QA. Price: 4p.

ST IVES TO FALMOUTH/available from Pendragon House UK Ltd, Penwartha, Perranporth, Cornwall. Price: 25p.

THE SHELL BOOK OF OFFA'S DYKE, by Frank Noble/Queen Anne Press Ltd. Price: 60p.

THE SOUTH DOWNS WAY/The Countryside Commission (leaflet). Free.

THE SOUTH DOWNS WAY/The R.A. Available from The Association at 1–4 Crawford Mews, York Street, London W1H 1PT. Price: 7½p (including postage).

THE SOUTH WEST PENINSULA PATH, by Michael Marriott/Queen Anne Press Ltd. Price: 60p.

WOLDS WAY/The R.A. East Riding Area. Obtainable from D. Rubinstein, Dept of Economics and Social History, The University, Hull HU6 7RX. Price: 5p (including postage).

PRINCIPAL NATURE CENTRES AND RESERVES IN ENGLAND, SCOTLAND AND WALES

1 Borralie (O)
2 Invernaver (O)
3 Strathy Bog (O)
4 Handa Island (B)
5 Inchnadamph (O)
6 Inverpoly (O, B)
7 Letherewe Woods (O)
8 Beinn Eighe (O)
9 Culbin (F)
10 Rassal Askwood (F)
11 Loch Druidibeg (B)
12 Rhum (O)
13 Craigellachie (F)
14 Arriundle (O)
15 Rannoch Moor (O)
16 Glenfeshie (O)
17 Sands of Forvie (O)
18 Kerloch Moor (B)
19 Caenlochan & Corrie Fen (O)
20 Ben Lawers (O)
21 Morton Lochs (B)
22 St. Cyrus (O)
23 Crarae (F)
24 Loch Lomond (F)
25 Gleann Diomhan (O)
26 Lady Isle (EB)
27 Ailsa Craig (O)
28 Tynron Juniper Wood (F)
29 Lochmaben (B)
30 Holy Island (EB)
31 Farne Islands (EF)
32 Caerlaverock (B)
33 Coom Rigg (O)
34 Moor House (O)
35 Castle Eden Denes (EF)
36 Upper Teesdale (O)
37 Ravenglass Dunes (B)
38 Calf of Man (B)
39 North Fen (O)
40 Russland Moss (OF)
41 Naddle Low Forest (F)
42 Neaming Wood (F)
43 Ling Gill (OF)
44 Meathop & Catrag Mosses (O)
45 Farndale (O)
46 Foulney Islands (B)
47 Askham Bogs (O)
48 Southpoty Sanctuary (B)
49 Ainsdale Sands (O)
50 Fairburn (B)

51 Humber Wildfowl Refuge (O)
52 Spurn Bird Observatory (OB)
53 Scotton Common (FO)
54 Saltfleet (B)
55 Lynwode Warren (B)
56 Rostherne Mere (O)
57 Cotterhill Clough (F)
58 Newborough Warren (O)
59 Coed Gorswen (O)
60 Cym Glas Crafnant (OF)
61 Coed Tremadoc (OF)
62 Coed Cymerau (OF)
63 Coed Camlyn (OF)
64 Rhinog (OF)
65 Bardsey Bird Observatory (B)
66 Cader Idris (O)
67 Wybunbury Moss (O)
68 Dove Dale Ash Woods (F)
69 Sherwood Forest (F)
70 Chartley Moss (O)
71 Gibraltar Point (O)
72 Blakeney Point (O)
73 Salthouse Broads (B)
74 Scotthead (B)
75 Horsey Mere (OB)
76 Hickling Dune Broad (OB)
77 Winterden Dunes (E)
78 Peakirk (E)
79 Borough Fen (E)
80 Caster Hanglens (F)
81 Holme Fen Wood (OF)
82 Walton Fen (E)
83 Monks Fen (OF)
84 Wicken (O)
85 Chippenham Fen (O)
86 Mickfield Meadow (OE)
87 Coed Raeidol (OF)
88 Cors Tregaron (O)
89 Nant Irfon (O)
90 Allt Ryd-y-Groes (OF)
91 Craig Cerrig Gleisiad (O)
92 Grassholm Island (B)
93 Skomer Island (B)
94 Skokholm Observatory (B)
95 Gower Coast (B)
96 Lundy (B)
97 Penmoeldlit (F)
98 Cym Clydach (OF)
99 Badgeworth (O)

100 Slimbridge Bird Observatory (OB)
101 Blackcliff (F)
102 Westonbirt (F)
103 Steep Holme (B)
104 Fyfield (F)
105 Walker's Hill (O)
106 Knap Hill (O)
107 Rodney Stoke (F)
108 Sharpham Moor (OF)
109 Wistmans Wood (F)
110 Black Tor Copse (F)
111 Yarner Wood (F)
112 Exe Estuary (OB)
113 Abbotsbury (B)
114 Portland Bird Observatory (OB)
115 Bramshaw (F)
116 Mark Ash (F)
117 Morden Bog (EF)
118 Arne (F)
119 Hartland Moor (O)
120 Blackmoor Copse (E)
121 Matley & Denny (OF)
122 Tring Reservoirs (O)
123 Knocking Hoe (O)
124 Epping Forest (F)
125 Ruislip (OB)
126 High Standing Hill (F)
127 Box Hill (O)
128 Alice Holt (F)
129 Old Winchester Hill (F)
130 Kingley Vale (F)
131 Bedgebury Pinetum (F)
132 Lullington Heath (O)
133 High Halstow (B)
134 Bradwell Bird Observatory (OB)
135 Wesleton Heath (OB)
136 Minsmore Level (B)
137 North Warren (B)
138 Orford Ness (O)
139 Blean Woods (F)
140 Stodmarsh (OB)
141 Wye & Crundale (O)
142 Hamstreet Woods (F)
143 Hales Wood (F)

O = Ornithological
F = Forest (Silviculture)
B = Botanical
E = Entomological

THE WOLDS WAY, by David Rubinstein/Dalesman Publishing Co. Ltd, Clapham (via Lancaster), Yorkshire. Price: 45p.

MAPS FOR WALKERS

Bartholomew's Maps
A complete catalogue of maps published by Bartholomew may be obtained by writing to JOHN BARTHOLOMEW & SON LTD, Duncan Street, Edinburgh EH9 1TA.

Although this company publishes a Lake District 1-inch Map, Bartholomew's most popular series is on the ½ inch to the mile scale. This is too small a scale for serious walking or hill-climbing but is most useful for route-planning and for cycling. Sixty-two sheets cover England, Scotland and Wales.

Ordnance Survey Maps
For most outdoor activities, Ordnance Survey maps on the scales of 1 inch and 2½ inches to the mile are the most suitable. Details of other scales may be obtained from Ordnance Survey (see below).

These maps may be obtained from any Ordnance Survey agent or from most booksellers or stationers. A list of retail agents in *England* and *Wales* may be obtained by writing to Ordnance Survey, Romsey Road, Maybush, Southampton SO9 4DH and for *Scotland* by writing to the Scottish wholesale distributors, Thomas Nelson & Sons Ltd, 18 Dalkeith Road, Edinburgh EH16 5BS.

Enquiries about maps of *Northern Ireland* should be addressed to the Chief Survey Officer, Ministry of Finance, Ordnance Survey, Ladas Drive, Belfast BT7 9FJ. Enquiries about maps of the *Irish Republic* should be addressed to the Assistant Director of Ordnance Survey, Phoenix Park, Dublin.

1 INCH MAPS (1:63,360)
The 1 inch series covers the whole of Great Britain in 189 sheets and is the most popular scale for walking, rambling and mountaineering. Each sheet covers an area of approximately

N.B. *For a note on map-lending facilities see p. 119.*

700 square miles. The sheets in this series are being constantly revised and about 12 revised sheets are published each year. The most important revisions are those concerning rights of way. The whole series (excluding Scotland) will eventually be revised to show rights of way with special red symbols. The unrevised sheets carry symbols showing footpaths and tracks, stating that such representation is no evidence of the existence of a right of way. At present all but 4 of the English and Welsh sheets show rights of way for at least some of the area covered. Details of the newly revised sheets appear regularly in RUCKSACK, the quarterly journal of the Ramblers' Association.

A map of the 1 inch sheet lines for the whole of Britain and for the areas of England and Wales for which the revised sheets are available is shown on p. 130.

Please note that on some sheets only part of the total area has been revised. This is because some county councils have not produced a definitive map for those areas. The cost of 1 inch maps is 44p folded or 38p flat.

1 INCH TOURIST MAPS
These cover specific tourist areas and are based on the 1 inch series described above. The following sheets are available:

GREATER	CAMBRIDGE	BEN NEVIS &
LONDON	NORTH YORKS	GLENCOE
THE NEW	MOORS	CAIRNGORMS
FOREST	PEAK DISTRICT	LOCH LOMOND
DARTMOOR		& THE
EXMOOR		TROSSACHS

In addition a 1-inch Tourist Map of the Snowdonia National Park is available.

The cost of Tourist Maps is 55p folded or 44p flat.

2½ INCH MAPS (1:25,000)
These maps are especially suitable for field studies, orienteering and other activities where greater detail is required. Many people prefer them for walking as they show field boundaries.

The First Series, in some 2,000 sheets, covers the whole of England, Wales and Scotland excluding the highlands and Islands. Some 70 sheets of the new Second Series are at present available: most of these cover *twice*

the area of the First Series (20 kilometres east to west by 10 kilometres north to south as opposed to 10 kilometres square) and are therefore extremely good value. Rights of way are shown on the Second Series if the information was available when the revision was prepared. An index for both series is available on request from Ordnance Survey or its Scottish wholesaler.

OTHER O.S. SCALES
Details of series at scales of 1:1,250, 1:2,500, 1:10,000, 1:10,560, 1:21,120, 1:100,000 and 1:625,000 may be obtained from Ordnance Survey or its Scottish wholesaler.

West Col Mountain Maps
West Col Productions is introducing a new series of large-scale mountain maps. The first in the series, specially designed for climbers and ramblers, covers Snowdonia in two sheets on the scale of 1:25,000 (approximately 2½ inches to one mile).

Other maps in this series are in preparation. *We do not advise use of these maps except in conjunction with O.S. sheets.*

Further details may be obtained from West Col Productions, 1 Meadow Close, Goring, Reading, Berkshire RG8 0AP.

Map Reading
EASY STEPS TO MAP READING, by G. H. Howard/J. M. Dent & Sons Ltd. Price: 25p.

ELEMENTARY MAP READING, by Thomas Pickles/J. M. Dent & Sons Ltd. Price: 35p.

INTERMEDIATE MAP READING, by Thomas Pickles/J. M. Dent & Sons Ltd. Price: 35p.

MAP READING (Know the Game Series)/Educational Productions Ltd. Price: 20p.

MAP READING, by Thomas Pickles/J. M. Dent & Sons Ltd. Price: 42p.

MAP READING AND INTERPRETATION, by P. Speak and A. H. C. Carter/Longman Group Ltd. Price: 80p.

MAP READING FOR THE COUNTRYGOER, by S. F. Marriott/The R.A. Price: 15p (including postage).

MAPS FOR WALKERS: Fact Sheet No. 3/The R.A. Free.

ORIENTEERING (Know the Game Series)/Educational Productions Ltd. Price: 25p.

National Park Guides

BRECON BEACONS NATIONAL PARK GUIDE/
HMSO. Price: 50p.
DARTMOOR NATIONAL PARK GUIDE/HMSO.
Price: 45p.
EXMOOR NATIONAL PARK GUIDE/HMSO. Price:
$32\frac{1}{2}$p.
LAKE DISTRICT NATIONAL PARK GUIDE/HMSO.
Price: $42\frac{1}{2}$p.
NORTHUMBERLAND NATIONAL PARK GUIDE/
HMSO. Price: $37\frac{1}{2}$p.
NORTH YORK MOORS NATIONAL PARK GUIDE/
HMSO. Price: 45p.
PEAK DISTRICT NATIONAL PARK GUIDE/HMSO.
Price: 45p.
PEMBROKESHIRE COAST NATIONAL PARK GUIDE/
HMSO. Price: 75p.
SNOWDONIA NATIONAL PARK GUIDE/HMSO.
Price: $32\frac{1}{2}$p.
YORKSHIRE DALES NATIONAL PARK GUIDE/
HMSO. Price: 45p.

GENERAL

The following series contain information on
the general background of the footpath systems,
but few contain great detail:
BATSFORD BRITAIN SERIES/B. T. Batsford Ltd.
COUNTY, PORTRAIT AND REGIONAL SERIES/Robert
Hale & Co.
NEW NATURALIST SERIES/Fontana Books.
THE TRAVELLERS' GUIDE SERIES/Darton, Long-
man & Todd Ltd.
    This series covers Suffolk and Essex,
Derbyshire and the Peak District, and the
Highlands of Scotland.
THE BACKPACKER'S HANDBOOK, by Derrick
Booth/Robert Hale & Co. Price: £2.00.
CAMPING LIST/available from The National
Trust, 42 Queen Anne's Gate, London SW1.
Free (send foolscap S.A.E.).
THE CAMP AND TREK BOOK, by Jack Cox/
Lutterworth Press. Price: 80p.
CAVES IN WALES AND THE MARCHES, by D. W.
Jenkins and Mason Williams/Dalesman Pub-
lishing Co. Ltd, Clapham (via Lancaster),
Yorkshire. Price: $52\frac{1}{2}$p.
THE CAVES OF DERBYSHIRE, by Dr Trevor D.
Ford/Dalesman Publishing Co. Ltd (as above).
Price: $52\frac{1}{2}$p (plus postage).

CAVING, by James Lovelock/B. T. Batsford
Ltd. Price: £1.25.
CLIMBING, by James Lovelock/B. T. Batsford
Ltd. Price: £1.70.
THE COUNTRY CODE/The Countryside Com-
mission. Free (send stamped, addressed label).
LAKELAND GEOLOGY, by E. H. Shackleton/
Dalesman Publishing Co. Ltd, Clapham (via
Lancaster), Yorkshire. Price: 75p (plus post-
age).
THE MOUNTAIN CODE/Central Council of Physi-
cal Recreation, 26 Park Crescent, London
W1N 4EE. Free (but send postage).
MOUNTAIN RESCUE HANDBOOK/available from
H. K. Hartley, 9 Milldale Avenue, Temple
Meads, Buxton, Derbyshire.
MOUNTAIN RESCUE, R.A.F./HMSO. Price: $62\frac{1}{2}$p.
MOUNTAINEERING, by Allan Blackshaw/Pen-
guin Books Ltd. Price: £1.00.
MOUNTAINS OF BRITAIN, by Edward C. Pyatt/
B. T. Batsford Ltd. Price: £1.25.
NATURE TRAILS IN BRITAIN/British Tourist
Authority, 64 St James's Street, London
SW1A 1NF. Price: 15p (including postage).
NATURE WALKS ON NATIONAL TRUST LAND/
available from The National Trust, 42 Queen
Anne's Gate, London SW1. Free (send foolscap
S.A.E).
PENNINE UNDERGROUND, by Norman Thornber/
Dalesman Publishing Co. Ltd, Clapham (via
Lancaster), Yorkshire. Price: $62\frac{1}{2}$p.
RAMBLING AND YOUTH HOSTELLING ('Know the
Game' Series)/Educational Productions Ltd,
17 Denbigh Street, London SW1. Price: 20p.
SAFETY ON MOUNTAINS/Central Council of
Physical Recreation, 26 Park Crescent, London
W1N 4EE. Price: 15p.
WILDERNESS CAMPING IN BRITAIN, by Eric
Hemery/Robert Hale & Co. Price: £1.75.

Snow in corries and hollows drifting :
Lives move slowly and feet are shifting.
Measuring the riffs for another to sing,
Clothe with loving the promise of another
spring.

BRIDGET ST JOHN

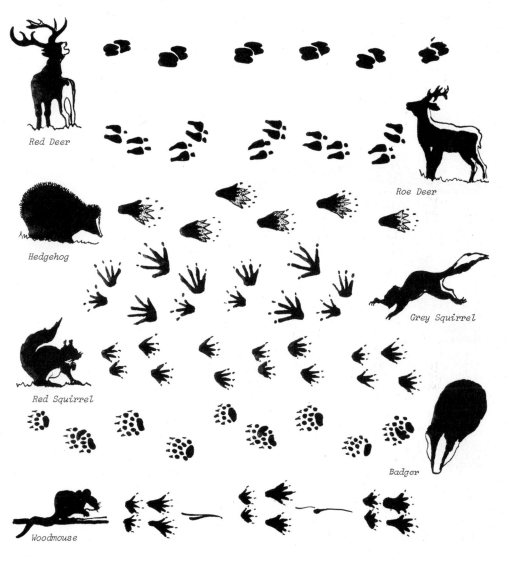

ANIMAL TRACKING

WHEN winter comes it is often thought that all the animals are fast asleep for all those cold snowy months, when in actual fact it isn't true at all. If any of you have walked over white fields and meadows after snow has fallen overnight, you may have seen the tracks of animals, criss-crossing in wild patterns on the snow. Now, with a bit of practice, you can begin to recognise the various animal tracks; of the little dormouse, the squirrel, the badger, the fox and many others, as well as innumerable bird tracks. The drawings shown are just a handful of the most common tracks you are likely to come across.

It is a worthwhile venture to immortalize these tracks by making Plaster of Paris casts which can then be brought home and painted. They will form an interesting addition to your other collections of natural bric-a-brac.

135

Stoat

Fox

Otter

Rabbit

Common Hare

Shrew

Mole

Rat

Equipment

The basic equipment needed is as follows:
1. A bottle of clean water.
2. A packet of Plaster of Paris (the quick-drying sort).
3. A bowl and mixing spoon.
4. A quantity of paper clips.
5. Some strips of thin, flexible card about 10 inches by 2 inches.
6. A pair of tweezers.
7. A clean rag.

METHOD

Having found a set of tracks, select the best impression i.e. one that has the clearest print with no caving in of snow. Remove any bits of twig or dirt should there be any, using the tweezers for this. Take one of the cardboard strips and roll it round bringing the two ends together, thus making a cardboard circle, and secure together with a paper clip. The actual size of the cardboard ring must be adjusted to the size of the track for it must completely enclose the impression within its circumference. Press the ring into the snow so that it forms a wall completely encircling the track. Next, mix up a fair amount of Plaster of Paris making it reasonably runny but not ridiculously so. Carefully pour the mixture into the ring in a steady flow. Never pour directly into the deepest part of the track as this causes air bubbles in the cast. After reaching the top of the ring with plaster, give it a few taps to ensure a clean removal. When set, remove the cast, clean it as much as possible with the rag and then wrap up well in some newspaper so that it is safe from breakage. Once home, the casts can be decorated realistically with colours true to the species of animal which made the tracks, or they can be daubed with brightly coloured paints and lacquers and given a coat of varnish as a nice finishing touch.

BIBLIOGRAPHY

BRITISH ANIMAL TRACKS, by J. S. R. Chard/C. Arthur Pearson Ltd.
ANIMAL TRACKS AND SIGNS, by Bang and Dahlstrom/Collins Sons & Co. Ltd.

137

The Trees of Life

White birch, give me thy peace,
So quiet thou art.
Give me thy strength, dark pine,
Thy fearless heart.
Give me thy sensitiveness,
And oak, I pray,
Thy wise endurance give—
So shall I be
More lovely in my life,
More like a tree.

TERESA HOOLEY

OF ALL the ecological and environmental acts of goodwill a citizen can do for his country, planting trees must be on top of the list. Our lives, if we stop to consider it, depend on the existence of trees for without forests, and woods and copses and spinneys and plantations and even single trees we would all die. Trees are essential because:

(a) They produce oxygen and help purify the air.
(b) They provide shelter for wild life, as well as food.
(c) They provide shade from the sun and help reduce noise.
(d) They retain moisture in the soil and keep the water table high.
(e) They are things of immense beauty inspiring contemplation and wonder in all passers-by.
(f) They are of immeasurable benefit to the appearance of city, town, village and individual houses and can be used as a barrier to mask ugly buildings etc.

Trees can be grown from seed or bought as saplings from a reliable nursery. Obviously, it is far easier to plant saplings as these will have a better chance of survival and will be of a more mature shape. On the other hand, growing trees from seed is immensely cheap and good fun and there is nothing more satisfying than planting a forest tree sapling that was grown and tended from a tiny seed.

What trees to grow—a suitable list:
Abbreviations used:
L. Need for light to produce satisfactory growth.
M.S.T. Moderate shade tolerated.
S.T. Shade tolerant
Ht. Maximum height in feet.
Sp. Maximum spread in feet.

The botanical name is followed by the common name and some features to aid choice.

Large growing forest trees
Acer platanoides: NORWAY MAPLE: L. smoke resistant, suitable for specimen or avenue.
A. p. schwedlerii: L. fast growing, rich leaf colour.
A. p. Drummondii: PURPLE NORWAY MAPLE: L. fairly fast growing, good for town use, Ht. 60 Sp. 40.
A. pseudoplatanus: SYCAMORE: L. hardy, Ht. 80 Sp. 50.

A pseudoplatanus purpureum: PURPLE SYCAMORE: L. purple leaves in summer, good autumn colour.
Aesculus hippocastanum: HORSE CHESTNUT: L. large head, 'candle flowers', var flore-pleno does not produce conkers. Ht. 90 Sp. 60.
A. carnea: RED HORSE CHESTNUT: L. smaller, Ht. 30.
Carpinus betulus: HORNBEAM: M.S.T. tolerant of soil conditions, may be used in place of Beech as a hedge in heavy soil. Resembles Beech, Ht. 60 Sp. 50.
C. betulus fastigiata: HORNBEAM: M.S.T. as above but more suitable in narrow sites where headroom is limited.
Fagus sylvatica: BEECH: S.T. dense foliage, excellent as specimen, shelter tree or hedge Ht. 80–100 Sp. 70.
F. Sylvatica purpurea: PURPLE BEECH: S.T. as above, good contrast to green foliage.
Fraxinus excelsior: ASH: L. heavy to medium soil, elegant, graceful, Ht. 90 Sp. 70.
Liriodendron tulipifera: TULIP TREE: L. greenish white, scented flowers in July.
Platanus acerifolia: LONDON PLANE: M.S.T. tolerant of atmospheric pollution.
Populus robusta: POPLAR: L. fast growing, slender, compact make good screens, roots may need to be controlled as they travel 30 or 40

feet and can invade drains.

P. tremula : ASPEN : L. used in gardens for the blind for scent and leaf movement, Ht. 40.

Quercus cerris : TURKEY OAK : L. dark foliage, faster growing than Common Oak, Ht. 100 Sp. 70.

Q. rubra : RED OAK : L. foliage turns dull red in autumn.

Q. coccinea splendens : L. not so vigorous as above, keeps bright purple-red leaves till December.

Tilia euchlora : LIME : L. withstands pollution, graceful, pendulous Ht. 40 Sp. 30, good street tree.

T. petiolaris : SILVER LIME : L. Ht. 60, Sp. 50.

T. platyphyllos rubra : RED TWIGGED LIME : Ht. 100.

Ulmus glabra : WYCH ELM : L. dense, Ht. 100 Sp. 50.

U. stricta var Wheatleyi : CORNISH ELM : L. erect, columnar. Ht. 100 Sp. 30.

Medium sized trees

Reaching an approximate height of 40 feet to 50 feet on maturity.

Alnus glutinosa : COMMON ALDER : Shallow roots, likes moisture, catkins in March.

Betula alba : SILVER BIRCH : L. good specimen tree, wind resistant, graceful, ornamental bark. Sparse foliage allows light to filter through.

B. pendula Youngii : WEEPING SILVER BIRCH : L. as above. Ht. 25–30 suitable for small garden.

Fraxinus excelsior diversifolia : SINGLE LEAVED ASH : L. withstands atmospheric pollution.

F. ornus : MANNA ASH : Panicles of white flowers in May.

Prunus avium : GEAN : L. white flowers in April–May, autumn tints, flore plena has double flowers.

P. padus : BIRD CHERRY : L. small, sprays of slightly scented flowers.

P. yodeoensis : YOSHINO CHERRY : L. single, white, early flowering.

Salix alba : CRICKET BAT WILLOW : L. pyramidal tree with white silvery foliage, quick growing, tolerates wind, dislikes dry shallow soil, makes good shelter.

S. vitellina : GOLDEN WILLOW : L. striking golden bark, less vigorous than most willows.

S. chrysocoma : WEEPING WILLOW : L. Hardy with graceful weeping habit.

S. daphnoides acutifolia : Fast growing, red stems, early catkins.

Small trees

Approximate height on maturity rarely exceeds 30 feet.

Cotoneaster cornubia : L. good for town conditions, abundance of red berries in autumn.

C. frigidus : Semi-evergreen, as above, fast growing.

Crataegus oxycantha : HAWTHORN : L. hardy, wind resistant.

Other varieties include: *C. oxy rosea-plena*, double pink flowers; *C. oxy plena*, double white flowers; *C. coccinea pleana*, red form.

Cercidiphyllum japonicum : Good autumn colour, liable to damage from spring frost.

Gleditchia triacanthus : Resistant to air pollution.

Ilex aquifolium : HOLLY : M.S.T. compact evergreen, many varieties.

Laburnum alpinum : SCOTCH LABURNUM : Hardy, graceful, pendulous flower heads, seeds poisonous.

L. Vosii : As above with semi-sterile seed pods and large flower heads.

Malus eleyi : FLOWERING CRAB : L. good foliage, decorative fruits in autumn.

M. floribunda : JAPANESE CRAB : L. a profusion of pale pink flowers and crimson buds.

Morus nigra : BLACK MULBERRY : Capable of great antiquity, suitable near historic buildings.

Prunus amanogawa : JAPANESE FLOWERING CHERRY : L. upright habit of growth, pink semi-double flowers.

P. amygdalis : ALMOND : L. pink flowers on bare stems in March.

P. avium flore-pleno : DOUBLE FLOWERING CHERRY : L. taller.

P. serrulata : JAPANESE CHERRY.

P. subhirtella autumnalis rosea : Winter flowers, autumn colour.

Pyrus atropurporea : FLOWERING PEAR : L. ornamental, purple foliage.

P. tremula : ASPEN : L. used in gardens for the blind for scent and leaf movement, Ht. 40.

Quercus cerris : TURKEY OAK : L. dark foliage, faster growing than Common Oak, Ht. 100 Sp. 70.

Q. rubra : RED OAK : L. foliage turns dull red in autumn.

Q. coccinea splendens : L. not so vigorous as above, keeps bright purple-red leaves till December.

Tilia euchlora : LIME : L. withstands pollution, graceful, pendulous, Ht. 40 Sp. 30, good street tree.

T. petiolaris : SILVER LIME : L. Ht. 60 Sp. 50, S5.

T. platyphyllos rubra : RED TWIGGED LIME : Ht. 100.

Ulmus glabra : WYCH ELM : L. dense, Ht. 100 Sp. 50.

U. stricta var Wheatleyi : CORNISH ELM : L. erect, columnar. Ht. 100 Sp. 30.

Trees from Seed

Many species of trees can be grown from seed that has either been collected in the autumn, or from a reliable seedsman. Horse Chestnut, Oak, Sweet Chestnut, Elder, Yew, Beech, Hawthorn, Plane, Sycamore and Maple are just some of the trees where the seed is of sufficient size to make collecting easy. Only full ripe seed should be collected—avoid green, under-ripe or damaged seeds.

The seeds of Horse Chestnut, Sweet Chestnut and Oak should be planted in a rich loamy peat soil as soon as they have been collected in the autumn as this helps break down the hard shells and makes germination easy. The soil should be kept slightly moist during the winter months but do not over-water as this may rot the seeds.

Other seeds can be stored in a dry, cool place and planted in the early spring in a good seed compost. Germination will be quicker if the seeds are kept indoors after planting, or under glass. As soon as the seedlings have pushed through the soil, and are a suitable size for transplanting, they should be split into separate pots and put outside to harden off. With large seeds, such as acorns and conkers, as soon as the seed has emerged from the soil, they should be put into separate 10-inch pots in a good loam or potting compost and put outside to harden off.

At the end of the first year, it is advisable to plant the young trees out into a prepared piece of ground at a distance of 2 feet apart. They should be allowed to mature there for 3–4 years, when they will then be a reasonable size to transplant to their permanent position. It may be necessary to dig up the trees each year during the first 4 years in the prepared ground to trim their roots, otherwise an extensive root system may prove difficult when digging them up for transplanting to their final position.

Ordering Trees

There are two grades of trees available, each suited to a particular purpose. In the first case, trees in bulk for plantations are ordered as 'transplants' and the size will range from 6 inches to anything up to 21 inches. The following table shows the method of describing such trees:

1 + 0 = *one-year-old seedling*
2 + 0 = *a two-year-old seedling*
1 + 1 = *a one-year-old seedling, transplanted and grown on for one year in a nursery.*

Individual trees are sold at a larger size and are older than the trees sold in bulk as described above. They come in three sizes: 'Bush trees', 'Standard' and 'Feathered' trees. Bush trees are the smallest having a stem ranging from 12 inches to 30 inches. Feathered trees consist of a straight stem with plenty of side or lateral shoots. Standards have no side shoots and come in 4 sizes:

Half standard = 3 feet 6 inches to 4 feet 6 inches.
Three-quarter standard = 4 feet 9 inches to 5 feet 3 inches.
Standard = 5 feet 6 inches to 6 feet.
Tall standard = 6 feet to 7 feet.

Conifers are not bound by any of the above grades but are ordered simply in height.

Soils and Preparation

Most trees grow for decades so it is worthwhile to make sure they have good soil suited to their needs and are planted correctly. It is very important to maintain the soil in good condition during the early years of growth otherwise drainage and air movement can be hindered.

There are four different types of soil:

CLAY SOILS
These soils are generally difficult to cultivate and poorly drained. To improve drainage, sharp sand or peat can be added which has the effect of opening up the soil, allowing the

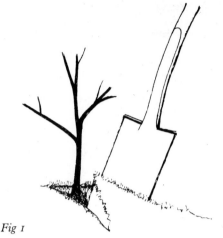

Fig 1

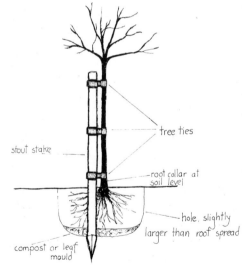

stout stake

tree ties

root collar at soil level

hole, slightly larger than root spread

compost or leaf mould

Fig 2

movement of water and air necessary for roots to breathe.

PEAT SOILS
These soils contain up to as much as 60% organic humus matter. Drainage can be improved by digging in sharp sand or gravel.

SANDY SOILS
These soils have easy drainage so that in drought conditions, the surface can become hard and baked. By digging in peat and manure, the water retention value can be increased and the soil improved.

LOAM SOILS
The best sort of soils as they contain a general mixture of humus, silt clay and sand, and drainage, as well as water retention, is good.

Time of Planting

Trees must be planted in the Autumn or Spring, when they are dormant and leafless. Never plant in bad climatic conditions, i.e. hard frost, snow, rain. Conifers are best planted in the Spring and the roots must not be disturbed too much when doing so.

Handling

Until such times as the tree will be planted, the roots must be protected. The roots can be 'dug in' to soft moist soil and left there until planting time. Keep the soil moist at all times.

Planting

There are two methods of planting trees; one method for young seedling called 'notch' planting, and the other method for larger trees called 'pit' planting.

Notch Planting

Make two cuts in the soil with a spade at right angles and lift the triangular piece of turf, inserting the roots of the seedling into gap. Next, press the turf back into its original position, making sure that the root collar of the seedling is at ground level *(fig 1)*.

Pit Planting (a) THE HOLE

The hole must be dug deeper and larger than the root spread and can be either square or

circular in shape. The soil at the bottom of the hole must be loosened with a fork to a depth of 6 inches. A little bone meal or compost can be worked in the bottom if wished.

(b) STAKING

As a general rule, a stout stake must be driven in to support the tree against strong winds etc. The stake should be driven in to the windward of the tree and to one side of the hole about 3 inches from the centre. It must be high enough when firmly hammered in, to reach above the level of the tree's lowest branches.

(c) PLANTING (fig 2)

It is very important to remember that all broken or damaged roots must be clearly cut away before planting. The tree should then be placed in the hole with the stem placed as near to the stake as possible. Fine top soil must then be sprinkled amongst the roots until covered and then the rest of the hole filled up with the soil that was taken out of it. Gently tread down the soil as it is shovelled in and when the hole has been completely filled, firmly trample down right up to the stem. Be careful to plant up to the earth mark at the bottom of the stem and do not plant lower than this mark.

(d) TYING

It is best to tie the tree to the stake in three places for large trees and at least two places for smaller trees. The correct places to tie are: (i) near the ground, (ii) in the middle of the trunk, (iii) in the crown or amongst the lower branches. Special tree ties can be bought in gardening shops which are nailed to the stake and are unbuckled gradually over a period of time to allow for the increase in the tree's girth.

Aftercare

Keep a circle of bare soil about 2 feet in diameter around the tree during its early years of growth. This will prevent other root systems of grass or weeds competing for soil sustenance. The ground for 6 feet round any tree must be kept free of any ashes, cement, asphalt etc. Keep the roots moist at all times during the year and in times of dry weather, give two or three gallons of water to each tree every day. It is a good idea to protect the bark by placing

round the tree and stake a tree guard, which can be constructed of a piece of chicken wire curled round. This will prevent cats and other animals ripping the stem.

Any damaged branch or twig must be clearly removed with a knife and pruning will be necessary during the first few years after planting. The leading shoot upwards must be left untouched but any side branch should be reduced by half, pruned to an outward facing bud. A tree should be made to develop as symmetrically as possible so that a well-balanced form will develop as it grows older. Study the forms of mature trees and try to encourage young trees to grow in the same way.

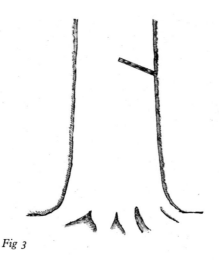

Fig 3

Laws Concerning Trees

Many fine trees are now protected by a Tree Preservation Order (see below) which means that no one whatsoever, even the owner, may cut it down or cut off any of its branches. If the tree dies, the owner must immediately replace it with one of the same species. Your local authority will have a list of preserved trees in your district, so check them out and keep a watchful eye for vandals who may attempt to fell or damage a listed tree.

Tree Preservation Orders

A Tree Preservation Order is made under the provisions of Section 29 of the Town and Country Planning Act, 1962. A Tree Preservation Order, therefore, becomes a registerable charge against a property with penalties for contravention as set out in Section 62(1) of the principle Act, as amended by Section 15 of the Civic Amenities Act 1967. These Sections of the Acts are framed to prevent the needless destruction or maltreatment of trees and are neither intended nor used to interfere with the requirements of good arboriculture or forestry. Properly administered, an Order can strengthen the hand of the discerning owner of trees, but the existence of a T.P.O. does not in any way exonerate the owner of a preserved tree from his responsibilities as established in Common Law.

All records of listed trees, protected with a T.P.O. can be found in your local Land Charges Office. The vigilance of the public is continually needed to get T.P.O.s put on fine trees. In this way, trees can be protected from developers and ignorant people who have no regard for them. Tree Preservation Orders are promoted by Local Planning Authorities and any enquiries or information should be dealt with by them only.

Apart from single trees, parklands, woodlands and whole landscapes in prominent positions in rural areas can be included in a T.P.O.

TAPPING TREES[1]

The sap of certain trees can be tapped and used as a nourishing addition to any diet. Delicious syrups can be obtained by boiling down the sap, and unique-tasting wines easily made by the natural fermentation of the sap, without sugar.

What Trees to Tap

The following list contains trees that have been successfully tapped. Only mature trees must be tapped otherwise severe damage will occur if young trees are used. There may be any number of different types of trees that could be tapped, but as to the quality of the sap, or whether the sap is safe to consume is another

[1] *We are indebted to John Allen of 35 Fairfield Avenue, Bollington, Macclesfield, for sending notes and information on this subject.*

matter. We suggest extreme caution when experimenting on new species, and to avoid those trees completely that have poisonous parts in their make-up, e.g. Yew and Laburnam.

SILVER BIRCH *(Betula Verrucosa)*
Birch trees were not only tapped in this country, but also in many parts of the Continent. The following extract is taken from *Natural History Rambles*, by M. C. Cooke, published in 1879. 'The sugary sap of the Birch as it rises in March is collected in some northern counties of Europe and converted into wine. Loudon states that a birch has been known to yield in the course of one season, a quantity of sap equal to its own weight. During the seige of Hamburg by the Russians in 1814 almost all the birch trees in the neighbourhood were destroyed by the Boshkirs and other barbarian soldiers in the Russian service by being tapped for their sap.'

LIME *(Tilia europaea)*
Produces a wonderful tasting syrup from its sap of great nourishing value.

SYCAMORE *(Acer pseudoplatanus)*
Again, quoting from *Natural History Rambles*, M. C. Cooke says, 'The sap of this tree contains sugar, and experiments have been made from time to time to obtain a kind of sugar from evaporation. Sometimes an ounce of sugar can be refined from a quart of sap, but the proportion varies. This sap has also been converted into a kind of wine.'

MAPLE *(Acer saccharum)*
A tree widely tapped commercially for its sap which is converted to maple syrup, of pancake fame.

How to Tap
All one needs for this is a beaker or some other container to collect the sap, some plasticine, a small hand-drill, with a drill bit of $\frac{3}{8}$ inch in diameter and a glass tube 6 inches long, the same diameter as the drill bit. Tapping can only be done between March and August when the sap is rising continually in the tree.

First, drill a hole with the drill about $1\frac{1}{2}$ to 2 inches deep into the tree trunk at chest height or below and at a 45° angle *(fig 3)*. Insert the tube into the hole and plug the point of entry into the trunk with plasticine which will prevent any sap leaking. The sap will immediately begin to trickle down the tube and there may be bits of wood chips at first from the drilling. If this happens, clean out the tube by blowing and re-insert in the hole. It is extremely important not to overlap any one tree so that once a pint or quart of sap has been collected, the tube should be removed and the hole firmly plugged with plasticine (this is very important). It is far better to take a little from a number of trees than to bleed one to death.

Making the Syrup
If the sap is left for too long after collection it will start to ferment because of its high sugar content and so it is advisable to turn it into syrup immediately on getting home. To make the syrup, simply boil the sap in a saucepan until the water has mostly evaporated, pour the residue into jam jars, and store until needed. The syrup is a delicious substitute for honey and can be spread on bread, pancakes or used in cooking.

Making the Wine
Because the sap has a high sugar content, it is not necessary to add more. The sap should be placed in a fermenting jar or a glass or earthenware jug with a little yeast (see p. 183, the wine-making chapter), and allowed to stand for 3 weeks. The liquid should then be strained through muslin, poured into wine bottles and left uncorked for a month. Finally, cork the bottles and keep at least six months before opening for use.

MAKING A TREE SURVEY[2]

A TREE SURVEY PROVIDES a record of the number, name and quality of the trees in a particular locality at a given time.

It's easy to see that such a survey can be enjoyable for its own sake and that the know-

[2] *Taken, with kind permission from the Council for the Protection of Rural England's leaflet 'Making a Tree Survey'.*

ledge of the locality gleaned from it can be fascinating. But how is it *useful*?

In the first place, the pressures on the countryside—housing and industrial developments, roads—mean that valuable assets are sometimes lost through lack of foresight. If local authorities don't know where the assets are—be they trees, hedgerows, historic sites, or whatever—they can't protect them. This isn't to say that recording the presence of a single oak will automatically preserve it in perpetuity—but the fact of a record will at least ensure that it is *considered*, when developments are mooted.

The other important justification for a tree survey is the state of the law. Over the past ten years, various legal provisions have made it clear that trees are now to be regarded as positive amenities. Devices such as the Tree Preservation Order, and government grants to aid local authorities in tree-planting schemes, record a welcome concern on the part of the government that England should stay green. *But the laws can only be made to work if information about the location and the state of trees is available.*

Much of such a recording must be a labour of love.

PLANNING THE SURVEY

1 Reasons for Survey
(a) To keep a check on the changing scenery of the locality.
(b) To make a record for historical purposes.
(c) To have available a record for a Branch of the Council for the Preservation of Rural England or amenity society to refer to when requests for help on preserving trees are made, and other purposes.
(d) To co-operate with County Planning Departments and in particular with their Landscape Sections.

2 Practical Considerations
The tree survey is best carried out by people living in or near the chosen areas so that a continual check can be made and changes easily recognised. It is more conveniently carried out by two people working together.

Spot checks by qualified people should be made.

MAPS

Grid system Ordnance Survey maps are recommended, covering 2 square kilometres, that is, on a scale of 1:2500 or 25 inches to a mile. It is useful for each surveyor to have two sheets, one for using in the field, and one for a fair copy to be returned to the County Planning Department (if working with their co-operation) or for your own permanent record.

It is most important that the map number and date are clearly visible on every record.

3 Field Techniques

The ideal form of field notebook is a small clipboard with loose-leaf ruled papers, previously columned and headed. It is best to use one map in the field and subsequently to transfer the results to another master or fair-copy map.

It has been found easier to begin a survey at the western edge of the map and, taking the major roads first, work up the left-hand side and down the right, labelling the trees in order and then following with the minor or cross roads.

The common name of the tree is normally used but one can be more specific if one wishes. Cultivated fruit trees and small mature flowering shrubs are not usually included.

It would be advisable to go over the same area at least every three years and record any changes that have taken place. The advantage of having someone living in the area, with responsibility for updating the records at regular intervals, is clear.

RECORDING

The trees are roughly classified under the following headings:

	Classification	*Code*
(a)	Single trees	T
(b)	Areas or linear belts with trees (e.g. hedges with significant trees)	A
(c)	Groups of trees (up to approx. 60)	G
(d)	Woods	W
(e)	Hedgerows	H

Single trees = T

These are recorded on the map as a dot with the letter code T and its sequential number, e.g. ·T₁ ·T₂ ·T₃ etc. The clip-board record gives the number, the name, trunk diameter at breast height and amenity value.

Areas or linear belts of trees = A

These are recorded on the map by outlining the area with a line and labelling with the letter A and its sequential number. They include belts or linear groups where there are too many to label singly and only one or two trees in depth. They can also include overgrown hedges which have significant trees in them.

Groups = G

These are recorded on the map by outlining the group with a line and labelling with the letter G and its sequential number. Groups are more than two trees in depth and up to about 60 trees in number.

All the tree types are listed.

Woods = W

These are recorded on the map by outlining the area and labelling with the letter W and its sequential number. They include large areas of trees or woodlands and they may be adjacent to groups or areas. One should name as many species as can be seen, either directly or through binoculars; add a question mark if the identity is in doubt.

Hedgerows = H

These are recorded on the map as vvvvv with the letter H and its sequential number. They include hedges without significant trees but do not include scrub. One should note the main species present in any one hedge.

Notes

Name This can be checked, if one is uncertain, by asking a specialist or visiting the tree at different times of the year so that leaves, flowers, fruit can be observed. Comment on any special features.

Height This can only be estimated and may be done by simple trigonometry or by taking the height of a person standing against the tree and seeing how many times that height goes into the height of the tree.

The diameter and height of the tree together give some idea of the age of the tree. (*A fairly accurate method of determining the age of a tree is as follows. Measure the diameter of the tree at chest height in inches and then multiply by four. Oaks and pines should be multiplied by six.*)

Diameter Usually measured at a point 4 feet above ground.

Amenity Value This is perhaps the most important factor from the point of view of the landscape situation and therefore of great concern to the CPRE, yet it is the most difficult to estimate. The following should be considered:

Is it a well shaped specimen?
Is it a healthy tree or is part of it dead or dangerous?
Does it suffer from fungal attack or is it just a poor specimen or over-mature?
Is it a rare species?
Does it add to the value of the locality?
Is it a landmark or has it 'local history' value?
Is it a young tree of good potential?

Amenity for the purposes of this survey has been divided into three grades, **A**, **B** and **C**.

A = fine specimens of trees or groups of trees, healthy and in a good position enhancing the surroundings. There is usually no difficulty in assessing such trees.

C = poor specimens, not growing well, often with dead branches and adding little or nothing to the surrounding scenery. There are also usually fairly easy to assess.

B = all remaining trees fall into this category.

THE FORESTRY COMMISSION[3]

On one level the Forestry Commission, started in 1919, is just another bullshit bureaucratic institution. On another level it is the only large-scale planter and preserver of trees and forests in Britain. It has planted 1,575,000 acres of trees on bare land that hasn't been woodland for centuries, though much of this—like the huge Kielder forests on the Northum-

[3] *Information kindly supplied by the now defunct Frendz magazine.*

berland/Scotland border—consists of ugly blankets of soft-woods, too dense to walk in and too monotonous to admire. That's because the Commission exists not to create beautiful forests but to plant forests with a quick money yield.

Certain Commission forests are open to the public. Others you need a special permit to visit, whether you want to just walk, ride, camp, picnic, study birds, fish, or just enjoy the peace of the wind in the pines. They are not difficult to get though, as long as you don't look like a pyromaniac. The thing to do is avoid the Commission's London headquarters, and go to the regional or district offices where the people are human and not just public relations men.

A side-effect of the Commission's work has been a vast increase in wild-life. There are now more varieties of wild deer in Britain than at any time since the Tudor and Stuart kings, and several extinct species of bird, such as the capercailzie, have returned.

Other good things provided by the Forestry Commission are:

Cottages: If you want to live for a while in a solitary forestbound cottage miles from anywhere, apply to any district office of the Commission. They usually lease them on a seven-year basis, but deals are negotiable and rents are reasonable.

Forestry Work: If you're interested in permanent forestry work, you should write for details to: Forestry Commission (Establishments Division), Priestley Road, Basingstoke, Hampshire. If you are looking for work of a more temporary nature, apply to the local district office.

Skins and Pelts: A friend tells me that you can get deer skins from the Norfolk office of the Commission, and this may well apply in other parts of the country.

Advice: As long as you're nice to them, your local Commission office will give you free and expert advice on all aspects of planting, growing, pruning, preserving, cutting and selling trees, etc.

Money: If you own any land, then the Commission will give you £23.50 for every acre of woodland that you plant. The idea is that you 'dedicate' your acre to forestry and nothing else, and this means that it cannot be compulsorily purchased except in the case of national need. If you plant over 100 acres, then you get an even better deal. There are also special schemes for farmers.

Schools : Any school near a Commission forest can approach the local Conservator of Forests with a view to 'adopting' a forest plot. This means that the Commission provides an acre or two where the school plants and tends the trees (with Commission help, of course). For schools that are not near any forests, the Commission will consider making a free gift of up to 100 young trees for planting for study purposes in school grounds. Application should be made to the local Conservator, during the summer preceding each autumn–spring planting season. The thing to do is to persuade a friendly member of the staff to talk to your headmaster.

Who To See : The Commission is organised on a three-tier system: the London headquarters at the apex, then the regional 'conservancy' offices, then the district offices. The best people to see for nearly anything are those at your local District Office. There are too many of them to list here, but you can get their addresses from the local regional offices which are listed below, or from the phone book.

Information : The Commission publishes numerous free pamphlets which you can pick up at any Commission office. They're mostly public relations, but they have some information. They also publish numerous technical booklets on all aspects of forestry, which can be had at varying prices from Commission headquarters or HMSO. Apply to any Commission office for a list of them, as printed in Forestry Commission booklet No. 31.

Forest Parks : The Commission has created seven 'Forest Parks' which are open to the public. They are: The Forest of Dean in Gloucestershire, Snowdonia in North Wales, Glen Trool in Galloway, Glen More in the Cairngorms, the Queen Elizabeth Forest Park between the Trossachs and Loch Lomond, Argyll Forest Park in Argyllshire, and the Border Forest Park covering parts of Cumberland, Northumberland and Roxburghshire.

There are also forest trails for walkers in over sixty Commission forests. Details of them are in the free Commission pamphlet 'See Your Forests'.

Forestry Commission Conservancy Offices

THE FORESTRY COMMISSION
25 Savile Row, London W1X 2AY.

ENGLAND
North West : Dee Hills Park, Chester.
North East : Briar House, Fulford Road, York.
East : Brooklands Avenue, Cambridge.
New Forest and SE England : The Queens House, Lyndhurst, Hampshire.
South West and Dean Forest : Flowers Hill, Brislington, Bristol 4.

SCOTLAND
North : 60 Church Street, Inverness.
East : 6 Queen's Gate, Aberdeen.
South : Greystone Park, Moffat Road, Dumfries.
West : 20 Renfrew Street, Glasgow C2.

WALES
North : Victoria House, Victoria Terrace, Aberystwyth.
South : Churchill House, Churchill Way, Cardiff.

SOURCES OF MATERIALS

Trees:
Trees can be obtained from the following people. Send away for free catalogues:
J. CHEAL & SONS LTD, Stopham Road, Pulborough, Sussex.
T. W. CHRISTIE, the Nursery, Forres, Morayshire, Scotland.
CIVIC TREES (SCOTLAND) LTD, The Gardens, Polton Lasswade, Midlothian, Scotland.
W. M. FERGUSON, 72 Campsie View, Kildrum, Cumbernauld, Scotland.
HILLIER & SONS, Winchester, England. *(Specialist in extra large trees.)*
JACKMANS NURSERIES LTD, Woking, Surrey.
MACDONALD BROS, Bogton Nurseries, 67 Muirend Road, Glasgow S4, Scotland.
ST BRIDGET NURSERIES, Old Rydon Lane, Exeter.
JOHN SCOTT, The Royal Nurseries, Merriot, Somerset.
SUNNINGDALE NURSERIES, Windlesham, Surrey.
Seeds : available from THOMPSON & MORGAN (IPSWICH) LTD, London Road, Ipswich.

SOCIETIES

ARBORICULTURAL ASSOCIATION, 59 Blythwood Gardens, Stanstead. Essex. *Aims to educate and inform on the practice of growing and looking after trees, as well as providing information concerning many other aspects of trees.*
ASSOCIATION OF BRITISH TREE SURGEONS & ARBORISTS, 11 Wings Road, Upper Hale, Farnham, Surrey. *Provides a consultancy service on tree care, which includes repair, maintenance and tree surgery.*
ASSOCIATION OF TREE TRANSPLANTERS, 91a High Street, Great Missenden, Buckinghamshire. *Concerns itself with all aspects of transplanting techniques, giving advice and promotion.*
THE FORESTRY COMMISSION, 25 Savile Row, London W1X 2AY. *Responsible for the production of timber for industry, as well as providing recreation for the public, and conservation for wild life in the forests. Carries out research into all aspects of forestry management, tree propagation and health.*
GLASGOW TREE LOVERS SOCIETY, 147 Blythswood Street, Glasgow C2. *Promotes a love and interest into all aspects of tree preservation and propagation.*
MEN OF THE TREES, Crawley Down, Crawley, Sussex. *Promotes understanding, education and interest in trees, as well as encouraging planting.*
ROYAL FORESTRY SOCIETY OF ENGLAND, SCOTLAND, WALES & NORTHERN IRELAND, 102 High Street, Tring, Hertfordshire. *Promotes good management of plantations and forests, as well as education on forestry and arboriculture.*

BIBLIOGRAPHY

THE ARBORICULTURALISTS COMPANION, by N. D. G. James, Blackwell Ltd.
THE COLLINS GUIDE TO TREE PLANTING AND CULTIVATION, W. Collins Sons & Co. Ltd.
DISCOVERING ENGLAND'S TREES, by Miles Hadfield, Shire Publications Ltd.

DISCOVERING FORESTS OF CENTRAL ENGLAND, by Jack Gould/Shire Publications Ltd.

THE INTERNATIONAL BOOK OF TREES, by Hugh Johnson/Mitchell Beazley Ltd.

THE NATURAL HISTORY OF AN ENGLISH FOREST, by Norman Hickin/Arrow Books Ltd.

THE OBSERVER BOOK OF TREES/Warne & Co. Ltd.

TREASURY OF TREES, by H. L. Edlin & M. Nimmo/Countrygoer Books Ltd.

TREE LOVER'S CALENDER/obtainable from Jarrold & Sons Ltd., Cowgate, Norwich, Norfolk NOR 50P.

TREES, by Andreas Feininger/Thames and Hudson Ltd.

The following publications are available from the ARBORICULTURAL ASSOCIATION, *59 Blythwood Gardens, Stanstead, Essex. Send for free details :*

THE ARBORICULTURAL ASSOCIATION ADVISORY LEAFLET NO. 1—Tree Preservation Orders.

THE ARBORICULTURAL ASSOCIATION ADVISORY LEAFLET NO. 2—Guide to Tree Pruning.

THE CARE OF TREES ON DEVELOPMENT SITES.

A GUIDE TO TREE PRUNING.

PLANTING AND PRUNING/The Glasgow Tree Lovers Society, 147 Blythswood Street, Glasgow C2. Available free.

RECOMMENDATION FOR TREE WORK, BS 3998: 1966/available from British Standards House, 2 Park Street, London W1.

SITE PREPARATION AND PLANTING.

TREES, by R. J. Morling/Estates Gazette Ltd, 151 Wardour Street, London W1V 4BN.

TREES & BUSHES IN WOOD & HEDGEROW, by H. Vedal & J. Lange/Methuen & Co. Ltd.

TREES IN TOWN AND CITY/Ministry of Housing & Local Government. Available from Her Majesty's Stationery Office.

THE TREE FOR THE SITE.

The following publications are available from the CIVIC TRUST, *17 Carlton House Terrace, London SW1Y 5AW :*

THE CIVIC TRUST TREES CAMPAIGN. Price: 15p (plus postage).

LARGE TREE TRANSPLANTING. Free.

PRACTICAL NOTES ON THE TRANSPLANTING OF SEMI-MATURE TREES. Price: 15p (plus postage).

TREES ON THE MOVE. Free.

The following publications are available from THE COUNCIL FOR THE PROTECTION OF RURAL ENGLAND, *4 Hobart Place, London SW1W 0HY. Send for free details :*

LOSS OF COVER (about the removal of hedgerows and its effects).

MAKING A TREE SURVEY.

PLANT A TREE THIS YEAR.

TREE SENSE.

TREES IN THE VILLAGE.

The following publications are available from THE FORESTRY COMMISSION, *25 Savile Row, London W1X 2AY. Send for free details :*

BEDGEBURY, Kent (National Pinetom) official guide.

BRITAIN'S NEW FOREST.

CONIFERS IN THE BRITISH ISLES.

EXOTIC FOREST TREES IN GREAT BRITAIN.

FOREST PARKS.

FORESTRY & THE TOWN SCHOOL.

FORESTRY IN THE LANDSCAPE.

KNOW YOUR BROADLEAVES.

KNOW YOUR CONIFERS.

RECREATION IN YOUR FORESTS.

SEE YOUR FORESTS.

STARTING A SCHOOL FOREST.

TREES AND PEOPLE.

The following leaflet is available free from THE SCOTTISH CIVIC TRUST, *24 George Square, Glasgow G2 1EF :*

THE PROPER CARE OF TREES.

The following books have been written by Dr Richard St Barbe Baker, founder of 'The Men of the Trees' society (see p.148) and the world's greatest living forester. All are available from him at THE LEAGATE HOUSE, *Bramley, Surrey :*

AMONG THE TREES/Privately by The Men of the Trees, 1935.

BROTHERHOOD OF THE TREES/Mondiale, 1930.

CARAVAN STORY AND COUNTRY NOTEBOOK/ Printed by McCorquodale, Wolverton, Buckinghamshire, 1969. *(Bedside book for a lover of caravan life.)*

DANCE OF THE TREES/Oldbourne Press, 1956.

FAMOUS TREES/Dropmore Press, 1952.

FAMOUS TREES OF THE WORLD: The Redwoods/ George Ronald, 1959. Famous Trees of New Zealand/George Ronald, 1963.

GREEN GLORY—FORESTS OF THE WORLD/Lutterworth Press, 1957. A. A. Wyn, New York, 1949. Wellington Books, Cambridge, Massachusetts, 1949.

I PLANTED TREES/Lutterworth Press, 1944.

MY HEALTH—MY WEALTH/manuscript awaiting publication. *(In response to numerous enquiries about the secret of his health.)*

MY LIFE—MY TREES/Lutterworth Press, 1970.

THE REDWOODS/George Ronald, 1943.

SAPOBA—UNLESS THE KING/manuscript awaiting publication. *(Silviculture in the mahogany forests of Nigeria.)*

SPIRIT OF THE TREES/Privately by The Men of the Trees, 1947. *(An anthology of poetry.)*

TREES BOOK OF THE SEASONS/Ernest Benn Ltd, 1940.

TREES OF BIBLE LANDS/manuscript awaiting publication.

TRUE BOOK ABOUT TREES/Frederick Muller Ltd, 1965.

MEN OF THE TREES/The Dial Press, New York, 1931.

MEN OF THE TREES/Stanley Unwin, 1932.

149

NED TOOKE

150

The Living Fence

The hedgerow is a fascinating place, I'm sure you will agree, but how much do you really know about the plants and animals which make up this intricately-balanced community? The hedgerow is a vast nature reserve: some counties have miles and miles of hedgerows, other areas have relatively little of this particular kind of habitat. The history of the hedgerow itself is rather an interesting one, so perhaps it might be a good idea to glimpse into its formation.

In early settlements the ground around the village was often afforested. Clearings were made, and increased in size as the population grew. These clearings were necessary for people to grow their crops. Generally there were three large fields, and these were sub-divided into a number of much smaller plots. One of the three large fields was left fallow each year, and crops were grown on each field for two successive years only. The third year it was given over to rough grazing, and in this way the field was also manured by the animals which fed there. Although the fields were, in turn, divided into strips, there were no hedges or fences and a man could hold pieces of land in different parts of the village without physical obstruction. As the population of the British Isles increased there was, quite naturally, the need to produce more food. There were always dominant characters in each village, either holding the title of Squire or Lord of the Manor. During the eighteenth and nineteenth centuries these influential people brought pressure to bear so that Acts of Parliament were passed so that the lands could be enclosed into farm fields: these were under the direct ownership of the Squire or Lord of the Manor. The 'poor' people had very little say in the matter, and suffered great hardship. However, the idea was, in principle, a sound one, in that the greater fields allowed for easier and more productive cultivation. With the increase in population it was vital that more food should be produced.

The Acts of Enclosure, to give these measures their correct name, saw the formation and widespread planting of hedges. These were useful in that they divided the larger fields, and also because they kept in, or out, farm animals. Other hedges grew up accidentally. Many hurdles and wooden-type fences had been, and still were, used between some strips of land. These also heralded the beginnings of the hedgerow as rough scrub and plants would grow up in this area, eventually developing into hedges. Many of the hedges which were purposely planted, were placed on the top of banks, on either side of which there were often drainage ditches. When landowners decided to plant hedges they needed to choose a species which would grow quickly and often they selected hawthorn, because it possessed these qualities. Once grown, it presented a virtually impenetrable barrier to animals by virtue of its thorny nature and dense growth. Unless checked, such hedges would grow wild, spreading into adjoining fields and periodically, usually every two or three years, perhaps more when fully grown, they would be trimmed. Layering was also a feature of the countryman's craft and branches would be partially cut through, being bent and interwoven to make a very strong hedge. Because the branches were not fully cut through they would continue to grow and many hedges are still to be found where hawthorn is the dominant plant. Within quite a short time of planting, other plants would be found. Animals would also seek a refuge in the hedge bottom, and birds would build their nests among the stable branches.

However, a hedgerow haunt is not a home for isolated species, but an interwoven network of living plants and animals, whose very livelihood and well-being will depend one on another. The species of plant which makes up the main part of the hedge will determine, to some extent, the animals and plants which will be found there. Hawthorn will, in a good season, provide a host of berries for many species of birds. Other plants will also provide an abundance of food for other birds, and for animals as well. Sloe, elderberry and dog rose are useful sources of food for birds and animals in Autumn.

Climbing plants will take advantage of the hedge, especially where the latter have been left unchecked. The flowers of the bindweed are a well-known feature of most hedges, and these will be joined by other climbing species like white bryony, traveller's joy, woody nightshade and ivy. The climbing plants are often accompanied by scrambling species like cleavers and the wild and dog rose. The latter will, in time, provide sturdy stems to support itself quite adequately, independent of the rest of the hedge. By Autumn most of the hedge foliage will have disappeared, and will re-appear in the following Spring, with new-found energy and growth. Some of the plants found here will occur in the hedge bottom, and will bear flowers before the main leaf canopy appears above, to blot out much of the sunlight so essential for plants to make their food. These plants which grow in the hedge bottom include those which grow quickly and spread outwards, so that the hedge does not shade them too much. Stinging nettles, hedge-parsley and jack-by-the-hedge are all perennials which fall into this category. Having grown quickly they will have a foothold in the hedge before the leaves appear above. There are only a few plants which can grow and flourish in the hedge bottom where there is little light. Such shade-loving plants include the primrose and the violet, together with cuckoo-pint. These plants will have produced their flowers before the main leaves appear on the hedge, clothing it in its suit of green.

Plants can be considered residents of the hedge, and there are many species of animals which are also residents. However, there are others which come and go, being regular visitors to the hedgerow habitat. The reasons for their comings and goings will vary from species to species, but there are two basic reasons why they visit the hedge: they will come in search of food and they will also look to the hedge for shelter.

Spiders are to be found in most hedgerows and their activities can best be observed during the Autumn when they are at their most active. It is a great delight to see a hedge adorned with a million sparkling strands of silk from a thousand spiders' webs, when the sun shines on the dew-encrusted hedge. There are many other invertebrate members of the hedgerow scene, and the caterpillars of many species of butterfly will be found feeding voraciously during late Spring through to early Autumn. It is interesting to note that some species of butterflies are to be found feeding exclusively on a single species of plant. Many such species may become extinct.

Mammals will also visit the hedgerow, and the very familiar hedgehog is one of these. He will choose a hedge bottom for his Summer retreat, and an even more sheltered one for his Winter hibernatory period. Sleeping in the hedge bottom by day, he will leave at dusk in search of food. Mice, voles, rabbits and shrews are all residents of the hedgerow habitat, and they are joined by birds, lizards and snails.

Visitors to the habitat include owls, searching for the abundance of wild mammals to be found and weasels and foxes are out to catch their prey. Butterflies and moths will frequent the area to sample the nectar from the many hedgerow flowers. Occasionally, visitors will include snakes and other species of birds. If there are trees in the hedge, then there is usually an even greater variety of wildlife: squirrels may build their dreys in its branches, and owls may nest in its trunk; caterpillars will feed on its leaves, and insects will lay their eggs in its flowers.

The hedge is an important wildlife refuge for birds. Some will sit on the highest boughs, singing and displaying, proclaiming that they have claimed the territory for their courtship period. Here the birds will build their nests, lay their eggs and raise their young. Long-tailed field mice will also make their nests in the hedge bottom, burrowing underneath the soil to make a number of chambers which will be used for sleeping and for storing food.

It is impossible to list all the species of the hedgerow, but as a habitat for wildlife it is of great importance. It has been considered as *the* most important wildlife reserve in the country, but each year it has been estimated that some 5,000 miles of hedgerow are removed, to make way for bigger fields to produce more food. This is not always an advantage, as many farmers have found in the Fenland area, where hedgerows have long since vanished in many parts. When dust storms occur they cause a great deal of damage, blowing away seeds, burying plants, and filling dykes.

Perhaps one day someone will understand more fully the intricate relationships which exist in the hedgerow, and instead of uprooting them they will plant more, so that future generations can enjoy the wealth of wildlife which the hedgerow habitat offers to the patient observer. *By Ron Wilson*

MAKING A HEDGE SURVEY[1]

Dating a hedgerow

Dr Max Hooper of the Nature Conservancy has established that in general it is possible to date a hedge by the number of kinds of shrub growing in it. Examine any 30-yard length of hedge: there will tend to be approximately one species of shrub for every hundred years. So a hedge with 5 species of shrub within a 30 yard length is probably about 500 years old; 9 species of shrub should mean roughly 900 years. And so on. Where the rule does not apply, there are likely to be other explanations. (Thus in part of Shropshire, Dr Hooper found five species of shrub in hedges he knew from documentary sources to be only 200 years old. The explanation for this apparent inconsistency was that, contrary to the national pattern—which is that hedges are originally planted as one species, generally hawthorn—in this part of Shropshire the original hedges were planted as *mixed* hedges. Or again, on the very acid soils in parts of the North and West of England, hedges are little more than gorse banks. Dr Hooper's rule does not apply where the acidity of the soil does not permit the ready growth of shrubs.) But in general, the dating of hedges by the Hooper method is reliable within certain margins of error (say 100 years either way).

Hedge survey

A hedgerow survey of a parish would be a most valuable contribution to local history, and could be welcomed by your County Archivist. In parts of England where hedges are especially at risk, it will probably be possible to get the co-operation of the Planning Authority. The intention of such a survey should be to draw together as much material as possible on the history of your parish hedges and to document it thoroughly.

Having checked with your CPRE branch and County Naturalists' Trust that no hedge survey has already been undertaken in your parish, you should follow the broad ground-rules set down here.

[1] *By kind permission of the Council for the Protection of Rural England.*

Many hedges can be recorded along public roadsides, bridle paths and footpaths. If you wish to examine a hedge on private land, it is vital that you first obtain permission from the owner or tenant.

For each hedge you survey, you will require a form which records the significant features in several 30 yard stretches of the hedge. The form was developed by the Cambridgeshire and Isle of Ely Naturalists' Trust.

The survey should clearly identify the hedges described. It is important to sketch a map (1) to give an Ordnance Survey map reference (2) and to give as much information as possible about the locality (3). Each hedge should be examined in 30 yard lengths (4) estimated by pacing out 30 yards on the ground. The dominant species (5) is the kind of tree or shrub which appears to be most abundant in the hedge.

Certain species of flowers, climbing plants and all rarities are of particular interest (6); be sure to record mercury, bluebell, oxlip, crested cow-wheat, if they are present. Remember, however, that for the purposes of hedge-dating, climbers, such as black bryony, white bryony, honeysuckle, and blackberry do not count. Under Further Comments (7) the kind and number of trees in the hedge should be identified. You should also note here whether the hedge appears to be planted (e.g. a hedge of mixed species surrounding a park), whether the hedge appears to be in immediate danger, whether it supports abundant fauna, etc.

Finally, Historical References (8). This section should include any additional *documentary* reference you are able to establish relating to a particular hedge. There are a number of available source documents: Anglo-Saxon charters, the records of medieval monasteries, parish maps, early estate maps, tithe maps, and early Ordnance Survey maps are some of them. Your County Records Office (and your County Archivist) will help guide you to sources for your parish. The relevant volumes of the *Victoria County History* will be indispensable.

But perhaps the most fascinating document of all is *the hedge itself*, using the Hooper method of dating by the number of shrubs contained in the hedge. The value of a hedge survey does not necessarily depend on its being tied into other historical matter.

How is a hedge survey useful? The survey is likely to be of great potential assistance to the Planning Authority. At present, nobody cares that an historic hedge may be lost, because nobody knows anything of its history. But an authoritative survey could provide details of its age and interest and such factors could weigh heavily in the decision of a Planning Authority or even, tactfully presented, of a farmer. So the survey will be a positive contribution to planning the survival of hedges that might otherwise be uprooted. Unlike trees, hedges *per se* are not subject to Preservation Orders. This makes it especially important to rouse and inform public opinion when hedges of particular interest are in jeopardy. Secondly, the survey will be welcomed as a contribution to local history, and as a source of material for other local historians. Finally, the survey will give you a deep and lasting understanding of the way in which the landscape of your parish reflects its varied history. The beauty of the English countryside is the product of hundreds, even thousands of years of man's endeavours. We must look after it.

SOCIETIES

THE COUNCIL FOR THE PROTECTION OF RURAL ENGLAND, 4 Hobart Place, London SW1W 0HY.

The CPRE is a registered charity formed to protect and enhance the beauty of the English landscape, and to ensure that changes, which are inevitable, are for the best whenever possible. The Council is concerned at the tendency in some areas for hedges to be uprooted and destroyed, regardless of their historic or amenity value. The Council has many affiliated bodies, all of which are listed on pp. 234–235.

BIBLIOGRAPHY

HEDGES AND LOCAL HISTORY/available from the Standing Conference on Local History, 26 Bedford Square, London WC1B 3HU. Price: 55p.

MAKING A HEDGE SURVEY/available from The Council for the Protection of Rural England (as above).

*Early autumn evening
is long, dark shadows
stroking the warm green richness
of the Kentish fields*

JOHN RICE

Every Garden Should Be One

How many gentle flowers grow
In an English Country Garden?
I'll tell you of some I know
And those I miss I hope you'll pardon.
There are daffodils, hearts season flocks,
Meadow sweet and lilies, stocks,
Gentle lupins and tall hollyhocks,
Roses, foxgloves,
Snowdrops and forget-me-nots
In an English Country Garden.

How many insects find their home
In an English Country Garden?
I'll tell you of some I know
And those I miss I hope you'll pardon.
There are dragonflies, moths and bees
Spiders falling from the trees
Butterflies sway in the mild, gentle breeze,
There are hedgehogs that roam
And little gnomes
In an English Country Garden.

How many song birds make their nests
In an English Country Garden?
I'll tell you of some I know
And those I miss I hope you'll pardon.
There are babbling coo-cooing doves
Robins and the warbling thrush,
Bluebird, lark, finch and nightingale,
We all smile in the spring
When the birds start to sing
In an English Country Garden.

THE PRESSURES on our wildlife are increasing yearly with alarming effects on both their food supplies and habitats. As urban expansion, encroaches slowly into the country-side, the creatures living there have little choice but to perish, move on, or adapt to the changes. Some have perished, some have moved on, but many have used their natural ingenuity to adapt to urban life and are flourishing quite well. It is therefore on this point of adaptation that we can be of real help to our wildlife. If nothing can be done to prevent the eating away of open land, at least something positive can be done to make life in the new towns and suburbs as attractive to wild creatures as possible. Most people own a garden, however, small and with little cost it can be transformed into a mini-nature reserve, the sort of place that will attract bees, birds, butterflies and perhaps the odd mammal or two.

Although many species are threatened, there are a number of things the individual can do:

The most important point to remember is that wildlife will need two basic requirements; food and shelter. Food must come from nectar-giving flowers, nut and berry bearing trees and shrubs, and shelter can be provided by planting trees and shrubs with thick or dense foliage. If the garden, or at least a good part of it, can be left 'wild', then all the better. This need not necessarily be a corner of tangled weeds, although this is very beneficial, but can be an area planted with specialist wild flowers, ornamental flowers and grasses, and shrubs which will only need a little attention now and again.

ATTRACTING BUTTERFLIES

One must approach this aspect of the ecological garden in two ways; firstly by providing nectar-bearing flowers for the butterflies and secondly by providing food for the caterpillars once the butterflies have been attracted and encouraged to lay eggs.

Caterpillar Food
A list will appear at the end of this chapter showing where the various flowers and plants can be purchased, as well as addresses of firms that actually sell eggs, caterpillars and pupae of butterflies. This means that once the garden has been stocked with suitable food plants, the actual insects can be introduced as well.

ASPEN *(Populus tremula)*
Food of the Poplar Hawk Moth.
ASH *(Fraxinus excelsior)*
Food for the Privet Hawk Moth.
BEECH *(Fagus sylvetica)*
Food of the Buff Tip.
BIRCH *(Betula)*
Food of the Kentish Glory, Camberwell Beauty.
BLACKTHORN *(Prunus spinosa)* Sloe
Food of the Gipsy Moth, Swallowtail, Black Veined White.
BRAMBLE *(Rubus fruticosus)*
Food of the Gatekeeper, Ringlet, Green Hairstreak, Brown Hairstreak, Whiteletter, Grizzled Skipper.
BUCKTHORN *(Rhamnus cathartica)*
Food of the Green Veined White, Brimstone.
BURDOCK *(Arctium minus)*
Food of the Painted Lady.
CABBAGE
Food of the Large White.
CARROT
Food of the Swallowtail.
CHERRY *(Prunus)*
Food of the Gipsy Moth.
CLOVERS *(Trifolium)*
Food of the Clouded Yellow.
DANDELION *(Taraxacum officinale)*
Food of the Tiger Moth.
DOCK *(Rumex)*
Food of the Small Copper, Large Copper, Tiger Moth.
ELM *(Ulmus)*
Food of the Camberwell Beauty, Large Tortoise Shell, Lime Hawk.
FENNEL *(Foeniculum vulgare)*

Food of the Swallowtail.
GORSE *(Ulex europaeus)*
Food for the Silver Shredded Blue.
GRASSES
Many caterpillars feed on the many types of grasses growing in the British Isles, including the Small Heath, Large Heath Speckled Wood, and Wall Brown.
HAWTHORN *(Crataegus monogyna)*
Food of the Lackey.
HOP *(Humulus lupulus)*
Food of the Comma.
HORSERADISH *(Armoracia rusticana)*
Food of the Green Veined White.
LILAC
Food of the Privet Hawk Moth.
LIME *(Tilia)*
Food of the Lime Hawk, Buff Tip.
LUCERNE *(Medicago falcata)*
Food of the Clouded Yellow.
MUSTARD, GARLIC *(Alliaria petiolata)*
Food of the Green Veined White, Orange Tip.
NETTLE, STINGING *(Urtica dioica)* —
Food for the Painted Lady, Peacock, Tortoiseshells, Red Admiral.
OAK *(Quercus)*
Food of the Buff Tip.
PLUM *(Prunus)*
Food of the Gipsy Moth.
POPLAR *(Populus)*
Food of the Poplar Hawk Moth, Eyed Hawk Moth, Puss Moth.
PRIVET *(Ligustram vulgare)*
Food of the Privet Hawk Moth.
SALLOW *(Salix)*
Food of the Eyed Hawk Moth, Puss Moth, Camberwell Beauty, Large Tortoiseshell, Purple Emperor, Kentish Glory, Buff Tip.
SCABIOUS *(Knautia arvensis)*
Food of the Bee Hawk Moth.
SCOTS PINE *(Pinus sylvestris)*
Food of the Pine Hawk Moth.
SORREL *(Rumex)*
Food of the Small Copper.
SPURGE *(Euphorbia)*
Food of the Spurge Hawk Moth.
THISTLE *(Cardaus and Cirsium)*
Food of the Red Admiral, Painted Lady.
WILLOW *(Salix)*
Food of the Eyed Hawk, Puss Moth, Camberwell Beauty, Large Tortoiseshell, Tiger Moth.

WILLOWHERB *(Epilobium)*
Food of the Elephant Hawk Moth.

Butterfly Food
Butterflies love sweet-scented flowers oozing with nectar and as a general rule, prefer small, rather simple flowers, such as the old cottage perennials. Take your choice from the following list:

ALLYSUM (white)	MALLOW
AGERATUM	MARJORAM
ARABIS (pink & white)	MIGNONETTE
AUBRETIA	MICHAELMAS DAISY
BLUEBELL	PINK THRIFT
BIRDSFOOT TREFOIL	PRIMROSE
BUDDLEIA (the	POLYANTHUS
butterfly bush)	PETUNIA
BRAMBLE	PHLOX
CATNIP	RUBUS
CANDYTUFT	RAGWORT
COMFREY	SWEET WILLIAM
CLOVER	SINGLE FRENCH
CAMPION	MARIGOLD
COWSLIP	SEDUM
DANDELION	SOAPWORT
DAISY	SEA HOLLY
EVERLASTING PEA	SENECIO
EGLANTINE ROSE	SCARLET GERANIUM
FOXGLOVE	(common)
GOLDEN ROD	SWEET ROCKET
HELIOTROPE	SWEET WILLIAM
HEBE	THYME
HEATHERS	THISTLE
HONEY SUCKLE	VERBENA
KNAPWEED	VALERIAN
LILAC	WALLFLOWER
LAVENDER	(purple & yellow)
LAVENDER	
MYRRH	
MEADOW CRANESBILL	

Many wild flowers can be bought as seeds (addresses of seedsmen are given at the end of this chapter) and either raised in a good quality seed compost under glass and transplanted out when of sufficient size, or the seeds raked lightly into the surface of the soil and allowed to germinate naturally. Some seeds may lie dormant in the soil for more than a year, so don't despair if nothing happens at first.

ATTRACTING BIRDS[1]

Somewhere to live
When replacing habitat for birds, you must fulfil two of their basic requirements—food and shelter. Food and shelter? Feeding birds and providing nestboxes does help. But there is more that you can do. You can provide a suitable habitat by growing plants on which the birds rely. Birds are part of nature—dependent like all animals and plants on other animals and plants. They are part of a food chain—a food chain which in turn depends on the soil and climate.

Planning for the birds
How do you set about planning out your garden nature reserve? The basic requirements of food and shelter often go together. Therefore, if you grow plants for food, you will provide shelter as well. Plants for food fall into two groups—those that are eaten by the birds and those that attract insects that are eaten by the birds. The birds that visit your garden can be divided into three basic categories—those that eat mainly vegetable matter, those that eat mainly animal matter such as insects and those that will eat almost anything.

No garden is flat
When planning your planting, remember that a garden has more than one level. It has a range of levels from the top of well-grown trees to the ground. So choose plants that will give you a wide range of heights.

The plants for the seed-eaters can range from the smaller varieties of daisies to the pyracantha that can grow up the walls of a house. Seeds of many herbaceous plants will attract members of the finch family. The most obvious of these is the sunflower. It is easy to grow and if left to go to seed is particularly attractive to goldfinches. Other suitable flowers include cosmos, china aster, scabious, evening primrose, antirrhinum and michaelmas daisy.

If you have a large garden and tolerant neighbours, you can leave a 'wild' area, where thistle, knapweed, teasel, groundsel and field

[1] *By courtesy of The Royal Society for the Protection of Birds.*

poppy can grow. Nettles are also valuable because they provide food for insects, which in turn provide food for birds.

Michaelmas daisies and other pink and mauve late-flowering plants such as ice plant, buddleia and veronica seem to be particularly attractive to butterflies and other insects. Amongst insect-attracting plants, one of the most successful is the giant hogweed. This will grow to 12 or 14 feet and will attract many flying insects, and therefore fly-catching birds. Remember to warn children not to play with this plant because it can cause very unpleasant skin irritation.

The berry-bearing shrubs are a valuable source of food for members of the thrush family in the winter. You may even attract the redwing and fieldfare, winter visitors from Scandinavia. Researches by the Royal Society for the Protection of Birds into the shrubs that birds prefer have shown the following to be most popular:

ELDER (mainly *Sambucus nigra*)
YEW *(Taxus baccata)*
Cotoneaster horizontalis
Cotoneaster simonsii
Cotoneaster waterii
AUTUMN OLIVE *(Elaeagnus umbellata)*
RUSSIAN OLIVE *(Elaeagnus augustifolia)*
RED CHOKEBERRY *(Aronia arbutifolia)*
BLACK CHOKEBERRY *(Aronia melanocarpa)*
BARBERRY *(Berberis darwinii)*
HOLLY *(mainly Ilex aquifolium)*
FLOWERING CURRANT (mainly *Ribes sanguineum)*
HONEYSICKLE *(Lonicera species)*
HAWTHORN (mainly *Crataegus monogyna)*
WAYFARING TREE *(Viburnum lantana)*
BLACKBERRY *(Rubus fruticosus)*
ROWAN *(Sorbus aucuparia)*
FIRETHORN *(Pyracantha coccinea)*
CRAB APPLE (mainly *Malus pumila)*
PRIVET (mainly *Ligustrum vulgare)*

Some of these plants make excellent hedges. Hawthorn is particularly effective because it provides both food and nest sites. In fact, some gardeners prefer it to the more usual privet hedge which can be a nuisance because it takes so much nutrient from the soil. Remember that some of the bushes suggested have berries that are harmful to man and domestic animals, but not to birds.

Birds which eat berries will also eat fruit in winter. They are not as fussy as humans and can be attracted by windfalls and damaged fruit put out during the cold weather.

Trees are a source of food as well as shelter for birds. If you want to plant trees, pick native rather than exotic species. Not only are they better adapted to the climate, they are also part of the pattern of our native flora and fauna. Of the native trees, the oak is undoubtedly the most productive; a mature oak supports so much life that it is almost a habitat in itself. However, oaks need space and take a long time to reach maturity. Therefore, you may prefer to choose a quicker-growing species such as ash, elm, silver birch or willow. Like other plants, trees do have a preference for certain soil types and therefore you should plant species already growing in your area or take a nurseryman's advice. Remember to ascertain how much room a tree takes up when fully grown before you plant it.

Ash seeds or 'keys' provide food for a number of species and have been proven to lessen the damage of bullfinches on buds in orchard areas. Silver birches attract numerous small insects which all the species of tits eat. Many insects, especially moths, lay their eggs on willow leaves and their grubs are eaten by robins, tits, wrens and dunnocks. If you buy an elm, make sure it is one of the varieties which are less susceptible to Dutch elm disease.

Dead trees can be left, unless they have died through a disease, such as Dutch elm disease. Rotting trees provide nest-holes and a plentiful supply of insect food in the rotting bark. If you think a dead tree is unsightly, grow a climbing plant such as clematis up it.

The importance of water

Throughout the year, birds need water for bathing and drinking. Birdbaths are the obvious way to do this. They can be purchased from garden shops and centres but often they are expensive, aesthetically unpleasing and badly designed, so that they do not fulfil their prime purpose. Basically, almost any receptacle is suitable as long as birds can reach the water and the sides are not slippery. A simple bath can be made from an upturned dustbin lid sunk into the ground or supported by three bricks.

In winter, freezing can be a problem. A small receptacle raised on bricks over a lighted nightlight can avoid this. If your birdbath is large or if you have a pond, you can use a thermostatic immersion heater designed for ponds. They can be bought from aquaria suppliers. Make sure you have a well-insulated lead. On no account use chemicals to lower the water's freezing point.

Your own pool

A garden pool is more effective than a birdbath as long as it has a shallow ledge around the edge. It will be used by birds for drinking and bathing. A pool very soon attracts a range of wildlife including creatures such as frogs, newts, and dragonflies. It also attracts other insects on which wagtails and flycatchers will feed.

Making a suitable pool is quite easy. First dig a hole approximately 5 feet by 4 feet. The deepest part should be between 1 foot and 2 feet but the bottom should slope gradually to a shallow end. Remove all sharp stones and lay a 9 feet by 8 feet sheet of 1,000 gauge polythene into the hole, allowing 2 feet spare around the edges. Trap the edges by replacing turf. Spread soil over the base of the pool to a depth of 3 or 4 inches, fill with water, allowing a week to settle before planting, and grow aquatic plants in the soil.

Nesting sites

Natural nesting places for birds are often not available in gardens. Hedges have been removed (or on modern estates just not provided), rotting trees which provide nest-holes have been chopped down and a thick undergrowth is not tolerated.

Many of the bushes and trees recommended for feeding birds also provide cover for nesting Particularly valuable are bramble and hawthorn which offer protection from predators.

The most obvious way to compensate for the lack of natural nest-sites is to put up nest-boxes. However these are only suitable for certain species. Many types are sold commercially and when you buy one, avoid those with ledges beneath the entrance which might help predators to get to the nest. Ornamentation is unnecessary from the birds' point of view—cupolas, balustrades, thatch or windows mean nothing to the birds. All they want is somewhere in which to nest safely.

Ideally, nestboxes should be put up in November but the early spring is not too late. Fix your nestbox to a tree or wall. For the birds' sake, avoid places which cats can easily reach and try not to have the hole facing south because the midday sun may be too hot for the nestlings. For your sake, find places where you can watch easily.

Tits, tree sparrows and house sparrows, starlings, nuthatches and pied flycatchers are all hole-nesters and will use nestboxes. For tits an entrance hole $1\frac{1}{3}$ inches in diameter is sufficient and too small for starlings and house sparrows. Spotted flycatchers, pied wagtails and robins will use nestboxes with open fronts. They will also nest in old kettles and flower pots. If you leave the door of your garden shed or greenhouse open throughout the breeding season, you may well attract robins, song thrushes, blackbirds, wrens, spotted flycatchers, pied wagtails or swallows to nest inside. Ensure that there are no open paint pots or tins of creosote because young birds may well fall into these when they leave the nest.

Many species will nest in holes in walls. If you remove a brick from a wall, you may well

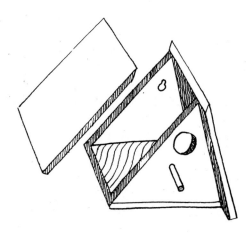

get pied wagtails, spotted flycatchers or wrens nesting in the hole. For details of the many types of nest-box that can be bought or made, you should read BIRD NEST-BOXING by Norman Hickin and the BTO GUIDE, NESTBOXES. Both are available from the RSPB whose address is given on p. 163.

At the end of each nesting season, clean out your nestbox in order to remove parasites. The remains of old nests may deter birds from nesting next year.

The making of the nest box
Get yourself some wood (plywood is best but it really doesn't matter) about $\frac{1}{4}$ inch thick, and cut out the front and back which are 8-inch-sided triangles. Drill the entrance hole in one of the two pieces; $2\frac{1}{2}$ inches below the apex and also a $\frac{2}{3}$ inch hole for the perch—4 inches below the apex. Cut a key-hole shape (using two drill sizes) in the other piece of wood directly opposite the entrance hole. Now for your sides. Cut two pieces of wood $8\frac{3}{4}$ inches by 6 inches and mitre the top edges. Glue and panel-pin the sides to the front and back, overlapping the front by 1 inch. Cut another piece of wood $8\frac{1}{4}$ inches by 5 inches for the base and bevel the edges to 60°. Screw the base to the front and back edges and then glue a $1\frac{5}{8}$ inches-long davel rod into the perch hole. Finally, paint the outside of the box thoroughly.

Nesting
When birds nest in your garden, leave them alone as much as possible. If you must look, make it a quick visit every other day. Be very careful not to leave signs of your visit such as broken twigs or trodden foliage because this might lead predators to the nest.

Leave young birds alone
Young birds away from the nest, apparently without their parents, have normally not been deserted. They have probably just left the nest and are not yet flying freely. Do not attempt to catch them, their parents will return when you leave. To try rearing them yourself would be difficult and would probably end in failure. It is also illegal to do this unless the bird has been deserted or was injured. Further details are available in TREATMENT OF SICK AND INJURED

BIRDS and WILD BIRDS AND THE LAW each of which can be obtained by sending 5p in stamps to the RSPB.

Birdtables and feeding devices
In very hard weather, feeding birds can be important in helping them to survive, but remember that during the rest of the year, the main value of feeding birds is making it easy for you to watch them.

A variety of birdtables is sold and they range from the elaborate 'rustic' type to simple platforms. Which you choose is really a matter of individual taste. Many birdtables have roofs and while these are not vital, they do give some protection to food, especially from snow.

You can suspend birdtables from a branch or from a wall bracket, or you can support the table on a post driven into the ground or on a movable stand. Avoid 'rustic' stands which are easily climbed by cats or grey squirrels.

Squirrels are inveterate birdtable feeders and it is difficult to keep them off the table. Many ingenious ideas have been tried but the squirrels' acrobatic ingenuity will often win. A table with a very smooth circular pipe around the post or a basket suspended on a long wire from a high branch will usually beat them.

House sparrows and starlings are considered nuisances on birdtables by some people and there is a variety of 'sparrow-proof' feeding devices—from baskets to coils of wire. They can be filled with nuts, fat or kitchen scraps. Unfortunately, some feeding devices can be dangerous and before you buy you should look carefully for sharp edges which can cut birds' feet, or springs which can trap birds by the feet or wings, or openings in which the birds themselves could become trapped.

Whatever feeding devices you choose, they should be moved occasionally because there is a danger that rotten food can accumulate in the ground, harbouring disease and encouraging rats.

Be considerate to your neighbours. Extravagant feeding can encourage birds to the extent that they become a nuisance.

HARD TIMES

When the ground is covered with a crust of
* frozen snow,*
Don't forget the hungry birds that flutter
* to and fro.*
Searching vainly for a worm, a berry
* or a seed,*
A sip of water and some crumbs will satisfy
* their need.*

Feed the feathered mendicants that gather
* at your door,*
They'll reward you with a song when
* Spring comes round once more.*
Feed God's little minstrels when the
* world is cold and white.*
Feed them and remember they were made
* for your delight.*

A FARM·HOUSE GARDEN

WILD FLOWERS: CONSERVATION AND SURVEYS

1   Don't pick wild flowers indiscriminately. Just as it is no longer the practice to encourage small boys to collect birds' eggs (a practice which was standard 40 years ago), so it is now important that the *picking* of unusual wild flowers should be discouraged. The Code of Conduct of the Botanical Society of the British Isles recommends: 'Pick only flowers known to be common or plentiful in the locality, but wherever you can, leave them for others to enjoy. If you wish to identify a plant, take the smallest adequate bit; often a photograph may serve the purpose.'

2   If you are seriously interested in wild flowers, join the BOTANICAL SOCIETY OF THE BRITISH ISLES (c/o The British Museum (Natural History), London SW7) and your COUNTY NATURALISTS' TRUST. You will quickly learn which plants are in danger, and which, if any, are plentiful.

3   The Association of Natural History Photographic Societies' CODE OF PRACTICE contains advice on photographing plants without harming them. It is obtainable from the RSPB, The Lodge, Sandy, Bedfordshire. Please enclose 5p in stamps.

4   Do not introduce plants into the countryside—and particularly into Nature Reserves—without the knowledge and consent of the appropriate conservation organisation. Indiscriminate introductions of wild plants will damage the ecology of the area. Certain species are very aggressive. Further guidance can be found in A POLICY ON INTRODUCTIONS, published by the SOCIETY FOR THE PROMOTION OF NATURE RESERVES, Alford, Lincolnshire.

5   Surveys. Detailed records of plant populations in particular habitats are valuable both as a means of *understanding* the flora, and for the archives of the BIOLOGICAL RECORDS CENTRE at Monks Wood, Huntingdonshire. There may already be surveys of this kind being undertaken in your area; your COUNTY NATURALISTS' TRUST or your local natural history society should be able to advise you. If in doubt, write to the BIOLOGICAL RECORDS CENTRE at Monks Wood, Huntingdonshire, which will always try to put you in touch. A number of County

Trusts have undertaken or might wish to undertake surveys of the wild plants on particular road verges.

THE BIOLOGICAL RECORDS CENTRE at Monks Wood welcomes details of certain specific plant populations and habitats:

(a) **Details of Cowslip meadows**
Does the meadow have ridge and furrow?
How wide an expanse does it cover?
How many other species of wild flower can you recognise growing in it?

(b) **Details of hedgerows** in which the following plants occur:
BLUEBELLS (*Endymion non-scriptus*)
DOG'S MERCURY (*Mercurialis perennis*)
PRIMROSE (*Primula vulgaris*)
WOOD ANEMONE (*Anemone nemorosa*)
YELLOW ARCHANGEL (*Galeobdolon luteum*)
WOODRUFF (*Asperula odorata*)

These wild flowers are primarily woodland plants; their presence in a hedgerow could indicate that the spot once fell within the boundaries of ancient forests.

SOURCES OF MATERIALS

MRS EMMERSON, Leeke, Limavady, Co. Derry, N. Ireland.
This lady supplies seedlings and young plants of many old-fashioned cottage perennials and wild flowers very cheaply.
MRS G. M. MILNER, Brompton Regis, nr Dulverton, Somerset.
Contact this lady for unusual strains of old-fashioned cottage perennials, as well as many other beautiful flowers.
JOHN SCOTT & CO., The Royal Nurseries, Merriot, Somerset.
For trees, shrubs and flowers, including many old-fashioned roses and cottage perennials.
THOMPSON & MORGAN, London Road, Ipswich IP20BA.
Many wild flowers can be obtained in seed form from this company.
The larvae, ova and pupae of all the butterflies mentioned can be obtained, along with breeding equipment and other sundries from :
THE BUTTERFLY FARM LTD, Bilsington, Ashford, Kent.
WORLDWIDE BUTTERFLIES LTD, Over Compton, Sherborne, Dorset.

Both of these firms supply information on how to breed butterflies and hatch out eggs etc. Their catalogues containing this information are free on request.
L. CHRISTIE, 137 Glenedon Road, Streatham, London SW16. *Supplies certain species of butterflies.*

SOCIETIES

THE AMATEUR ENTOMOLOGIST SOCIETY, c/o R. D. Hilliard, 18 Golf Close, Stanmore, Middlesex. *Caters for the young and amateur entomologists. Enclose a 6p stamp when enquiring please.*
BRITISH BUTTERFLY CONSERVATION SOCIETY, Tudor House, Quorn, Leicestershire LE12 8AD.
FAUNA PRESERVATION SOCIETY, c/o The Zoo, Regents Park, London N1. *A society that cares for the whole British animal kingdom.*
THE ROYAL ENTOMOLOGIST SOCIETY, 41 Queens Gate, London SW7.
THE ROYAL SOCIETY FOR THE PROTECTION OF BIRDS, The Lodge, Sandy, Bedfordshire. *The most popular wild life charity in Britain which does an excellent job in helping to protect birds as well as encouraging interest and respect for wild life. Its monthly bulletins,* BIRDS *and* BIRDLIFE, *are issued free to members. The Society also runs film shows and gives lectures on bird conservation. Write for details.*
THE SOUTH LONDON ENTOMOLOGIST SOCIETY, 14 Rochester Row, London SW1.
TEEN INTERNATIONAL ENTOMOLOGY GROUP, c/o Mr J. Wilson, 67 Harcourt Road, Thornton Heath, Surrey CR4 6BS. *An international society for teenage entomologists which organises day trips, camps and newsheets. Membership is free to those genuinely interested in entomology.*
THE WILD FLOWER SOCIETY, c/o Mrs C. M. R. Schwerdt, Rams Hill House, Horse Monden, Tonbridge, Kent. *The Society aims to encourage a love of wild flowers amongst both children and elders. Competitions and expeditions are arranged as well as a bulletin entitled* WILD FLOWER MAGAZINE.

BIBLIOGRAPHY

BIRDS/The Royal Society for the Protection of Birds. (Alternate months.) Annual subscription: £2.00.
BIRDS AND COUNTRY MAGAZINE/available from 79 Surbiton Hill Park, Surbiton, Surrey. (Quarterly.) Price: 15p. Annual subscription: 75p.
BIRD LIFE/The Royal Society for the Protection of Birds. (Quarterly.) Price: 12½p. Annual subscription: 60p.
BULLETIN OF THE AMATEUR ENTOMOLOGIST SOCIETY/available c/o K. H. Bobe, 50 Winn Road, Lee, London SE13.
ENTOMOLOGIST GAZETTE/353 Hanworth Road, Hampton, Middlesex.
ENTOMOLOGIST MONTHLY MAGAZINE/c/o Nathaniel Lloyd & Co. Ltd, Burrell Street Works, Blackfriars, London SE1.
THE ENTOMOLOGIST RECORD/c/o F. W. Buyers, 59 Gurney Court Road, St Albans, Hertfordshire. *A monthly illustrated magazine devoted to insects with reports on collecting trips, distribution habits and study techniques. Write for a specimen copy.*
THE BIRD TABLE BOOK, by Tony Soper/Pan Books Ltd.
COLLINS BOOK OF BIRDS/Collins Sons & Co. Ltd.
CREATE A BUTTERFLY GARDEN, by L. Hugh Newman/Cedar.
LOOKING AFTER WILD BIRDS, by Clare Abrahall/Corgi Books Ltd.
THE UNOFFICIAL COUNTRYSIDE, by Richard Mabey/Collins Sons & Co. Ltd. *An account of the natural history of the city and suburbia.*
Publications available from the Butterfly Farm Ltd, Bilsington, Ashford, Kent :
BUTTERFLIES IN BRITAIN, by G. Hyde.
BUTTERFLY FARMER, by L. Newman.
PICTURE REFERENCE SERIES: *This series includes the following titles :* BERRIES & FRUITS; BUTTERFLIES, MOTHS AND THEIR CATERPILLARS; INSECTS; WILD FLOWERS IN THE AUTUMN; WILD FLOWERS IN THE SPRING; WILD FLOWERS IN THE SUMMER; TREES.
Publications available from The Royal Society for the Protection of Birds, The Lodge, Sandy, Bedfordshire :
THE BIRDS IN YOUR GARDEN. Price: 10p (plus postage). *Free on request if joining the Society.*
NEST BOXES, by Norman Hickin. Price: 30p.

For any plant, be it tree, bush, flower or vegetable, to live and flourish in the soil, there must be a good supply of humus in that soil, for the simple reason that humus (decayed organic matter or compost) contains essential nutrients which plants need, and what is more important, these nutrients are in the right proportion for plants to absorb. Humus also improves the condition of soils; breaking down heavy clay soils and giving body and life to sandy and chalky varieties so that root systems can get a good anchorage to feed the plants they serve. Added to this there is the fact that a soil rich in humus retains moisture more readily than a soil lacking in organic matter, so that the need for constant watering of plants is eliminated.

every garden should have one

What now follows is a comprehensive guide to making compost using six different methods: ranging from the very simplest of techniques to those more complicated so that at least one will be found suitable for your needs.

WHAT AND WHAT NOT TO COMPOST

A good compost, when it is ready, should be a deep brown or black colour and should have no bad odours, indeed, it will generally have a sweet smell. However, care must be taken as to what sort of stuff is put on the compost heap because certain materials will not rot or if they do, may need certain conditions in which to do so. All the following will make good compost: leaves, grass cuttings, dead flowers, nut shells, egg shells, tea leaves, weeds, cuttings from most herbs and shrubs, sawdust, wood-clippings, shredded rags, hair, wood ash, fish bones, seaweed, all animal manures, hay, straw, paper (provided it is thoroughly shredded and soaked in water) and waste from the vacuum cleaner. Never put the following on a compost heap: metal, glass, plastic, bulk paper, thick twigs or branches, oily or greasy materials.

Bulky material such as old swedes and turnips etc., will need shredding into small pieces before it will rot down. Bearing in mind that a compost heap is at its most efficient when constructed of a mixture of materials, never put a mass of one sort of material in one place to rot down, as nine times out of ten it will take ages to do so and the finished result will not be pleasing.

SOURCE OF MATERIALS

Apart from weeds, leaves and cuttings from your own garden, always save the vegetable waste from the kitchen. Neighbours are a good source of material—get them to dump their own waste into a pile in your garden (provided, of course, that they aren't composting themselves). If you live in the countryside, or near stables you will be able to get manure for next to nothing. If you live in the town, greengrocers are a good bet. Go down to your local man with a barrow and bring home his cabbage, cauliflower, sprout cuttings etc. Also, when the trees in your street begin to shed their leaves in Autumn, there will be tons of leaves for the taking, but get there before the road sweepers come around.

1st Method
This is just about as basic as you can get. Simply spread the waste and leaves etc. on the surface of the soil or dig it in. This method makes the soil look a bit unsightly, but it works. This is composting at its most fundamental.

2nd Method
Once a good bucketful of waste has been collected, dig a hole about 1 foot deep and bury it. Do this for every bucketful, systematically over the whole plot of ground. Alternatively, dig a trench and spread the waste along the bottom before covering with soil.

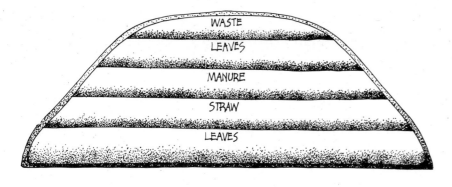

WASTE

LEAVES

MANURE

STRAW

LEAVES

Fig 1

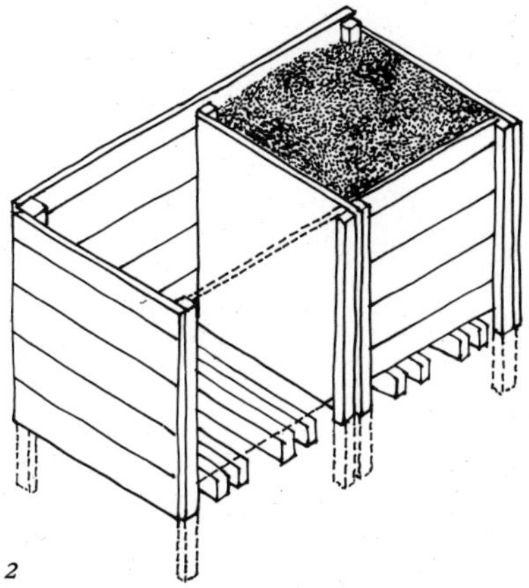

Fig 2

3rd Method

From the two methods just described, the next step up in composting is to make piles of waste, thoroughly mixed and if possible, shredded. Covering it with black plastic sheeting will aid decomposition as this keeps the heat stable—an essential factor in the breaking down of organic matter.

4th Method

This is known as the 'indoor' method and it works on the theory that a heap of organic material will decompose more readily if it is constructed of layers of different types of material. Construct the heap with 6 inch layers of material and try to work in a layer or two of some animal manure *(fig 1)* as these will act as an 'activator' and help to break down the heap quickly. Other 'activators' to use if manure is not available are: dried blood, bone meal, sewage sludge and wood ash.

Any weeds or diseased plants should be placed in the centre of the heap as the heat generated there through decomposition will kill off bacteria and destroy seeds. When the pile has reached about 3 feet high, leave it and begin another: don't make compost heaps too high. Also, to give extra aid to decomposition, air holes must be made and these can easily be constructed by driving in a stake or crowbar at various places. Keep the compost heap moist at all times as a dry heap will not decompose. Conversely don't drown it either, as this prevents a heap from building up a good heat.

5th Method

This is known as the anaerobic method, and for this a large box should be constructed as in *(fig 2)*, consisting of a double compartment with the bottom of each compartment lined with bricks in two double rows which act as air-draughts. The box can be constructed of any old timber or logs and it is a good idea to coat the finished job with a wood preserver or creosote.

Before building the compost heap, begin with a fair amount of twiggy material which will act as a false bottom, thus preventing organic material from blocking up the air draughts. Build up the heap in layers (as in Method 4). When the first box has been filled, start building up in the other compartment and what is most important, cover each finished compartment with black polythene sheeting. This is by far the best method of producing good quality compost.

6th Method

This method utilises specialist activators which can be bought on the market and which are sprinkled on every 6 inch layer of material. These activators are mostly of a chemical origin but there are one or two herbal types and these are to be preferred if possible. The benefit of commercial activators is the speed with which they break down organic matter into rich compost. If you feel lazy and don't mind paying the price, then perhaps this method will suit you.

SOURCES OF MATERIALS

The following list of firms sell compost-grown flower and vegetable seed or untreated seed:

CHASE COMPOST SEEDS, Benhall, Saxmundham, Suffolk.

JAMES HUNTER LTD, Chester, Cheshire (bulk orders only).

Untreated seeds available from:

D. T. BROWN & CO. LTD, Station Road, Poulton le Fylde, Blackpool.

HURST GUNSON COOPER & TABER LTD, Coggeshall, Essex.

E. W. KING & CO. LTD, Colchester, Essex.

MILN MARSTERS, Chester, Cheshire.

J. W. MOLES, Stanway, Colchester, Essex.

FRANK PERTWEE & SONS LTD, Harbour House, Witham, Essex.

SAMUEL DOBIE & SONS LTD, 11 Grosvenor Street, Chester, Cheshire.

THOMPSON & MORGAN (IPSWICH) LTD, London Road, Ipswich, Suffolk.

Organic Activators available from:

CHASE COMPOST SEEDS LTD, Benhall, Saxmundham, Suffolk.

SOCIETIES

BIO-DYNAMIC AGRICULTURAL ASSOCIATION, Broome Farm, Clent, Stourbridge, Worcestershire.

THE GOOD GARDENERS ASSOCIATION, Arkley Manor, Arkley, nr Barnet, Hertfordshire.

HENRY DOUBLEDAY ASSOCIATION, Bocking, Braintree, Essex.

SOIL ASSOCIATION, Walnut Tree Manor, Houghley, Stowmarket, Suffolk.

SERVICES

E. F. DIDCOT, ORGANIC GARDEN SERVICES, 117 Landseer Avenue, Bristol 7. *Advisory organisation on organic gardening as well as supplying organic sundries (i.e seeds, pesticides etc.).*

BIBLIOGRAPHY

JOURNAL OF THE SOIL ASSOCIATION/The Soil Association, Walnut Tree Manor, Houghley, Stowmarket, Suffolk. *(Quarterly)* Price: 25p. Annual subscription: £3.00.

SPAN—SOIL ASSOCIATION NEWS/New Bells Press, Walnut Tree Manor, Houghley, Stowmarket, Suffolk. *(Monthly)* Price: 5p. Annual subscription: 60p.

STAR & FURROW—Bio-Dynamic Agricultural Association, Broome Farm, Clent, Stourbridge, Worcestershire. *(Bi-monthly).*

ABOUT ORGANIC GARDENING, by G. J. Binding/Thorsons Publishers Ltd., Denington Estate, Wellingborough NN8 2RQ.

ASPECTS OF ORGANIC FRUIT CULTURE, by D. Macer Wright/The Soil Association (as above).

THE BASIC BOOK OF ORGANIC FARMING, by Robert Rodale & Brian Furner/Pan Books Ltd.

BOUND TO THE SOIL, by B. Kerr/John Baker (Publishers) Ltd.

CHEMICALS, HUMUS AND THE SOIL, by Donald P. Hopkins/Faber & Faber Ltd.

COMMONSENSE COMPOST MAKING, by M. E. Bruce/Faber & Faber Ltd.

THE COMPLETE BOOK OF COMPOSTING, by J. I. Rodale/The Rodale Press.

COMPLETE VEGETABLE GROWER, by W. E. Shewell-Cooper/Faber & Faber Ltd.

COMPOST : FOR GARDEN PLOT OR THOUSAND ACRE FARM, by F. H. Billington and Ben Casey/Faber & Faber Ltd.

COMPOST MAKING, by Maye Bruce/available from Chase Compost Seeds Ltd, Benhall, Saxmundham, Suffolk. Price: 16p (plus postage).

CONTROL OF SOIL FERTILITY, by G. W. Cooke/Crosby Lockwood & Son Ltd.

DARWIN ON HUMUS AND THE EARTH WORM, introduced by Sir Albert Howard/Faber & Faber Ltd.

DOWN TO EARTH GARDENING, Lawrence D. Hills/Faber & Faber Ltd.

AN ENGLISH ORGANIC FARM, by Sam Mayall/The Soil Association (as above).

FERTILITY FROM TOWN WASTES, by J. C. Wylie/Faber & Faber Ltd.

FERTILITY WITHOUT FERTILISERS, by L. D. Hills/available from The Henry Doubleday Association, Research Association, Bocking, Braintree, Essex. Price: 18p.

FRESH FOOD FROM SMALL GARDENS, by Brian Furner/Stuart & J. M. Watkins Ltd.

HOW TO GROW VEGETABLES & FRUIT BY THE ORGANIC METHOD, by J. I. Rodale/The Rodale Press.

ORGANIC FARMING, by Hugh Chorley/Faber & Faber Ltd.

ORGANIC FERTILIZERS/Fertilizer Journal Ltd.

THE ORGANIC FOODFINDER & DIRECTORY/The Rodale Press.

ORGANIC GARDENING WITHOUT POISONS, by Hamilton Tyker/Van Nostrand-Reinhold Co.

SILENT SPRING, by Rachel Carson/Hamish Hamilton Ltd & Penguin Books Ltd.

SOIL FERTILITY & ANIMAL HEALTH, by William Albrecht/Faber & Faber Ltd.

WORLD OF THE SOIL, by Sir J. Russell/Fontana Books.

The following publications are available from the Henry Doubleday Association (see above). Send for free leaflet :

THE BASIC FOOD GUIDE.

BIOLOGICAL PEST REPORT (Nos. 1 & 2).

COMFREY REPORT (Nos. 1, 2, 3, 4 & 5).

COMPOSTING OF THE TROPICS.

FERTILITY FINDER.

FERTILITY WITHOUT FERTILISERS.

GIVE UP SMOKING BONFIRES.

GOOD TASTE GUIDE.

HOUSEWIVES HELP.

NO DIGGERS REPORT.

OPERATION NIGHTLIGHT.

OPERATION TIGGY WINKLE.

PERFUMES AGAINST PESTS (Parts 1 & 2).

PESTS CONTROL WITHOUT POISONS.

REPORT ON MANURE.

SLUGS & THE GARDENERS.

THE TAGETES EXPERIMENT.

(VARIOUS SPECIALIST REPORTS ON DISEASES.)

WEEDKILLERS WITHOUT WORRY.

COURSES

EWELL COUNTY TECHNICAL COLLEGE, Reigate Road, Ewell, Surrey. *The Department of Biological Studies at the College runs Summer courses on biological approaches to soil husbandry, composting, soil fertility, cultivation, weed control, soil structure and many other subjects.*

THE SOIL ASSOCIATION, Walnut Tree Manor, Haughley, Stowmarket, Suffolk, *runs courses and lectures and produces bulletins and newssheets etc.*

WWOOF (Working Weekends on Organic Farms), 143 Sabine Road, London, SW11. *This organisation arranges weekends whereby people can get practical knowledge of organic husbandry.*

Companion Plants

THERE EXISTS in the vegetable kingdom, a natural relationship between various plants which is both sympathetic and beneficial, enabling one plant to help another in the process of germination, flowering and bearing fruit. Technically this relationship is known as symbiosis but it is commonly known under the heading of 'companion planting' for the simple reason that some plants act as companions to others. What is even more remarkable is the fact that the whole process can be reversed so that a plant will not grow very well when next to one particular species, but will indeed flourish again when placed next to another variety. This indicates that there is both a repelling and attracting influence between all plants. Different forms of plant interaction have now been discovered and this information can be used to advantage, not only in gardening, but in farming as a whole, to produce higher yields and healthier crops, thus eliminating to a greater extent, the need for excessive feeding and pesticides.

This process is known as Bio-Dynamic farming or gardening and is now being practiced more and more because it really works. So next time you come to plan out the vegetable or flower garden, whether by planting seedlings or sowing seeds, take note of the following list and do yourself and your plants a favour.

APPLE TREES (*Malus*)
Plant chives round the base to prevent scab. Plant nasturtiums round the base to prevent woolly aphis. Potatoes and apple trees repel each other.

ANISE (*Pimpinella anisum*)
Anise and coriander aid each other.

ASPARAGUS (*Asparagus officinalis*)
Plant tomatoes next to asparagus. Parsley also aids asparagus.

BASIL (*Ocimum Basilicum*)
Rue hates basil so plant them well away from each other.

BEANS (*Phaseolus and Vicia*)
Plant carrots next to beans. Other aids are beets, cucumbers, cabbages, leeks, celeriac and corn, but carrots are best, except for early potatoes. Runner beans are suppressed by onions.

BEECH TREES (*Fagus*)

BEETS (*Beta vulgaris*)
Beets grow better if sown alongside dwarf beans, kohlrabi, and onions, but are repelled by beans.
Ferns and beech trees repel each other.

BIRCH TREES (*Betula*)
These trees produce leaves that help kill disease in soils. Always add the leaves to a compost heap as they aid decomposition.

BORAGE (*Borago Officinalis*)
Strawberries and borage aid each other and bees love borage.

CABBAGE (*cauliflowers, broccoli, savoys, kale, Brussel sprouts, kohlrabi*)
All the cabbage family are aided by strongly aromatic plants. Early potatoes are an aid as well. Cabbages and strawberries repel each other, as do cabbages and tomatoes.

CHAMOMILE (*Matricaria Chamomilla*)
Chamomile aids onions and cabbages.

CARRAWAY (*Carum Carui*)
Carraway aids peas but repels fennel.

CARROTS (*Daucus carota*)
Carrots suffer greatly from carrot fly, which is diminished by the presence of leeks, salsify, rosemary, wormwood and sage. Do not store apples near carrots as they turn the carrots bitter.

CAULIFLOWER (*Brassica oleracea*)
Cauliflower is aided by celery.

CELERIAC (*Apium graveolens rapeceum*)
Both scarlet runner beans and leeks aid celariac.

CELERY (*Apium graveolens*)
Dwarf beans, leeks, tomatoes and cabbages aid celery.

CHERRY TREES (*Prunus*)
Potatoes are less prone to blight when grown near cherry trees but wheat is suppressed by this fruit.

CHERVIL (*Anthriscus cerefolium*)
Chervil and radishes are companions.

CHIVES (*Allium schoenoprassum*)
Chives aid carrots.

CORN (*Zea mays*)
Sweet corn aids early potatoes and is aided by peas, beans, dill and cucumbers.

CUCUMBERS (*Cucumis sativus*)
Cucumbers are aided by sweet corn, lettuce, celeriac, radishes, kohlrabi and sunflowers. But don't plant potatoes next to cucumbers.

DANDELION (*Taraxacum Officinale*)
Dandelions inhibit the growth of many plants because they emit ethylene gas.

DEAD NETTLE (*Lamium Album*)
Dead nettle is generally beneficial to most vegetables.

DILL (*Anethum graveolens*)
Dill aids cabbages, lettuce, onions and cucumbers.

ELM TREES (*Ulmus*)
Grapes trained on elm trees bear excellent fruit.

EUPHORBIA (*Euphorbiaceae*)
Euphorbias or 'spurges' as they are commonly known, protect tender plants because of the warmth they stimulate in the soil. One species of spurge, *Euphorbia lactea*, helps repel moles, mice and rats if planted in the vicinity of the animals' territory.

FENNEL (*Foeniculum Vulgare*)
Fennel repels carraway, tomatoes, dwarf beans, kohlrabi, coriander and wormwood.

FERNS (*Pteridophyta*)
Compost made from ferns is beneficial to tree seedlings, except beech (*Fagus*) which it repels.

FLAX (*Linum usitatissimum*)
Flax aids the growth of carrots and helps reduce the possibility of disease in potatoes.

FOXGLOVE (*Digitalis purpurea*)
The cut flowers of foxgloves infused in water and used for the drinking water of other cut flowers will help to prolong their life. Foxgloves also aid the growth of many trees.

FRENCH MARIGOLDS (*Tagetes Patula*)
Marigolds aid tomatoes, roses and most vegetables.

FRUIT TREES
Fruit trees in general are aided by tansy, chives, horseradish, nasturtiums, southernwood and stinging nettles.

GARLIC (*Allium sativum*)
Garlic is a great aid to roses, but repels peas and beans.

GLADIOLI
Gladioli are a strong repellent to peas and beans.

GOOSEBERRY (*Ribes grossularia*)
Gooseberries are aided by tomatoes.

GRAPES (*Vitis*)
Hussop, mustard and elm trees aid grapevines.

GRASS
Grass suppresses the root growth of fruit trees.

HERBS
A great many herbs are beneficial additions to any plot of flowers or vegetables by controlling biologically the diseases and insect pests peculiar to individual flowers or vegetables. Such herbs as basil, borage, chervil, chives, dill, hyssop, lavender, parsley, sage and thyme are just some that are worth planting apart from the fact they are delicious for cookery.

HORSERADISH (*Cochlearia armoracia*)
Horseradish aids potatoes.

HYSSOP (*Hyssopus officinalis*)
Hyssop aids grapevines but repels radishes.

KOHLRABI (*Brassica*)
Kohlrabi is aided by beets and onions but repels tomatoes.

LAVENDER (*Lavendula officinalis*)
A beneficial plant to most vegetables.

LEEKS (*Allium porrum*)
Carrots and celery both love leeks.

LETTUCE (*Lactuca sativa*)
Lettuce is aided by strawberries, carrots and radishes. Lettuce aids onions.

LILY OF THE VALLEY (*Convallaria majalis*)
Lily of the valley repels mignotte and narcissus.

MAPLE (*Acer*)
The leaves of maple are an excellent preservative if stored with apples, potatoes, carrots and other root vegetables during Winter.

MARJORAM (*Origanum*)
Marjoram aids most vegetables.

MINT (*Spearmint, applemint, eau-de Cologne mint, etc.*)
The mint family strongly repel ants, moths and other bugs and insects.

NASTURTIUM (*Tropaelum Majus*)
Nasturtiums aid apple trees, radishes and potatoes and strongly repel many insects and bugs.

OAK (*Quercus*)
The leaves of oak are an excellent repellant of slugs, snails and other garden pests, if used as a mulch among plants.

ONIONS (*Allium*)
Onions love beets, chamomile, lettuce and carrots but repels peas and beans.

PARSLEY (*Petroselinum Crispum*)
Parsley aids roses and tomatoes.

PEAS (*Pisum*)
Peas are aided by cucumbers, carrots, sweetcorn, radishes, beans and turnips, and especially by potatoes.

PINE (*Pinus*)
Pine needles aid the growth of strawberries and wheat.

POTATO (*Solanum tuberosum*)
Early potatoes love sweetcorn, beans, peas and cabbage. Horse radishes, if only one or two are planted, aid potatoes. Potatoes increase in the likelihood of getting blight when planted near tomatoes, raspberries, cucumbers, cherry trees and sun flowers.

PUMPKINS (*Cucurbita pepo*)
Pumpkins repel potatoes but aid sweet corn.

RADISHES (*Raphanus sativus*)
Radishes aid peas and lettuce but are repelled by hyssop.

RASPBERRY (*Rubus*)
Raspberries repel blackberries.

ROSEMARY (*Rosmarinus Officinalis*)
Rosemary loves sage and aids carrots.

ROSES (*Rosa*)
Roses are aided by parsley, garlic and mignonette. Boxwood suppresses roses.

RUE (*Ruta graveolens*)
Rue repels basil.

SAGE (*Salvia Officinalis*)
Sage aids cabbage, rosemary and most other vegetables.

SAVORY (*Satureia Hortensis*)
Summer savory aids onions and green beans.

SHALLOTS (*Allium ascalonicum*)
Shallots repel peas and beans.

SOUTHERNWOOD (*Artemesia Abrotanum*)
Southernwood aids fruit trees and cabbages.

SPINACH (*Spinacia oleracea*)
Spinach and strawberries love each other.

SPRUCE (*Picea*)
A mulch of spruce needles aid strawberries.

STINGING NETTLE (*Urtica Dioica*)
Stinging nettles make most plants more resistant to disease.

STRAWBERRIES (*Fragaria*)
Strawberries are aided by lettuce, spinach, dwarf beans, borage, pine needles and spruce needles. Cabbage and strawberries repel each other.

SUNFLOWER (*Helianthus annus*)
Sunflowers stunt the growth of potatoes and are inhibited themselves when grown near this root crop. Cucumbers grow well next to sunflowers.

TANSY (*Tanacetum Vulgore*)
Tansy repels many harmful insects.

THYME (*Thymus Vulgaris*)
Thyme is beneficial to most plants in the garden.

TULIP (*Tulipa*)
The growth of wheat is suppressed by tulips.

TOMATOES (*Lycopersicon esculentum*)
Tomatoes aid cabbages, parsley and asparagus. Tomatoes repel apricot trees, gooseberries and lower the resistance of potatoes to blight.

TURNIPS (*Brassica rapa*)
Turnips aid peas.

VALERIAN (*Valeriana Officinalis*)
Valerian is beneficial to most vegetables.

WALLFLOWER (*Cheiranthus*)
Wallflowers aid apple trees.

BIBLIOGRAPHY

COMPANION PLANTS, by Helen Philbrick & Richard B. Gregg/Robinson & Watkins Ltd.

GARDENING WITHOUT WORK, by Ruth Stout/ The Devin-Adair Company, 1 Park Avenue, Old Greenwich, Connecticut 06870.

HOW TO ENJOY YOUR WEEDS, by Audrey Wynne/ Frederick Muller Ltd.

SOIL FERTILITY, by E. E. Pfeiffer/Faber & Faber Ltd.

USING WAYSIDE PLANTS, by Nelson Coon/ Hearthside Press, 445 Northern Boulevard, Great Neck, N.Y. 11021.

WEEDS AND WHAT THEY TELL, by E. E. Pfeiffer/ The Bio-Dynamic Farming & Garden Association.

The following publications are available from THE HENRY DOUBLEDAY ASSOCIATION, Bocking, Braintree, Essex:

PERFUMES AGAINST PESTS.

THE TAGETES REPORT.

Drying, Pressing and Preserving Flowers

Care and patience are all that are needed for this craft as a hurried, clumsy job can ruin specimens. Almost any flower, grass, leaf or berry can be preserved in some way and although we have listed suitable specimens to try out, in some of the processes you should experiment with whatever you can obtain.

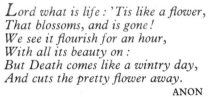

Lord what is life: 'Tis like a flower,
That blossoms, and is gone!
We see it flourish for an hour,
With all its beauty on:
But Death comes like a wintry day,
And cuts the pretty flower away.
                                      ANON

PRESSING

You will need the following materials, according to which method you use:

1 Botanical drying paper or blotting paper.
2 Some sheets of glass about 6 inches square to 1 foot square.
3 A bookbinder's press, a cool iron, or book weights etc.
4 Sheets of cardboard.

1st Method

On a piece of cardboard, lay a sheet of the botanical or blotting paper that has been heated gently in an oven. Lay on top of this your specimen taking care to arrange the leaves and flowers in a pleasing way (prune any leaves or stems if necessary). Lay over the specimen another sheet of hot drying paper and finally top the whole lot with a sheet of cardboard. Next, either place the 'sandwich' in a press under gentle pressure, or weight down under some heavy books or other suitable objects. Every day for the next four weeks, remove from the pressure and replace the drying paper with fresh, hot sheets. An expensive but perfect method of pressing flowers.

2nd Method

On a sheet of drying paper, lay out your specimen nicely and cover with another sheet of drying paper. Apply a cool iron and press until most of the moisture has been removed, replacing the sheets of drying paper as it becomes necessary. Finally, put the specimen under pressure between sheets of drying paper and cardboard for 1 week. This method is more suitable for fleshy specimens.

3rd Method

On a sheet of drying paper, lay out your specimen and cover with another sheet of drying paper. Sandwich this between sheets of newspaper and lay the lot under a carpet. Leave it there for six weeks to three months according to the specimen (i.e. more fleshy specimens will need longer to dry out). With this method, leaves, sprays and autumn foliage can be suitably pressed.

4th Method

On a sheet of drying paper, lay out your specimen and then carefully lay on top a sheet of glass. With this method, you can see just how the specimen will look after pressing, and final alterations can be made before finally covering with newspaper and putting in the press, or under a weight of books. This method takes about 6–8 weeks to dry according to the fleshiness of the specimen.

Almost any specimen can be dried and pressed with one of the above methods. When pressing leaves, remember to use only mature specimens otherwise blistering can occur.

DRYING

Most people have a reasonable access to a piece of countryside and even on grass verges by roadsides or on building sites, plenty of material can be found. When out on your travels, look out for the following:

FLOWERS (WILD)	FRUIT & CATKINS
Bullrush	Alder
Carraway	Ash
Chervil	Beech
Cow Parsnip	Crab Apple
Dill	Dogrose
Hogweed	Hawthorn
Lovage	Hazel
Masterwort	Juniper
Ribwort Plantain	Larch
Rosebay	Maple
Saxifrage	Mistletoe
Sweet Cicely	Oak
Tansy	Pine
Teasle	Snowberry
Thistle	Silver Birch
Travellers Joy	Woody Nightshade
Yarrow	

FOLIAGE
Grasses and Sedges
Ferns
Maple
Beech

Most of this material will have dried naturally so will be ready to use, but should any further drying be necessary, simply stand in a jar in a warm room for a few weeks. Berries may be varnished when completely dry.

1st Method

This is for drying flowerheads. Flowers should be bunched together and tied at the stems, using no more than half a dozen flowerheads per bunch. Hang each bunch upside down in a cool, dark place such as a cellar or shed. Always keep out of sunlight and prevent the bunches from getting damp.

The only special treatment necessary applies to Hydrangea flower heads. Wait until the flowers have begun to 'flush' in the Autumn whilst still on the plant before attempting to cut them for indoor use. The flowers should then be placed upright in a vase containing a 2-inch depth of water and when all this water has been used up, they should then be left to dry naturally.

The following cultivated flowers are well suited for drying purposes:

Acroclinium	Eryngium
Achilea	Helichrysum
Amaranthus	Solidago
Astilbe	Monkshood
Anaphalis	Stachys Lanata
Delphinium	Rhodanthe
Echinops	Stachys

2nd Method

This is for drying grasses, rushes, sedges and ferns. With some of these, nature drys them out naturally but if further drying is necessary, hang them up in small bunches as with the flower heads. A good point to remember is to try and pick specimens of grass when the stamens are just beginning to appear at the bottom of the spike. Never pick anything on a wet or damp day or when there has been a heavy dew.

The following is just a few names of the many grasses, rushes, sedges, etc., to be found growing in most areas quite commonly:

GRASSES	SEDGES
Cats Tail	Moor Sedge
Crested Hair Grass	Bottle Sedge
Crested Dogs Tail	Pond Sedge
Common Couch	Drooping Sedge
Common Cord Grass	Common Sedge
Meadow Fescue	
Ratstail Fescue	FERNS
Cocksfoot	Bracken
Purple Moor Grass	Hard Fern
Heath Grass	Harts Tongue
Giant Fescue	Black Spleenwort
Red Fescue	Common Spleenwort
Quaking Grass	Male Fern
Wood Melick	Lady Fern
Hairy Brome	Common Poly-pody
Bearded Couch	
Wild Oat	
Meadow Oat	
White Bent.	

PRESERVING

Sometimes, a very fleshy specimen will not press or dry successfully and so artificial preserving is the answer. However, these three following methods can be used to preserve almost anything.

1st Method (GLYCERINE)
This method is more suited to evergreen foliage with shiny leaves such as laurel, holly, rhododendron etc. Glycerine has an unusual effect on specimens for, after treatment, those stored in the dark will have a different colour from those left in the light. In this way, a whole range of colours can be achieved.

Specimens must be chosen from plants which are fully mature—never use any damaged, blotched or diseased leaves. Dilute the glycerine in hot water at the rate of two parts of water to one part glycerine. Crush the end of the stems of the specimens and after standing them overnight in water, put them upright in a vase of the cold glycerine mixture. The length of time needed for this process to complete will vary considerably as some leaves such as Beech will take nearly a month, whilst Rhododendron and Holly will only take about four days. The sign to watch out for is when the glycerine can be seen clearly in the veins of the leaves. Then the whole specimen should be removed from the mixture and allowed to dry for a few days in a cool, dark place.

The following plants can be preserved in this way:

Berberis	Laurel
Beech	Lime
Box	Camellia
Cotoneaster	Mahonia
Choisya	Magnolia
Eucalyptus	Pear
Holly	Rhododendron
Oak	Sweet Chestnut

2nd Method (BORAX)
This method is more suited to fleshy specimens and those with delicate petals. A quantity of powdered borax and an airtight box will be needed. Put a good quantity of the borax in the bottom of the box and then lay the specimen in the powder, making sure that it is thoroughly covered, especially the petals. Shut the box tightly and leave it for about 3–4 weeks. Then the specimen should be removed and all the excess borax carefully blown off it.

3rd Method (SILICA GEL)
This method is used in exactly the same way as with borax, except that more care must be taken to keep it from the light. This process takes only about two weeks to complete.

Both borax and silica gel will need sifting after use to prevent lumping.

Dyeing Specimens
Should you wish to colour seedheads, grasses and ferns etc. after they have been dried, then there are a number of ways of doing so. The easiest and by far the cheapest, is to use a fabric dye such as a Dylon cold-water dye, or Procion M dye. In both cases, these dyes are cold-water dyes—never use a hot-water dye otherwise you will absolutely ruin the specimens. The flowerheads or grasses must be tied in small bunches and left submerged in the dye for a couple of hours but before plunging them into the dye bath, soak the specimens thoroughly for 12 hours as this helps the dye to penetrate into the fibres. After dyeing, the bunches should be hung up to dry somewhere warm.

Another way to colour specimens is to dip them in paint and good effects can be had from using both oil- and water-bound paints. Try using lacquers, emulsion, gloss and varnish as well. Some wood stains can also give pleasing colours. Apart from dipping in paint, brushing the paint on is a good way and much more economical, but more care must be taken.

The recipe for Procion dye will be found on p. 66. For dyeing with vegetable dyes, use the method described at the end of the basketry chapter (see p. 108).

Other Uses
There is a definite craft in mounting wild flowers, leaves and grasses under glass and then framing them to form a picture. It would take time to give a detailed plan on how to do this but here are a few rules which can be remembered as well as a couple of ways to mount the specimens:

1 Always allow a reasonable space around the arrangement otherwise the finished picture may look out of proportion.

2 Dried flowers have delicate colours so avoid mounting them on lurid, bright-coloured card. White and black are the most successful 'colours', but experiment with dark greens, dark blues and other sombre colours.

3 Use the tiniest amount of glue to stick specimens to the mount and always use a clear glue such as Bostik. The glueing is the hardest part of the whole process so be very, very careful as delicate wild flowers fall to bits in clumsy hands.

4 Choose a simple frame and avoid heavy or pompous frames as these will kill the delicacy of the mounted specimens.

As well as mounting under glass, specimens can be glued to card and then covered with a layer of clear self-adhesive cellophane or plastic such as Transpaseal or Fablon. This method of mounting is ideal for making use of specimens when constructing greetings cards, as the clear plastic coating gives perfect protection from handling.

SOURCES OF MATERIALS

Unless bookbinding is being considered as well, buying a book press is an expensive business as books themselves are just as effective for pressing botanical specimens.

Botanical paper, blotting paper and card can be obtained from a local handicrafts shop or from :
KETTLES, 127 High Holborn, London WC1.
NATURAL FERN DISPLAY, 73 Monmouth Street, London WC2H 9DG. *(Big selection of dried grasses, seedheads, ferns and flowers for sale.)*

See the dyeing chapter for addresses of stockists selling dyes to colour plants.
A very good selection of papers can be found at :
PAPER CHASE, 216 Tottenham Court Road, London W1. *Or try making your own paper (see pp. 110–111).*

BIBLIOGRAPHY

COLLINS POCKET BOOK OF WILD FLOWERS, by D. McClintock & R. S. Fitter/Collins Sons & Co. Ltd.
THE CONCISE BRITISH FLORA *in colour*, by Keeble Martin/Ebury Press.
DRIED FLOWER ARRANGEMENT, by Winifride

Morrison/B. T. Batsford Ltd.
DRIED FLOWER ARRANGEMENT, by Edwin Rohrer/Van Nostrand Reinhold Co., New York.
DRIED FLOWERS FOR DECORATION, by Edwin Rohrer/Van Nostrand Reinhold Co., New York.
DRIED FLOWERS FOR DECORATION, by Violet Stevenson/David & Charles Ltd.
DRYING AND PRESERVING FLOWERS, by Winifride Morrison/B. T. Batsford Ltd.
ENCYCLOPAEDIA OF FLOWER ARRANGING, by Sheila McQueen/Faber & Faber Ltd.
THE OXFORD BOOK OF WILD FLOWERS, by S. Wary & N. Gregory/Oxford University Press.

PRESSED-FLOWER CRAFT STUDIOS TO VISIT

England
BUCKINGHAMSHIRE
WINIFRIDE MORRISON, Bolter End Cottage, Lane End, nr High Wycombe. Tel. High Wycombe 881621 (off B482 Marlow to Stokenchurch Road)
British flowers and foliage pressed and dried, then used to make individual pictures, signed by the artist and never duplicated.
CORNWALL
MAURICE AND MARGARET LEADBETTER, Hustyn Mill, Burlawn, Wadebridge. Tel. Wadebridge 2540
Specialists in high-quality colourful floral collages. Selection of framed pictures and unframed panels always available.
Resident, call any time.
HERTFORDSHIRE
PATRICIA BESWICK, Thele, Great Amwell, nr Ware. Tel. Ware 870040
Dried flower pictures and wall decorations.
Wales
ANGLESEY
ANGLESEY CRAFTWORKERS, High Point, Llanfairpwll. Tel. Llanfairpwll 342
Floral pictures using dried flowers, grasses and leaves from the countryside.
Northern Ireland
TYRONE
THE PIPER'S CAVE, Cady, Cookstown. Tel STD 064-872 3615
Dried floral arrangements, some with wooden bases.

Leaf Lace

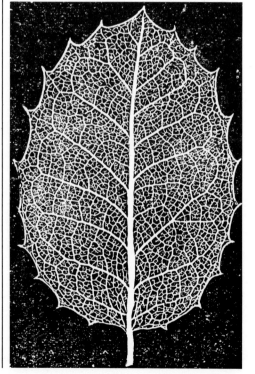

The best sort of leaves to skeletonise are those that are evergreen, i.e. holly, laurel, mahonia and rhododendron, but any thick, veiny leaves will do: magnolia, for instance, skeletonises beautifully.

There are two ways to remove the fleshy tissue from a leaf. One is to put it in a saucepan with a handful of washing soda, cover it with water and after bringing it to the boil, allow it to stand for about $1\frac{1}{2}$ hours. The second way is to mix together 4 tablespoonfuls of caustic soda and $\frac{1}{2}$ pint sodium hypochlorite with one pint of water and bring to the boil. Drop in the leaf and simmer until the leaf is limp whereupon it should be removed by first running cold water into the pot to displace the soda solution (don't put your hands in it).

With both of these methods, the leaf, after boiling, must then be gently scraped with a tooth-brush to remove the tissue. Great care is paramount because the leaf veins are very delicate. When all the tissue has been removed, place the skeleton between two layers of blotting paper to dry. If a light-coloured skeleton is desired, it can be dropped into a solution of domestic bleach overnight and then thoroughly rinsed and dried.

177

posies, petals, & pot-pourris.

This gripping scent is theme and subject,
Whereas—however well they look—
The flowerbeds, the lawn, the garden,
Are but the cover of a book.
FROM 'JULY', BY PASTERNAK

There may have been many occasions when you wished that you could bring indoors the smells of the countryside and garden; new-mown hay and the smell of the fields, or the sweet perfumes of the herbery and herbacious border, and keep these smells with you into winter. Well, to a certain extent, you can do this if the flowers and leaves of your choice are preserved in a potpourri or sachet. Many ancient peoples knew how to do this with their incense and perfumes, and there has always been a need for sweet odours in the home, especially so today. In some cases, the scents of certain flowers will help repel insects, while others help to ward off mould and other bacteria which might well destroy books and clothing.

There are two ways to use these flower mixtures. In the first case, a potpourri, is normally a varying mixture of spices, herbs and dried leaves and flowers and is left in open bowls around the house so that its sweet odours fill the room or rooms. In the second case, a sachet, is normally either one special herb or flower, e.g. lavender, or a special mixture, which is packed into a muslin bag and then left in clothes drawers, under pillows, in book cases and to scent bed linen or repel insects etc.

MATERIALS

Apart from the flowers or leaves chosen to dominate the general odour of a mixture, other types of botanicals will be needed as 'fixatives' which help prolong the life of a mixture. A general list is now shown of all the common fixatives available, as well as other botanicals which may be included to add colour to a mixture.

Allspice: Used as a fixative for spicy mixtures.

Ambrosia: Use the herbal scented leaves only as a blending influence in a mixture.

Bachelor's Buttons: Use the flowers as a colourful additive to a mixture.

Balsam of Peru: Use as a fixative.

Balsam of Tolu: Use as a fixative.

Basil: Use the leaves of common basil in mixtures to give a spicy scent. Purple basil is a good colour additive.

Bay: Use the leaves to give a 'carnation' aroma to mixtures.

Black Malva: Use the deep purple flowers as a colour additive.

Borax: Use as a fixative.

Cardomon: Use the whole seeds as a spicy, fragrant addition to mixtures.

Calamus: This root has many uses. It is most commonly used as a fixative for prolonging the strengths of other botanicals, but is equally good as an insect repellant.

Calendula: Use the flowers as a colour additive.

Carraway: Use the seeds as a spicy ingredient in mixtures.

Cedarwood Chips: Cedarwood has a strong aroma so care must be taken that it does not overpower more delicate scents. A good fixative and an equally good repellant.

Cloves: One of our strongest fragrant spices and a good fixative.

Coriander: Use the seeds as a spicy ingredient to mixtures.

Cinnamon: Use as a fixative. Commonly used in rose potpourris.

Costmary: Use the leaves in mixtures. Gives linen a pleasant smell if used in a sachet.

Gum Benzoin: A common fixative usually applied at the rate of 1 oz of gum to 2 quarts of flowers.

Gum Storax: A common fixative used at the same rate as gum benzoin. Both these gums are better if finely ground.

German Rue: A lovely addition to any mixture.

Hollyhock: Use the flowers to colour mixtures.

Lavender: Best if used on its own in sachets for scenting linen etc., or used with discretion in mixtures.

Lemon Geranium: Use the leaves or dried stems in mixtures and sachets for scenting linen.

Lemon Fruit: Use the dried peel as a fixative.

Lemon Verbena: A sweet fragrance that must be used with subtlety in mixtures.

Mace: A spicy smell for a spicy mixture.

Marjoram: A herbal scent very useful in a herb-dominant mixture.

Mint *(Eau de Cologne, Apple, Orange, Spearmint)* : All the mints are very strong and care

'The Approach' by Betty Swanwick, A.R.A.

must be taken when adding them to any mixture.

Nutmeg: A spicy addition to a mixture.

Oils (*i.e. Oil of Bergamot, Oil of Lavender, Oil of Eucalyptus*) : Use these oils very sparingly as fixatives.

Orange Fruit: Use the dried peel as a fixative.

Orris: Use the root as a fixative. Thoroughly recommended as its fragrance improves with age.

Patchouli: Another powerful fragrance. Use the leaves with discretion.

Rose: The most popular and perhaps the most beautiful addition to any mixture. The best aromas come from the Damask and Old English roses such as: Ispahan, Omar Khayyam, Belle Amour, Hebes Lip, Boule de Neige, Madame Isaac Pereire, Celestial, Zephirine Drouhin, Ruskin, Moss Salet, Musk Buff Beauty and Alba Celestial.

Rose Geranium: A wonderfully delicate fragrance which goes well with other geraniums and lemon verbena.

Rosemary: Use the leaves in herbal mixtures. It also goes well with Rue.

Sage: Use the leaves in herbal mixtures.

Sandalwood: The wood chips are best used as a fixative for rose mixtures.

Southernwood: Use on its own in sachets as a good moth repellent and for scenting sheets and line, or as an additive to mixtures.

Sweet Fern: Use the leaves in mixtures to give a pine-type fragrance.

Sweet Melilot: Can be used alone in sachets or the vanilla-fragrant flowers can be in pot-pourri mixtures.

Tangerine Fruit: Use the dried peel as a fixative.

Woodruff: A lovely fragrance, reminiscent of new-mown hay. Use on its own in sachets or in mixtures.

Winter Savoury: A good insect repellant, especially against fleas. Use in sachets for the bedding of pet dogs and cats etc.

Wormwood: A good moth repellant. Use alone in sachets or as an additive to mixtures.

Vetiver: Use the root as a fixative.

HARVESTING THE BLOSSOM AND LEAVES

As a general rule, never pick bruised, damaged or infected flowers and leaves as this will almost certainly ruin a mixture. Flowers are best picked just before their peak of opening. The day must be dry, and always try to collect material about mid-morning, when the sun has dried up the dew. Never pick anything in the afternoon as the strength of the fragrance will have begun to diminish.

Drying off the blossom and leaves is important too. Lay the leaves or blossom in single layers on sheets of paper in a cool, dry place; turning every day for 2–3 weeks until they are perfectly dry. Avoid piling them in heaps as this will brown and rot blossom and leaves alike.

RECIPES

Pot Pourris

We will give some standard recipes but you can experiment yourself with your own favourite ingredients. Apart from the ingredients mentioned, you will need a number of wide-necked glass or earthenware jars (never use plastic containers).

Several pounds of coarse salt are also needed, but cooking salt is just as good except that it is more expensive. Incidentally, all the jars must have air-tight lids.

ROSE POT POURRI   Damask rose petals are best, but pick what you will. Put 2-inch layers with a light covering of salt in a glass or earthenware jar until it is absolutely full and then tightly cover it with the lid. Store it in a cool dark place for one week. After storing, empty the mixture out on to a big sheet of paper and loosen all the petals from the salt into a bowl. Mix together the following ingredients:

1 oz orris root (ground or at least finely crushed); $\frac{1}{2}$ teaspoon ground cloves; $\frac{1}{2}$ teaspoon ground cinnamon; $\frac{1}{2}$ teaspoon ground mace; 6 drops Oil of Geranium; 20 drops Oil of Eucalyptus; 10 drops Oil of Bergamot.

Add the petals to this mixture, thoroughly mix and return all of it to the jar. Cover it tightly and store it for 2 weeks before using.

ANOTHER ROSE POT POURRI   Put an equal quantity of rose and lavender blossom in a large bowl and add $\frac{1}{2}$ lb ground orris root. To every 2 lb of this mixture add 2 oz each of crushed cloves, ground cinnamon, ground allspice and lemon peel. Mix thoroughly and then it is ready for use.

OLD ENGLISH POT POURRI   Mix in a bowl, equal amounts of rose petals, lemon verbena leaves, geranium leaves and any other flowers or leaves of your choice. To every 1 lb of this mixture, add $\frac{1}{4}$ lb salt, $\frac{1}{4}$ lb Barbados Sugar, and $\frac{1}{2}$ oz each of ground orris root, cinnamon, cloves, gum storax and gum benzoin. Put the whole, thoroughly-amalgamated mixture in to a jar and store it with the lid off for a week, stirring every day. After this, pour it into a bowl for use.

ANOTHER OLD ENGLISH POT POURRI   Take two bowls. In one put flower petals of your choice with an equal amount of mixed rose and lavender blossom. In the other bowl, mix together 4 oz ground orris root, 4 oz gum benzoin, 2 oz ground cinnamon, 2 oz whole cloves, 1 oz cardomon seeds and 6 lb of coarse salt. Next, fill each glass or earthenware jar with alternate 1-inch layers of mixture No. 1 and mixture No. 2 until full. Compress each layer down firmly with a flat piece of wood. Fasten the lids tightly and leave the mixture to mature for 3 months by which time the pot pourri should be ready for use.

A SPICY POT POURRI   Mix together in a bowl $\frac{1}{2}$ oz each of cloves, ground cinnamon, ground nutmeg, allspice, borax and ground orris root. Add 1 lb of salt and a handful of either orange, tangerine or lemon peel. Thoroughly mix and the pot pourri is then ready for use.

Sachets

Almost anything will be O.K. on its own in a sachet, but more common ones generally contain eau-de-cologne mint, spearmint, lavender or woodruff.

LAVENDER SACHET   The whole flowerhead plus about 1 foot of the stem must be cut from the plant and bunches tied together at the stems and hung upside down, should be stored in a cool dark place until absolutely dry. The flowerheads when nice and brittle, can then be broken off the stems and packed into muslin bags, ready for use.

The following two recipes are for special sachets:

VIOLET SACHET Mix together 4 lb wheat starch, 1 lb ground orris root, 1 drachm oil of cloves and 1 drachm oil of bergamot. Mix thoroughly and fill muslin bags with the mixture, carefully sealing them. This mixture will strongly resemble the perfume of violets, especially if attar of lemon is added.

ROSE SACHET Mix together 1 lb rose petals, ½ teaspoonful of rose oil, ½ lb sandalwood chips, and 3 oz of rose geranium leaves. Fill muslin bags with this mixture as above.

Oil Extraction

The oils of various botanicals can be obtained either from a chemist or a good herbalist, but if you would like to extract them yourself, the following method is a good one.

Obtain a fair amount of cotton tissue or wadding from a chemist. Saturate the wadding with olive oil and cut it up into 1 foot-square pieces. Take a metal or glass tray and place on it one of the saturated pieces of wadding. Sprinkle on top a layer of whatever botanical you intend extracting the aroma from, and on top of this place another piece of saturated wadding. Go on like this, layer by layer until you have used up all the flowers or leaves. The oil-sodden wadding will then soak up the odour of the botanicals. Ideally, the flowers or leaves should be replaced with fresh ones each day but this may be impossible. After three days, press the oil from the wadding and store it in covered bottles until ready for use.

Pomanders

These are oranges impregnated with whole cloves and lightly dusted with cinnamon orris root or allspice and are generally used to scent clothes in wardrobes and linen etc. They are very easy to make, cheap to produce and can either be left as they are, or encased in a decorative pottery shell.

Materials

You will need some good-sized oranges, a fair quantity of whole cloves, some ground cinnamon, ground orris root or ground allspice, a roll of ¼ inch wide Sellotape, some lengths of coloured ribbon, a bradawl, a small screwdriver or some other pointed instrument, and a roll of silver paper.

METHOD

Leave the oranges to dry and thus dehydrate for a couple of weeks. Next, put a band of Sellotape round the middle of each orange (this is to mark the place where you will secure and tie the ribbons to hang the finished pomanders by). Then, making holes about ⅛ inch to ¼ inch apart, pierce the surface of each orange with the bradawl or screwdriver, leaving the Sellotape band untouched. The distance between each hole must be such that when the cloves are pressed into them, there should be a very small space between each clove to allow for further shrinkage of the orange. When all the oranges have been impregnated with cloves so that only the Sellotape band remains showing, lightly dust the orange with cinnamon or the spice of your choice, and wrap up each one in silver paper. Store them in a dry place for about 6–8 weeks. Finally, remove the pomanders from their silver paper and tie round each a length of pretty ribbon and finish it in a bow.

The clay shells mentioned earlier, should be made in two halves. After firing, they should be glued together with a pomander inside. Each clay ball must have a number of holes about ¼ inch in diameter to allow the aroma to escape. Decorate them as you wish.

SOURCES OF MATERIALS

You can grow many of the herbs yourself, in a garden, an allotment or even a window box. The following suppliers will stock seeds and in some cases, young plants, and will send them through the post:

LAXTON AND BUNYARD NURSERIES, Brampton, Huntingdon.
THE OLD RECTORY HERB GARDEN, Ightham, Kent.
JOHN SCOTT, THE ROYAL NURSERIES, Merriot,

Somerset.
STOKE LACY HERB FARM, Bromyard, Herefordshire.
THOMPSON AND MORGAN (IPSWICH) LTD, London Road, Ipswich, Suffolk.

The more unusual spices and fixatives, as well as oils and extracts, can be purchased from the more specialist herbalists, but check your local man before writing to the following people:
G. BALDWIN, 173 Walworth Road, London SE17.
   Apart from being one of Londons oldest herbalists, this shop boasts a very wide range of unusual and less unobtainable extracts, oils and fixatives. Mail order by arrangement.
MARGARET BRUCE, Station House, Wolsingham, Co. Durham.
   Stocks perfume oils, rare herbs, incenses, extracts, fixatives and other unusual materials. Write for a detailed catalogue, price 30p.
PERFUME GARDEN OILS, 56a Lancaster Road, London W11. Tel. 01-270 6310
   These people sell the widest selection of oils anywhere in the country and at a reasonable price. Rosemary, patchouli, orange, lemon, peppermint, resins, gums and lots more.

BIBLIOGRAPHY

THE HERBALIST, by Joseph E. Meyer/The Oak Tree Press.

PLACES TO VISIT

NORFOLK LAVENDER LTD, Caley Mill, Heacham. Tel. Heacham 384
Growers and distillers of lavender oil. Perfumery products, lavender perfume, talcum powder, toilet soap, bath salts and bath cubes. Hand-made sachets. Lavender for men, after-shave etc. Open daily 9 am–5 pm Monday to Friday.

Wayside Wines and Other Delights

From claret and burrage
Are fain to encourage
That mystic high-stepper,
Professor von Pepper,
To show (by the proxy
Of hydrogen-oxy)
The horrible features
Of all the dread creatures
That foes to wine bottles
Would pour down our throttles.

OLD TEETOTAL POEM
W. S. GILBERT

ALTHOUGH WRITERS ABOUT wine have involved themselves in a lot of pomp and circumstance, the basic processes involved are simple and whether expensive wine-making equipment, or second-hand make-do material is used, the fundamentals of the art are the same. Wine can be made from virtually anything edible growing in the field, wayside or garden: from the leaves, stems, flowers, fruit or roots of wild and cultivated plants so that the range of wine available, given a good cross-section of recipes, is almost infinite. By keeping to, and sticking to, one or two important rules, subtle and beautiful wines can be made at all times of the year so that a continuous stock is available for use.

Terminology and processes

CLARIFIERS

Sometimes a wine will remain cloudy even after a number of strainings so that a *'clarifier'* has to be added to induce the floating particles to sink to the bottom of the jar or bottle so that the clear liquor can be strained off. There are a number of clarifiers good for this purpose:

(a) EGGWHITES
One white of an egg beaten into a pint of new wine and well dissolved should be added to the main stock of liquor at the rate of one eggwhite to every 15–20 gallons.

(b) EGG SHELLS
The shells must first be baked in a slow oven until they are brittle and then crumbled into a fine dust. To each bottle of new wine, one good pinch is added which should be sufficient to clear the cloudiest wine.

(c) ISINGLASS
Isinglass can be obtained from any chemist. Only one quarter of an ounce must be used to every 10 gallons of liquor as too much isinglass can have a detrimental effect on the wine. The isinglass should first be dissolved in a little warm wine and then added to the main stock.
  With both eggshells, eggwhites and isinglass, the effect on the wine does not alter the taste.

(d) SUGAR CANDY
Add a small piece to each bottle but allow for the extra sweetness when working out the sugar content for a sweet, medium, or dry wine.

(e) PECTIC ENZYME
This is used generally for fruit wines such as apple, pear, plum and cherry which are difficult to clear after the fermenting process. A teaspoonful of pectic enzyme should be added to each gallon of liquor at the onset of fermenting.

Fermenting

This is simply the action of the yeast on the prepared liquor or *'must'*. During this process, the yeast feeds on the sugar and gives off carbon dioxide which rises up in bubbles to the surface of the liquid. It also gives off alcohol. The ratio of carbon dioxide to alcohol is roughly 50–50.

Flavouring

This comes from the plants or parts of edible plants that form the flavour of the wine. A more detailed analysis follows later on in the chapter.

Lees

This is the sediment that forms at the bottom of the jars during fermentation.

Must

The *'must'* is the prepared liquid which ferments and contains the flavouring, water, and possibly a clarifier. Sugar and yeast are added to the must later.

Nutrient

A yeast nutrient is added to a wine to boost the action of the yeast where the liquor may have a deficiency in trace elements, especially acid. To overcome this, a whole lemon's juice should be added during the fermentation process.

Racking

By *'racking'* is meant the syphoning off clear wine from the lees. All wines should be racked *at least* twice before use.

Sugar

The amount of sugar per gallon of liquid determines the sweetness of a wine, i.e. sweet, medium or dry. As a general rule, 2 lb of sugar per gallon will produce a dry wine and 3–3½ lb of sugar per gallon will produce a sweet wine.

Yeast

Yeast is a tiny plant organism which feeds off the sugar content in the wine. The yeast feeds until the sugar content is exhausted, or, until there has been so much alcohol produced that the yeast is then killed. In dry wines the yeast has exhausted the sugar supply and in sweet wines the yeast has been killed off by a high alcohol content.
  There are a number of yeasts available that are used for the fermentation process. Most are easily obtained from bakers, health food shops or wine-making specialists. The basic types are:

(1) BAKER'S YEAST:
Use only fresh baker's yeast as it tends to deteriorate quickly. This is a fast-acting yeast and is generally the cheapest.

(2) DRIED YEAST:
Available from health food shops and some grocery shops. With dried yeast, there is the advantage of it not 'going off' as it keeps for ages.

(3) WINE YEAST:
There are now a number of special wine yeasts available which have been specially cultivated for the fermenting of specific wines. For instance, there are champagne yeasts, sherry yeasts and so on. There is also an all-purpose wine yeast which is suitable for making most wines. With all these special yeasts, the instructions (which are usually on the pack) *must* be followed carefully.

(4) NO-YEAST RECIPES:
Some fruit wines such as plum or apple may be made without the addition of a prepared yeast to the must because there may be wild yeast on the skins of the fruit. Using a no-yeast recipe is strictly a hit-and-miss business because some strains of wild yeast are of poor quality and will produce a low alcohol content. If one of these recipes is being used, then the fruit *must* be absolutely fresh, i.e. picked and prepared the same day. Also, as wild yeasts tend to grow only on fruit, then only fruit wines can be made this way.

Water
For most recipes the water must be lukewarm for the yeast to work properly, with an ideal temperature of 65°–75°F. This temperature must be kept constant during the fermenting process.

Equipment essential for the job (see diagram)
(1) Large, deep bowls or plastic pails for holding the must.
(2) Glass or polythene funnels in two sizes: 5 inch for fermentation jars and 2½ inch for bottles.
(3) Fermentation jars. These are special jars obtainable from wine suppliers with a special airlock or fermentation trap fitted in the neck. Although one can improvise with empty cider flagons and use three layers of cotton material tightly tied over the necks as a substitute for an airlock, it is well worth obtaining the proper equipment because it helps to keep out harmful bacteria that can ruin a good wine.
(4) A measuring jug.
(5) A plastic strainer of a good-quality fine muslin.
(6) Three feet of rubber or plastic ½-inch tubing for racking purposes.
(7) A large saucepan for boiling the flavouring if necessary.
(8) New corks and foil caps.
(9) A good quantity of wine bottles of varying sizes up to 1 gallon capacity.

The Basic Process of Producing a Standard Wine
(1) The flavouring, whether it be fruits, nuts, berries, roots, leaves or flowers must first be crushed, pressed, boiled or soaked to extract the flavour.
(2) Water is added to the flavouring in a plastic pail (never use metalware for wine making) and if necessary, the pectic enzyme should be added as well. Stir thoroughly and cover tightly with a lid. Keep the must warm.
(3) The sugar and yeast should be added to the lukewarm must. If bakers yeast is being used, it should first be creamed with some of the warm must. Generally, one heaped teaspoon per gallon is a good guide for an all-purpose yeast. Stir the whole contents of the must thoroughly and leave for three days to 'short' ferment. Keep the air out by keeping a lid on the bowl or pail.
(4) On the 4th day, the must should be strained through muslin into the fermentation jars by means of a large funnel. If necessary, add a clarifier at this stage. Never fill the jar right to the brim but allow an inch of air below the air lock or cloth covering.
(5) Topping up. Always keep some of the must back to top up the level of liquor as during the second or 'long' fermentation process, the level will decrease.
(6) The wine should be left in the fermentation jar until the fermenting of the must has finished. The best way to determine this if an airlock is being used, is to listen out for any hissing or 'singing', i.e. the escaping of carbon dioxide gas. While hissing is to be heard, the fermenting process is still going on. Another way of testing is to look out for the carbon dioxide bubbles rising to the surface. When no more bubbles can be seen, the fermentation is over.
(7) Racking. Immediately following fermentation, the new wine must be syphoned off from the lees into clean sterilized wine bottles. The best way to do this is to place the fermentation jar on a table and using the length of rubber or plastic tube, draw the liquid (by sucking) into 1 gallon wine bottles placed on the floor or lower level. If the wine still appears cloudy after syphoning, then add a clarifier to each bottle. Leave the wine in a cool place, firmly corked, for three months.
(8) Second racking. After three months, repeat the syphoning process and this time syphon into sterilized wine bottles firmly corked.
(9) Leave for another three months and rack a third time and then bottle for use. The corks must be brand new and firmly inserted into the bottles by using a wooden mallet or similar tool. Corks are more easily inserted if they are first soaked in cold water for a few hours and then dipped into boiling water immediately prior to use. Incidentally, a good way to drive a cork firmly home is to push the bottle firmly against a hard surface like a wall, twisting it as you push.
(10) Store the bottles on their sides for 4–6 months at least before use. Remember to label each bottle with the name of the wine and any other details such as the date of bottling etc.

Some Important Points to Remember
(1) Cleanliness is essential. Sterilize all equipment such as corks, bottles, pails and jars before use, otherwise harmful bacteria may affect the wine. Boiling water is the best medium for sterilizing.
(2) All fruit and flowers etc. must be harvested on a warm sunny day and pick only perfect fruit and undamaged flowers and leaves.
(3) In the first days of fermenting it is essential that air is kept out of the pail or bowl by covering firmly with a lid.

(4) Never use metalware in any part of a wine-making process.

(5) Always use brand new corks and undamaged wine bottles.

(6) Never bottle wine that is still heavily fermenting (see later).

(7) Rack all wines at least twice and preferably three times.

(8) Keep wines stored for at least 4–6 months before use after corking.

(9) Don't use too much sugar in a recipe.

(10) Don't ferment a small amount of wine in a large jar as the air may ruin the wine.

APPLES
Wash and boil the fruit before preparing the must, mashing well. Pectic enzyme will probably need to be added. Don't forget to remove the apple stalks.

BILBERRIES
Simply squeeze and mash, adding pectic enzyme.

BLACKBERRIES
Squeeze the fruit by hand.

BLACKTHORN (Sloes)
Mash thoroughly.

BLUEBERRIES
Mash and add pectic enzyme.

COWSLIP FLOWERS
The green parts of the flowers, the 'receptacles', should be removed. Generally, cowslip wine improves with the addition of the juice and rind of an orange or two.

ELDER FLOWERS
The florets must be first removed from the heads before preparing a must.

FENNEL
Fennel wine needs the flavouring of beetroot juice to bring out its flavour. To each handful of fennel, 3 lb of beetroot is needed. The beetroot must first be sliced and boiled in $1\frac{1}{2}$ gallons of water, strained and mixed with the sugar and then poured on to the fennel to make the must.

HAWTHORN BERRIES
The hard berries must be thoroughly mashed. A mallet is useful for this purpose.

MAY BLOSSOM
Remove all twigs and foreign bits before adding to the must.

NETTLES
The addition of root ginger improves a nettle wine.

Flavourings
Here are a few tips concerning some flavourings that are commonly used. When using wild fruit and flowers be careful to avoid poisonous species (see Bibliography, p. 246). A complete guide to wild flavourings is featured on p. 186.

PRIMROSE FLOWERS
Should be treated like cowslips by removing the green parts of the flowers. The addition of the rind of an orange or two will greatly enhance the quality of primrose wine.

A Guide to Possible Wild Flavourings: Fruit
BARBERRY *(Berberis vulgaris)*
BILBERRY *(Vaccinium myrtillus)*
BLACKBERRY *(Rubus fruiticosus)*
BLACKCURRANT *(Ribes nigram)*
BIRD CHERRY *(Prunus padus)*
BLACK BULLACE *(Prunus domestica)*
CHERRY PLUM *(Prunus cerasifera)*
CLOUDBERRY *(Rubus chamaemorus)*
COWBERRY *(Vaccinium vitis)*
CRANBERRY *(Vaccinium oxycoccus)*
CROWBERRY *(Empetrum nigrum)*
CRAB APPLE *(Malus sylvestris)*
DEWBERRY *(Rubus caesius)*
ELDER *(Sambucus nigra)*
GOOSEBERRY *(Ribes uva-crispa)*
GUELDER *(Viburnum opulus)*
HAWTHORN *(Crataegus monogyna)*
JUNEBERRY *(Amelanchier intermedia)*
JUNIPER *(Juniperus communis)*
MEDLAR *(Mespilus germanica)*
OREGON GRAPE *(Mahonia aquifolium)*
PEAR *(Pyrus communis)*
RED CURRANT *(Ribes rubrum)*
RASPBERRY *(Rubus idaes)*
ROWAN *(Sorbus aucuparia)*
ROSE-HIP *(Rosa canina)*
SLOE *(Prunus spinosa)*
STRAWBERRY TREE *(Arbutus unedo)*
WHITEBEAM *(Sorbus aria)*
WILD SERVICE TREE *(Sorbus forminalis)*
WILD STRAWBERRY *(Fragaria vesca)*

Flowers
Although we have listed many flowers, it will be impossible to make a wine from the rarer sorts as there will not be enough flowers to make a must. In any case, picking wild flowers is, on the whole, to be discouraged, but with the excessively common wild flowers, as well as those which have become naturalised in gardens, it is possible to produce beautiful and delicate flavoured wines.
BROOM *(Sarothamnus scoparius)*

COWSLIP *(Primula veris)*
CHAMOMILE *(Chamomile nobile)*
DANDELION *(Taraxacum officinale)*
ELDER *(Sambucus nigra)*
HAWTHORN *(Crataegus monogyna)*
HEATHER *(Calluna vulgaris)*
HOP *(Humulus lupulus)*
HARDHEAD *(Centaurea nigra)*
LIME *(Tilia europaea)*
PRIMROSE *(Primula vulgaris)*
SWEET VIOLET *(Viola odorata)*
WILD ROSE *(Rosa canina)*

Special Flavourings and Fragrances
Many botanicals such as certain leaves, nuts, bark, seeds etc., which possess the property of imparting a special flavour or fragrance, can be used to give a wine character, or be utilised in the production of brandies and liqueurs. The best way to draw out a flavour or fragrance in any part of a plant is to steep it for some time in either alcohol or water. With water steeping, the liquid can be added to a wine must and in this way the wine will be enriched. With alcohol steeping, however, the spirit must not be added to any part of the wine making process but used as a drink in its own right, i.e. liqueurs or brandy etc. Flowers and leaves and especially strong-flavoured materials need less steeping time than such hard materials as barks, nuts, berries, seeds, roots, gums, resins etc. The following list is a rough guide to just some of the many botanicals available. Where direct steeping in the finished wine is possible we have mentioned this:

ALKANET *(Anchusa)*
Use the root, steeped in alcohol only. An excellent colouring for port wine as the root imparts a deep red colour.

ANGELICA *(Angelica sylvestris)*
Use the root and seed in cordials and liqueurs to impart a subtle flavour and mellow fragrance. Can be steeped in finished wine.

BALM *(Melissa officinalis)*
Imparts a delicate flavour to wines with the added pleasure of a pleasing aroma. Use the leaves only. Can be steeped in finished wine.

BASIL *(Osymum basilicum)*
Use the leaves to give relish to a wine.

BURNET *(Poterium sanguisorba)*
The stalks of this herb give a spicy flavour to wine.

CALAMUS
Use the root, steeped in water or spirits. Imparts an aromatic taste to wine and beer. Can be steeped in finished wine.

CARRAWAY *(Carum carvi)*
The oil and seeds imparts a pleasing flavour to spirits, liqueurs and wines. Can be steeped in finished wine.

CARDOMON *(Elettaria cardamomum)*
The seed imparts a strong aromatic fragrance and a bitter flavour to wines, spirits and beer. Can be steeped in both water and alcohol. Can be steeped in finished wine.

CHAMOMILE *(Anthemis nobilis)*
The flowers impart an aromatic fragrance to wine.

CLARY *(Salvia horminoides)*
Use the flowers to flavour beer. The use of clary in wine has the effect of sweetening the flavour.

CLOVES
Steep the cloves in alcohol or in finished wine.

CORIANDER *(Coriander sativum)*
Use the seed and steep in alcohol. Gives a lovely flavour to brandies. Can be steeped in finished wine.

DAMIANA
The aromatic leaves should be steeped in alcohol only. Good for flavouring liqueurs. Can be steeped in finished wine.

FLAXSEED *(Radiola linoides)*
The seed should be used to give body to wines. Instead of steeping, the seed should be boiled which releases the mucilage.

DOGWOOD *(Thelycrania sanguina)*
Steep the ripe fruit of this flowering shrub in

randy which gives a unique flavour.

AGE *(Salvia officinalis)*
se the whole of this herb in making beer,
eeping it in the must with the rest of the
gredients.

ENTIAN
 bitter flavour is imparted by this plant. Steep
 water or alcohol.

NSENG ROOT
teep in alcohol only. Can be steeped in
nished wine.

YSSOP *(Hyssopus officinalis)*
se the leaves and flowers only which impart
 unique flavour to wines and cordials. Can be
eeped in finished wine.

JNIPER *(Juniperus communis)*
Jse the berries for flavouring gin. The flavour
 imparted in water or alcohol. Can be steeped
 finished wine.

EADOW SWEET *(Filipendula vulgaris)*
oth the flowers and the leaves of this plant
npart a delicate almond odour which can be
tilised in both liqueurs and wines. Use only
he leaves for steeping.

AK *(Quercus robur)*
he bark of this tree can be used for colouring
ll sorts of drinks as steeping will produce a
ovely brown colour. The bark also yields a
lightly bitter flavour.

RANGE
Jse the peel of fresh, unsprayed and undyed
ranges to impart a distinctive orange aroma
 wines and other liquors. Instead of steeping
 water, the peel can be added to the prepared
quor and left for a few days before removing.

OSEMARY *(Rosemarinus officinalis)*
he leaves of this lovely herb should be
teeped in white wine and left until the liquor
as drawn out the flavour.

AFFRON *(Colchicum autumnale)*
he bright orange pollen of this crocus-like

flower can be used to colour wines and other
drinks. It should added afterwards when
fermenting has finished.

SLOE *(Prunus spinosa)* Blackthorn
Use the berries to flavour gin or in the preparation of raisin or currant wines. The berries
have a distinctive acid taste and impart a lovely
red colour to some wines. Can be steeped in
finished wine.

WOODRUFF *(Galium odoratum)*
Steep the whole of this herb, excluding roots,
in any dry white wine and remove when the
desired flavour has been acquired.

WORMWOOD *(Artemesia absinthium)*
When used with Angelica, Fennel and Carda-
mon, a good tasting Vermouth can be made.
Can be steeped in finished wine.

YARROW *(Achillea millefolium)*
Use the leaves in the preparation of beers,
adding a few leaves to the must.

RECIPES

Flower Wine Recipes

ROSE PETAL WINE: 3 quarts scented roses
(petals); 3 lb sugar; juice of two lemons; $\frac{1}{2}$ pint
fresh strong tea; 1 teaspoon of dried yeast;
seven pints of water. ($\frac{3}{4}$ oz of bakers yeast may
be used for this and other recipies.)

The petals should be picked when they drop
off easily from the bush when shaken. Spread
the petals on to a piece of muslin and gather up
into a bag. Place the bag in a pail or bowl and
pour on 4 pints boiling water. Put the sugar and
3 pints of water in a saucepan and dissolve over
a slow heat after which the liquid should also
be poured into the pail. Add the tea, yeast and
lemon and proceed as for a normal wine.

ELDER FLOWER WINE: 2 pints elder flowers;
3 lb sugar; $\frac{1}{2}$ lb sultanas; juice of 2 lemons;
$\frac{1}{2}$ pint fresh strong tea; 1 teaspoon of dried
yeast; seven pints water.

Gather up the flowers in muslin as for the
rose petals and proceed exactly the same way.

DANDELION WINE: 3 quarts dandelion petals;
juice of 2 lemons; juice of 1 orange; $\frac{1}{2}$ pint fresh
strong tea; 1 teaspoon dried yeast, 7 pints of
water. For sweet wine use 3 lb sugar; dry wine
use 2 lb.

Place all the petals in a pail and cover with
4 pints boiling water. Add all the ingredients
except the sugar which should be dissolved in
2 pints of boiling water, and the yeast and
added afterwards. Proceed as for normal wine.
The yeast must only be added after the must
has cooled.

CLOVER WINE: 1 gallon clover blossom (red or
white); 1 gallon water; 3 lb sugar; 2 lemons;
2 oranges; 1 teaspoon dried yeast.

Crush the lemons and oranges and place in
the pail with the flower heads. Pour over them
the water, which has been boiled with all the
sugar. Allow to cool to lukewarm and add the
yeast. Proceed as for normal wine.

COLTSFOOT WINE: 1 gallon coltsfoot flowers;
1 gallon water; 2 lemons; 2 oranges; $3\frac{1}{2}$ lb
sugar; 1 teaspoon dried yeast.

Proceed as for clover wine.

GOLDEN ROD WINE: 1 pint golden rod flowers;
1 gallon water; $3\frac{1}{2}$ lb sugar; $\frac{1}{2}$ lb crushed raisins;
6 oranges; a teaspoon dried yeast.

Proceed as for clover wine except the raisins
must be added to the must with the other
ingredients.

LIME BLOSSOM WINE: 3 pints lime tree blossom;
1 gallon water; 1 lb crushed raisins; 1 lb
washed whole wheat; 2 teaspoons dried yeast.

The blossom must be dried in the sun
which brings out the flavour. Boil the blossom
in all the water for 30 minutes and when cool,
place in a pail and add the wheat, sugar and
raisins. Stir well and then add the yeast.
Proceed as for normal wine but keep for at
least 1 year before use. An exquisite wine.

Fruit Wines

BARLEY WINE: 1 lb pearl barley; 1 lb raisins;
1 large potato; 1 lemon; 1 orange; 1 gallon
water; 4 lb brown sugar; 1 teaspoon dried
yeast.

Crush the orange and the lemons finely and

...ace in a pail with the potato which must be ...ashed and diced. Pour over these the water, ...oiling, and add the wheat, raisins and sugar. ...dd the yeast when cool and proceed as for ...ormal wine.

...LACKBERRY WINE: 1 gallon blackberries; 1 ...allon water; 4 lb sugar; 1 teaspoon wine yeast.
   Boil the fruit in the water for a few minutes ...nd let it stand in a pail for seven days. Strain ...e contents through muslin on to the sugar ...hich has been put in another pail, and add ...e yeast. Proceed as for normal wine.

...HERRY WINE: 6 lb cherries; 1 gallon water; ...lb sugar; 1 teaspoon sugar.
   ...ice and stone the cherries and boil in all the ...ater for $\frac{1}{2}$ hour. Strain through muslin into ...e pail and when lukewarm, add the sugar and ...east. Proceed as for normal wine.

...RAB APPLE WINE: 1 gallon crab apples; $3\frac{1}{2}$ lb ...rown sugar; $\frac{1}{2}$ lb raisins; 1 gallon water; 1 ...aspoon dried yeast.
   Wash and slice the crab apples and pour ...ver them all the water in a pail. Stand for two ...eeks and then strain through muslin on to the ...ugar and raisins in another pail. Add the yeast ...nd proceed as for normal wine.

...RANBERRY WINE: 2 lb raisins; 1 gallon cran-...erries; 1 gallon water; $3\frac{1}{2}$ lb sugar; 1 slice of ...ast; 1 teaspoon dried yeast.
   The cranberries must be crushed and placed ...a pail. Pour over boiling water and leave for ...week, thoroughly stirring every day. Strain ...e mixture through muslin into another pail ...ith the rest of the ingredients and proceed as ...r normal wine.

...LDERBERRY WINE: 1 gallon elderberries; 12 lb ...ugar loaf; 3 oz bruised whole ginger; 2 gallons ...ater; 1 teaspoon yeast.
   Boil everything, except the yeast, in all the ...ater for $\frac{1}{2}$ hour and strain through muslin. ...dd the yeast and proceed as for normal wine.

...AWTHORN BERRY WINE: 4 lb berries; 4 oranges; ...lemons; 6 lb brown sugar; 2 gallons water; ...teaspoon dried yeast.
   Put the berries in a pail and pour over all the water which must be boiling. Stand for 1 week and stir thoroughly every day. Crush and dice the oranges and lemons and place in another pail with the sugar and strain the berries through muslin on to these ingredients. Add the yeast and proceed as for normal wine.

Other Wines, Meads, Beers and Liqueurs etc.

OAK LEAF WINE: 1 gallon oak leaves; 2 oranges; 1 lemon; 4 lb sugar; 1 gallon water; 1 teaspoon yeast.
   Stand the oak leaves in a pail for 24 hours after covering with the gallon of boiling water. Strain into another pail with the rest of the ingredients and proceed as for normal wine. (Use only young oak leaves).

BRAMBLE TIP WINE: 1 gallon young bramble tips; 3 lb sugar; 1 gallon water; 1 teaspoon dried yeast.
   Boil the tips in all the water for $\frac{1}{2}$ hour and strain into a pail. When cool, add the sugar and yeast and proceed as for normal wine.

CARROT WHISKY: 6 lb carrots; 1 lb raisins; 1 lb whole wheat; 2 oranges; 2 lemons; 4 lb sugar; 1 gallon water; 1 teaspoon dried yeast.
   Boil the washed carrots whole in all the water until tender. Crush and dice the oranges and lemons and put in a pail over which the strained, boiling carrot juice should be poured. Add the sugar and stir thoroughly. When cool, add the rest of the ingredients and proceed as for normal wine.

CELERY WINE: 4 lb celery; 1 gallon water; 2 lemons; 1 orange; $3\frac{1}{2}$ lb sugar; 1 teaspoon dried yeast.
   Cut the celery into small pieces after washing and boil in all the water until tender with the lemons and oranges which must be crushed and diced. Strain into a pail with the sugar and when cool, add the yeast, proceed as for normal wine.

DAMSON GIN: Damsons; cloves; sugar-candy; essence of almonds; unsweetened gin.
   Preserving jars will be needed to make this drink. First prick holes in all the damsons with a fork and half fill each preserving jar with the fruit. To every bottle, add 2 oz crushed sugar candy, 1 whole clove and a few drops of almond essence.
   Fill up now to the brim of each jar with the unsweetened gin and keep firmly airtight in a warm place for three months. Strain the mixture through muslin and firmly cork in wine bottles, storing until needed for use.

NETTLE BEER: 2 lb young nettle tips; 2 lemons; 1 lb brown sugar; 1 oz cream of tartar; 1 gallon water; 1 teaspoon dried yeast.
   Boil the nettles and the lemons, crushed and diced, in all the water for 15 minutes. Strain into a pail with all the sugar and cream of tartar. When cool, add the yeast. Ferment for 3 days in a warm place, then 2 days in a cool place and strain into strong wine bottles. Cork firmly and tie-down the works with wire fasteners (champagne fasteners obtainable from wine specialists are ideal). Keep one week and drink—don't leave this beer bottled longer than this.

CIDER: 12 lb apples; 1 lb raisins; 1 gallon water; 1 teaspoon dried yeast.
   Mince the apples and place in a pail with the water and the rest of the ingredients. Leave in a warm place for 2 weeks, stirring thoroughly each day. Strain through muslin and proceed as for normal wine.

ROSE HIP MEAD: 3 lb rosehips; 4 lb honey; 2 lemons; 1 gallon water; 1 teaspoon dried yeast.
   Boil the hips in all the water for 10 minutes and allow to cool. Thoroughly mash the hips in the water and then strain through muslin. Pour the liquid into a pail, add the honey and juice of the lemons and after stirring thoroughly, add the yeast. Proceed as for normal wine.

ELDERFLOWER CHAMPAGNE: 1 pint elderflowers; 2 lemons; $1\frac{1}{2}$ lb sugar; 2 tablespoons wine vinegar; 1 gallon of water.
   Pour the boiling water on to the sugar in a pail and when cool, add all the other ingredients. Leave standing for 24 hours and then strain. Bottle and cork in strong bottles using champagne wire fasteners.

obtained quite easily by making a 'plant' which will give a continuous supply of beer over a period of time.

Mix $\frac{1}{2}$ oz bakers yeast in 1 pint warm water in a big jug. Then for every day in the following week, feed the mixture with one heaped teaspoon of ground ginger and one of sugar. Leave now for 24 hours and then strain through a double thickness of muslin. Place the sediment back into the jug, add four cups of cold water and divide into two separate plants. The plant must be separated each week otherwise it will suffocate and die. The plants are then fed in exactly the same way for another week and divided again etc. Obviously, one plant will have to have a home found for it or be destroyed otherwise one ends up with a thousand and one plants in no time at all.

The strained liquor from the plant must be placed in a pail, with four pints of water, the juice of two lemons and 1 lb of sugar dissolved in boiling water. Mix thoroughly and bottle in strong bottles, being careful not to bring the level of beer higher than within 2 inches of the cork. Keep bottled for one week before drinking.

HOME-MADE BEER: 1 lb malt extract; 2 handfuls good dried hops; $\frac{1}{2}$ lb sugar; 1 gallon water; 1 teaspoon dried yeast.

Dissolve the malt extract in 4 pints of warm water, adding the sugar afterwards and stirring well. Take 1 pint of the remaining $\frac{1}{2}$ gallon of water and boil all the hops in it, simmering for ten minutes. Strain the liquid into the malt and sugar solution and repeat with each of the remaining 3 pints of water until all the flavour has been extracted from the hops. While the must is lukewarm, add the yeast. The fermentation will be strong so be ready for any frothing over the top of the fermenting jar. When the bubbles are just barely rising in the liquor (after about three days), bottle in strong jars and use after a week, though the beer will keep for two months or so.

SOURCES OF MATERIALS

Check out your local hardware shops, chemists, health food shops and departmental stores for all the winemaking equipment mentioned. Other

specialist suppliers such as the following, can be found in a local telephone directory:

THE AMATEUR WINEMAKER, North Croye, The Avenue, Andover, Hampshire.

CONTINENTAL WINE EXPERTS LTD, The Winery, North Walsham, Norfolk.

GREY OWL LABORATORIES LTD, Morley Road, Staple Hill, Bristol.

M. AUGUSTI HIDALGO (LONDON) LTD, 81 Ledbury Road, London W11.

LEIGH-WILLIAMS & SONS, Tattenhall, nr Chester.

LOFTUS, 16 The Terrace, Torquay, Devon.

W. R. LOFTUS LTD, 1–3 Charlotte Street, London W1.

SEMPLEX HOME BREWS LTD, Old Hall Works, Stuart Road, Birkenhead.

HOCK: 6 medium-sized potatoes; 3 lemons; 2 oranges; 4 lb sugar; 1 lb raisins; 1 gallon water; 1 teaspoon dried yeast.

Crush the raisins, potatoes and fruit and place in a pail with all the other ingredients. Proceed as for normal wine.

TEA WINE: 4 pints tea; 2 lb sugar; $\frac{1}{2}$ lb raisins; 2 lemons.

Crush and dice the lemons, chop up the raisins and place in a pail with all the other ingredients. Leave standing for 1 month and then strain and bottle. Proceed as for normal wine.

GINGER BEER PLANT: Ginger beer can be

SOUTHERN VINYARDS LTD, Brighton, Sussex.
VINA LTD, 63–65 St Johns Road, Waterloo, Liverpool 22.
VINAIDE, 28 Swan Street, Manchester 4.
WINEMAKERS EQUIPMENT, 242 Deansgate, Manchester.

Oak casks for maturing wine available from:
THOS. TREVIS SMITH LTD, Cooperage, Hollybush Street, Cradley Heath, Warley, Worcestershire.

Yeasts:
ALLINSON LTD, 210–214 Cambridge Heath Road, London E2. *(For yeasts only.)*

SOCIETIES

AMATEUR WINEMAKERS NATIONAL GUILD OF JUDGES, c/o Wing Commander R. W. Woodley, Chalk Pit Lane, Monxton, Andover.
BREWERS SOCIETY, 42 Portman Square, London W1.
NATIONAL ASSOCIATION OF AMATEUR WINE-MAKERS, c/o Mrs L. K. Lucus, Molburn House, Ferndown Drive, Ferndown, Wimborne, Dorset.
NATIONAL ASSOCIATION OF CYDER MAKERS, Georgian House, Trinity Street, London SW1.
SOCIETY OF FRIENDS OF WINE, 1 Vintners Place, London EC4. *Sets out to stimulate the knowledge and appreciation of wine.*

BIBLIOGRAPHY

AMATEUR WINEMAKER/C. J. J. Berry and M. F. Berry, South Street, Andover, Hampshire. (Monthly) Price: 10p. Annual subscription: £1.75.
HOME BEER AND WINE MAKING/Foremost Press Ltd, P.O. Box 1, Wirral, Cheshire L46 0TS. (Monthly) Price: 15p. Annual subscription: £2.40.
HOME-MADE COUNTRY WINES, by Dorothy Wise/Hamlyn Ltd.
HOME-MADE WINES, by F. W. Beech/The Women's Institute.
HOME WINE & BEER RECIPES/available from Allinson Ltd, 210–214 Cambridge Heath Road, London E2.
HOME WINEMAKING & BREWING, by B. C. A.

Turner/Wolfe Publishing Ltd.
HOME WINE MAKING AND VINE GROWING, by H. E. Bravery/Macdonald & Co. Ltd.

The following publications are all available from AMATEUR WINEMAKER *(see above). Send for a free price list:*
ADVANCED HOME BREWING, by Ken Shales.
'AMATEUR WINEMAKER' RECIPES, by C. J. J. Berry.
BREWING BETTER BEERS, by Ken Shales.
DURDEN PARK BEER CIRCLE BOOK OF RECIPES, by Wilf Newsom.
FIRST STEPS IN WINEMAKING, by C. J. J. Berry.
THE GOOD WINES OF EUROPE, by Cedric Austin.
GROWING GRAPES IN BRITAIN, by Gillian Pearkes.
GROWING VINES, by N. Poulter.
HINTS ON HOME BREWING, by C. J. J. Berry.
HOME BREWED BEERS AND STOUTS, by C. J. J. Berry.
HOME BREWING SIMPLIFIED.
HOW TO MAKE WINES WITH A SPARKLE, by J. Restall and D. Hebbs.
LIGHTHEARTED WINEMAKING, by Duncan Gillespie.
MAKING MEAD, by Brian Acton and Peter Duncan.
MAKING WINES LIKE THOSE YOU BUY, by Brian Acton and Peter Duncan.
ONE HUNDRED AND THIRTY NEW WINEMAKERS RECIPES, by C. J. J. Berry.
PLANTS UNSAFE FOR WINEMAKING, by T. Edwin Belt.
PRESERVING WINEMAKING INGREDIENTS, by T. Edwin Belt.
PROGRESSIVE WINEMAKING, by Peter Duncan and Bryan Acton.
RECIPES FOR PRIZEWINNING WINES, by Bryan Acton.
SCIENTIFIC WINEMAKING, by J. R. Mitchell.
WHYS AND WHEREFORES OF WINEMAKING, by Cedric Austin.
THE WINEMAKER'S COOKBOOK, by Tilly Timbrell and Brian Acton.
THE WINEMAKER'S DINING BOOK, by Tilly Timbrell.
THE WINEMAKER'S GARDEN, by Duncan Gillespie.
THE WINEMAKER'S RECITER, by Philip Delmon.
WINEMAKING AND BREWING, by Dr F. W. Beech and Dr A. Pollard.

WINEMAKING WITH CANNED AND DRIED FRUIT, by C. J. J. Berry.

COURSES

WEST DEAN COLLEGE, Chichester, Sussex. *Short courses on wine making.*

192

No doubt there are quite a few folk who have chewed over the idea of keeping some hens behind the potting shed. If you are one of them, the most important factor to consider at the beginning is the amount of space available in your garden. An area approximately 6 feet by 4 feet should be set aside for the housing of your birds, plus about 5–6 feet for use as a run. This run isn't necessary if you fancy the idea of a few hens goosestepping around your garden, but don't forget they have some bad habits and one of them is scratching holes all over the place and eating new and tender shoots once they've been unearthed.

Siting

When choosing a site it is essential for the comfort of the birds, to construct the house facing south, with plenty of window space on the side where most light can enter. Do not forget to choose a position in your garden which is high and relatively dry—not a low, damp spot. Now, as mentioned before, the ideal size for keeping six hens in comfort should be 6 feet by 4 feet and a house of this size or thereabouts can be bought for £30 to £40, which is incredible as it can be made for easily half that much with timber from your local wood yard.

Chicken Shack

Remember, when building your house that light and warmth is essential for your hens—not to mention the egg supply—so be meticulous about the construction. Have the windows built so that they can easily be opened wide or shut tight depending on the weather. If wire netting is fixed behind the window frames, they can be kept open night and day during the Summer. Also, if possible, build a window below the roosting perches and a droppings board at the end of the house as near the floor as you can, so that the hens will have plenty of light in the mornings to see to scratch around

Chickens From Scratch

193

other day and remove any droppings or matted portions which may accumulate, and change this litter without fail every three months.

On the Nest

A good laying hen will spend something like six or seven hours a week in her nest box, so it must be made as comfortable as possible and well-protected from draughts. Check the nests regularly for any hard or harsh nesting materials and check also to see if it is big enough for the hen to sit at ease: the nest should never be less than 12 to 14 inches square or she may suffer from cramp. Some egg producers, for fear of insects invading their nest boxes, spray or squirt insect powder all over the place, but this should be avoided at all costs. Instead, change the nesting material as often as possible, at the same time scrubbing it out with hot water and vinegar should there be any bugs around.

As with other household pets (and presumably this is what they will become), pullets should be house-trained too and in this case they must be taught to lay their eggs in the proper place instead of dropping them anywhere which could lead them to being smashed. Simply place one china egg (the sort we all used to use in egg and spoon races and available possibly from your local sports shop) in each

in. This will keep them warm and contented while waiting for you to roll off your hammock and give them their breakfast. For some reason, chickens love to scratch and scuttle around, so a section must be allocated in the house or pen for such a purpose. Ideally, the house should have a wooden floor and in the pen, grass, but whatever the case, the litter should be piled up to a depth of about 6 inches —especially in the Winter months. This litter can be of coarse sawdust, bracken, dry leaves, straw, chaff or peat—any of which will make fine scratching material. Rake it over every nest box and good old Mother Nature will do the rest.

Little Boxes

Construct the nest boxes about 1 foot off the floor at the end of the hen house to allow more room for the hens to pursue their favourite pastimes. At the same time place a strip of wood across the bottom of the nests to stop the nesting material from falling out. For a quiet life, allow one box for every two fowls you decide to keep, as normally the majority of eggs are laid before mid-day so the last thing you want is to have three egg-bound chickens all squawking and clambering for the same nesting box. Ideally it would be good to have one box per hen but this isn't always possible. Another important requirement which can be overlooked is a droppings board. This should be fixed about 2 feet from the floor and 2 to 3 inches below the perch. Clean it each day if possible by scraping the droppings into a bucket and lightly cover the board with either sawdust or sand. Never let the droppings build up on the board as this can harbour disease.

There are many little details to watch out for when building the house and one of these concerns the perches. Keep all perches the same height, for if not, all the hens will scramble for the highest and trouble could easily develop. Also remember to allow about 9 to 10 inches per bird when making the perch as this is a nice comfortable space for them to roost. There are various thicknesses recommended for perches, but the favourite seems to be one of 2 inches square with the top edges well rounded off and the lower edges only very slightly rounded. It is very important to secure the perch firmly at each end so that there isn't the slightest hint of a wobble, as this is extremely disturbing for your hens and not too good for the egg supply. Never allow your hens to sleep in the nesting boxes at night. One way of doing this is to quietly visit the house after dark and gently put the culprit back on the perch. A couple of nights of doing this should see the end of this habit. One other important factor to watch out for is the food container. This must be large enough to allow all the birds to eat at the same time for if not, a timid bird that has to fight its way to the grub will never get close enough and will certainly become ill. Construct a simple trough for the food as this is much better than a bowl. A strip of wood across the top will stop the hens from fouling or scattering the contents about the house or run.

The water trough, and especially its positioning is quite important as this can determine a good or bad egg supply. To begin with, the water trough must be in such a position that it is impossible for the hens to kick dirt or litter into it and one nice idea is to attach it to the outside of the house if possible. But should this prove too troublesome, another method is to have the trough fixed on the wall at a suitable height so the birds can drink easily from it but find it impossible to foul it up. Either method is fine but you must remember to change the water daily or some dreaded disease may set in. Also, and this only applies to the winter months or when frost is in the air, empty it each night and in the morning before the birds wake up and fill the trough with tepid water. This will ensure that the hens drink sufficient for the production of eggs and their own personal requirements. The making and laying of eggs gives our feathered friends quite a thirst and if they are forced to drink very cold water they will become ill. In the Summer the drinking water can be washed out and filled with clean water in the evening all ready for the hens the next morning. But keep the trough in a shady spot—never in the sunlight.

Beside the water trough you must also build a shallow box with two sections in it for holding a quantity of grit and oyster shell. Flint is a *must* for all fowls as it is used to grind up the food in the gizzard and the oyster shell or limestone provides the pure lime necessary for the hen to make egg shells.

Chicken Feed

We now come to foodstuffs which, naturally it is just as important to keep clean. One idea which you may find useful is to hang a netted bag from the roof of the run or house the same height as the chickens' heads. This can then be filled with all sorts of goodies which cannot be fouled up. Once again, the cold months can be a bit of a swine as you must on no account feed chickens with any kind of frozen food until it is well thawed out. If you have any trouble keeping the food away from the icy mornings, a couple of good, fresh mangel-wurzels or swedes chopped in half and nailed to the wall of the house will suffice till mid-day. Never toss food on to the ground—the nailing method is both clean and simple and at the end of the day the empty mangel shells can be cleaned and chopped up for the stock-pot as a special treat later in the week. In actual fact the general feeding of your hens is quite a simple matter as the majority of foodstuffs are kitchen scraps. Any stale bread or cake should be baked or dried in an oven and then crushed before being used and any which isn't going to be used immediately can be stored in an old biscuit tin for later. Potato peelings and small potatoes can be given but they must be boiled first. Naturally, not everyone will have enough spare green food and leftovers to keep 6 hens in trim, but don't forget there is an unlimited supply at your local market place, and sackfuls can be collected at the end of the day, all free of charge.

When making a stock-pot out of all the odds and ends, use as little water as possible and on no account serve the hens with sloppy food.

A crumbly, moist consistency is their favourite and your birds will enjoy every beakful. Check, when serving, that the hens will each receive about 8–10 oz twice a day: once in the morning and once in the late afternoon. The afternoon meal should be given in time for the birds to eat it in comfort and to allow them ample time to find their roosting perches before it gets dark. Never let your hens go to roost with an empty or half empty crop. In actual fact it's probably better for them to have a slightly bigger meal in the afternoon, so they will still have a full crop when they eventually settle down for the night. Unlike us, they won't be troubled with indigestion. One of the most basic and stable foods to give your laying hens is mash, and good mash is made up with the following ingredients: 3 parts of bran, 3 parts of ground oats, 3 parts of maize meal, 1 part of alfalfa meal and 1 part of fish meal plus a sprinkling of salt.

The Runs

We now come to the run, and for this an area of 5–6 feet must be marked out preferably covered with grass. Earth is fine but it must be dug over frequently. In the case of a grass run, it would be best to keep the grass very short and, providing you don't feed the hens on it, it will last quite a long time.

Admittance to the run should be by means of a pop-hole for the birds to come and go, but for the convenience of access to the run, there should also be a door leading from the house to the run and the pop-hole should be built in the door. On the inside of this door, fix a well-made slide so that the pop-hole can be securely held every night to keep your neighbours' cat and other predators at bay. This also helps to prevent draughts from coming into the hen house. Across the top of the run build some kind of roof and attach some canvas or sacking to it that can be drawn down over the sides in a storm.

Lastly, sprinkle a liberal amount of scratching litter plus some oyster shell or limestone grit in the run to keep your hens amused and at the same time provide some useful exercise.

Well, that's about it really for the house and

pen—just remember that chickens are like us in that they like to be warm and cosy in the Winter and cool in the Summer so a few well-built windows and shutters wouldn't come amiss.

Stocking

Now to the most difficult part—the actual stocking of the hen house.

Probably the simplest method of stocking your house will be with hens that are already laying, as opposed to buying 16–20 week-old pullets or even 8-week-olds which are a little more difficult (we shall come to these little characters in a minute).

The first point to remember after buying your chickens is that it's quite reasonable not to expect them to lay for a little while as the change in surroundings upsets them a bit: but here are a couple of tips which may be of help. Try as much as you possibly can to keep the birds under the conditions to which they have been accustomed and to give them similar food. But in an attempt to cut out trial and error feeding methods, check first on what food they have been getting so that you can match it—in time you will be able to alter it to your own requirements.

There are many birds on the market that will do you proud but we suggest that you buy a breed which is not too active and will be content in a small house or run. Possibly the most likely choice would be Rhode Island Red or Light Sussex or even a cross between the two would be fine. Both breeds are hardy, quiet and docile and normally make good layers, but make sure you give them 2 feeds per day as well as plenty of fresh green food and water. Protect them too from very cold or wet conditions as laying hens should *never* get cold or wet feet! There isn't a great deal of difference between keeping laying hens or 16–20 week-old hens except that the latter should be made even more comfortable with plenty of fresh, clean litter and for the first few days anyway, should be given food as tempting as possible. They won't begin laying their eggs for at least 6–12 weeks so don't start worrying.

Eight-week-old chicks are a different matter

and although they won't need a broody hen for comfort and warmth, they will need some kind of heating plus plenty of clean straw mixed with fresh, dry litter to snuggle into. For the first few weeks it would be a good idea to give them greater warmth and a feeling of security by sectioning off a part of the house for their use—not forgetting of course to cover up the nest boxes as these fluffy little characters will soon foul them up. Perches aren't really necessary at this stage as the chicks won't use them until they are at least 3 months old. Eight-week-old chicks can have similar food to that recommended for the older birds except in this case it should be finely chopped up and given to them in a large bowl—making sure it stays reasonably clean. Allow them to play in the garden or run if they want to but not if the ground is damp as this can cause them harm.

Complaints Dept.

Here are a few remedies for the commonest of complaints likely to affect your hens:

COMMON COLD: Mix together 4 oz syrup of scillae, 4 oz syrup of mulberry, and $\frac{1}{2}$ oz of the following—vin. ipecac., spirit of nitre, chlorodyne and paregoric, making 10 oz in all.

Dose: One or two dessertspoonfuls of the mixture in half a pint of water or stirred into 2 lb of mash.

BRONCHITIS & WHEEZING: Exactly the same mixture as above but give one teaspoonful to the patient on a little scalded milk and bread (moist *not* soggy) or the same amount in a drop of warm water.

DIARRHOEA: Mix together 1 oz of bismuthi carb, and $\frac{1}{4}$ oz salol.

Dose: Give as much as will cover a $\frac{1}{2}$p piece on a little scalded milk and bread (moist *not* soggy).

GAPES CURE: Mix together $\frac{1}{4}$ oz pure creosote in 4 oz of pure glycerine.

How to apply: Dip a small feather into the mixture and carefully thrust it down the hen's throat, twisting the feather while slowly withdrawing it so as to dislodge the gape worms from the throat and windpipe.

RED MITE KILLER: To 1 pint of paraffin, add 2 oz of oil of camphor or 4 oz of creosote.

How to apply: Scrub all perches and woodwork etc.

SOURCES OF MATERIALS

Local livestock auctions are the best source of poultry, but check what's happening and when in FARMERS WEEKLY and POULTRY WORLD (see below), both available from your local newsagent.

Breeders:

ABBOT BROS, Thuxton, Norfolk.
K. ALLAN, 9 Tennant Road, Paisley, Renfrewshire.
BIRCHALS, Church Lane, Leek, Staffordshire.

STANLEY BROWN AND SON, Poultry Farm, Chearsley, nr Aylesbury, Buckinghamshire.
WILLIAM COOK & SONS, Bylaugh, East Dereham, Norfolk.
FAWCETTS CHICKS, Longton, Lancashire.
VIC FELL, 68 Pentrich Road, Swanwick, Derbyshire.
GLENMANOR CHICKS, 1 The Nook, Great Glen, Leicester.
A. J. HOADLEY, 10 Vernon Road, Uckfield, Sussex.
GEOFFREY MARSTON, Biddenden, Kent.
MAYFIELD CHICKS LTD, Bunkers Hill, Colne, Lancashire.
MAURICE MILLARD (CHICKS) LTD, Pelpards Farm (No. 2), Freshford, Bath, Somerset.

THE POULTRY MAN, 68 Pentrich Road, Swanwick, Derbyshire.
D. A. ROWE, Sudan, Bulmer Street, Sudbury, Suffolk.
MR STAFFORD, 70 Tyresal Crescent, Bradford.
TURBARD, 4 Lee Chapel Lane, Laindon, Essex.
R. J. WOOD, Albrighton 3327 (day time) or 2586 (any time).
Litter for chickens (woodchips, woodshavings or woodflakes) can be obtained from woodyards, timber merchants, or specially prepared from:
D. L. GILLESPIE LTD, Market Drayton, Shropshire.
JOHN INKSTER LTD, The Chippings, Chigwell Row, Essex.
MARSHALL'S WOODFLAKES, Downside, Backwell, Bristol.

SOCIETIES

BRITISH CHICKEN ASSOCIATION, 52–54 High Holborn, London WC1.
NATIONAL INSTITUTE OF POULTRY HUSBANDRY, Newport, Salop.
POULTRY CLUB OF GREAT BRITAIN, 72 Springfields, Great Dunmow, Essex.

BIBLIOGRAPHY

FARMERS WEEKLY/Agricultural Press Ltd, 161–166 Fleet Street, London EC4P 4AA. Price: 12p. Annual subscription: £10.25.
POULTRY WORLD/Agricultural Press Ltd (as above). Price: 10p weekly. Annual subscription: £7.50 (including postage).

DISEASES OF POULTRY, by P. Seneviratna/John Wright & Sons, Bristol BS8 1EX.
HERBAL HANDBOOK FOR FARM AND STABLE, by Juliette de Bairacli Levy/Faber & Faber Ltd. *(Includes a section on herbal cures for chicken illnesses.)*
THE LITTLE BROWN EGG BOOK, by David Eno/The Juniper Press. *(A lovely little book full of things to do with eggs.)*
NATURAL POULTRY KEEPING, by Jim Worthington/Crosby Lockwood & Son Ltd.
THE RIGHT WAY TO KEEP HENS, DUCKS, GEESE & TURKEYS, by Robert H. Holmes/Elliot Right Way Books, Kingswood Building, Kingswood, Tadworth, Surrey.

NANNY, BILLY & KIDS

When you consider the small amount of cash needed to keep a goat in comfort for one week (probably no more than a medium-sized dog) and in the case of a nanny, the good fortune of being rewarded with at least four pints of good wholesome milk a day, it is odd that the humble goat has rarely been welcomed by people with a patch of spare ground in their gardens.

BREEDS AVAILABLE IN THIS COUNTRY:

THE ANGLO NUBIAN Nicknamed the 'Jersey Cow of the goat world' (due to its high butter-fat percentage), is a large beast with a fine skin and glossy coat. Its only handicap is that the top teeth tend to overlap the bottom set, thereby making the biting of grass and twigs difficult. This can be overcome in stall-fed animals by chopping or grinding their foodstuffs.

THE TOGGENBURG Once bred in the valley of Toggenburg in Switzerland, this animal is now very popular in England due mainly to its quiet and gentle temperament and fine looks. The Toggenburg is a rather small animal and has white or light fawn markings down each side of the face and from the knees (or hocks) to the feet. There is also a wide strip of white round about the tail and rump that spreads towards the thighs. These animals, although not very heavy milkers are extremely consistent in their yields and pride themselves in their long lactation (milking) periods. The Toggenburg butter-fat percentage is about average.

BRITISH TOGGENBURG Normally thought of as an improved version of its Swiss brother, this goat, although identically marked, is in fact larger and more finely coated. Unlike its Swiss equivalent the British Toggenburg is a good milker with a reasonably high butter-fat percentage.

THE SAANEN This is yet another Swiss breed, similar in many ways to the Toggenburg especially in its size and nature. This breed is ideal for anyone with limited space for its placid nature makes it content with less-than-ideal grazing. These goats are excellent milkers and well known among goat handlers for their

extremely long lactation periods. Their butter-fat percentage is about average.

BRITISH SAANEN These goats are rather heavily built in comparison with other breeds. They are nevertheless very good milkers with a fine length of lactation.

THE BRITISH ALPINE Fully bred in England, these goats, although black in colouring, have white or fawn markings similar to the Toggenburg. The British Alpine is a fairly large beast and is quite striking due to the high colour contrast in its appearance. This goat has a gentle nature and is nice to work with, but it probably needs more exercise than most of the other breeds. They are extremely good milkers with an average butter-fat percentage.

BRITISH Really quite attractive in appearance, these goats can be of any colour and often have white markings on the body. They are very good milkers both in quantity and quality and are well known for some of the highest recorded yields in this country.

ENGLISH These goats are stocky little characters, with thick coats in varying shades of greys, fawns and browns. Unfortunately they are not very good milkers.

HOUSING A GOAT

Although it is an extremely hardy creature, the goat, like the rest of us, cannot stand draughts and is therefore very susceptible to colds: so please bear this in mind when you decide on its shelter. An unused garage or shed would naturally be ideal, but if you have no outbuildings available, one will have to be constructed.

Basically the sort of stall needed is just the same as a dog kennel except it must of course be much larger (at least six feet or so square) with a door similar to that found on a horse's stable. To this can be added as many windows as can sensibly be constructed. In the summer they can be sprayed or painted with lime-wash or green distemper to keep the goat house cool. Inside the goat's house it is necessary to build a trough and hay-rack plus a strong wooden bench or platform for sleeping. Although it need only be a couple of inches off the ground, the goat prefers this to the cold floor. Always keep the floor covered with a good layer of

straw and never allow the stall to turn into a smelly heap.

If more than one milker is to be kept, then separate stalls must be provided as it is not advisable to allow them to run loose together in case one should dominate the house. Stalls are advisable too, as it is necessary to feed each goat according to her milk yield. These really only need to be 4 feet high and 2–2½ feet wide. Inside them there should be small hay-racks about 15 inches deep and 12 inches wide at the top, with wooden slats constructed at 1½-inch intervals. To the left of the stall, a metal ring should be fastened for tying the goat up when milking. This can vary in height according to the height of the goat, but generally it will need to be some 2 feet off the ground. Don't forget to allow enough rope to enable the goat to move its head freely up and down but not enough for it to back out of the stall. Keeping water in the stalls should be avoided as it can become rather messy if spilt.

FEEDING

On the question of foodstuffs, you will find no problem at all in keeping your goat content and happy as long as you realize that it eats quite a lot. If you live in the countryside this food situation will be very easy to deal with, but in town you will have to be a bit more ingenious. All sorts of vegetables can be got very cheaply by visiting market places or green-grocers, asking at cafes and restaurants or just knocking on people's doors. Even from your own home, foodstuffs like boiled potatoes, dried bread, cabbage leaves and pea-pods etc. will help maintain a steady diet. Hay and straw can be a problem for town dwellers because the prices can be fairly steep, so if possible, it will be best to buy in bulk.

The supply of straw or hay can always be bought from market harvesters who are the suppliers of shops and stalls in the towns. Should you be fortunate enough to live in the country, it will be a very simple matter to give your goats an added treat by taking them for a regular walk along any country lane and allowing them to nibble at the trees, hedgerows and grasses. Be careful, however, as there are some shrubs which can be dangerous to your animals such as yew trees, foxglove, privet berries, ivy berries, ragwort, deadly and woody nightshade, rhododendrons, acorns, laburnum, walnut and any variety of bulbs. In Winter, due to seeding, the grasses and weeds lose their food value, to such an extent that some produce will have to be cultivated in your garden. A nice batch of kale and carrots should be grown if possible along with oats and peas and fed to the animals whilst still green. Small branches and pieces of bark can be dried and sorted for the winter months too.

KIDDING

Kidding (in theory), possesses no more problems than any other animal that you may have at home. Altogether you will have something like 145 days from mating to prepare not only yourself, but the goat house and a few pieces of equipment too. Try if you can not to leave this till the last minute as the last thing your goat will want if she needs help when delivering her young, is to wait while you flap around.

The simple essentials needed for a normal delivery is a sterilized bucket (for washing your hands and arms in thoroughly), disinfectant, soft tissue paper and towelling (for the cleaning of the new born kid[s]). You will soon become aware that your goat is about to come into labour by a marked increase in her appetite, especially for hay. Other signs include the tightening up of the udder due to an influx of milk. Her tail will be carried much higher than normal and she will become fidgety as well as breathing rapidly or even panting. She will show definite signs of being in pain by making distress noises and will insist on ruffling up her straw and lying down only to rise in a few minutes and start the procedure all over again. There isn't a great deal you can do at this point but to show kindness and sympathy.

After a while a thick, white discharge will appear only to be followed by another similar in appearance to the white of an egg. It is at this stage that you must quickly, but thoroughly, wash your hands because soon your goat will begin kidding. Shortly after the second discharge, she will begin to show signs of straining —nothing much at first but gradually building up until at long last a shiny substance (mucus) is exuded followed soon after by the water bag in which the kid is huddled. Don't break the bag even though the goat appears to be in great pain as this will hinder not help the delivery. After a few moments your goat will begin to strain much harder causing the water bag to break internally, thereby allowing the kid's forefeet and the tip of its nose to become visible. Should your goat appear to be in great pain, it is essential for you to help. Simply take hold of the kid's two feet pulling them gently downwards as the goat strains. In case they are much too slippery to hold on to, it's a good idea to wrap a towel around them and then continue. Sadly the goat may cry out when the head fully appears, but by then the delivery will soon be over and you should comfort her as much as possible.

Once the head is free, your goat may wish to rest for a while before continuing to strain with renewed energy, when she will then give birth to the remainder of her kid.

In most cases when a second kid is delivered, it tends to come hind-feet first. This is quite normal but speed is of the essence for if there should be a delay it may suffocate. As soon as the hind-feet become visible, take a firm hold as described before and gently pull.

The two methods described are for normal births but it's very easy for something to go

Anglo-Nubian

Saanen

wrong, such as the failure of the kid to appear due to some slight malpositioning or its size. If this is the case don't hang around but contact a vet immediately.

As soon as the kid(s) has been born, all the mucus should be removed from its mouth and nose to enable it to breathe properly. If the delivery has been rather a long affair, the little chap may be extremely weak and unable to breathe, in which case the kid must be carried into the fresh air and given artificial respiration. This is done by holding the front legs and slowing pressing them backwards and forwards causing the kid to gasp, thereby filling its lungs. Once this has been done, the kid can then be helped back to its mum and she will clean him.

After cleaning away the afterbirth and laying down fresh straw, give your proud mum a warm oatmeal drink with a tablespoonful of treacle (if she's partial to it) or some honey.

SOURCES OF MATERIALS

The best way to get a good quality, healthy goat is to go to a livestock auction and have a word with a local farmer who will be able to give you a tip or two on what's worth buying. *For addresses of local goat breeders, contact your nearest branch of* THE BRITISH GOAT SOCIETY *(see below) or write to its head office.*

Alternatively, contact the following:
J. M. ABBOT, Thuxton, Norwhich, Norfolk.
MRS E. ANDREWS, 4 Palace Road, Hawleys Corner, Westerham, Kent.
MISS Y. DRUCE, Bewkes, Lamberhurst, Kent.
MRS S. HINES, Pine Lodge, Maesmaur Road, Tatsfield, Westerham, Kent.
FRED RITSON, Goat Appliance Works, Longtown, Carlisle. *Sells everything for the goatkeeper including literature.*

SOCIETIES

THE BRITISH GOAT SOCIETY, c/o Mrs May, Lion House, Rougham, Bury St Edmunds, Suffolk. *This society gives out information on all aspects of keeping and breeding goats and produces books and leaflets on subjects related to goat-keeping. There are also many affiliated goat societies, all of which are listed as follows:*
BINGLEY & DISTRICT GOAT SOCIETY: D. Robinson, 3 Uplands Grove, Clayton Heights, Queensbury, Buckinghamshire.
BUCKINGHAMSHIRE GOAT CLUB: N. C. Nichol-son, Chequers Home Farm, Butlers Cross, Buckinghamshire.
CAMBRIDGESHIRE GOAT CLUB: Mrs R. M. Masters, Flint Cottage, Westley Waterless, Newmarket, Cambridgeshire.
COLCHESTER, SUDBURY & DISTRICT GOAT CLUB: Miss P. V. Minter, The Chestnuts, Ipswich Road, Ardleigh, Colchester, Essex.
DERBYSHIRE GOAT CLUB: Mrs M. M. Hollis, Greenacre, Duckmanton, Chesterfield, Derbyshire.
CORNWALL GOAT CLUB: A. F. Mylam, Hillcrest Farm, Hick Mill, Bissoe, Truro, Cornwall.
DEVON GOAT CLUB: Mrs B. Short, Cothland Barn, Lustleigh, Newton Abbot, Devon.
HAMPSHIRE GOAT CLUB: Miss M. E. K. Pennington, 52 Broad Street, Alresford, Hampshire.
IPSWICH & DISTRICT GOAT CLUB: E. P. Appleton, Hazlemere, Burcklesham Road, Ipswich, Suffolk.
KENT GOAT CLUB: Mrs E. A. Moon, Oakwood, Dean Street, East Farleigh, Kent.
LANCASHIRE DAIRY GOAT KEEPERS ASSOCIATION: K. B. Turner, 28 Bradley Lane, Wigan, Lancashire.
MID-ESSEX GOAT CLUB: Mrs E. V. Trigg, The

Anchorage, Nathans Lane, Wittle, Chelmsford, Essex.

NORFOLK & SUFFOLK GOAT CLUB: Miss C. Loveridge, Sandylands, Waxham, Norwich.

NORTHAMPTONSHIRE & DISTRICT GOAT CLUB: Mrs R. M. Lock, 2 Brickhill Lodge, Stanion Road, Brigstock, Northamptonshire.

NORTHERN IRELAND GOAT CLUB: Miss E. Gibbins, Finlarig, Furren Ballynahinch, Co. Down.

NORTH STAFFORDSHIRE GOAT CLUB: Mrs B. White, Fairview Farm, Thorny Edge, Bagnall, Stoke-on-Trent, Staffordshire.

NOTTINGHAM GOAT CLUB: C. B. Morrison, 8 Sheppards Row, Queen Street, Southwell, Nottinghamshire.

OXFORDSHIRE GOAT CLUB: Miss B. M. Barton, Elmfield, Witney, Oxfordshire.

PENNINE GOAT CLUB: Mrs J. Myrard, Stubbing Lock House, Hebden Bridge, Yorkshire.

PONTEFRACT & DISTRICT GOAT CLUB: Mrs M. E. Husband, Pear Tree House, Holme Lane, Bentley, Doncaster, Yorkshire.

RUTLAND & DISTRICT DAIRY GOAT SOCIETY: Miss M. Cheaney, Marboro Cottage, Hambleton, Oakham, Rutland.

SCOTTISH GOAT KEEPERS FEDERATION: Mrs E. M. Adamson, 58 Queen's Road, Aberdeen.

SOMERSET & WILTSHIRE GOAT SOCIETY: Miss J. G. McLeod, Chestnut Tree Cottage, Doynton, Bristol, Wiltshire.

SURREY GOAT CLUB: Miss P. E. Goldsmith, Hadresham, Outwood, Redhill, Surrey.

SUSSEX GOAT CLUB: Miss P. E. Paris, Willow Cottage, East Chiltingdon, Lewes, Sussex.

SWAFFHAM & DISTRICT GOAT CLUB: A. E. Curry, The Forge, West Bradenham, Thetford, Norfolk.

VALLEY GOAT CLUB: Mrs Philips, Leacroft, Westerham Hill, Kent.

WARWICKSHIRE GOAT CLUB: Mrs M. Townsend, High Cross Farm, Shrewley, Warwickshire.

WELSH GOAT SOCIETY: Mrs G. Festing, Heol Gerrig House, Llanellen, Abergavenny, Monmouthshire.

WESSEX GOAT CLUB: Mrs E. P. Clark, Yonder Hill, Coalton-Raleigh, Sidmouth, Devon.

WORCESTER GOAT CLUB: Mrs C. M. Wickett, The Orchards, Harvington, Evesham, Worcestershire.

YORKSHIRE GOAT CLUB: Mrs Harben Williams, Field House, Gomersal, Cleckheaton.

SERVICES

Members of THE BRITISH GOAT SOCIETY *can obtain milking buckets, churns, butter churns, agricultural seeds, milk cartons, kid's teats, trimming knives (for hoof trimming) and many other items.*

BIBLIOGRAPHY

THE HERD BOOK/The British Goat Society. Price: £1.00 (plus postage). (Published annually.)

THE MONTHLY JOURNAL/The British Goat Society. Price: 15p (plus postage). Annual subscription: £1.50.

THE YEAR BOOK/The British Goat Society. Price: 50p (plus postage). (Previous issues are available at a reduced rate.)

GOAT HUSBANDRY, by David Mackenzie/Faber & Faber Ltd.

GOATS, by H. E. Jefferey/Cassell & Co. Ltd.

HERBAL HANDBOOK FOR FARM & STABLE, by Juliette de Bairacli Levy/Faber & Faber Ltd. *Includes a section on herbal cures for goat illnesses.*

PRACTICAL GOATKEEPING, by Mrs A. Abbey/Cassell & Co. Ltd.

The following publications are available from The British Goat Society:

BREEDS OF GOATS. Price: 10p (plus postage).

COMMON AILMENTS OF THE DAIRY GOAT (S.G.F.). Price: 5p (plus postage).

DAIRY WORK FOR GOATKEEPERS. Price: 10p (plus postage). (Includes butter and cheese-making.)

GOAT PRODUCTION IN THE TROPICS, by C. Devendra and Marca Burns. Price: £2.50 (plus postage).

GOAT-KEEPING. Price: 10p (plus postage).

GOATS MILK DIET SHEET (S.G.F.). Price: $1\frac{1}{2}$p (plus postage).

GOATS MILK FOR HEALTH. Price: 20p per hundred leaflets (plus postage).

GOATS MILK IN MODERN MEDICINE. Price: 5p (plus postage).

I-SPY BOOK OF FARM ANIMALS. Price: 9p (plus postage). (Includes goats.)

LIFE STORY OF A GOAT. Price: 2p (plus postage).

A Crystal Garden

A crystal garden is a delicate piece of beauty that can be made very easily and costs next to nothing in materials. It can be made in a small goldfish bowl, a glass jar, or even a bottle, and can be very simple in design, or as involved as you like. Apart from the container, the only other essential materials are coarse sand, a tin of water glass (the stuff thrifty mothers preserved eggs with in the old days) and a few packets of various crystals. The best crystals to use are as follows: Epsom Salts, Zinc Sulphate, Ferrous Sulphate, Cobalt Nitrate, Manganese Sulphate and Cadmium Nitrate. (Although these crystals are pretty well harmless, they don't taste very nice so avoid getting any in your food and keep them out of the way of children.)

METHOD

Fill the bottom of the glass container with a layer of coarse sand. Coloured sand and the ornamental chippings sold in tropical fish shops can be also used, but remember that crystal trees are very delicate and beautiful in themselves and any brightly-coloured material may over-power their effect. There are, however, a number of ways to set the crystal growths off. For instance, a miniature garden can be made out of plasticine and carefully positioned in the sand. By making little trees, garden seats, ornamental birds etc., a fantasy world can be created, especially if pieces of coral, shells and pebbles are incorporated in the design.

Before actually making the garden grow, decide whether the crystal growths are to form ad lib all over the bottom of the jar, or whether they are to grow in selected places. If it is the latter that is desired, then the crystals must first be carefully positioned in their respective places. Absolutely beautiful effects can be got by making little plasticine trees and bushes, and pressing a few crystals into the branches. (Be careful not to press the crystals right in otherwise they cannot grow.) The next step is to mix up a solution of water and water glass, which is made by dissolving three tablespoon-fuls of waterglass to a pint of hot water. Make sure that enough solution has been mixed to fill the container and then very carefully, pour it gently into the container until it is full. If the crystals have already been positioned, they will immediately start to grow but if a wild garden is desired, then the crystals are dropped into the jar and will start to grow wherever they fall.

After about ten minutes, the crystals will have grown into beautiful tree-like forms. It is best to avoid moving the container around too much in case any of the growths get damaged, so try to have the container as near to its position as possible when actually making the garden.

SOURCES OF MATERIALS

All the crystals mentioned here can be obtained for a few pence from your local chemist.

Coarse sand is obtainable from the sea shore or a builders' merchant.

Waterglass is obtainable from most hardware shops.

A Taste of Honey

Normally when one considers the role of bees in this country, one usually thinks of them as only producers of honey and wax; but this is small compared to the part they play as pollinators of flowers and many varieties of hard and soft fruits. Many farmers today realize the importance of keeping bees in their gardens, for they have discovered that their presence means heavier fruit crops as each year progresses. In actual fact, bee keeping has never been as popular as it is now: even people in large towns are keeping apiaries on their rooftops where the bees will fly over two miles to collect nectar from flowers and crops in gardens and outlaying districts. Naturally the quantity of honey collected is not near as much as country bees who are within easy reach of orchards and heather crops, but the joy of eating good fresh honey is the same.

Although there are many intricacies in bee-keeping, many problems will work themselves out with practice and clear thinking. But so you don't get ploughed under with too many difficulties, we suggest that you start with only one hive. In due course, as you get more acquainted with working with bees, you can then purchase a second or even a third.

There are quite a few manufacturers of bee equipment in this country who, once they realize that you are a beginner, will try and persuade you into buying the 'essentials' needed for successful bee keeping; but do your utmost to ignore them.

For example—there is a small hand-tool on the market which the manufacturers will insist on is absolutely essential for the dismantling of your hive and which no other tool will achieve—this is rubbish. A hefty screwdriver from your shed will do exactly the same job. There are a couple more examples which we could give but you will realize what they are once you get your hive. There is only one hand-tool which, to our knowledge cannot be improvised, and that is a 'smoker'. This is a tin with bellows attached and once it has been filled with either dried bark, 'cow-chips', peat or old rags will, once it has been set alight,

smoulder all the time that you are working with your bees. In short, when bees smell smoke they automatically think of fire. This in turn leads them to stuff themselves with honey which in turn makes them lazy and less inclined to sting.

Proper clothing is another essential, but can be overcome by just making sure that you don't have any gaps for the bees to enter, e.g. trouser bottoms, shirt or blouse sleeves, fly-holes (could be very nasty) and even button-holes! A veil must be worn at all times to protect your eyes, ears, nose and mouth, so instead of buying one at a ridiculous price, why not make one? It is quite easy and only needs one and a half yards of black Bretonne net and a stiff-brimmed hat to keep the net away from your face. (Black net is best as it gives much clearer vision than white or green). Sew the net into a long bag and drape it over the hat. Thread a long piece of elastic round the back of the veil so that the middle will fit into the back of the neck. The ends are then brought through to the front (about 5 inches apart), passed under the arm pits and tied behind the back. Gloves should be avoided if possible as they are too clumsy for such delicate work. Unfortunately you will get stung at first, but as time goes on you'll know how to handle the bees and the occasional sting will be no more than a minor irritation.

Whilst on the subject of stings, never pull out the sting between your forefinger and thumb because attached to each sting there is a small sac of poison and if you're not careful, you will squirt all the poison into the wound. If you have time, simply push the sting out with a finger nail or failing that, just rub it out against your clothing.

The positioning of your hive is extremely important, not just for your bees, but your neighbours too. If you can, have your hive facing south so that the bees have the advantage of the morning sun; but *never* face them towards the north. Keep your hive away from heavy shade, busy roads or livestock as it has been known for bees to sting an animal to death. A good idea is to face the hive towards a high hedge or clump of trees so they have to fly high as they leave, thereby flying well over the heads of neighbours and animals alike.

Also put your hive where the bees have easy access to water as they require it for keeping the hive cool in summer; in winter you will probably have to supply the water yourself.

The hive is the costliest piece of equipment needed, but there are many different designs on the market so you will have no difficulty in choosing one. The average price for a good hive is around £25, but if you advertised for a second-hand one in the various bee-keeping journals you should pick one up for much less. This price includes all the interior equipment essential for the harvesting of honey and can be bought direct from the makers. (See p. 209 for books on hive-making.)

In most cases when you buy a hive, you will also get a colony of bees. This will contain (dependant on the price) a young queen, 12,000 workers, a few hundred drones and a brood in all stages of development. But should you want to buy your bees separately (as in the case of a second-hand hive) you can expect to pay about £9 for 24,000 workers (in all cases a young queen, drones and brood are included): £8.50 for 18,000 and £6.50 for 12,000 workers. A good queen can be purchased for around £1.30 but the price varies slightly during the year.

The function of the queen (or mother) is simply to populate the hive. She is the only perfectly-developed female in the hive and in the summer months may lay up to two thousand eggs per day which hatch out into drone and worker bees. She can be recognised by her sheer size in comparison with the rest of the colony.

The worker bee, on the other hand, is an undeveloped female and the smallest in the hive. She spends all her time building cells for the queen to lay more eggs in; collecting nectar and pollen: feeding the young larvae and any other household chores which may arise.

But in the case of the drone bees they are simply there to fertilise the young queen. Towards the end of the honey season, when their services are no longer required, the drones are turned out of the hive by the workers and left to die. They can be distinguished quite easily by their size—they are smaller than the queen but larger than the workers.

There are in fact four different species of bees available, the most common and favourite of which is the Italian variety. They are especially suitable for the beginner because due to its slowness of action, it is less inclined to sting, therefore making it easier to work with. The other varieties are nowhere near as docile and are much quicker and hot-headed that normally only professional keepers know how to handle them.

There are many essential factors to consider when the important time of wintering down your bees arrives. This should be done in September, so that by the time Spring arrives they will be in such good condition that they will be ready when the nectar flow begins.

1 A good supply of food is of course a must and during these winter months 25 lb of food is consumed. But just in case there is a really cold Spring, the bees must be bedded down with at least 30 lb of supplies or they might possibly starve to death.

During the summer months the bees will provide you with something like 35 to 40 lb of honey (or more) but out of this, 30 lb must be given back for the colony to survive, so make sure that you don't take more than your quota.

In most cases, the professional keeper takes 35 lb of honey from each hive, gives back 51 lb and substitutes the other 30 lb with white sugar mixed with water. Although there are lots of books which recommend this practice, we must stress the importance of *not* using this method. The use of white sugar is totally wrong in any situation but even the use of brown sugar must be avoided as this can cause dysentery amongst the bees and is still no exchange for their proper food—honey.

2 Keep your hive as weatherproofed as possible. Do not put it beneath a tree as the continual dripping of rain will cause unrest amongst the bees. In snow, to prevent too much sun-light reflecting up into the hive, place a small fence or something similar in front of the opening. (Bees have been known to fly out in such conditions, thinking it Spring, but dying in the cold air.)

3 Keep all openings free from leaves etc. as this can cause bad ventilation, resulting in the bees becoming ill. In some cases you will find a few dead bees in the entrance, but don't worry as this is quite normal. Simply clear them away so that they don't hinder the air circulation.

4 Try not to disturb your bees at all. If you must check the hive, do it quickly and quietly. Make sure that the hive is firmly fastened down and the roof secure.

5 If needed, renew your queen bee before the winter. There is no set time as to how long a queen should be kept, but bear in mind that she will have to give you plenty of young during these six months ready for the spring.

6 Make sure that you check for disease just before the last bee settles in for Winter. The most common malady is European Foul Brood (EFB). In this disease, the worker, and the drone larvae die giving off a nasty 'glue-pot odour'. Nosema is another serious complaint and is quite similar to dysentery. But if you're in any doubt at all about recognising or curing a disease, contact your nearest veterinary surgeon who, if unable to help, will put you in touch with someone who can.

There is one setback which you must expect to come across when you own a hive, and that is swarming. At any time during the summer the queen can summon her workers and drones and together they will disappear over the rooftops.

There are many reasons for this. One could be lack of space in their hive, or a decline in nectar in their area; even the weather can cause swarming. Real prime swarms generally appear from mid-May to mid-June and unfortunately there isn't a great deal you can do about it except perhaps to rub a few leaves of lemon balm (Mellissa officinalis) around the inside of the hive which I'm told tends to attract bees and therefore may deter them from leaving.

Another method is the clipping of the queen's wings. In so doing, should her bees swarm, it is impossible for her to fly with them; and as they are her subjects, they would not leave without her. But this is horribly cruel because all you need to do is to collect the swarm (once it has settled) is to place an open box beneath them and brush the cluster of bees into it with a branch.

Honey is produced in two forms—comb and extracted. If the honey is required for bottling, a 'super' (designed for the collecting of surplus honey) should be used; each one holding some shallow frames and fitted with a sheet of wired wax foundation. As the honey flow gets under way, the worker bees build out the cells, fill them up with honey and secure (cap) them with a thin layer of wax. These cappings are then sliced off the supers with a knife, placed in a honey extractor and by centrifugal force, separated from the cappings and the honey drained off.

On the other hand, comb honey can be got by fitting square wooden sections to the supers, each containing a thin piece of wax foundation. In the same manner as above, the bees build out the foundation, fill the cells with honey and seal them over. When finished, the comb honey is cut away from the wooden frames in one piece and is equally as nice to eat.

The first thing to remember when dealing with honey is not to collect it too early from the hives; the simple reason being that the surplus honey is needed for the expansion of the colony. The best time is when the honey flow is at its highest. No precise time can be given for this occurrence, so you will have to use your own observation and discretion when judging the time to begin collecting from the hives.

Although it is not absolutely necessary to have a suitable workshop where you can store your extracting equipment, it is best to keep all your activities well away from your house as the wasps and bees will soon make it their business to enter and forage around for goodies. If you have a small shed, this will be ideal except one or two modifications will be needed.

In the first place make sure there are no holes in the wood or around the door for the bees to enter and secondly, a bee escape will have to be installed in the window. This can be easily done by fixing a piece of glass half an inch shorter than the window frame, so that there is a space at the bottom. Half an inch outside this, another strip of glass should be fixed, but this time only 2 inches deep. What happens is that if any bees are carried into the workshop they will automatically make for the light, climb up the inside glass, but on reaching the top, drop to the bottom and start climbing again: this time they will climb up the small piece of glass and so get out. For some reason, bees rarely reverse their actions so it is quite bee-proof.

Inside your shed, a small bee-proof cupboard should be constructed in which your supers and honey can be kept quite safely.

The essential extracting equipment is a bit expensive but should you want some pure honey to slap between your bread you don't really have any alternative.

The only necessary piece of machinery needed is the extractor itself. For one capable of producing 36 lb of honey you will probably not get it for less than £16; other extractors in this price range are £18 and suitable for holding 46 lb of honey, or £22 for a 63 lb extractor. For only one hive the £16 one will be fine. In each case the basic principle is the same: the rapid revolution of the combs inside the extractor causes the honey to fly outwards against the tank wall and run down to the bottom, where it is drained off into tins ready for cleaning.

Here again, if you are not careful, you may be persuaded into buying equipment which you don't really need—the storage tank is a prime example. This tank, priced around £8 is designed for the separating and straining of honey, but the same result can be got by straining the honey through a cone-shaped strainer and into the waiting honey jars: all the honey impurities will be trapped and can be disposed of in due course.

The removing of the honey from the supers is quite straightforward and if you follow a set pattern you should have no trouble at all. Before you open the hive to take out the supers it is advisable to make sure that the hive is relatively free from bees and a way this can be done is by fitting a 'Porter escape' over the entrance to the brood chamber in the morning. This simple mechanism is designed to allow the bees to fly out of the hive but completely prevents them from returning.

Carefully take out the supers (this technique will vary according to the make of hive) and carry them into your workshop. This should be done preferably when the weather is warm, but not too hot as the heat may melt the honey before it can be extracted properly. With a hot knife (one which has stood in hot water for a few minutes) cut off the honey combs from the supers and place them in the extractor until the

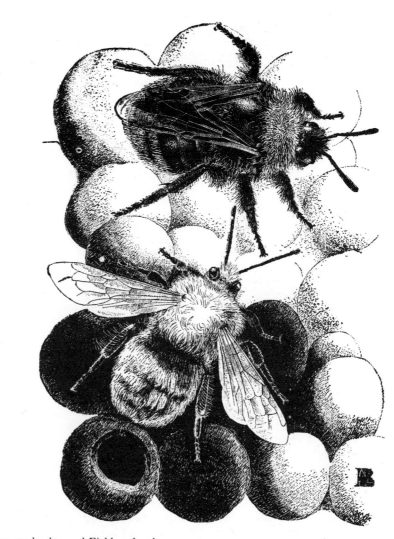

Common garden bee and Field cuckoo bee.

machine is full. Slowly turn the extractor handle until you begin to hear the honey pattering against the cylinder sides and then increase the revolutions for a while until the combs are empty. Whilst this is taking place, the honey in the base of the extractor must be drained off into some large tins and put aside for straining.

Once all the honey has been extracted from the combs and drawn off, the equipment must

then be cleaned out. This can be done by closing the valve where the honey has drained out and filling it with a gallon of cold water. Keep swilling this round until the inside is spick and span and drain off. (This water can be saved to make mead or honey vinegar later on.) Carefully dry the inside with a clean cloth and store the extractor away with another piece of cloth draped over it for protection.

The method by which the bees wax can be

207

obtained is as follows. Wash the combs in warm water and place them in a pan of hot water over a low flame. As it melts, the finer impurities will rise to the top where they should be skimmed off. Leave both the wax and water to cool, pour off the water and remove the wax from the pan. This wax can then be moulded into small cakes by placing it in a small pan, set into a larger one of boiling water. Once it has melted it can then be poured into a mould and left to set. The choice of mould is up to you but a jelly mould or a cup is good enough.

Bees-wax mixed with other ingredients is ideal for many household uses as the examples here show:

Beeswax & Turpentine Polish: Melt one pound of beeswax, and as it cools down, stir in a quart of turpentine. If it seems too thick, more turpentine can be added.

Furniture or shoe cream (a): Cut into small pieces, 8 oz beeswax, 1 oz white wax, 1 oz Castile soap and boil for twenty minutes in a quart of rain water. When the mixture is nearly cold, add a quart of turpentine and shake until a good cream is formed.

Furniture Cream (b): 1 pint turpentine, 1 pint of rain water, 2 oz white wax, 3 oz beeswax, 2 oz Castile soap, $\frac{1}{3}$ oz spermaceti. Melt all the wax and stir in the pint of turpentine. Boil the soap in the rain water, mix it all well together and add the spermaceti when cool.

Black Wax: Melt together 2 oz beeswax and $\frac{1}{2}$ oz burgundy pitch and add $1\frac{1}{2}$ oz of fine ivory black.

Fruit Bottle Covers: 2 oz beeswax, 4 oz resin, $\frac{1}{2}$ oz vaseline. Melt these together in a tin and brush evenly over pieces of linen or calico. When a cover is required for use, apply to the hot jar and press down firmly.

Country folk in all the four corners of the world recognise honey as containing many medicinal characteristics. Lots of people think of honey as the best cure for a sore throat (which it probably is) and, due to its antiseptic qualities,

is one of the most useful things to apply to abrasions and burns.

Honey Tea: For severe digestive disorders a tablespoon of honey dissolved in a cupful of hot water will be beneficial to take several times a day. Sip it slowly on an empty stomach.

Honey and Lemon Tea: Add the juice of half a lemon to a tablespoonful of honey dissolved in a cupful of hot water. This is very good for liver disorders and complexion blemishes. If it is taken as hot as possible before going to bed, it will often ward off a cold.

Honey and Yarrow: To an infusion of yarrow, add a good teaspoonful of honey and drink it hot at bedtime and on rising in the morning. This is widely recommended for influenza and as a tonic.

Honey and Milk: Mix a teaspoonful of honey with a cupful of warm milk and take it last thing at night as an ideal cure for insomnia. It is also highly recommended for stomach ulcers and anaemia.

Honey and Glycerine: A really nice cure for a cold or a sore throat is a mixture of 2 teaspoonfuls of honey and 1 teaspoonful of glycerine in a cupful of hot water.

Linseed and Honey: Boil 1 oz of linseed in a pint of water for half an hour. Strain, add the juice of a lemon and sweeten the mixture with honey. Drink this hot at bedtime.

Cough Candy: Boil horehound leaves in water, strain through muslin and add as much honey as desired to the liquor. Boil until the candy can be made into a soft ball when dropped into water. Pour the mixture into greased tins and leave it to set.

Honey is also ideal for ointments and cosmetics and is widely known as having great value in curing certain skin troubles.

Honey and Glycerine: In equal parts this mixture is ideal for bruises, and chaps on the face or hands.

Cure for Chilblains: Mix 1 tablespoonful of honey with an equal quantity of glycerine, the white of an egg and enough flour to make a fine paste. (A teaspoonful of rose water is helpful.) Wash the affected parts well with pure soap and warm water, dry thoroughly and spread the paste over. Wrap up with a cotton cloth, as this ointment is very sticky.

As with other natural foods like milk, fruit, green leaves and nuts, honey is at its best when eaten raw, but that doesn't mean to say it isn't beneficial when mixed with other good things and baked in an oven.

Grapefruit and Honey: Simply scoop a hole in the pulp of the fruit and put in two or three teaspoonfuls of honey. (Very nice this one.)

Honey Plum Butter: Wash some plums and cook them gently in water till soft. Pass them through a sieve and for each cup of pulp add half a cup of honey. Cook slowly until thick and jelly-like and then pour the mixture into hot sterilised jars, sealing them securely.

Plain Honey Cake: Beat together well $\frac{1}{2}$ pint of sour milk, 6 oz Barbados sugar and 4 oz of honey. Work all this well into 10 oz of wholemeal flour and bake the mixture in buttered tins from a half to three-quarters of an hour and serve hot.

Honey Gems: Add 6 oz honey to 1 pint of sour milk. Mix in enough wholemeal flour to make a soft dough and bake the mixture in heated tins.

Mead: There are numerous recipes for this drink, some of which contain herbs, spices and fruit etc., but the simple fermented liquor is equal to anything more complicated.

If made with fresh honey, 4 lb should be used to each gallon of water and some folk think it improves the flour if lemon peel is added. Boil the honey and water for an hour, skim any frothy impurities from the surface and pour it into a tub or any large receptacle. Add 1 oz of yeast per gallon either by mixing it first in warm water or floating it on the liquor on a piece of toast. When fermentation has started, strain off the liquor into a clean vessel, but keep it lightly covered until it has stopped working. When the fermentation has stopped, pour the liquor into bottles and cork them securely. You should then leave the mead in a temperature of about 70°F for a year. (A kitchen is probably the ideal place for storing.)

Honey and Oatmeal: This non-alcoholic drink is made by putting 2 tablespoonfuls of oatmeal into a quart jug nearly filled with fresh boiling water. Cover the jug and let it stand for 24 hours. In another jug dissolve 3 tablespoonfuls of honey in a little boiling water and the juice of 2 lemons. Strain the oatmeal water into this and it is ready for use. This drink may be made with pearl barley instead of oatmeal and lime juice instead of lemons.

SOURCES OF MATERIALS

There are only a few manufacturers of bee-keeping equipment in this country, and although we have listed them we cannot say how reputable they are, but they certainly have the widest ranges:

BIRDWOOD APIARIES, Hawkers Lane, Wells, Somerset.

BURTT & SONS, Stroud Road, Gloucester.

ROBERT LEE LTD, Beehive Works, George Street, Uxbridge, Middlesex.

E. H. TAYLOR LTD, Welwyn, Hertfordshire.

E. H. THORNE LTD, Beehive Works, Wragby, Lincolnshire.

SOURCES OF MATERIALS IN THE USA

THE WALTER T. KELLEY CO. Inc., Clarkson, Kentucky.

SOCIETIES

THE BEE RESEARCH ASSOCIATION, c/o London Zoological Gardens, Regents Park, London N1.

THE BRITISH BEEKEEPERS' ASSOCIATION, 55 Chipstead Lane, Riverhead, Sevenoaks, Kent.

This society was formed to educate and help those keeping and breeding bees whether they be amateur or professional. The society produces a magazine called BEECRAFT (see below).

DEVON BEEKEEPERS' ASSOCIATION, 36 Seaton Down Road, Seaton, Devon.

FEDERATION OF IRISH BEEKEEPERS, Boston Park, Cork, Eire.

THE SCOTTISH BEEKEEPERS' ASSOCIATION, 1 Kennilworth Avenue, Foxbar, Paisley.

BIBLIOGRAPHY

APICULTURAL ABSTRACTS/Bee Research Association, Hill House, Chalfont St Peter, Gerrards Cross, Buckinghamshire SL9 0NR. (Quarterly) Annual subscription: £9.50.

BEE CRAFT/The British Beekeepers' Association. Available from the Secretary, 17 West Way, Capthorne, Sussex. (Monthly) Price: 9½p. Annual subscription: £1.15 (including postage).

BEE WORLD/Bee Research Association, Hill House, Chalfont St Peter, Gerrards Cross, Buckinghamshire SL9 0NR. (Quarterly) Annual subscription: £2.50.

BEEKEEPING/ Devon Beekeepers' Association, 36 Seaton Down Road, Seaton, Devon. (Eight times a year) Price: 5p. Annual subscription: 60p.

IRISH BEEKEEPER/Federation of Irish Beekeepers, Boston Park, Cork, Eire. (Monthly) Price: 4p. Annual subscription: 70p.

SCOTTISH BEEKEEPER/Standard Printing Works, Grange Place, Kilmarnock. (Monthly) Price: 7½p. Annual subscription: 90p.

THE ART OF BEEKEEPING, by William Hamilton/The Herald Printers.

BEEKEEPING UP TO DATE, by A. B. Flower/Cassell & Co. Ltd.

THE DANCING BEES, by Karl Von Frisch/Methuen & Co. Ltd.

HERBAL HANDBOOK FOR FARM & STABLE, by Juliette de Biaracli Levy/Faber & Faber Ltd. *Includes a section on herbal cures for bee illnesses.*

THE LIFE OF THE BEE, by Maurice Maeterlinck/Allen & Unwin Ltd.

THE LIVES OF WASPS & BEES, by Sir Christopher Andrews/Chatto & Windus Ltd.

MY BEE BOOK, by W. C. Cotton/Kingsmead Reprints, Rosewell House, Kingsmead Square, Bath, Somerset.

BEES, by Karl Von Frisch/Cape Editions.

A TREATISE ON THE MANAGEMENT OF BEES 1770, by Thomas Wildman/Kingsmead Reprints, Rosewell House, Kingsmead Square, Bath, Somerset.

QUEEN REARING/available free from Badgerdell Apiaries, Hambrook Grange, nr Chichester, Sussex (Booklet and catalogue.)

The following books are published by Beecraft Books, which is affiliated to The British Beekeepers' Association:

APIARY RECORD BOOK & GUIDE.

THE BEE COMMUNITY, by F. H. Metcalfe.

THE BEE CRAFTSMAN, by H. J. Wadey.

BEES & HONEY, by G. A. Carter.

THE BEHAVIOUR OF BEES—AND OF BEEKEEPERS, by H. J. Wadey.

THE PHILOSOPHY AND PRACTISE OF BEEKEEPING, by A. L. Gregg.

QUEEN BREEDING FOR AMATEURS, by C. P. Abbott.

THE VENTILATION OF HIVES, by E. B. Wedmore.

The following publications are available from branches of Her Majesty's Stationery Office, or by post from HMSO, P.O. Box 569, London, SE1:

BEEKEEPING (Bulletin No. 9).

DISEASES OF BEES (Bulletin No. 100).

SWARMING OF BEES (Bulletin No. 206).

The following HMSO publications concern hive construction:

BEEHIVES (Bulletin No. 144).

Also ADVISORY LEAFLETS Nos. 367, 411, 445, 468 and 549.

Courses

CROYDON TECHNICAL COLLEGE, Surrey and DULWICH COLLEGE, London, provide courses in beekeeping.

SURREY BEEKEEPERS' ASSOCIATION (Epsom Division) runs its own courses for members. The address may be obtained from the head office of the British Beekeeping Association (see above).

The Home Dairy

The number of people moving out into the country increases yearly and many of them are keeping goats and perhaps the odd cow or two. The whole economics of the backyard dairy have been superbly recorded in a small book by Len Street and Andrew Singer[1] so there is no need to go any further on that point, but what we have written about are the various ways of making cheese, butter, yoghurt and cream in the home, with limited kitchen equipment, using milk or cream from your own goat or cow or from the milkman.

[1] See Bibliography p. 212.

Cheese is simply the curd of milk coagulated, separated from the whey and pressed into a mould or processed into many differing forms. There are, however, two basic types of cheese: *'Lactic cheese'* which needs no rennet to coagulate the curds and is produced by allowing milk to sour for a certain time and then straining, and *'Rennet'* cheese, a normally hard cheese that has rennet as a ripening agent to coagulate the curds. As vegetarians we will only deal with easily-produced soft *'lactic'* cheeses, because rennet is a substance obtained from animal sources. However, there are one or two ways of separating milk using a rennet 'substitute'. Both marjoram and sorrel (when crushed and their juices extracted) will coagulate the curds. The juice of one or the other herbs can be used, or mixed together, and by experimenting with different quantities and mixtures, an efficient substitute can be prepared.

There may arise certain difficulties where pasteurised milk from the milkman is concerned. If left to sour, it may go bad and end up smelling highly unpleasant. This is because the process of pasteurisation kills off the natural bacteria in the milk and so becomes highly susceptible to outside bacteria. To overcome this, the juice of one or two lemons should be added to every gallon of milk. If the milk still goes bad, try using more lemon juice.

Cottage Cheese (1ST METHOD)
Allow a quantity of milk (*preferably skimmed : skimmed milk is what is left after the cream has been removed*) to sour well until it begins to coagulate and then strain through muslin. The remaining curds can either be mixed with cream and served as a delicious cottage cheese, or pressed between two flat bread boards or plates so that a solid form is made.

Cottage Cheese (2ND METHOD)
Use only soured skimmed milk. Heat the milk gently until the curds begin to appear and after removing from the heat, allow to cool naturally. Strain as described above.

Pot Cheese
Add together in a saucepan, 2 quarts of sour milk and 1 quart of buttermilk. Heat till nearly boiling and the curds appear. Remove the curds from the whey and put them in a muslin bag, tie tightly and allow to drain for an hour or longer. Remove the curds from the bag, add a little salt and then mould the pieces into balls. Let the balls cool for a few hours and then serve.

Cream Cheese
(1) DOUBLE-CREAM CHEESE
Obtain as much double cream as you can (1 lb of cheese is obtained from about 1 pint of double cream) and lay a piece of muslin around the inside of a sieve or colander and pour the cream into it. Keep at a temperature of about 40°F (fairly low) for about 12 hours. Place a lid or some other flat object over the cream and add weights to lightly press it for about 4 hours, then serve.
(2) ORDINARY CREAM CHEESE
To your muslin-lined sieve or colander add as much single cream or rich fresh milk as you can add and simply leave for three or four days. Nothing to it, and ready to eat.

Quark Cheese
Obtain as much natural yoghurt as possible and let it sour. Drain the yoghurt through muslin bags and serve as desired.

Indian Soft Cream Cheese
For this cheese, tartaric acid is needed (available at many chemists). Heat a quantity of milk to the boil and then remove from the heat. Stir in a cupful of tartaric acid and hot water ($\frac{1}{4}$ of a teaspoonful to each cup) at the rate of one cupful to every $1\frac{1}{2}$ pints of milk, and stir well until the curds appear. Strain the mixture into muslin bags and press the curds to form 'hard' blocks.

With all these cheeses, chopped herbs such as sage, chives and garlic etc., can be added in the final stages which will produce delicious alternatives to the plain recipies.

CREAM
Cream is the fatty part of milk that separates and rises to the surface. It has to be skimmed from the top of the milk and this is possible in a number of ways. The easiest way is to pour the fresh milk into a wide shallow pan and leave it for about 24 hours until the cream has separated. By using a saucer, the risen cream can then be scooped off the surface. Another method is to pour the milk into a large glass container like a wine fermenting jar and leave again for 24 hours. Then, using a rubber tube, and by inserting it down into the jar just below the bottom level of the cream, the skimmed milk can be syphoned off, leaving just the cream behind. For both these methods, the milk must be left to separate in a cool place. Use the remaining skimmed milk for cheese making.

Clotted Cream
Stand the fresh milk in a heat-proof pan in a cool place for 24 hours. Only allow 8 inches depth of milk for each pan. Next, heat the milk very gently to 160°F until the cream begins to form at the sides. Remove from the heat and allow to cool. The clotted cream can then be skimmed from the surface.

BUTTER
Butter is obtained from cream by '*churning*', i.e. shaking the cream until it coagulates into a lump. What is left is called buttermilk and should not be thrown away as it can be used to make cheese. Butter can be made from either ordinary skimmed cream or clotted cream.

METHOD
To make butter successfully, the temperature for churning needs to be correct, about 50°–60°F, and slightly warmer in cool weather and cooler in warm weather. The simplest way to make butter is to put the cream in a bottle and shake it for a couple of hours. This invariably is a tiring process and it is easier to put the cream in a bowl and activate it with a spoon for about half an hour until the colour changes. The grains of butter will then soon appear and after straining through a muslin bag, wash them in water to remove the buttermilk and squeeze the grains into one lump.

If you own a foodmixer, this is by far the easiest method. Set the machine up on the slowest speed with the cake-mixing attachment fitted. Add the cream slowly, mixing all the while until all the cream is in the mixing bowl. Wait for the colour change again and when the butter grains have appeared, strain as described above, and wash with water. The remaining grains are then similarly squeezed into one lump.

Home-made butter will be a very pale colour and if the familiar golden yellow colour is desired, then annatto, a vegetable colouring, can be added. Salt can also be added if desired. The rate of salt per 1 lb of butter is a matter for personal taste but normally, 1 teaspoonful is used for each 1 lb.

YOGHURT

Yoghurt is made by adding a 'culture' or bacteria to milk, which then breeds in the milk and produces a creamy substance with a distinctive soured flavour. There are a number of cultures available on the market, the most easily available being *Lactobacillus Bulgaris*, a culture supposedly originating from Bulgaria. There are also innumerable yoghurt culture kits, yoghurt making machines and yoghurt thermos activators etc. available, but they are all totally unnecessary and a gross waste of money. If you can just get hold of a few lumps of the culture, that is all that is needed, for it breeds in milk reasonably quickly so that after a few weeks, large quantities of yoghurt will be produced and the culture will then have to be split and one half given away to a friend. A culture I was given about two years ago has been split in this way about two dozen times and the culture sent all over the country.

Having obtained the culture all one needs is a glass bowl (don't use steel or plastic). Pour in a pint of milk and add the culture. The culture looks rather weird—white lumps rather like pieces of polystyrene. Part cover the bowl with a plate and put it in a warm place. The quantity of resulting yoghurt will vary according to the proportion of culture to milk and the temperature at which they are left. For instance, a little culture in a lot of milk in a cool place will create yoghurt very slowly. As a general guide, half a cupful of the culture to 1 pint of milk in a warm place will take about 24–30 hours to make a solid bowl of yoghurt.

To separate the culture from the yoghurt a metal strainer or sieve is needed. Simply pour the contents of the bowl into the strainer and work the yoghurt through gently with a wooden spoon. All that will be left in the strainer will be the lumps of culture, which are then placed back in the bowl and covered with another pint of milk. A sort of greyish mould will appear on top of the milk when the culture is working but don't worry about this as it is all good stuff and disappears on straining. One important point is to try and get a strainer with a medium-sized mesh: too fine a mesh will tend to liquify the yoghurt.

The strained yoghurt can then be eaten immediately, or left for another day which tends to thicken its consistency.

There are other methods for yoghurt making, but all of them involve special temperatures and other complications: anyway, no yoghurt tastes as good as that which is obtained from a culture.

SOURCES OF MATERIALS

Information on suppliers of *anatto*, used for colouring butter and cheese, and on supplies of *yoghurt cultures* may be obtained from: J. RODALE & CO LTD, Chestnut Close, Potten End, Berkhamsted.
Butterchurns, milking buckets, milk cartons and other sundries can be obtained from:
THE BRITISH GOAT SOCIETY, c/o The Secretary, Rougham, Bury St Edmunds, Suffolk.

SOCIETIES

BUTTER INFORMATION COUNCIL, 735 Salisbury House, London Wall, London EC2.
CHEDDAR & CAERPHILLY FARMHOUSE CHEESE MAKERS ASSOCIATION, Havyatt Farm, Langford, Bristol.
STILTON CHEESE MAKERS ASSOCIATION, 44 Asfordby Road, Melton Mowbray, Leicestershire.

BIBLIOGRAPHY

ALL ABOUT YOGHURT/The Milk Marketing Board. *A free leaflet on how* not *to make good yoghurt.*
THE BACKYARD DAIRY BOOK, by Len Street and Andrew Singer/Whole Earth Tools, Mill Cottage, Swaffham Road, Cambridge. *Highly recommended. Price: 40p (plus postage).*
THE STORY OF CHEESE—MAKING IN BRITAIN, by Bal Cheke/Routledge & Kegan Paul Ltd.

COURSES

WEST DEAN COLLEGE, Chichester, Sussex. *Provides short courses on butter and cheese making.*

Further Useful Information

CRAFT ASSOCIATIONS, GUILDS AND SOCIETIES

NATIONAL

ARCHITECTURAL METAL CRAFTSMENS ASSOCIATION
Lenning House, Masons Avenue, Croydon, Surrey.
ART WORKERS' GUILD
Secretary: Richard Murry, Art Workers' Guild, 6 Queen Square, London WC1N 3AR. Tel: 01-837 3474
ASSOCIATION OF GUILDS OF WEAVERS, SPINNERS AND DYERS
Acting Hon. Secretary: Mrs Connie Laycock, Five Bays, 10 Stancliffe Avenue, Marford, nr. Wrexham, North Wales. Tel: Gresford 2386
BLADON SOCIETY OF ARTS AND CRAFTS
Curator/Secretary: George Burton, Bladon Gallery, Hurstbourne Tarrant, Andover, Hampshire. Tel: Hurstbourne Tarrant 278
BRITISH SOCIETY OF MASTER GLASS PAINTERS
Hon. Secretary: Mrs Caroline Swash, 113 Albert Palace Mansions, Lurline Gardens, London SW11. Tel: 01-622 4859
BRITISH STONE FEDERATION
37 Soho Square, London W1
Director: Miss Susannah Robins, British Crafts Centre, 12 Waterloo Place, London SW1Y 4AY. Tel: 01-839 5263
and
BRITISH CRAFTS CENTRE
43 Earlham Street, London WC2H 9LD. Tel: 01-240 3327
The aim of the British Crafts Centre is to show the best work by leading British craftsmen. The Centre runs a gallery at the Earlham Street address, displaying examples of jewellery, silver, glass, ceramics, textiles, weaving, woodwork, furniture, leatherwork and other crafts. One-man and group exhibitions are held frequently and all items on display are for sale. Craftsmen wishing to obtain details of the selection procedure should get in touch with the Membership Secretary, at 43 Earlham Street, London WC2.
BRITISH TOYMAKERS' GUILD
Chairman: Peter Greenhill, British Toymakers' Guild, Guild Centre, 32–34 Ridgeway, London SW19 4QW. Tel: 01-947 5662
COLLEGE OF MASONS
Hon. Secretary: R. A. Golland, April Cottage, Withyditch, Dunkerton, Bath. Tel: Timsbury 70493
CRAFTS ADVISORY COMMITTEE INDEX AND REGISTER OF CRAFTSMEN
12 Waterloo Place, London SW1Y 4AU
The Crafts Advisory Committee has set up a Register of craftsmen, which will be a record of craftsmen showing name, address and craft, and a selective Index of craftsmen, illustrated with colour slides. All Exhibiting Members of the British Crafts

Centre are eligible for inclusion in the Index. It is, however, possible for a craftsman to be included even if he does not wish to become a member of the British Crafts Centre, although his work must go through the same selection procedure. The Register and the Index are planned to provide a link between craftsmen and members of the public who may wish to commission work.
CRAFTSMEN POTTERS ASSOCIATION OF GREAT BRITAIN
Hon. Secretary: David Canter, Craftsmen Potters Shop, William Blake House, Marshall Street, London W1. Tel: 01-437 5117
DESIGN & RESEARCH CENTRE FOR THE GOLD, SILVER AND JEWELLERY INDUSTRIES
Director and Secretary: J. Francis Coote MVO, FRSA, Saint Dunstan's House, Carey Lane, London EC2. Tel: 01-606 7260
DESIGNER BOOKBINDERS
Hon. Secretary: Miss Elizabeth Greenhill, 12 Cornwall Mansions, 33 Kensington Court, London W8 5BG. Tel: 01-937 2943
EMBROIDERERS' GUILD
Secretary: Miss A. N. Beale, Embroiderers' Guild, 73 Wimpole Street, London W1M 8AX. Tel: 01-935 3281
FEDERATION OF BRITISH CRAFT SOCIETIES
Secretary: Miss Anne French, c/o British Crafts Centre, 12 Waterloo Place, London SW1Y 4AU. Tel: 01-839 5263
GALPIN SOCIETY
Secretary: Dr Maurice Byrne, Department of Physics, University of Warwick, Coventry CV4 7AL.
GLASS ADVISORY COUNCIL
6 Mount Row, London W1Y 6DY.
MASTER THATCHERS ASSOCIATION
6 Cheynes Walk, Northampton.
NATIONAL MASTER FARRIERS, BLACKSMITHS AND AGRICULTURAL ASSOCIATION
48 Spencer Road, Leeds.
GUILD OF LETTERING CRAFTSMEN
Hon. Secretary: Thomas Langley, c/o Art Workers' Guild, 6 Queen Square, London WC1N 3AR.
INSTITUTE & COLLEGE OF CRAFT EDUCATION
The P.R.O., 52 Locarno Avenue, Gillingham, Kent.
THE MARQUETRY SOCIETY
Hon. Secretary: Mrs G. M. Walker, 113 Kingsway, Petts Wood, Kent BR5 1PP. Tel: Orpington 23581
NATIONAL ASSOCIATION OF MASTER MONUMENTAL MASONS
Secretary: Mrs N. White, National Association of Master Monumental Masons, 215 Abbey House, Victoria Street, London SW1. Tel: 01-437 0328
NEW EMBROIDERY GROUP
Organiser: Mrs Ione Dorrington, 137 Colney Hatch Lane, Muswell Hill, London N10. Tel: 01-883 6046
RED ROSE GUILD OF DESIGNER CRAFTSMEN
Secretary: Miss Patricia Henderson, Northern Crafts Centre Ltd., 35 South King Street, Manchester 2. Tel: 061-832 5718
62 GROUP OF THE EMBROIDERERS' GUILD
Secretary: Miss Susan James, Embroiderers' Guild, 73 Wimpole Street, London W1M 8AX. Tel: 01-935 3281

SOCIETY OF DESIGNER-CRAFTSMEN
Secretary: Miss Jill Bundy, 3 Springfield Close, Lymington, Hampshire. Tel: Lymington 5506
SOCIETY FOR EDUCATION THROUGH ART
Hon. Secretary: Mrs Val Shillington, 131a Bedford Square Court Mansions, Bedford Square, London WC1B 3AH. Tel: 01-636 9973
SOCIETY OF CHURCH CRAFTSMEN
Hon. Secretary: Malcolm Fry, Royal Watercolour Society Galleries, 26 Conduit Street, London W1. Tel: 01-629 8300
SOCIETY OF ORNAMENTAL TURNERS
Hon. Secretary: W. A. Bourne, 2 Parry Drive, Rustington, Littlehampton, Sussex. Tel: Rustington 5430
SOCIETY OF PAINTERS IN TEMPERA
Hon. Secretary: Miss Rosamund Borradaile, 28 Eldon Road, London W8. Tel: 01-937 6573
SOCIETY OF SCRIBES AND ILLUMINATORS
Assistant Secretary: Miss Wendy Gould, 270 Trinity Road, London SW18. Tel: 01-870 0408
TIMBER BUILDINGS MANUFACTURERS ASSOCIATION
4 High Street, Epsom Surrey.
WORLD CRAFTS COUNCIL—BRITISH SECTION
Hon. Secretary: Brian Marshall, c/o British Crafts Centre, 12 Waterloo Place, London SW1Y 4AU.

REGIONAL—ENGLAND

Berkshire
BERKSHIRE CRAFT CENTRE ASSOCIATION
Secretary: W. Vincent, 15 Crescent Road, Wokingham, Berkshire RG11 2DB.

Buckinghamshire
BUCKINGHAMSHIRE GUILD OF WEAVERS, SPINNERS & DYERS
Hon. Secretary: F. J. Ruck, The Meads, 22 Millshot Drive, Amersham, Buckinghamshire. Tel: Amersham 7619
BUCKINGHAMSHIRE POTTERY & SCULPTURE SOCIETY
Hon. Secretary: Mrs E. Scott-Taggart, 96 Gregories Road, Beaconsfield, Buckinghamshire.

Cambridgeshire
IMPINGTON VILLAGE COLLEGE CRAFTSMEN'S GUILD
Hon. Secretary: E. F. Osborne, 10 College Road, Histon, Cambridge CB4 4PD. Tel: Histon 2366

Cheshire
CHESHIRE GUILD OF HANDLOOM WEAVERS
Hon. Secretary: Mrs Louise Littleton, 26 Glebelands Road, Knutsford, Cheshire WAL6 9DZ. Tel: Knutsford 2137

Cornwall
CORNWALL GUILD OF WEAVERS, SPINNERS & DYERS
Hon. Secretary: Mrs Vera Lyne, Boskerys, 52 Falmouth Road, Truro, Cornwall. Tel: Truro 4988

Devon
THE DEVON GUILD OF CRAFTSMEN
Hon. Secretary: Lt Col T. P. Honnor RM, Broomhill Cottage, Harford, Ivybridge, Devon PL1 0JG.

Tel: Ivybridge 2228

DEVON GUILD OF WEAVERS, SPINNERS & DYERS
Hon. Secretary: Mrs H. M. Lee, 16 Whiteway Road, Kingsteignton, Newton Abbott, Devon. Tel: Newton Abbott 5540

Dorset

DORSET COUNTY ARTS & CRAFTS ASSOCIATION
Exhibition Secretary: John Rome Esq., Lydlinch Studio, Lydlinch, Sturminster Newton, Dorset. Tel: Sturminster Newton 375
DORSET GUILD OF WEAVERS, SPINNERS & DYERS
Hon. Secretary: Mrs M. Richmond, 16 Parkstone Avenue, Parkstone, Poole, Dorset BH14 9LR. Tel: Parkstone 746538

Gloucestershire

THE CRAFTSMEN OF GLOUCESTERSHIRE
Hon. Secretary: Mrs M. Smith, 66 Prestbury Road, Cheltenham, Gloucestershire. Tel: Cheltenham 52782
GLOUCESTERSHIRE GUILD OF WEAVERS, SPINNERS & DYERS
Hon. Secretary: Mrs B. G. Martin, Victoria Villa, Cotswold Close, Brimscombe, Stroud, Gloucestershire GL5 2UA.
GUILD OF GLOUCESTERSHIRE CRAFTSMEN
Treasurer: W. G. Brotherton, Hambutts Barn, Edge Lane, Painswick, Gloucestershire. Tel: Painswick 3559

Hampshire

HAMPSHIRE GUILD OF WEAVERS, SPINNERS & DYERS
Secretary: Miss Nancy Goschen, 36 Shortheath Road, Farnham, Surrey. Tel: Farnham 5312
ISLE OF WIGHT GUILD OF BLACKSMITHS
Secretary: J. G. Fraser, CoSIRA, 'Venture Fair', Lower Padworth, Reading, Berkshire. Tel: Woolhampton 2350

Herefordshire

GUILD OF HEREFORDSHIRE CRAFTSMEN
Clerk: H. O. Williams, 25 Castle Street, Hereford. Tel: Hereford 2307
HEREFORDSHIRE ART & CRAFT SOCIETY
Hon. Secretary: Mrs H. F. Jackson, Yew Tree House, Wellington, Hereford.
SOCIETY OF CRAFTSMEN—HEREFORD
Hon. Secretary: Mrs C. Bulmer, Old Kemble Galleries, 29 Church Street, Hereford. Tel: Hereford 66049

Hertfordshire

WELWYN CRAFTWORKERS GUILD
Hon. Secretary: Miss Philips, 22 Howard House, Welwyn Garden City, Hertfordshire.
WEST HERTFORDSHIRE GUILD OF WEAVERS
Hon. Secretary: Mrs Monica George, 38 Orchard Drive, Watford, Hertfordshire WD1 3DY. Tel: Watford 22660

Kent

INSTITUTE & COLLEGE OF CRAFT EDUCATION
The P.R.O., 52 Locarno Avenue, Gillingham, Kent ME8 6ES.
KENT GUILD OF SPINNERS
Hon. Secretary: Mrs J. E. Church, Kent Bridge Lodge, Kingsdown, Deal, Kent.

Lake District

GUILD OF LAKELAND CRAFTSMEN
Secretary: Mrs J. Williams, Low Holme, Kentmere, Kendal, Westmorland. Tel: Staveley 505
LANCASHIRE & THE LAKES GUILD OF WEAVERS, SPINNERS & DYERS
Secretary: Miss M. Scragg, 69 Brookhouse Road, Caton, Lancaster.

Lancashire

ARTS & CRAFTS CENTRE
Secretary: Mrs A. West, Ribchester Road, Clayton-le-Dale, Nr. Blackburn, Lancashire.
LANCASHIRE & THE LAKES GUILD OF WEAVERS, SPINNERS & DYERS
See under Lake District.

Lincolnshire

THE GUILD OF LINCOLNSHIRE CRAFTSMEN
Hon. Secretary: G. P. Ginno, CoSIRA, 35 Orchard Street, Lincoln LN1 1XX. Tel: Lincoln 25282 x 305
LINCOLNSHIRE RURAL CRAFTWORK COMMITTEE
Hon. Secretary: J. I. Gordon, Lindsey & Holland Rural Community Council, 86 Newland, Lincoln. Tel: Lincoln 24020
MEN OF THE STONES
The Rutland, Tinwell, Stamford, Lincoln.

London

CLERKENWELL GREEN ASSOCIATION FOR CRAFTSMEN
Secretary: R. Barnes, 298 Upper Street, London N1 2TU. Tel: 01-226 2822
LONDON & HOME COUNTIES GUILD OF WEAVERS, SPINNERS & DYERS
Registrar: Miss Raie Barnett, 7 Ralston Road, London SW3 4DT. Tel: 01-352 8740

Midlands

MIDLAND GROUP GALLERY
Director: Miss Sylvia Cooper, Midland Group Gallery, 11 East Circus Street, Nottingham. Tel: Nottingham 48981
MIDLAND HAND WEAVERS ASSOCIATION
Hon. Secretary: P. B. Chawner, 51 Westridge Road, Kings Heath, Birmingham B13 0DU. Tel: 021-777 7980

Norfolk

THE BLAKENEY GUILD OF MANY CRAFTS
Clerk: Miss W. S. Ridley, 9 Weynor Gardens, Kelling, Holt, Norfolk. Tel: Weybourne 634
GREAT YARMOUTH GUILD OF ARTISTS & CRAFTSMEN
Hon. Secretary: Miss D. Hazel, The Hazels, Runham, nr. Filby, Great Yarmouth, Norfolk. Tel: Fleggburgh 221
NORFOLK RURAL CRAFTSMEN'S GUILD
Hon. Secretary: Mrs M. Chapman, The Charters, Fleggburgh, Great Yarmouth, Norfolk.
NORFOLK & SUFFOLK GUILD OF SPINNERS, WEAVERS & DYERS
Hon. Secretary: Miss I. M. Sturgeon, Naini Tal, 21 Cotmer Road, Oulton Broad, Lowestoft, Suffolk. Tel: Lowestoft 5958
See also under Suffolk.

Northumberland

NORTHUMBRIA GUILD OF WROUGHT IRON CRAFTSMEN
Secretary: I. Atkinson, CoSIRA, Hallgarth House, Hallgarth Street, Durham. Tel: Durham 3511

Oxfordshire

OXFORD GUILD OF WEAVERS, SPINNERS & DYERS
Secretary: Mrs P. Baines, 23 St Margarets Road, Oxford OX2 6RX.

Staffordshire

STAFFORDSHIRE GUILD OF WEAVERS, SPINNERS & DYERS
Secretary: Miss M. Lewis, 11 Green Lane, Bilston, Staffordshire.

Somerset

THE SOMERSET GUILD OF CRAFTSMEN
Hon. Secretary: Mrs M. Smith, 9 Ganges Hill, Fivehead, Taunton, Somerset. Tel: Isle Brewers 416
THE SOMERSET GUILD OF WEAVERS, SPINNERS & DYERS
Hon. Secretary: Mrs Joan Williamson, 120 West Street, Bridgwater, Somerset.

Suffolk

NORFOLK & SUFFOLK GUILD OF SPINNERS, WEAVERS & DYERS
See under Norfolk.
SUFFOLK CRAFT SOCIETY
Hon. Secretary: Charles Hocking, Suffolk Rural Community Council, County Hall, Ipswich, Suffolk. Tel: Ipswich 55801

Surrey

WESTCOTT ARTS & CRAFTS SOCIETY
Chairman: J. E. Allen, Cradhurst, Westcott, Dorking, Surrey. Tel: 0306 2612

Sussex

DITCHLING HANDWORKERS GUILD
Hon. Secretary: Mrs E. M. Warman, Underhill Cottage, Westmeston, Hassocks, Sussex BN6 8XG. Tel: Hassocks 3505
EAST SUSSEX GUILD OF CRAFT WORKERS
Hon. Secretary: Miss Gertrude Ennis, Flat 1, 18 St Helens Park Road, Hastings, Sussex. Tel: Hastings 2304
GUILD OF SUSSEX CRAFTSMEN
Hon. Secretary: W. T. Elliott, Sussex House, 212 High Street, Lewes, Sussex. Tel: Lewes 3422
SUSSEX GUILD OF WEAVERS, SPINNERS & DYERS
Hon. Secretary: Miss D. M. Ablett, Wantage House, 76 Dean Court Road, Rottingdean, Sussex. Tel: Brighton 32530

Warwickshire

BIRMINGHAM GUILD OF WEAVERS, SPINNERS & DYERS
Hon. Secretary: Mrs L. F. Stringfellow, 680 Evesham Road, Crabbs Cross, Redditch, Worcestershire.

Wessex

THE GUILD OF WROUGHT IRONWORK CRAFTSMEN OF WESSEX
Hon. Secretary: A. Newson, CoSIRA, County Hall, Exeter, Devon EX2 4QD. Tel: Exeter 77977 x 477
THE WESSEX GUILD OF BOOKBINDERS
Hon. Secretary: Miss W. M. Allen, 10 Denby Road, Poole, Dorset. Tel: Poole 6250

Wiltshire

WILTSHIRE GUILD OF SPINNERS, WEAVERS & DYERS
Hon. Secretary: Mrs P. M. Haynes, Moat Cottage, Siddington, Cirencester, Gloucestershire. Tel: Cirencester 3113

Worcestershire

WORCESTERSHIRE GUILD OF ARTIST-CRAFTSMEN
Secretary: Alan Knight, 27 Lickey Square, Rednal, Birmingham B45 8HB. Tel: 021-445 1678
WORCESTERSHIRE GUILD OF WEAVERS, SPINNERS & DYERS
Hon. Secretary: Miss V. L. Lockyer, 41 Howsell Road, Malvern Link, Worcestershire.

Yorkshire

GUILD OF YORKSHIRE CRAFTSMEN
Secretary: Richard Gill, Purey Cust Chambers, York. Tel: York 24778
HALLAMSHIRE & DISTRICT GUILD OF WEAVERS, SPINNERS & DYERS
Secretary: Miss O. M. Brown, 115 Stubley Lane, Dronfield-Woodhouse, Sheffield S18 5YL.
INSTITUTE OF CRAFT EDUCATION
Hillside, Little Weighton, Hull, Yorkshire.

WELSH NATIONAL SOCIETIES

GUILD OF WROUGHT IRONWORK CRAFTSMEN IN WALES
Secretary: R. Morris, CoSIRA, Community House, Severn Place, Newtown, Montgomeryshire. Tel: Newtown 6564
THE LACE SOCIETY OF WALES
Secretary: Mrs E. Brenton, 14 Balmoral Park, Chester.
WELSH WEAVERS ASSOCIATION
Secretary: Gareth Poulson, Glyn Taf, Login Whitland, Caernarvonshire.

REGIONAL SOCIETIES IN WALES

NORTH WALES

GUILD OF NORTH WALES CRAFTSMEN
Chairman: Russell Matthews, Grenor Farm Cottage, Bethal, Caernarvonshire.
GUILD OF NORTH WALES POTTERS
Hon. Secretary: John Stopes, The Old Shop, Lower Street, St Asaph, Flintshire.

SOUTH WALES

EMBROIDERERS' GUILD—SOUTH WALES & MONMOUTHSHIRE
Secretary: Mrs Dorothy Bowden, 87 Lavernok Road, Penarth, Glamorgan.
MONMOUTHSHIRE GUILD OF WEAVERS, SPINNERS & DYERS
Hon. Secretary: Mrs I. McGraghan, 30 Allteryan Court, Newport, Monmouthshire NPT 5GF.
SOUTH WALES POTTERS
Hon. Secretary: Dr Garrod Thomas, 54 Clairewain, New Inn, Pontypool, Monmouthshire.

SCOTLAND

SCOTTISH CRAFT CENTRE
Acheson House, Canongate, Edinburgh.

MASTER CRAFTSMEN ASSOCIATIONS

MASTER CARVERS ASSOCIATION
8a Gunters Grove, London SW10.
MASTER CLOTH WORKERS ASSOCIATION (London) LTD
65 Beak Street, London W1.
MASTER BUILDERS FEDERATION
33 John Street, WC1.
MASTER BOOKBINDERS ALLIANCE OF LONDON
11 Bedford Row, London WC1.
MASTER LOCKSMITHS ASSOCIATION
39 Waterloo Road, Epsom, Surrey.
MASTER MUSIC PRINTERS & ENGRAVERS ASSOCIATION
Plantation Road, Amersham on the Hill, Buckinghamshire.
MASTER PHOTOGRAPHERS
33 Bedford Street, WC2.
MASTER SIGN MAKERS ASSOCIATION
30a St George Street, Hanover Square, W1R 8EJ.
MASTER TANNERS ASSOCIATION
80–86 Lord Street, Liverpool 2.
MASTER THATCHERS ASSOCIATION
c/o G. E. Gunkley, 25 Little Lane, Yardley, Hastings.
NATIONAL MASTER FARRIERS, BLACKSMITHS & AGRICULTURAL ENGINEERS ASSOCIATION
48 Spencer Place, Leeds.

EDUCATION

At the end of each chapter of this book details have been given of colleges which provide courses or tuition in the various crafts featured. There are however one or two institutions which deserve fuller mention:

THE REYNTIENS TRUST LTD, BURLEIGHFIELD HOUSE, Loudwater, Buckinghamshire.

The Reyntiens Trust was formed in 1970 to encourage education in the arts, and to promote courses and exhibitions at Burleighfield House Studios and Gallery. It is administered by Patrick Reyntiens and Anne Bruce.

Burleighfield House was built in 1864 by Ford, the inventor of blotting paper, whose factory until lately existed in Loudwater. The house is set in a 7-acre romantic over-grown Victorian garden, and its stables and buildings have been converted to make a variety of well-equipped studios. A recent addition is a large new studio complex under one roof in its grounds.

Courses are intended to provide tuition and facilities for students of all ages and at different stages of development, including the professional. Subjects include Drawing, Painting, Pottery, Construction and Stained Glass. Lithography and Etching are taught in the studios of Burleighfield Printing House. The major course at Burleighfield is Stained Glass and although it is possible to attend this course by the day, it is generally understood to be a residential course. A children's weekend art school is also held at Burleighfield.

For further details of the courses available at Burleighfield write to the address above.

WEST DEAN COLLEGE, Chichester, Sussex.

West Dean College, owned by the Edward James Foundation, is unique for the vast range of courses it offers in traditional crafts, many of which are now threatened with extinction. The Foundation also owns approximately six thousand acres of farms and woodlands; some one-hundred-and-fifty farmhouses and cottages; two country houses, magnificent collections of paintings, furniture and other objets d'art, some of which are on loan to the Tate Gallery, the Royal Pavilion at Brighton, the Victoria and Albert Museum and the Worthing Museum and some of which are in the College. An arboretum of seventy acres adjoining the lands of the Foundation contains many rare and magnificent trees and has been made available to the Foundation for the furtherance of its education work. The Foundation has leased areas of land to the National Environmental Council for a nature reserve and to the Weald and Downland Open Air Museum at Singleton.

A selection of the following list of subjects will be used in future programmes as the College develops:

GROUP 1 *(subjects which lend themselves to short courses)*
Basketry, Butter making, Calligraphy, Candle making, Car and cycle maintenance, Cheese making, Clog making, Collage, Cookery: country fare, national, international, Crochet, Crook making, Fan making, Flower arrangement, Glove making, Horn—working in, Knitting, Millinery, Netting, Pipe making, Raffia work, Rope work, Rug making, Rush weaving, Smock making, Soft furnishing, Straw crafts, Straw marquetry, Tortoiseshell—working in, Toy making, Trug making, Upholstery, Walking stick making, Wax—working in, Willow work, Wine making.

GROUP 2 *(subjects which may be taken at various levels)*
Angling crafts: Fly, rod and tackle making, Archery crafts: bow making and fletching, Blacksmithing, Boat building, Bookbinding, Brazier's work, Canoe making, Cartography, Carving: various media, Ceramics, Chair making, Design for crafts, Drawing—general course, Dress and fashion, Dye making and dyeing, Embroidery—machine, Wall panels and fabric pictures, Modern Embroidery design, Embroidery—hand (various types), Fabric printing, Farriery, Furniture making, Goldsmithing, Hand papermaking, Heraldry, Illuminating, Jewellery—general and lapidary, Lace-making (various types), Leatherwork, Letter cutting—metal, stone, wood, Marquetry, Metal casting—fine, Metal inlay work, Musical instrument making, Painting (various types), Pewter work, Picture print making, Puppetry and marionettes, Sculpture (various media), Sign making, Silversmithing, Spinning, Taxidermy, Weaving, Welding, Wire working (gold and silver), Wood turning and treen, Woven tapestry, Wrought iron-work.

GROUP 3 *(subjects to be studied in depth on extended courses)*
Armourer's work, Glass and crystal making, Glass engraving, Clock making, Gunsmithing, Millwrighting, Organ building, Porcelain, Saddlery and harness making, Stained glass work, Stone masonry—advanced, Wheelwrighting.

GROUP 4 *(major subjects which must be subdivided to make up a course)*
Antiques—conservation of: ceramics and china, furniture, pictures, objets d'art,
Building and restoration: Bricks, handmade, Brickwork, Chalk—building in, Cob—building in, Cobble paving, Drystone walling, Flint walling, Gesso work, Gilding for inscriptions, Lead moulding, Painter-stainer's work, Pargetting, Pisé, Plaster work, Slate work, Stone masonry—including restoration, Wattle and daub,
Home maintenance: Carpentry, Electrical maintenance, Heating systems, Painting and decorating, Plaster work.

GROUP 5 *(mainly out-door activities)*
Archery, Beekeeping, Coppice work, Coracle making, Fence making, Fencing, Field archaeology, Gamekeeping, Gate making, Hedging, Hurdle

making, Ladder making, Natural History (with outings), Sheep shearing, Stile making, Thatching.

GROUP 6 *(general interest subjects mainly lecture based)*
Archaeology, Architecture, Art appreciation, Astronomy, Costume design (theatre) and make-up, The English Country Church, The English Country House, The English Country Life, Fashion design, Folk art: general, canals, circuses, fairgrounds, gipsies etc.
History of: Antiques, Art, Ceramics, Church brasses, Costume and fashion, Crafts, Falconry, Gardens, Heraldry, Horology (including sundials), Horse brasses, Jewellery, Mills—wind, water and tide, Musical instruments, Puppets and marionettes, Signs—inn, shop and ships' figureheads, The theatre, Weather vanes, Industrial archaeology, Interior decoration, Local history, Meteorology, Monuments and church brasses, Musical appreciation, Photography, Production and organisation of craft workshops, Theatre design.

Write to the College at the address given above for details of courses in which you are interested.

DESIGN COURSES IN THE U.K.

At the time of writing this book, the structure of art education in this country is being radically changed. We suggest that if a career in art is being considered, you should write to the college in question first to see what the current situation is. A full list of colleges can at present be obtained from the National Council for Diplomas in Art and Design, 16 Park Crescent, London, W1N 4DN.

Grants

COSira: Council for Small Industries in Rural Areas

COSira is a Government-sponsored advisory service, set up in 1921 to co-ordinate and encourage local craftsmen and to maintain traditional crafts. It has compiled a register of all known and recommended specialist craftsmen in rural areas.

The Council's services to small firms in rural areas of England and Wales are grouped under three main headings: finance in the form of loan facilities; business or technical advice and help with general problems such as power supplies, apprenticeship schemes and the recruitment of labour. Agriculture, horticulture and retail trading are not eligible for assistance.

The Council runs courses in the following subjects:
Agricultural machinery repair
Estimating courses for country builders and joiners
Estimating courses for small engineering firms
Furniture restoration
Saddle making
Vehicle hydraulics and electrics
Welding
Woodworking machinery instruction
Wrought ironsmithing

It will also give technical advice on:
Clay product technology
Electrical specifications
Furniture making and antique furniture restoration
Machine shop reorganisation
Machinery and equipment evaluation
Product value analysis and development
Saddlery and saddle-making
Semi-automatic welding techniques
Structural designs
Textile industries
Thatching
Timber utilisation
Woodworking machinery
Workshop design and plant layout
Wrought ironwork

For a free leaflet, HOW COSIRA HELPS SMALL FIRMS write to the Council at 35 Camp Road, Wimbledon Common, London SW19 4UW.
Similar services to rural industries are offered in Scotland by the Small Industries Council for Rural Areas of Scotland, 27 Walker Street, Edinburgh and in Northern Ireland by the Local Enterprise Development Unit, 21 Linenhall Street, Belfast 2.

Crafts Advisory Committee, Design Council, 28 Haymarket, London SW17 5SU.

Write to the CAC for leaflets which explain in full the following categories of financial assistance which are available to craftsmen living in England or Wales:

Training Grants

This scheme aims at providing practical workshop experience for graduate students and others wishing to make a career as an artist craftsman, by awarding grants to established workshops which are able to take on such trainees.

The scheme is divided into two parts:
Part A Grants to workshops prepared to take on a student who has just left college or art school and who wishes to gain practical experience in a workshop
Part B Grants to workshops wishing to train an apprentice assistant

Although the grants will be paid to the workshop or studio, the Committee is prepared to offer advice to students seeking such training on the approved workshops to which they might apply. The relative value of the student to the workshop and the training to the student will be estimated, and the amount of the grant to remain with the workshop and the amount to be spent on wages will be recommended by the sub-committee handling the scheme.

Grants to New Craftsmen

This scheme gives financial aid in the form of a non-recurring grant to artist-craftsmen at the outset of their career for either or both of the following purposes:
(a) Equipment for a first workshop
(b) Maintenance for the first year of business
The Committee is also prepared where appropriate to put craftsmen in touch with organisations offering consultative services to help in the establishment of their workshop business.
A similar type of scheme for Scotland is operated by the Crafts Entrants Committee of the Scottish Craft Centre, Edinburgh.

Grants to Established Craftsmen

This scheme of non-recurring grants is to provide craftsmen with capital to develop their workshops. Priority is given to recently-established craftsmen whose workshops are still in a formative stage, but the Committee is concerned that any scheme submitted to them is directed towards improving the quality of work produced.

Scotland administers separate funds through the Joint Crafts Committee in Edinburgh.

Craft Outlets

An alphabetical county list of retail craftshops which may be willing to sell your work. Try them and see.

Bedfordshire

BEDFORD CRAFTS CENTRE, Emma Russell, 6 Newnham Street, Bedford.
A large selection of craftwork, hand made by British craftsmen and craftswomen, including pottery, glass, rush-work, woodware, jewellery, lamps, alabaster, hornware, hand-woven ties, soft toys and many other items.
DOREEN CHETWOOD, Woodlands Craft Centre, Thurleigh Road, Milton Ernest, Bedford.
Craftwork from Bedfordshire—pottery, jewellery, toys, hobby-horses, woodwork, mobiles, crochet, rush-work, corn-dollies, lace and Woodlands pottery.
Art exhibitions are often held.
SERENDIB, 15 Market Place, Woburn. Colin and Marianne Mulrenan.
A wide range of hand-crafts from all over Britain, including work by many local craftsmen. Serendib was the name given to Ceylon by Arab traders of 1,500 years ago where they found many exotic and rare products.
CARRIE LOVELL, ARTS AND CRAFTS, Slicketts Lane, Edlesborough, nr Dunstable.
Shed in the garden containing large stock of pottery (by Brendan Maund), pillow lace, tatting, crochet jewellery, soft toys, corn-dollies, basket-work, shell pictures, candles, etc.
THREEHOUSEHOLDS GALLERY, Threehouseholds, Chalfont St Giles.
Local artists and craftsmen display paintings, pottery, enamels, woodcraft, etc., in a seventeenth-century setting.
GRAHAM & ANNE FLIGHT, The Craft Shop, 12 High Street, Bassingbourn.
Stoneware and earthenware pottery, prints, enamels, embroidery and collage pictures, toys, knitted and crochet goods and a selection of hand-made craft goods.
PRIMAVERA, 10 King's Parade, Cambridge.
Famous for pottery, glass, textiles, jewellery, toys, lamps.

Cornwall

'THE BARBICAN', Battery Road, Penzance Harbour.
Craft workshops, crafts direct from the makers. Silver jewellery, weaving, needlework, leatherwork, ceramic tiles. Also a craft and pottery shop and a gallery for local paintings and sculpture.
THE SLOOP CRAFT MARKET, St Ives.
Here you can see craftsmen at work.
CARNSEW GALLERY, 15 Penpol Terrace, Hayle.
The work of Cornish artists and craftsmen: ceramic sculpture and murals; paintings; fine studio pottery and porcelain by Tolcarne Pottery, Newlyn.
CELTIC CRAFTS (CORNWALL), Tregony, Truro.
A full range of hand-made West Country craft goods.
CELTIC CRAFTS (LLYSWEN WELSH CRAFT CENTRE): Church Street, Mevagissey,

Couch's Great House, Polperro, 30 Fore Street, St Ives.
Wide range of tapestry clothing, including capes, skirts and anoraks. Tapestry handbags and purses, sheepskin rugs, sheepskin coats, hats, gloves and slippers.
CONTEMPORARY CRAFTS, 5 The Esplanade, Fowey.
Hand-made copper, pewter and silver jewellery, copper enamelling.
THE CRAFT SHOP, 'Private Bag', 2 Mill Road, Padstow, Cornwall.
Specialists in hand-crafts of all descriptions.
THE CRAFTSMEN'S CENTRE, The Quay, Polperro.
Specialising in West Country craftware. Studio pottery, sheepskin slippers, gloves, etc. Tweeds, ties, rugs, wooden tableware, lamps and toys.
THE CRAFTSMEN'S SHOP, 30 Fore Street, St Ives.
Quality baskets, toys, weaving and jewellery.
CRIFTCRAFT, St Germans, Saltash.
Comprehensive range of Cornish craft-made goods including woodwork, pottery, toys, etc.
CRITERION HOTEL, Cawsand, nr Plymouth.
High-class pottery, jewellery, wood and stoneware, lamps and tweeds, etc., hand-made in the West Country.
FOGOU KNITWEAR AND CRAFTS, Withy Cottage, Porthallow, nr St Keverne, Helston.
Knitwear, basketry, hand-made toys, studio pottery, crochet work, dolls' clothes, camphor-driven model ships, all locally made. Garments knitted to order including Aran.
KERNOWCRAFT ROCKS & GEMS LTD, 9 Old Bridge Street, Truro.
Everything for the lapidary enthusiast—rough and polished gemstones, polishing machines and accessories, jewellery mounts, polished agate dishes and paperweights, stone carvings, books and mineral specimens. Illustrated catalogue available.
MAYFIELDS, The Wharf, St Ives.
West Country stoneware and earthenware, ceramic jewellery. Tiles, mosaics, table-lamps, silver and pewter jewellery.
NEW CRAFTSMAN, 24 Fore Street, St Ives.
Contemporary furniture and kitchenware, glass, pottery and weaving.
THE SALT CELLAR, Coverack.
Old fisherman's loft converted into shop to sell Cornish craftwork, including hand-made studio pottery, glassware, wood sculpture, silver jewellery, etc. Miniature camphor-propelled model ships are made and sold on the premises.
TAMAR RIVER GALLERY, The Quay, Calstock.
Museum of ship-building, salmon fishing, mining, horticulture and other local interests.
Crafts shop selling a wide range of local hand-made goods.
THIRTY-EIGHT, The Wharf, St Ives. E. H. & M. S. Popple.
Robin Nance hand-made furniture, standard-lamps, turned wooden bowls. West Country hand-thrown pottery, weaving and batik.
TREMAEN CRAFT MARKET, Market House, Penzance.
Retailing all varieties of Cornish craftwork.
TROIKA SHOP, 61 Fore Street, St Ives.
Cornish crafts, pottery, jewellery, clothes, dolls and boutique.

Cumberland

BARKERS OF LANERCOST, Holmefoot, Lanercost, Brampton.
Hand-made goods produced by local craftsmen: couture knitwear, silverware, jewellery, ceramics, fine prints, soft toys and dolls, Roman reproductions in bronze, resin and pot, collage and embroidered pictures. Hookie rugs, Cumbrian bonnets, weaving, stained glass, leatherware, candles.
FINE DESIGNS (RICHARD & ALLAN FISHER), 22 St John's Street and 35 Lake Road, Keswick.
Workshops for woodsculpture, also jewellery in fine metals and stone-setting. Retail craft shops specialising in studio pottery—art metalwork, etc. Producers of reproductions of lakeland wood-carvings. Editions of animal sculptures in bronze and silver.
GREENRIGG POTTERY AND HANDMADE CRAFTS STUDIO, Caldbeck.
A specially selected collection of handcrafts—pottery, Herdwick knitted goods, jewellery, leather and suède work, lamp-shades and local stone products.
KESWICK INDUSTRIAL ARTS, Greta Bridge, Keswick.
Craftsmanship in silver, stainless steel, copper and brass, hand-made by local craftsmen. Brochures of tableware, jewellery and church furnishings posted by return.
LAKELAND RURAL INDUSTRIES, Grange-in-Borrowdale, Keswick.
Old-established specialists in hand-beaten stainless steel and copper in many decorative and practical forms made on the premises. Church and other furnishings designed and made to order. Other Lakeland craftwork on permanent display, e.g., pottery, hand-woven rugs, scarves, etc., pictures, wood-turning, jewellery, soft toys, horn goods, hand-wrought ironwork, local slate and other items.
THE OLD SMITHY, Caldbeck, Wigton.
An unusual craft shop specialising in locally made hand-knitted garments, crochet, pebble jewellery, clogs, shell-work, pottery, Aran and Icelandic knitting wools. Icelandic and Norwegian garments, sheepskins, slippers, baskets, toys, tweeds. Shetland knitwear, pure wool suits, dresses and trouser-suits from the Scottish glens and islands.
ROOKIN HOUSE FARM, Caravan Site and Pony Riding Centre, Troutbeck, nr Penrith.
A wide range of local crafts, of particular interest to horse enthusiasts.

Derbyshire

THE SMITHY, Water Street, Bakewell DE4 1EW.
Crystal, bone china, porcelain and pottery. Antique and reproduction objets d'art. Wrought-iron brackets, lamps, screens, wind-vanes, gates, candelabra, etc.
TIDESWELL DALE ROCK SHOP, Commercial Road, Tideswell.
Jewellery and ornamental work in natural stone. Mineral specimens for the collector, supplies and materials for the lapidary.

Devonshire

CASTLE CRAFT CENTRE, Joan & Basil Elliott, 25 South Street, Torrington.

Decorative candles, pottery, leathercraft, turned wooden goods and rag dolls.
'LITTLE MEADOW COTTAGE INDUSTRY', Mr & Mrs B. P. Hutchins, 'Little Meadow', Venton Lane, Widecombe in the Moor.
Specialists in cane and wicker : cribs, chairs, ottomans, linen-boxes and allied furniture. Other local craftsmen's work offered when available, i.e. plant-troughs, stonework, woodwork and local pictures.
BETTINA MERRIAM, 46 High Street, Honiton.
Craft and kitchen shop offering pictures, pottery, woodcraft, glassware. Kitchen co-ordinates including famous 'Muff' tea-cosy.
CHAGFORD GALLERIES, 20 The Square, Chagford.
British original paintings and hand-made goods. Pottery by leading craftsmen, jewellery, alabaster, weaving, toys, pinewood furniture, wood turnery, glass and enamelling.
DOONE VALLEY WOOCRAFTS, Brendon (4 miles Lynton), North Devon.
Wide selection of West Country crafts. Decorative hand-made pottery. Coffee-sets, vases, table-lamps, ovenware, Sheepskin goods. Large stock of Dartington tweeds and rugs. Woodware, turned bowls, platters, coffee-tables, etc.
GALLERIE MARIN, Appledore.
Original marine paintings by Mark Richard Myers and Peter M. Wood. Wood-carvings by Jack Whitehead and Norman Gaches. Glass engraved by John Ford. Ship jugs and traditional pottery by Harry Juniper. Nautical books, locally made rope mats, traditional Appledore jerseys, ships in bottles, nautical gear and a variety of small gifts in the same connection.
HAND-MADE GOODS, 11 Sycamore Avenue, Dronfield, Derbyshire.
THE LILIAN GALLERY, West Country Arts & Crafts, 15 Market Street, Appledore.
Pottery, basketry, wood-turnery, paintings, original brass-rubbings, art candles. Cottage crafts: sewn, knitted and crocheted. Ceramic cartoons. Sheepskins and leathercrafts. Small wrought-iron items, picture framing.
LOTUS GALLERY, Stoke Gabriel, Totnes.
West Country crafts, pottery, paintings and sculpture.
SERENDIPITY OF SHALDON, nr Teignmouth.
Hand-made glass, pottery, candles, paintings, garden furniture by local craftsmen, hand-made modern jewellery, soft toys. A changing scene of other crafts, kitchenware and many other items of interest.
SIDMOUTH POTTERY & CRAFT SHOP, 74 Temple Street, Sidmouth.
Specialising in pottery but has a range of other craft work.
OTTERY POTTERY, Mill Street, Ottery St Mary.
A wide variety of pottery and other craftwork including batik silk scarves, corn-dollies, turned wood, basketware, glass and candles.
WOODTURNERS (SOUTH DEVON), New Road, Modbury, South Devon.
Quality hand-made fruit- and salad-bowls, bread- and cheese-boards, table- and standard-lamps, furniture, coffee-tables, bench-stools, name-boards, etc. Also pottery, weaving, basket-work, painting, screen-printed fabrics, sheepskins, tapestry work, etc. You may watch

woodenware being made.

Dorset
GUILD CRAFTS (POOLE) LTD, The Brewery, Fontmell Magna, nr Shaftesbury.
Potters and woodworkers. Workshop tours. Retail shop.
PILGRIMS CRAFT CENTRE, Shillingstone, nr Blandford.
Hand-made chunky pine furniture in refectory style. Tables, chairs, benches, dressers and four-poster beds. Also a display of paintings and pottery. All goods made by local village craftsmen. Furniture made on the premises.
DAVID EELES (THE POTSHOP), 18 Barrack Street, Bridport.
Pottery, stoneware, slipware and porcelain ovenware, tableware lamps, cider- and wine-jars, platters, small and large individual pieces hand-made furniture, jewellery.
'FLEURSEC' (primary producers and retailers), The Studio, West Street, Corfe Castle.
Dried flowers, grown and processed on the premises. Also pottery, jewellery and many other hand-crafts from the four South-Western counties.
GALLERY 24, Bimport, Shaftesbury.
Paintings, pottery and selected work by artists, craftsmen and designers.
WEST COUNTRY CRAFTS CENTRE, Top of the Hill, Charmouth.
A wide range of craftsmen-made goods, including pottery, jewellery, toys, coffee-tables and stools, Dartington Tweeds, rugs and glass, original oil-paintings and prints.

Durham
MEANDER, 58 Saddler Street, Durham.
The purpose of Meander is to promote local art and craft by providing a place where these can be exhibited and sold. Exhibits cover a wide range of skills, including paintings, prints, tapestries, pottery, decorative candles, hand-made jewellery, leather craft, brass-rubbings, historic seals, etc.
Special exhibitions are held from time to time.

Gloucestershire
CAMPDEN POTTERY & CRAFT SHOP, Leasbourne, Chipping Campden.
Hand-thrown pottery made on the premises. Other crafts available including weaving, wood and stone carving, corn-dollies, baskets and costume jewellery. Wooden toys a speciality.
COUNTRY CRAFTS, The Chestnuts, Bourton-on-the-Water, also at Welsh Crafts, High Street, Bourton-on-the-Water, and Celtic Crafts, Digbeth Street, Stow-on-the-Water.
Wide range of tapestry clothing, including capes, skirts and anoraks. Tapestry handbags and purses, sheepskin rugs, hats, gloves and slippers.
RIVERSIDE STUDIO POTTERY, Riverside, Priding, Saul.
Craft pottery centre, work by many well-known potters. Hand-made pottery, tankards, lamp-bases, jugs, traditional frog-mugs, high-temperature tableware, extruded ceramics, pottery animals, birds.

Hampshire
COUNTRY COUSINS, Commercial Road, Bournemouth.
HEAD RETAIL STALL, Tricorn Market, via Clive Rogers, 70 Marmion Road, Southsea.
Studio pottery, Welsh tapestry clothing and other British tweeds. Hand-woven shawls and rugs. Ceramic jewellery. Suèdecraft.
THE POTTERY & CRAFTS SHOP, High Street, Bishop's Waltham.
A wide range of pottery and stoneware, both functional and decorative. Wooden tableware, hand-carved leather stools, handbags, belts, etc., suèdecraft, candles, sheepskin rugs, jewellery in silver, pewter, copper and wood, original paintings in watercolour and oils.
STRAWBERRY FAYRE, High Street, Stockbridge.
Traditional village industry. Hand-made patchwork, crochet, medieval furniture and children's toys.

Herefordshire
'CEEJAY', 5 High Street, Ross-on-Wye.
Baskets, wrought iron, wooden ware, pottery, jewellery, leather handbags. Welsh tapestry goods and tweeds, sheepskin rugs, hand-beaten stainless steel and copper, glass and hornware and numerous types of toys.
THE CRAFTS SHOP, Bell Square, Weobley.
Hand-made crafts by British craftsmen. A wide selection of corn-dollies, toys, basketware, stoneware, slipware, jewellery, woven goods, hornware, woodware, etc.
SELDA, The Bridge, Leintwardine.
Pottery, weaving, wood, glass, baskets, toys hand-made by studio craftsmen and the handicapped.
THE SOCIETY OF CRAFTSMEN'S SHOP AT THE OLD KEMBLE GALLERIES, 29 Church Street, Hereford.
Work by members of the Society, many of them local, including pottery, jewellery, metal and ceramic sculptures, weaving, pictures, gloves and greetings cards. A small gallery is available for exhibitions.
THE SPINNING WHEEL, 25 Church Street, Hereford.
Wide range of tapestry clothing, including capes, skirts, and anoraks. Tapestry handbags and purses, sheepskin rugs, hats, gloves and slippers.

Kent
BARRONNE CRAFTS, 126a High Street, Edenbridge, Kent.
Domestic and creative pottery, jewellery, leather and basket-work, candles, soft toys and dried flower plaques.
KENT CRAFT, 37 Upper Stone Street, Maidstone.
Pottery, jewellery, toys, corn-dollies, candles, wrought iron. Lapidary section includes polished gemstones, rough rock, tumblers, findings and specimens.

Lancashire
THE OLD SMITHY, Cartmel, nr Grange-over-Sands.
Hand-beaten stainless steel and copper for the home, and certain church furnishings, hand-wrought ironwork, pottery, hand-weaving, soft toys, and many other local crafts.

Lincolnshire
'THE GREEN PARROT', Arts and Crafts Centre, Tealby.
Craft-work from Lincolnshire and neighbouring counties includes pottery, wood-craft, leatherwork, furni-

ture, lamp-shades, jewellery, soft toys and paintings.
NEWSONS OF ENFIELD, 1 Windmill Hill, Enfield.
A very large range of hand-thrown stoneware and earthenware, domestic and purely decorative, collected from potters' studios all over the country; dolls and toys.

Norfolk
THE 'COUNTRY & COTTAGE CRAFTS' PROJECT, Coltishall.
Cottage, period and contemporary furniture in oak, pine, etc. Domestic and studio pottery; turned woodware; wrought iron; local stone jewellery; rush-work; basketry; brass-rubbings; flower pictures; soft toys; corn-dollies; tweeds; chess-sets and boards: needlecraft.
SAXTHORPE POTTERY (KEITH & JOAN CORRIGAN), Norwich NOR 15Y.
Hand-made pottery, kitchenware and other hand-made pieces. Exhibitions of paintings, weaving, hand-made furniture and allied crafts of Norfolk.
ELM HILL CRAFT SHOP, 12 Elm Hill, Norwich NOR 70K.
Pottery, rush-weaving, jewellery, toys, etc.
THE KELLING STUDIO, Kelling, nr Holt.
Collection of local artists' and craftsmen's work including paintings, pottery, wrought iron, wood carving and jewellery.
MATELLA, 17 High Street, Sheringham.
Pottery, corn-dollies, wooden and soft toys, jewellery and leather goods, pictures and prints, etc.
PALGRAVE CRAFTS AND ART GALLERY, 25 St Nicholas Street, Diss.
Hand-made goods, wrought iron, pottery, toys, firebacks, jewellery, fancy goods, copper canopies, firebacks and baskets.
THE PILGRIMS CRAFTS CENTRE, Bacton-on-Sea.
Pottery, weaving baskets, toys, jewellery, woodwork, antiques, etc.
STUDIO 69, 40 Elm Hill, Norwich NOR 70K.
Contains a department entirely devoted to the needs of brass-rubbers, with a permanent exhibition of rubbings in the Cellar Gallery. The first floor galleries display the works of local artists.

Northamptonshire
THE CRAFTS CENTRE, Pilton Lane, Wadenhoe.
Patchwork, pillow lace, original oil-paintings and watercolours, old needlework restored, wrought iron, wood-turning, dried flowers, enamel on copper, knitting, crochet and tatting, smocking children's clothing.

Northumberland
THE CRAFT CENTRE, Harbottle, Morpeth.
Country saleroom, hand-work from Northumbrian craft-workers, professional and amateur.
THE HORSELESS CARRIAGE, Warkworth, Morpeth.
Hand-woven and hand-printed fabrics, bygones, pottery, Lindisfarne liqueur honey and marmalade, Elsenham & Ledbury high-quality preserves, Border knitwear, old prints, books on Northumbria, maps for tourists, walking-sticks.

Oxfordshire
MICHAEL & HEATHER ACKLAND, Coniston House, New Street, Deddington.

Jewellery, pottery, basketware, glass, wooden bowls, picture-framing, including work by local craftsmen. Silver jewellery designed and made on the premises.
HAND-MADE, St Michaels Street, Oxford.
MADE BY HAND, George Street, Oxford, Oxon.
THE OLD FORGE, Lower High Street, Burford.
Local pottery, weaving, metal work, paintings, rugs, knitting and crochet.
MRS A. G. RHODES, Hill House, Hardwick Road, Whitchurch-on-Thames, Reading RG8 7HH.
Small private gallery which features hand-crafted things for household and personal use. Emphasis on usefulness, few-of-the-kind.
STOCKLANDS, Little Clarendon Street, Oxford.
'THE TABLE SHOP', 25 Couching Street, Watlington.
A wide selection of tables, benches and chairs, together with pottery and other hand-made goods.

Shropshire
DRAGON CRAFTS, St Alkmund's Square and 5 St Mary's Street, Shrewsbury.
Local and Welsh crafts: hand-thrown pottery, woodwork, art, wrought ironwork, Welsh tapestry quilts and clothing, sheepskin products, perfume, jewellery, etc.
LUDLOW WELSH CRAFT CENTRE, 13 Tower Street, Ludlow.
Bedspreads, handbags and purses, pottery, sheepskins and gloves, jewellery and perfume. Specialists in tapestry clothing, including coats, capes, skirts and anoraks.
STANDISH-TAYLOR, School Gardens, Shrewsbury.
British crafts including hand-thrown pottery by master craftsmen. Antique stripped pine furniture, Shropshire yew tables, rush log and shopping-baskets. Norfolk rush-mats, runners and carpets made to order. Jewellery, large selection of British basketry, hand-woven ties and head-squares, salad-bowls and toys, kitchenware, etc.
WELSH & TRADITIONAL CRAFTS (G. M. NEAL), Shrewsbury Market, Barker Street, Shrewsbury.
Honeycomb and tapestry quilts, coats, capes, anoraks, purses and stoles. Sheepskin slippers and mitts. Celtic jewellery, Cambrian tweeds and socks, perfume and pomanders.

Somerset
MUCHELNEY POTTERY (JOHN LEACH), Muchelney, Langport.
Hand-made stoneware, domestic shapes, stewpots, casseroles, mixing-bowls, jugs and store-jars. Craft shop open, displaying high standard of Somerset and West Country crafts, woodwork, leather, hand-loom weaving, hand-screen printed fabrics. Batik scarves, baskets and pottery.
THE BANTAM SHOP, Dunster, nr Minehead.
Wide selection of hand-made goods. Pottery made on the premises.
CELTIC CRAFTS, The Avenue, Minehead.
Tapestry clothing, including capes, skirts and anoraks. Tapestry handbags and purses, sheepskin rugs, hats, gloves and slippers.
THE CRAFT SHOP, Blagdon, Bristol BS18 6TH.
Specialises in unusual cane furniture. Complete range Welsh tapestry; tweed and lambswool skirts, skirt

packs, matching sweaters, Suède garments. Silver and craft jewellery. Pottery, Ceramic figurines. Pewter ware, wood-, leather goods, handbags, Sheepskin slippers, kitchen sets. Baskets of all types.*
DAVID EELES (THE POT SHOP), Watergore, nr South Petherton.
Pottery, stoneware, slipware and porcelain, ovenware, tableware, lamps, cider- and wine-jars, platters, small and large individual pieces.
GIFTCRAFTS, 46 High Street, Glastonbury.
KITCHENCRAFT, Union Street, Yeovil.
Craftsman-made local pottery, woodware, glassware, candles.
JEAN & PETER MARTIN, 15–16 Pulteney Bridge.
Coloured and scented candles, jewellery, wooden toys, hand-made clothes, pottery, cards, hand-woven rugs, natural perfume oils, wickerware, hand-printed silk scarves, etc.
MILVERTON CRAFT WORK SHOP (Beth Designs), Fore Street, Milverton, nr Taunton.
Somerset crafts, corn-dollies, pottery, basketwork, woodware, weaving, toys, ties, tweeds, leather-crafts, lamps, etc. Specialising in unusual, quality hand-made soft toys, furnishings and pressed flower pictures.
THE TINKER'S BAG (JIM LEE), 27b Belvedere, Lansdown Road, Bath.
British hand-made pottery, woven goods, hornwork, etc.
WESSEX CRAFTS, Langport.
West Country craftware, basketry in natural and stained willow and cane (including the traditional 'shacklebasket' and 'Willow Queen' rattlewattles), pottery, wood- and stone-carvings, jewellery, enamels, ropecraft, knitted and crochet work, unusual hand-made toys and dolls, thatch animals and models, corn-dollies, framed old maps.

Staffordshire
ALSTONFIELD CRAFT CENTRE, The George Inn, Alstonfield, Dovedale.
Hand-thrown pottery, leather goods, watercolours, collages, woven and crocheted goods, jewellery, toys, basketware, wrought ironwork, shelves, tables, lamps.
W. E. M. TILDESLEY, ARTS, CRAFTS & HOME INDUSTRIES, 38b High Street, Eccleshall, Stafford.
Soft and wooden toys, tapestry and picture-framing, our own design tapestry frames, silver and enamel jewellery, lace bobbins, fancy goods, ironwork, pictures, lamp-shades, Staffordshire alabaster, horn work, harness, carts, etc, for model horses.

Suffolk
ALDRINGHAM CRAFT MARKET, Leiston Road, Aldeburgh, East Suffolk.
MARY LOE, High Street, Nayland.
Useful things made by craftsmen mostly in East Anglia, including pottery, woodware, rushwork, baskets, corn-dollies and jewellery.
THE POTTERS WHEEL, Walberswick, Suffolk.
ST EDMUNDS POTTERY & COUNTRY CRAFTS, 74–75 Whiting Street, Bury St Edmunds.
Corn-dollies, beaten copperware, pewter, enamelled and silver jewellery, soft toys, leather, tweeds, tapestry garments, tie and dye, semi-precious stones cut and polished, pottery, rushwork.

SNAPE CRAFT SHOP, Snape Bridge, Saxmundham, Suffolk.

J. B. TOYS, 'Gayhurst', Hitcham, nr Ipswich.
Hand-made wooden toys and pine furniture manufactured on the premises. A variety of other craft products for sale.

VOUT, LAND O' GREEN GINGER, 74 Whiting Street, Bury St Edmunds, Suffolk.

Surrey

ALICAT CRAFTCENTRE AND GALLERY, 52 Friars Stile Road, Richmond.
Jewellery, pottery, glass, woodwork, wall-hangings, rushwork and toys. Regular exhibitions of the work of leading British potters.

CRAFTWORK, 38 Castle Street, Guildford, Surrey.
Pottery, jewellery, glass, silver, rugs and wall hangings.

THE HARRIS CRAFT SHOP, 21 West Street, Reigate.
Pottery, jewellery, woven scarves, ties, etc. Wrought iron, original pictures, lamps, small sculptures.

'TOBYCRAFT GALLERIES', High Street, Ripley, nr Guildford.
Original paintings, lamps, jewellery, pottery, wrought iron, leather goods. Welsh tapestry, ponchos, jackets, spreads, etc.

Sussex

THE DOVECOTE, Michelham Priory, Upper Dicker, nr Hailsham.
Wide range of traditional Sussex crafts, including pottery, ironwork and trugs. August exhibition sponsored by Sussex Small Industries Committee, with demonstrations of potting, thatching, weaving and other crafts.

FORUM GALLERY, 16 Market Street, Brighton.
Gallery specialising in original contemporary prints and drawings, hand-made jewellery, wood-carving and pottery figures, chess-sets, and individual pottery. Also good selection of standard ware.

Warwickshire

PETER DINGLEY, 16 Meer Street, Stratford upon Avon.
A selection of modern British crafts—pottery, woodcarving, fabric pictures, wall-hangings, hand-blown glass, and other products. Also silk squares, hand-painted on the premises.

GRUMMEL DESIGN (R. & J. E. MAVER), 61 Smith Street, Warwick.
Wide range of hand-made designs in teak, rosewood and local woods. Pottery, silver jewellery, soft toys, lamps, thread pictures, ornamental candles and holders, animal carvings, etc.

(RAY & LIZ KEY) 'KEY CRAFTS', 1C Clay Lane, Coventry (from March: 19 Vine Street, Evesham, Worcestershire).
Quality hand-made wood-turning made on the premises by Ray Key. Bowls, platters, table- and standard-lamps, cheese-boards, ash-trays, egg-cups, candle-holders, etc. Other crafts, studio pottery, candles, basketware, corn-dollies, jewellery, rushware, etc.

Wiltshire

ABBEY CRAFTS & TEA ROOMS, Market Cross, Malmes-bury (Jean & David King).
Rural crafts in pottery, stone, leather, suède, deer skin, horn, reed, wicker, wood, pewter, metals, wrought iron, linen, wool, corn, flowers, and hand-made toys.

CHATTELS, 19 Sheep Street, Devizes.
Toys, pottery, Victorian-style aprons, woodwork, jewellery, macramé, corn-dollies, greeting-cards, brass-rubbings and home-made preserves and chutneys. Furniture and other articles in wood can be made to order and customers' own designs if required.

'INSPIRE GALLERY', 40 Fisherton Street, Salisbury.
Contemporary paintings (changing exhibitions); prints, posters, stoneware goblets, etc, earthenware houses; enamel and silver jewellery, candles, exotic oils, chess-sets, modern furniture, immortal flowers, lights.

THE OLD FORGE, Bridge Street, Bradford-on-Avon.
Country crafts, hand-thrown pottery, tapestry blankets, hand-made glass, teak, leather and suède, basket-work, corn-dollies, books, toys, candles and pine furniture.

Worcestershire

THE BIRD CAGE, 6a Market Place, Evesham.
Stoneware, ceramics, corn-dollies, hand-weaving, jewellery, soft toys, hornware, wood-turner, rushwork, basketry.

Yorkshire

COUNTRYCRAFTS, 44 Lower Petergate, York.
Hand-woven ties, scarves, knee-rugs, hand-thrown pottery and woodcraft.

CRAFTSMEN, 33 Goodramgate.
Hand-thrown pottery, weaving, rush-work, hand-made jewellery, wooden toys.

THE JAM POT, Slaidburn, Via Clitheroe (J. & M. Bolton).
Cutters and polishers of semi-precious stones, makers of lapidary machinery, mineral specimens of the British Isles and world wide, lapidary supplies, wood-turnery and wood-craft in a wide range.

THE POTTER'S WHEEL, Minster Gates, York.
Craft-work made exclusively in Yorkshire. Hand-thrown earthenware and stoneware pottery, woodware and stainless steel jewellery.

LES & AUDREY ROBINSON, The Craft Centre, Thorpe in Balne, nr Askern, Doncaster.
Weaving, basket-work, pottery made in the centre. Other hand-made goods. Practical work facilities available for visitors by arrangement.

THE VILLAGE CRAFT CENTRE, Hungate Lane, Hunmanby, nr Filey.
Hand-forged ironwork, cane chairs, rocking-chairs, hand-thrown pottery, leatherwork, woodwork, etc.

WALES

Anglesey

GLEASON & JONES, The Cottage Crafts Shop, Castle Street, Beaumaris.
Welsh tapestry and honeycomb quilts. Ladies' and children's clothing and accessories in Welsh tapestry, tweed and flannel, Sheepskin gloves, rugs, slippers and coats, oil-paintings of local interest. Welsh pottery, dolls and horse-brasses. Local honey in local pottery a

speciality.

W. & E. HORNER, Ship's Bell, Moelfre Bay.
Welsh tapestries, coats, suits, dresses, capes, handbags, purses, bedspreads and cushion-covers. Pottery, jewellery, ships' hanging and table-lamps, etc.

Breconshire

CLOTH HALL CRAFTS, Llanwrtyd Wells.
Decorative candles, pottery, ceramics, enamelled jewellery, leather belts, bags and other hand-made articles.

CURIO AND WELSH CRAFT SHOP, Groe Street, Builth Wells; and at 7 Lion Street; and 22 High Street, Kington.
Welsh tapestry and honeycomb quilts, ladies' and children's clothing and accessories in Welsh tapestry, tweed and flannel. Sheepskin gloves, rugs, slippers and coats, oil-paintings of local interest. Welsh pottery, jewellery, dolls and horse-brasses. Local honey in local pottery.

LLYSWEN WELSH CRAFT CENTRE, Llyswen, Brecon.
Tapestry bedspreads, handbags and purses, hand-made Welsh pottery, sheepskins, sheepskin slippers, jewellery, tapestry clothing, including coats, capes and skirts. Children's tapestry capes, hats and tweed caps and a wide range of Welsh perfumes.

Caernarvonshire

BRYN AFON STUDIO, Trefriw.
Jewellery made in our own workshop in sterling silver, pewter and stainless steel. Also pottery, Welsh slate goods, sheepskin slippers, corn-dollies, carved Welsh love-spoons, walking-sticks, hand-made dolls, miniature spinning-wheels, pressed-flower pictures, hand-knitted sweaters, bags, etc.

BRYNKIR WOOL SHOP, Castle Square, Caernarvon.
All products of the Brynkir Woollen Mill.

CRAFTCENTRE CLOTHES, 8 St George's Place, Llandudno.
Welsh tapestry clothing. Welsh tweed, flannel and tapestry by the yard. Sheepskin mitts and hoods.

CRAFTCENTRE CYMRU, 8 Pool Street, Caernarfon.

CRAFTCENTRE CYMRU, Stanley Buildings, Castle Street, Conway.

CRAFTCENTRE CYMRU, 45 High Street, Criccieth.

CRAFTCENTRE CYMRU, 6 St George's Place, Llandudno.

CRAFTCENTRE CYMRU, 75 High Street, Porthmadog.
Pottery, Welsh tapestry clothing, slate goods, house name-plates and model ships made to order; sheepskin rugs, mitts, hoods and slippers, carved wooden love-spoons, tapestry quilts, wrought iron sculptures, Welsh dolls, books, honey, fudge and beauty products.

WELSH CRAFTS, 10 High Street, Conway.

WELSH CRAFTS, 92 High Street, Porthmadog.

GWYNEDD CRAFTS, Beddgelert.
Pottery, tapestry, clothes, quilts, sheepskin products, jewellery, slate-craft, perfumes, cosmetics, woodcare, dolls. Anglesey fudge, honey, etc.

R. & E. HUMPHREYS, Siop-y-Plas, Llanbedrog.
Welsh crafts, small tapestry hand-crafts, sheepskin rugs, pottery, glass, copper, brassware jewellery, shells and shell-craft. Blenders of Arandelle perfumes—Hwyrnos Haf, Lelog Wen, Grug-y-Mynydd, etc.

HANNAH JONES LTD, Welsh Woollen Mills, Pen-

machno, Betws-y-Coed.
Pure wool tweeds, tapestry cloth, tapestry quilts, tailored garments, craft goods.
Mill open to the public all year round.
F. & V. PHILIPSON, The Log Cabin, Station Square, Betws-y-Coed.
Sheepskins, sheepskin slippers, gloves and hats. Welsh tapestry bed-covers, Welsh tapestry and tweed clothing, cane- and basket-work.
'SANDBACH'S', 78a Mostyn Street, Llandudno.
Pottery, slate clocks, lamps and tables. Jewellery ranging from inexpensive stone to sterling silver.
THE WEAVER'S LOFT, 7 Castle Street, Conway.
Tapestry and tweed clothing, tapestry bed-covers, pottery, slate-craft including house-names. Sheepskin rugs and slippers. Celtic jewellery. Baskets and wood-work, honey.
YR EFAIL, Gwyndy, Llanystumdwy, Criccieth.
Craft gifts in slate, pottery and jewellery. Hand-made toys. Paintings. Antiquities and bric-à-brac.

Cardiganshire
THE CRAFT CENTRE, 11–13 Terrace Road, Aberystwyth.
CRAFT DESIGN CENTRE OF WALES, Rhan o Atom.
A permanent exhibition and sales showroom for artist-craftsmen producing high-quality items in Wales. Traditional and contemporary design in clay, wood, stone, metal, glass, precious metals and gems.
CORNEL CREFFT, 5 Stryd y Baddon (5 Bath Street), Aberystwyth.
Welsh tapestry clothing ('Lili Lon' for children), tapestry quilts, handbags, table-mats, Pottery, wood, stone, slate crafts.
QUIXOTE (MONA & GARTH HATHERLEY), 4 College Row, Cardigan.
Craft shop specialising in local pottery and tweeds, tapestry made-ups, woodware, rugs. Woodwork and pottery made on the premises.
WELTEX SPORTSWEAR, The Welsh Wool Shop, 11 Bridge Street, Aberayron.
Welsh thorn-proof tweed fishing hats, deerstalkers and skirts. Flannel shirts and dresses. Tapestry coats, anoraks, capes and skirts. Also tapestry and honey-comb quilts and blankets and a variety of Welsh pottery, woodware and other crafts.

Carmarthenshire
CORGI WELSH CRAFTS, Wind Street, Ammanford.
Wide range of Welsh crafts including hand-tailored garments, made to measure and exclusive 'Corgi' sweaters and socks.
THE OLD FORGE, Abergorlech.
Crafts: antiques, pottery, old maps and prints. Old oil-lamps, globes and spare parts, electrified lamps, lamps repaired, tapestries. Sheepskin rugs, slippers, etc.
THE SPINNING WHEEL, 2 King Street, Carmarthen.
Wide range of tapestry clothing, including capes, skirts and tabards. Tapestry handbags and purses, bed-spreads, sheepskin rugs and slippers.

Denbighshire
'STUDIO 69', Station Road, Llanrwst.
All original work in the form of paintings, sculpture, copperware, pottery, taxidermy.
BETTINA CRAFTS, Bridge Street, Llangollen.
Wide range of tapestry clothing, including capes, skirts and anoraks. Tapestry handbags and purses, sheepskin rugs, sheepskin coats, hats, gloves and slippers.
CRAFTCENTRE CYMRU, 28 Penrhyn Road, Colwyn Bay.
Pottery, Welsh tapestry clothing, tapestry quilts and handbags, slate lamps, ash-trays, fans; carved wooden love-spoons; Welsh dolls, fudge, honey and books; sheepskin rugs, mitts, slippers and hoods.
NICE THINGS, 20 Market Street, Llangollen.
Kitchenware and pine furniture.
SIOP CLWYD, Vale Street, Denbigh.
Welsh tapestry quilts, made-up garments, wood-craft, love-spoons, leather goods, slate work, ornamental candles, local-made pottery.
WELSH SHOP OLD MILL AND COTTAGE IN THE VILLAGE, Tynllan, Llanarmon Dyffryn Ceiriod, nr Llangollen.
Welsh tapestries, honeycombs, travel-rugs, pottery, wrought iron, basketware, walking-sticks, sheepskin, garments in tapestry, ladies' and gents' hats in Welsh tweed, skirts, socks, golf-hose, purses, handbags, perfumery, slate craft, etc. Local honey.
'WELSHCRAFTS', Abbey Road, Llangollen.
Welsh tapestry, quilts, honeycomb blankets, travel-rugs, tweeds, hand-woven scarves, squares, ties, etc. Baskets, woodwork, old maps and prints, hand-made pottery, wrought ironwork, etc. Copper, pewter and silver jewellery.

Flintshire
BARROW CRAFTS, High Street, St Asaph.
Welsh tapestries and tweeds, sheepskin clothing and rugs, knitwear, pottery and china.
CELTIC CRAFTS LTD, Nannerch, nr Mold and 36 Well Street, Ruthin.
Wide range of tapestry clothing, including capes, skirts and anoraks. Tapestry handbags and purses, sheepskin rugs, hats, gloves and slippers. Paintings and prints.
CRAFTS UNLIMITED, The Old Mill, Nanarch, nr Flintshire.

Glamorganshire
DINAS WELSH CRAFTS, Ewenny, Bridgend.
Tapestry quilts and clothes (coats, capes, skirts, dresses, etc), tweed, flannel and tapestry by the yard; honey, pottery, jewellery, woodwork, perfume.
INTERCRAFT, Boverton Road, Llantwit Major.
Tapestry, tweed and flannel, local-made soft toys, pottery, woodware, jewellery, perfume, honey, slate, prints, etc.
THE POTTER'S WHEEL, Cathedral Green, Llandaff, nr Cardiff.
Traditional Welsh copper lustre jugs and grey stone glazed tableware. Welsh tapestry and Celtic jewellery, Welsh perfume and love-spoons.
WELSH COTTAGE CRAFT SHOP, Oystermouth, Swansea.
Specialists in Welsh fashion—Welsh tapestry garments and accessories, tapestry by the yard. Jewellery in silver, pewter, copper and stainless steel. Welsh pottery, Welsh perfumes, honeys, ties and scarves.

Locally carved love-spoons, leather goods.
WELSH COTTAGE CRAFT SHOP, Pennard, Gower, Swansea.
Welsh tapestry garments and accessories, tapestry by the yard. Welsh pottery, perfume. honey, ties, scarces, love-spoons. Good selection of leather goods.
WELSH COTTAGE CRAFT SHOP, Sketty, Swansea.
Welsh tapestries, new soft flannels in bright modern colours, Welsh tweeds, large range of garments and accessories, handbags, purses, etc. Hand-made jewellery, Welsh pottery in stoneware, copper lustre, and earthenware. Locally carved love-spoons—love-spoons made to order.
WELSH FASHION CRAFT, Marments Ltd, Queen Street, Cardiff.
Welsh tapestry and flannel—coats, capes, suits, dresses, maxi-skirts, evening-dresses, wedding-dresses, etc.
WELSH FASHION CRAFT, Oystermouth, Mumbles, Swansea.
Welsh tapestry and flannel—coats, capes, suits, dresses, max-skirts, evening-dresses, wedding-dresses, suède garments.

Merionethshire
PHILIP WILSON, Furniture Maker, Llyn, Barmouth Road, Harlech.
Hand-made furniture, individually designed. Carved woodware.
BRAICHGOCH SLATE QUARRIES LTD, Corris, Machynlleth.
Manufacturers and distributors of slate craftwork, clocks, lamps, sundials, barometers, jewellery, etc.
CILDERI CRAFTS AND CURIOS, Tan-y-Bwich, nr Maentwrog.
Welsh handcrafts, local honey and preserves, sheepskin rugs, pictures, books on handcrafts and the district.
CRAFTCENTRE CYMRU, Copper Hill Street, Aberdyfi.
CRAFTCENTRE CYMRU, Cambrian House, Bala.
CRAFTCENTRE CYMRU, 91a High Street, Bala.
CRAFTCENTRE CYMRU, High Street, Barmouth.
Pottery, Welsh tapestry clothing. Slate clocks and fans; house name-plates and model ships made to order; sheepskin rugs, mitts and slippers; carved wooden love-spoons; suède clothing and handbags; tapestry quilts and table-mats; wrought iron sculptures; Welsh dolls, honey, fudge and perfume.
MEREDITH & SMITH LTD, Y Tanws, Dolgellau.
Sheepskin rugs, mitts, gloves and coats. Leather and suède coats, wallets and purses, etc.
QUARRY TOURS LTD, Llechwedd Slate Caverns, Blaenau Ffestiniog.
Slate-craft pottery and jewellery, candles, tapestries and Welsh perfumes. Geological samples on sale.
Y CREFFTWR, High Street, Bala.
Pottery, jewellery, weaving, walking-sticks, candles, leather goods, wrought ironwork, paintings, etc. Hand-made corn-dollies, wild-flower pictures, period costume dolls, original prints, etc. Also sheepskins, Welsh honey.

Monmouthshire
CRAFTS OF BRITAIN, Mrs D. G. Bonelle, 3 St Mary Street, Monmouth.
High-quality hand-crafts all made in Britain.
THE OLD FORGE CRAFT SHOP (NANCY E. JAMES),

Llanellen, nr Abergavenny.
Ladies' and children's fashions in Welsh tapestry and tweed, hand-made pottery, jewellery, glassware, rushwork, sheepskin leather goods, cashmere, etc.
WELSH COUNTRY CRAFTS, Tintern, nr Chepstow.
Traditional Welsh tapestry, capes, etc., bed-covers, blankets, local hand-woven ties, head-squares and tweeds. Welsh natural sheepskins, mitts, slippers, etc. Welsh national dressed dolls. Hand-worked copperware, jewellery, woodware, hand-thrown pottery.
WELSH CRAFTS SHOP (WYNFORD WEST), 416 Chepstow Road, Newport NPT 8JH.
Tapestry quilts, high-class fashion-wear to measure, hats, bags, purses, Welsh dolls, pottery, yew tables, horse- and pony-brasses, perfumes, jewellery, honey, socks.
WELSH RURAL CRAFTS SHOP, Rhadyr, nr Usk.
Antique prints and maps. Celtic jewellery, perfumes, local paintings, pottery and woodcrafts, tapestries and tweeds. Welsh national-dressed dolls.

Montgomeryshire
CRAFTCENTRE CYMRU, Llangurig, nr Llanidloes.
Welsh tapestry clothing, quilts, handbags. Slate lamps, ash-trays, clocks, Caldey perfume, Aberaeron honey and fudge, Welsh books, dolls, carved wooden love-spoons. Rush and wicker work, antique maps and prints of Wales, sheepskin slippers, rugs, mitts and hoods. Pottery.
'CREFFTAU CAIN', High Street, Llanfyllin.
Pottery, bellows, Celtic jewellery, stone, copper, pewter, steel and silver jewellery. Welsh tapestry quilts, handbags, purses, etc. Tapestry and tweed 'tailored' garments, also by the yard. Sheepskin rugs and slippers. Basketry. 'Natural' walking-sticks, ties, brassware. Tweed hats, mohair.
'DAVEY', Welsh Crafts, 6 Short Bridge Street, Newtown.
Welsh tapestry, tweed, sheepskin, pottery, paintings and jewellery. Hand-knitted Arans, etc.
Y GIST DDERW, Llangynog.
Welsh tapestry, rushwork, slate lamps, clocks, etc. Horse-brasses, copperwork, honey, marmalade, fudge. Dolls, perfumed, decorated candles, Welsh honeycomb cot-blankets, Welsh tapestry items. Skirt lengths. Locally made Welsh wool socks. Flannel shirts. Local oil-paintings. Gemstone jewellery.

Pembrokeshire
THE CRAFT SHOP, The Pebbles, St Davids.
Materials by the yard, clothing with matching accessories, traditional quilts, pottery, Caldey perfumes and silver Celtic jewellery.
ANN & MARK JEFCOATE, The Strand Craft Shop, Saundersfoot.
Welsh woollen goods, hand-thrown pottery and other country workshops' products.
THE PEMBROKESHIRE CRAFT & GIFT SHOP, 27 Bridge Street, Haverfordwest.
Quality craftwork, most of which are made in Pembrokeshire or have a direct connection with Pembroke.
E. A. WINN-JONES, THE WELSH SHOP, 1 Bridge Street, The Harbour, Tenby.
Welsh tapestry quilts, coats, capes, skirts, table-mats,

etc. Pottery, slateware, Welsh tweed garments, ties, woollen blankets, rugs, Welsh flannel, knitwear, perfumes, costume dolls and wrought ironwork.

Radnorshire
LLANDRINDOD WELSH CRAFT CENTRE, Lindens Walk, Llandrindod Wells.
Tapestry bedspreads, handbags and purses, hand-made Welsh pottery, sheepskins, sheepskin slippers, jewellery. Tapestry clothing including coats, capes and skirts. Children's tapestry capes, gents' tweed caps and hats and a wide range of Welsh perfumes.
BRYAN W. POCOCK, Ithon Craft Shop, Llanbister, Llandrindod Wells.
Welsh tapestry products, sheepskin, suède and leather goods and garments. Welsh studio pottery, woodware, jewellery, perfumes, toys, copperware, Welsh cloth by the yard, love-spoons, candles.

SCOTLAND
Argyllshire
THE CRAFT CENTRE, 5 Hillfoot Street, Dunoon PA23 7DR.
Scottish, Welsh and Irish crafts. Hand-made porcelain and stoneware, sheepskin rugs, mohair rugs and stoles. Hand-woven tapestry and honeycomb quilts, hand-woven place-mats. Pewter, silver and ceramic jewellery.

Berwickshire
SEA CREATURES (JOHN AITCHISON), 'West Winds', Burnmouth, Eyemouth.
Real shellfish preserved for ornaments and displays, lobster, hermit, spider, green crabs, etc, world-wide shells, mother-of-pearl, tropical shell and gemstone jewellery. Shellcraft, marine paintings, ships-in-bottles, paper-weights, marine antiques and curios, model lobster-pots. Woollens, pottery and various other craftwork.

Inverness-shire
CASTLEWYND STUDIOS LTD, Inverdruie, Aviemore.
Earthenware and stoneware, made and decorated by hand. Figures, animals and a range of pots (saut-buckets, mugs, jugs, plates, etc).
CULLODEN CRAFT CENTRE, Little Cullernie Balloch, nr Inverness.
Crafts and produce made in the Highlands and elsewhere.

Midlothian
HIGHLAND HOME INDUSTRIES LTD, 94 George Street, Edinburgh EH2 3DQ.
Head Office and main showroom for hand-knitted woollens and tweeds made in the Highlands and Islands. Only authentic Scottish craft goods and productions in twelve retail shops throughout Scotland. Mohair, woollen and tweed weaving centre, Morar, Inverness-shire. At Aberdeen, Elgin, Fort Augustus, Gairloch, Glenesk, Golspie, Iona, Lochboisdale, Morar, Strathpeffer, Ullapool, Poolewe.

Morayshire
FINDHORN STUDIOS LTD, Pineridge, Findhorn Bay,

Forres.
Health food and craft shop. As part of a community venture, hand-made craftwork in original designs will be made available. These include leatherwork, weaving, macramé, candle-craft, pottery, woodwork, screen-printing.
BATA BEG, Findhorn.
Hand-made gifts collected from all over Scotland. Articles of sea-side and yachting interest.
LAICHMOOR, 24 Batchen Street, Elgin.
Tweeds, tartans, knitwear, kilts and skirts tailored. Scottish crafts of every description.

Perthshire
GLENOGLE TWEEDS, The Shieling, Lochearnhead.
Knitwear in cashmere and lambswool. Extensive range of Scottish hand-woven tweeds and tartans, also Harris, Shetland and Fair Isle products. Rugs of cashmere and wool mohair and sheepskin. Horn work, pottery and jewellery.
PERTHSHIRE CRAFTS LTD, The Ell Shops, The Square, Dunkeld.
Deerskin and tilt marble articles made in Dunkeld. All Scottish products including engraved crystal, woollen goods, etc, also work of other Scottish craftsmen.
THE STABLE GIFT SHOP, Kilmahog, Callander.
Specialists in sheepskin and deerskin rugs and Scottish craft goods. This company also manufactures the 'Clan' range of game fishing-rods.

NORTHERN IRELAND
Antrim
BALLINDERRY ANTIQUES, Ballinderry Upper, Lisburn.
GIFTS AND CRAFTS, 2 Castle Street, Carrickfergus.
THE IRISH CRAFTS SHOP, 71 Main Street, Portrush.
NATIONAL TRUST INFORMATION & CRAFT CENTRE, Giants' Causeway, Bushmills.

Armagh
LITTLE ORCHARD POTTERY, Cranagill, Portadown.

Belfast
JOHN MAGEE LTD, 4 Donegall Square West.
NATIONAL TRUST INFORMATION & CRAFT CENTRE, Malone House, Barnett Demesne, Belfast BT9 5PU.
NATIONAL TRUST INFORMATION & CRAFT CENTRE, 10 Royal Avenue
ULSTER BOUTIQUE, 60–64 Wellington Place, 29 College Street, Belfast.

Down
COUNTY CRAFTS, Heather Garrett, 4 Shore Street, Donaghadee.
MAGPIE TWEEDS, 40 High Street, Bangor.
NATIONAL TRUST INFORMATION & CRAFT CENTRE, Castle Ward, Strangford.
THE TWEED SHOP, 12 Main Street, Hillsborough.

Fermanagh
FERMANAGH COTTAGE INDUSTRIES, 14 East Bridge Street, Enniskillen.

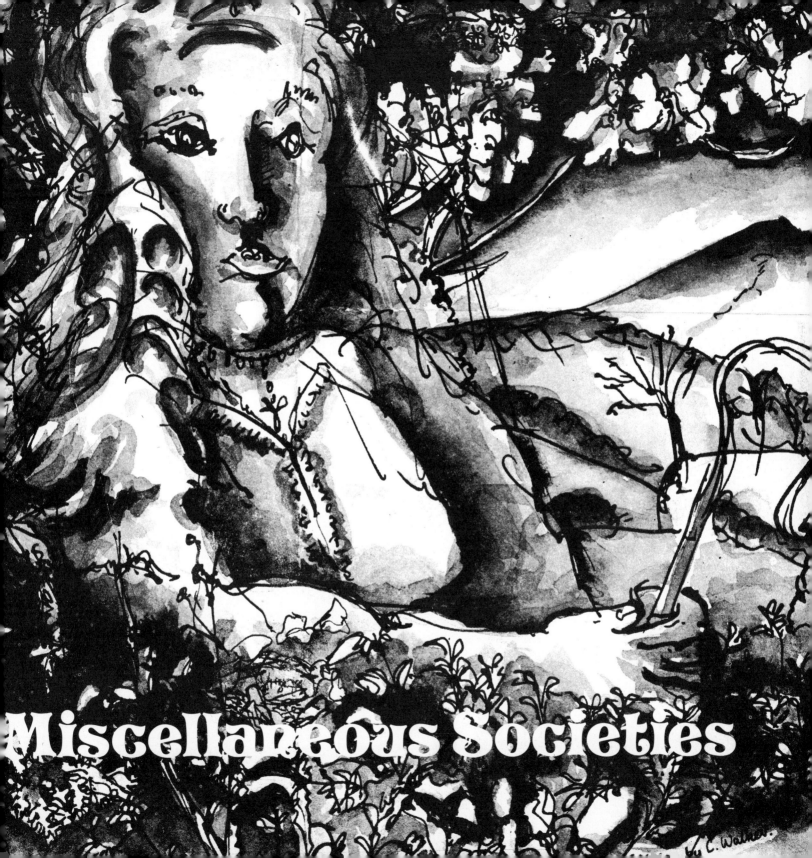

Miscellaneous Societies

Agriculture

BRITISH PLOUGHING ASSOCIATION, 41 Washington Street, Workington, Cumberland.
COUNTRY LANDOWNERS' ASSOCIATION, 7 Swallow Street, London, W1R 8EN.
CROFTERS COMMISSION, 4/6 Castle Wynd, Inverness, Scotland.
FARM BUILDINGS ASSOCIATION, Twineham, Haywards Heath, Sussex RH17 5NH.
FARMERS' UNION OF WALES, Llys Amaeth, Queen's Square, Aberystwyth.
HIGHLANDS AND ISLANDS DEVELOPMENT BOARD, Bridge House, Bank Street, Inverness, Scotland.
MINISTRY OF AGRICULTURE, FISHERIES AND FOOD, Whitehall Place, London SW1.
MINISTRY OF AGRICULTURE, GOVERNMENT OF NORTHERN IRELAND: FORESTRY DIVISION, Dundonald House, Upper Newtownards Road, Belfast BT4 3SB.
NATIONAL FARMERS' UNION, Agriculture House, Knightsbridge, London SW1.
YORKSHIRE FARM MACHINERY PRESERVATION SOCIETY, 42 Northgate, Walkington, Beverley, Yorkshire HU17 8ST.

Air Pollution

CLEAN AIR COUNCIL, Department of the Environment, Queen Anne's Chambers, 28 Broadway, London SW1.
CLEAN AIR COUNCIL FOR SCOTLAND, Scottish Development Department, 21 Hill Street, Edinburgh EH2 3JY.
NATIONAL SOCIETY FOR CLEAN AIR, 134–137 North Street, Brighton, Sussex BN1 1RG.
ROYAL COMMISSION ON ENVIRONMENTAL POLLUTION, Church House, Great Smith Street, London SW1P 3BL.

SOLID SMOKELESS FUELS FEDERATION, York House, Empire, Wembley, Middlesex.

Animals (specific)

THE BRITISH DEER SOCIETY, Haybridge Deer Sanctuary, Bouth by Ulverston, Lancashire.
BRITISH GOAT SOCIETY, Rougham, Bury St Edmonds, Suffolk.
BRITISH FRIESIAN CATTLE SOCIETY OF GREAT BRITAIN & IRELAND, Scotsbridge House, Rickmansworth, Hertfordshire WD3 3BB.
BRITISH HORSE SOCIETY, National Equestrian Centre, Kenilworth, Warwickshire.

BRITISH RABBIT COUNCIL, 302 Farnborough Road, Farnborough, Kent.
BRITISH SPOTTED HORSE & PONY SOCIETY, Nash End Farm, Bisley, Stroud, Gloucestershire.
BRITISH WATERFOWL ASSOCIATION, The High House, Long Green, Epping Upland, Essex.
THE CAT CLUB, c/o Mrs Goudy, Summers Lodge, Summers Leys Road, Princes Risborough, Buckinghamshire.
PONIES OF BRITAIN, Brookside Farm, Ascot, Berkshire.
PONY CLUB, National Equestrian Centre, Kenilworth, Warwickshire.

Animal Welfare & Protection

ANIMAL DEFENCE SOCIETY & ANTI-VIVISECTION SOCITY LTD, 52–53 Dean Street, London W1V 5HO.
BLUE CROSS, 1 Hugh Street, London SW1.
CATHOLIC STUDY CIRCLE FOR ANIMAL WELFARE, Catholic Rectory, Goring, Reading.
CATS PROTECTION LEAGUE & TAIL WAVERS, 29 Church Street, Slough, Buckinghamshire. Also: 435 Caledonian Road, London N7.
COUNCIL OF JUSTICE TO ANIMALS, 42 Old Bond Street, London W1.
DOG RESCUE SOCIETY, Denewood, Totteridge.
FAUNA PRESERVATION SOCIETY, Zoological Gardens, Regents Park, London N1.
FUND FOR THE REPLACEMENT OF ANIMALS IN MEDICAL EXPERIMENTS, 312a Worple Road, Wimbledon, London SW20 8QU.
HORSES & PONIES PROTECTION ASSOCIATION, 1 Station Parade, Balham, London SW12.
THE HUNT SABOTEURS, c/o Dave Wetton, 11 Brunswick Grove, Kingston-on-Thames, Surrey.
LEAGUE AGAINST CRUEL SPORTS, 1 Reform Row, London N17 9TW.
THE NATIONAL ANIMAL RESCUE KENNELS, 51 Harley Street, London W1N 1DD.

NATIONAL SOCIETY FOR THE ABOLITION OF FACTORY FARMING, c/o Hon. National Organiser, 42 Mount Pleasant Road, Lewisham, London SE13.

PERFORMING & CAPTIVE ANIMALS DEFENCE LEAGUE, 11 Buckingham Street, London WC2.

THE RARE BREEDS SURVIVAL TRUST, c/o J. Henson, The Rare Breeds Survival Centre, Cotswold Farm Park, Guiting Power, Gloucester. *A society devoted to the preservation of rare and unusual breeds of livestock.*

ROYAL SOCIETY FOR THE PROTECTION OF ANIMALS, 105 Jermyn Street, London SW1.

ROYAL SOCIETY FOR THE PROTECTION OF BIRDS, The Lodge, Sandy, Bedfordshire.

R.S.P.C.A. REFORM GROUP, 'Savannah', 15 Stratford Road, Preston Plucknett, Yeovil, Somerset.

STOP FACTORY FARMING LEAGUE, Old Beams, Stoodleigh, nr Tiverton, Devon.

THE UNIVERSITIES FEDERATION FOR ANIMAL WELFARE, 230 High Street, Potters Bar, Hertfordshire.

WILD ANIMAL PROTECTION SOCIETY, c/o S. Goddard, Resident Flats, Guys Hospital, London SE1.

WORLD WILDLIFE FUND, 7 Plumtree Court, London EC4.

Architecture (general)

CENTRAL COMMITTEE FOR THE ARCHITECTURAL ADVISORY PANELS, 4 Hobart Place, London SW1.

CIVIC TRUST, 17 Carlton House Terrace, London SW1Y 5AW.

FARM BUILDINGS ASSOCIATION, Twineham, Haywards Heath, Sussex RH17 5NH.

MEN OF THE STONES, The Rutlands, Tinwell, Stamford, Lincolnshire.

ROYAL FINE ART COMMISSION, 2 Carlton Gardens, London SW1.

ROYAL FINE ART COMMISSION FOR SCOTLAND, 22 Melville Street, Edinburgh EH4 1PL.

ROYAL INSTITUTE OF BRITISH ARCHITECTS, 66 Portland Place, London W1N 4AD.

SALTIRE SOCIETY, Gladstone's Land, 483 Lawnmarket, Edinburgh 1.

SCOTTISH GEORGIAN SOCIETY, 41 Castle Street, Edinburgh EH2 3BH.

SOCIETY OF ARCHITECTURAL HISTORIANS OF GREAT BRITAIN, 8 Belmont Avenue, Melton Park, Newcastle-upon-Tyne NE3 5QD.

WELSH OFFICE, Cathays Park, Cardiff CF1 3NG.

Architecture (Historic and Conservation)

ANCIENT MONUMENTS SOCIETY, 11 Alexander Street, London W2.

CIVIC TRUST, 17 Carlton Terrace, London SW1Y 5AW.

CIVIC TRUST FOR THE NORTH EAST, 34/35 Saddler Street, Durham.

CIVIC TRUST FOR THE WEST, 56 Oxford Street, Manchester M1 6EU.

CIVIC TRUST FOR WALES/TREFTADAETH CYMRU, 6 Park Place, Cardiff CF1 3DP.

THE CONSERVATION SOCIETY, 34 Bridge Street, Walton-on-Thames, Surrey.

COUNCIL FOR BRITISH ARCHAEOLOGY, 8 St Andrew's Place, Regents Park, London NW1.

FRIENDS OF FRIENDLESS CHURCHES, 12 Edwardes Square, London W8.

THE GEORGIAN GROUP, 2 Chester Street, London SW1.

HISTORIC BUILDINGS BUREAU, Department of the Environment, 25 Savile Row, London W1X 2BT.

HISTORIC BUILDINGS COUNCIL FOR ENGLAND, 25 Savile Row, London W1X 2BT.

HISTORIC BUILDINGS COUNCIL FOR SCOTLAND, Argyle House, Lady Lawson Street, Edinburgh EH3 9SF.

HISTORIC BUILDINGS COUNCIL FOR WALES, Summit House, Windsor Place, Cardiff.

HISTORIC CHURCHES PRESERVATION TRUST, Fulham Palace, London SW6.

NATIONAL ASSOCIATION OF ALMSHOUSES, Billingbear Lodge, Wokingham, Berkshire RG11 5RU.

NATIONAL MONUMENTS RECORD (ENGLAND), Fortress House, 23 Savile Row, London W1X 1AB.

NATIONAL MONUMENTS RECORD (SCOTLAND), 52–54 Melville Street, Edinburgh EH3 7HF.

NATIONAL MONUMENTS RECORD (WALES), Edleston House, Queen's Road, Aberystwyth, Cardiganshire.

SCOTTISH CIVIC TRUST, 24 George Square, Glasgow G2 1EF.

SCOTTISH GEORGIAN SOCIETY, 41 Castle Street, Edinburgh EH2 3BH.

SOCIETY OF ARCHITECTURAL HISTORIANS OF GREAT BRITAIN, 8 Belmont Avenue, Melton Park, Newcastle-upon-Tyne NE3 5QD.

SOCIETY FOR THE PROTECTION OF ANCIENT BUILDINGS, 55 Great Ormond Street, London WC1N 3JA.

THE VICTORIAN SOCIETY, 29 Exhibition Road, London SW7.

ULSTER ARCHITECTURAL HERITAGE SOCIETY, 30 College Gardens, Belfast BT9 6BT.

Book Societies

COUNTRY & GARDENERS' BOOK SOCIETY, Dept L831, PO Box 6, Newton Abbot, Devon TQ12 2DW.

Camping & Touring

THE CAMPING CLUB OF GREAT BRITAIN & IRELAND, 11 Grosvenor Place, London SW1W 0EY.

YOUTH CAMPING ASSOCIATION, c/o E. G. Lawrence, Upper Flat, 14 East Road, Enfield, Middlesex.

YOUTH HOSTELS ASSOCIATION (England and Wales) Membership, sales, travel and service departments: 29 John Adam Street, London WC2.

National office: Trevelyan House, St Stephens Hill, St Albans, Hertfordshire.

Communes
THE COMMUNE MOVEMENT, c/o Richard Secombe, 3 Longfellow Avenue, Bath, Somerset BA2 4SJ.

Canals
BRITISH WATERWAYS BOARD, Melbury House, Melbury Terrace, London NW1 6JX.
INLAND WATERWAYS ASSOCIATION LTD, 114 Regent's Park Road, London NW1 8UQ.
RAILWAY AND CANAL HISTORY SOCIETY, 174 Station Road, Wylde Green, Sutton Coldfield, Warwickshire.
TRANSPORT STUDIES SOCIETY, 12 The Glebe, Denman's Lane, Lindfield, Sussex.

Conservation
ASSOCIATION FOR THE PRESERVATION OF RURAL SCOTLAND, 39 Castle Street, Edinburgh 2.
ASSOCIATION OF RIVER AUTHORITIES, Grosvenor Gardens House, Grosvenor Gardens, London SW1W 0BS.
BERKSHIRE, BUCKINGHAMSHIRE & OXFORDSHIRE NATURALISTS TRUST, Shirbourne Lodge, Watlington, Oxfordshire.
BRITISH TRUST FOR CONSERVATION VOLUNTEERS, Zoo-

logical Gardens, Regent's Park, London NW1 4RY.
CENTRAL COUNCIL FOR RIVERS PROTECTION, Fishmongers' Hall, London EC4.
CENTRE FOR ENVIRONMENTAL STUDIES, 5 Cambridge Terrace, Regent's Park, London NW1 4JL.
CIVIC TRUST, 17 Carlton Terrace, London SW1Y 5AW.
CIVIC TRUST FOR THE NORTH EAST, 34/35 Saddler Street, Durham.
CIVIC TRUST FOR THE NORTH WEST, 56 Oxford Street, Manchester M1 6EU.
CIVIC TRUST FOR WALES, 6 Park Place, Cardiff CF1 3OP.
THE CHEPSTOW SOCIETY, 41 Hardwick Avenue, Chepstow.
COMMITTEE FOR ENVIRONMENTAL CONSERVATION, 4 Hobart Place, London SW1W 0HY.
CONSERVATION SOCIETY, 34 Bridge Street, Walton-on-Thames, Surrey.
COUNCIL FOR THE CARE OF CHURCHES, 83 London Wall, London EC2M 5NA.

COUNCIL FOR THE PROTECTION OF RURAL ENGLAND, 4 Hobart Place, London SW1W 0HY. *This society has many affiliated bodies, all of which are listed below. The addresses of these affiliated bodies are obtainable from the C.P.R.E.'s address (unless already listed).*

  Arboricultural Association
  Ashtead Residents Association
  Association of Friends of Cannock Chase
  Barnes Amenities Committee
  Bath Preservation Trust
  Bathavon Rural District Council
  Beaulieu Residents Association
  Bedfordshire Association of Parish Councils
  Bedfordshire Preservation Society
  Berkshire Association of Parish Councils
  Betchworth Society
  Bexleyheath and District Ratepayer's Association
  Biggleswade Rural District Council
  Birmingham School of Planning
  Bosham Association
  Boston Preservation Trust
  Bournville Village Trust
  British Archaeological Association
  British Caravanners' Association
  British Horse Society
  British Naturalists Association
  Brockley Hill Residents Association
  Bromsgrove Rural District Council
  Buckinghamshire Association of Parish Councils
  Campden Trust
  Carshalton Amenities Society
  Caterham & District Residents Association
  Chiltern Club of Arts and Handicrafts
  Chiltern Society
  Chipstead Residents Association
  Commoners of Croxley Green
  Conservation Society
  Crawley (Hants) Owners Resident's Association
  Cudham Residents' Association
  Cyclists Touring Club (Northumberland) and Durham District) Association
  Dalton-on-Tees Parish Council

Darlington Society of Arts
Dartmoor Preservation Association
Dartmouth and Kingswear Society
Dedham Vale Society
Ditchling Preservation Society
Dorking and Leith Hill District Preservation Society
Dorking Urban District Council
Dorset Association of Parish Councils
Durham Association of Parish Councils
East Coulsdon Residents Association
East Dean with Friston Residents' Association
Eastcote Residents' Association
Eastern Federation of Amenities Society
Enfield Preservation Society
English Speaking Union
Fell & Rock Climbing Club of the English Lake District
Finchingfield Parish Council
Findon Village Preservation Association
Forest of Galtres Society
Friends of Box Hill Association
Friends of Brockenhurst Society
Friends of the Lake District
Galleon World Travel Association Ltd
Godalming Trust
Great Warley Conservation Society
Guild of St George
Guildford Borough Council
Guildford Natural History & Literary Society
Guildford Society
Hampshire Association of Parish Councils
Hampton Residents' Association
Harpenden Society
Harting Society
Haslemere and District Preservation Society
Hayes (Kent) Village Association
Hertfordshire Association of Parish Councils
High Beech Green Belt Association
Historic Churches Preservation Trust
Holiday Fellowship (London Group)
Holyport (Berks.) Preservation Society
Home Counties Rambling Association
Horsham Society
Huddersfield Art Society
Hurst Green Women's Institute
Hurstmere County Secondary Boys' School (Sidcup)
Island Development Committee (Jersey)
Isle of Wedmore Society
Kennet and Avon Canal Trust Ltd
Keston and District Branch, C.P.R.E.
Kingswood District Residents' Association
Lands Improvement Company
Leatherhead and District Countryside Protection Society
Leicestershire & Rutland Trust for Nature Conservation Ltd
Little Chalfont Rural Preservation Society
London C.H.A. Club Ltd
London Society
Lyme Regis Society
Lyminster Society
Malling Preservation Society (Kent)

Men of the Trees
Mendip Society
Midhurst Society
Mill Hill Preservation Society
New Forest Rural District Council
North Bedfordshire Preservation Society
North London Mountaineering Club
Northumberland Federation of Women's Institutes
Norton St Philip Society (Bath)
Nottingham, Derby and Lincoln Society of Architects
Ockley Society
Orpington and District Amenity Society
Orwell Preservation Society
Oxfordshire Association of Parish Councils
Oxshott Heath Conservators
Oxted and Limpsfield Amenities Association
Park Langley Ratepayers' Association
Pedestrians' Association for Road Safety
Penn County Branch, C.P.R.E.
Petersfield Society
Pin Mill Preservation Society (Suffolk)
Piscatorial Society
Potters Bar Society
Pulborough Society
Ramblers' Association (Southern Area)
Ramblers' Association (Wessex Area)
River Thames Society
Rottingdean Preservation Society
Royal Archaeological Institute
Royal Institute of British Architects, Tyneside Branch
Royal Institute of British Architects, Yorkshire Region
Royal Society of St George
Ruislip Residents' Association
Ruskin Society and Friends of Brantwood
Saffron Walden Countryside Association
St Helen's Park Preservation Society
Sanderstead Preservation Society
Sawbridgeworth Preservation Society
Sherborne Urban District Council
Shere and District Rural Preservation Society
Shoreham Preservation Society
Sid Vale Association
Society for the Preservation of Lindfield
South Bedfordshire Preservation Society
South Hams Society
South Nutfield and Nutfield Conservation Association
Southend-on-Sea County Borough
Southern Pathfinders
Stanmore Society
Storth Women's Institute (Westmorland)
Suffolk Association of Architects
Sussex Rural Community Council
Sussex Vigilant Association
Sutton and Cheam Society
Teignmouth and Shaldon Environment Society
Theydon Bois and District Rural Preservation Society
Totteridge Manor Association
Turville Society

Ullswater Preservation Society
Ulster Society for the Preservation of the Countryside
Wadhurst Area Society for Protection and Preservation
Warninglid (Sussex) Residents' Society
Warwick Society
West Chiltington and District Rural Preservation Society
West Surrey Society
West Wickham Residents' Association
Wild Brooks Society
Wiltshire Archaeological and Natural History Society
Wiltshire Association of Parish Councils
Wimborne and Cranborne Rural District Council
Wirral Society
Wisbech Society
Women's Farm and Garden Association
Yorkshire Federation of Women's Institutes
Youth Hostels Association (Lakeland Regional Group)
Youth Hostels Association (Leicestershire and Rutland Sub-Regional Group)
Youth Hostels Association (Midland Regional Group)
Youth Hostels Association (South-Eastern Countryside Committee)

COUNCIL FOR THE PROTECTION OF RURAL WALES, Meifod, Montgomeryshire.
COUNTRYSIDE COMMISSION, 1 Cambridge Gate, Regent's Park, London NW1 4JY.
COUNTRYSIDE COMMISSION FOR SCOTLAND, Battleby, Redgorton, Perth.
DARTMOOR PRESERVATION SOCIETY, c/o Mr B. J. Rider, Cedar Cottage, Crapstone, Yelverton, Devon.
DEPARTMENT OF THE ENVIRONMENT, 2 Marsham Street, London SW1P 3EP.
ENTERPRISE YOUTH, 29 Queen Street, Edinburgh EH2 1JK.
ENVIRONMENTAL CONSORTIUM, 14 William IV Street, London WC2N 4DW.
THE EXMOOR SOCIETY, c/o E. A. Roberts, Y Garn, Llanychaer, Pembrokeshire.

FRIENDS OF THE EARTH, 9 Poland Street, London W1. Regional offices listed below:
Cambridge: Richard Brown, Trinity Hall, Cambridge, CB2 1TX.
Cheshire: FOE Birkenhead, 108 Argyle Street, Birkenhead.
Cornwall: Roy Bennett, The Workshop, 4 Lower Green Street, Newlyn.
Sally Willington, Riverside Herb Garden, Hessenford, Torpoint. Tel: Downderry 352.
Devon: Richard Jennings, St Clare, St Andrews Road, Exwick, Exeter, EX4 2AF. Tel: 0392 73954.
Dorset: Simon Gapper, 1 Tallbay Road, Parkstone, Poole.
East Anglia: Ray Mumford, 59 Earsham Street, Bungay, Suffolk. London tel. contact: Linda Silk 01-623 1964.
Essex: Simon Dodson, The White House, 11 Manor Close, Great Horkesley, Colchester, CO6 4AR.

Tel: Gt Horkesley 406.

Terry Hurlstone, 24 Linton Court, Pettits Lane, Rise Park, Romford.

Dave Dryer, 9 Grove Road, Rayleigh.

Linda Proud, PO Box 44, Chelmsford. Tel: Chelmsford 59839.

T. J. Birtchnell, 8 Lynton Close, Dovercourt, Harwich. Tel: Harwick 4342.

Alan Martin, 37 Rigby Gardens, Chadwell St Mary.

John Matthiessen, 237 Eastern Avenue, Redbridge, Ilford. Tel: 01-550 2003.

Mary Hollywood, 36 Mark Hall Moors, Harlow.

Graham Penfold, 168 North Crescent, Southend.

Hampshire: John Worley, 16 St George's Avenue, Havant, PO9 2RX. Tel: 07012 3217.

Mr D. Parkins, 18 Latimer Road, Winton, Bournemouth.

Philip Chandler, 13 Sycamore Avenue, Chandler's Ford.

John Mickerson, 51 Westwood Road, Southampton, SO2 1DJ.

Hertfordshire: Arthur Puffett, 56 Pondfield Crescent, Marshalswick, St Alban's. Tel: St Albans 58913. Secretary: Pearl Holder, Tel: St Albans 51634.

Doug Scott, c/o Watford & District YMCA, 37 Clarendon Road, Watford, WD1 1JQ. Tel: Watford 24287.

Mrs Margaret Whiting, 28 Catlin Street, Hemel Hempstead.

Joanne Duncan, 20 Port Hill, Hertford. Tel: Hertford 3742.

Ireland: Ellen Riorden, An Taisce, 126 Baggot Street, Dublin 2.

Kent: Ian Kemp, 54 Burns Crescent, Tonbridge.

Lancashire: FOE Merseyside, 3 Devonshire Road, Liverpool 8. Tel: 051-727 2456.

Stephen Harvey, c/o Fylde College, University of Lancaster.

Leicestershire: Bob Moloney, Leicester Polytechnic Students' Union, Newarke Street, Leicester. Tel: Leicester 27652.

Lincolnshire: John Jackson, 16 Wyredale Road, Ashby, Scunthorpe.

London: Sue Chapman, 46 Haldan Road, London E4. Tel: 527 7660.

John Wielgosz, 7 Baron's Court Mansions, Gledstanes Road, London W14.

Tony Williams, Flat 1, 101 Devonport Road, London W12.

Pat Rosenwald, 9 Bracken Gardens, Barnes, London SW13. Tel: 748 5072.

Dr David Sharon, Dept. of Applied Biology, South Bank Polytechnic, London SE1. Tel: 928 8989 Ext. 395.

Jill Hall, 23 Kenilworth Road, Penge, London SE20 7QG. Tel: (home) 659 0588, (office) 822 3117.

John Garley, 42 Kings Road, South Norwood, London SE25 4ES.

Geoff Leigh, 30 Woodside, London SW19. Tel: 947 4094.

Dave Cooper, 27 Elderlie Road, London SE9 1UD.

Jenny Sullings, 1 Christchurch Avenue, London NW6. Tel: 629 8144 X 26.

Gerry Coward, 3 Essex Road, London E12.

Joanna Gibson, 4 Abercorn Mansions, London, Abercorn Place, London NW8. Tel: (office) 487 4455.

London FOE Shop: 'It's Your Problem', 59 Skinner Street, London EC1. Tel: 837 7733.

Norfolk: Julian Blackmore, 36 College Road, Norwich.

Mr & Mrs D. Hicks, 7 Woodlands Drive, Thetford.

Northamptonshire: Ken Strong, Cherry Orchard High School, Birchfield Road East, Weston Favell.

Northumberland: Susan Turner, Hancock Museum, Newcastle-upon-Tyne, NE2 4PT. Tel: 22359.

Northern Ireland: David J. Paul, Students' Union, Queens University, Belfast N1.

Nottingham: Brian Grout, Dept. of Zoology & Botany, University of Nottingham.

Oxfordshire: Patricia Keel-Diffey, 72 Reading Road, Henley-on-Thames. Tel: Henley 4081.

Scotland: Geoff Kearsley, University of Glasgow, Glasgow W2. Tel: 041 339 8855 Ext. 213.

Ann Cohen, 19 Dundas Street, Edinburgh. Tel: 031-556 1872.

Somerset: Brian Price, Brunel House, St George's Road, Bristol 1. Tel: 0272 290485.

Suffolk: Tim Bell, The Mill House, Cavendish, Sudbury. Tel: Clare 463.

Surrey: Denise Wyllie, 10A Crescent Road, Norbiton, Kingston. Tel: 01-546 3893.

Sussex: Wendy Marlar, c/o Active Recovery Ltd, Martins Thakeham, Nr pulborough. Tel: W. Chiltington 2704/2252.

Mrs Pauline Gordon-Clarke, Itchingfield House, Nr Horsham. Tel: Slimfold 393.

Mrs B. Johnson, Bryckden Place, Waldron. Tel: Heathfield 3094.

Mr M. Beale, Rise Holding, Rise Farm, Lewes. Tel: Lewes 6319.

Warwickshire: John & Carol Parks, 95 Anderton Park Road, Moseley, Birmingham 13. Tel: 021-449 6276.

Wiltshire: Sue & Dick Capel, Greywethers, Bath Road, W. Overton, Marlborough.

Worcestershire: Dr. Alison Brown, Flat 5, 53 Graham Road, Malvern, WR14 2HU.

Yorkshire: Stewart Hildred, 161 Victoria Road, Leeds 6.

Robin & Alison Ramsey, 113 Coltman Street, Hull, HU3 2SF.

Keith Lowe, 56 St George's Road, Anlaby Road, Hull.

Vicky Kilner, 5 Heathmount Hall, Crossbeck Road, Ilkley.

David Fletcher, Netherclough, Cragg Vale, Hebden Bridge.

V. C. Staples, Waveney, Church Lane, Bardsey, Nr Leeds, IS7 9DH.

Mrs Beryl Schofield, 104 Howard Crescent, Durkar, Wakefield.

LAKE DISTRICT NATURISTS' TRUST LTD, 5 Annisgarth Close, Windermere.

NATIONAL HERITAGE, Bedford Chambers, Covent Garden, London WC2E 8HA.

NATIONAL TRUST, 42 Queen Anne's Gate, London SW1.

NATIONAL TRUST FOR SCOTLAND, 5 Charlotte Square, Edinburgh EH2 4DU.

NATURE CONSERVANCY, 19–20 Belgrave Square, London SW1X 8PY.

PILGRIM TRUST, Millbank House, 2 Great Peter Street, London SW1.

SCOTTISH CIVIC TRUST, 24 George Square, Glasgow G2 1EF.

SOCIETY FOR THE PROMOTION OF NATURE RESERVES, The Manor House, Alford, Lincolnshire.

SURREY NATURISTS TRUST, Juniper Hall Field Centre, Dorking, Surrey.

ULSTER SOCIETY FOR THE PRESERVATION OF THE COUNTRYSIDE, West Winds, Carney Hill, Holywood, Co. Down.

Cycling

BRITISH CYCLING BUREAU, Greater London House, Hampstead Road, London NW1 7QP.

THE BRITISH CYCLE FEDERATION, 26 Park Crescent, London W1.

THE CYCLIST TOURING CLUB, 69 Meadrow, Godalming, Surrey.

THE FELL CLUB, 12 Ravenswood Crest, Stafford.

THE 40-PLUS GROUP, T. Wooder, 425 Upminster Road North, Rainham, Essex.

THE ROUGH STUFF FELLOWSHIP, H. G. Robson, 23 Spring Terrace, North Shields, Northumberland.

SOUTH EASTERN ROAD CLUB, Mrs J. Oborne, 13 Amherst Drive, St Mary, Kent.

SOUTHERN VETERAN-CYCLE CLUB, c/o I. Cowan, 8 Shrubbery Road, Gravesend, Kent.

TANDEM CLUB, Hon. Secretary, 71 Exeter Road, Welling, Kent.

THE VEGETARIAN CYCLING AND ATHLETICS CLUB, 18 Mill Lane, Kilburn, London NW6.

ROYAL NATIONAL ROSE SOCIETY, Chiswell Green Lane, St Albans, Hertfordshire.

Flowers

ALPINE GARDEN ASSOCIATION, 58 Denison House, 296 Vauxhall Bridge Road, London SW1.
BRITISH FUCHSIA SOCIETY, 72 Ash Lane, Hale, Altrincham, Cheshire.
BRITISH GLADIOLUS SOCIETY, 223 Frindsbury Hill, Frindsbury, Rochester, Kent.
BRITISH IRIS SOCIETY, 72 South Hill Park, London NW3.
BRITISH NATIONAL CARNATION SOCIETY, 1 Evelyn Road, Worthing, Sussex.
BRITISH ORCHID GROWERS ASSOCIATION, 1 Crutched Friars, London EC3.
BRITISH PANSY & VIOLA FLORAL SOCIETY, 43 Northfield Lane, Horbury, Wakefield, Yorkshire.
BRITISH PELARGONIUM & GERANIUM SOCIETY, 129 Aylesford Avenue, Beckenham, Kent.
DAFFODIL SOCIETY, College of Ascension, Selly Oak, Birmingham 29.
DELPHINIUM SOCIETY, 5 Park Lane, Sevenoaks, Kent.
THE HARDY PLANT SOCIETY, 10 St Barnabas Road, Emmer Green, Caversham, Reading RG4 8RA.
NATIONAL AURICOLA & PRIMULA SOCIETY, 584 Edenfield Road, Rochdale, Lancashire.
NATIONAL BEGONIA SOCIETY, 50 Woodlands Farm Road, Birmingham 24.
NATIONAL CHRYSANTHEMUM SOCIETY, 65 St Margarets Avenue, London N20.
NATIONAL DAHLIA SOCIETY, 26 Burns Road, Leamington Spa, Warwickshire.
NATIONAL SWEET PEA SOCIETY, 33 Priority Road, Rustingdon, Sussex.
NATIONAL VIOLA & PANSY SOCIETY, 16 George Street, Birmingham.
NORTHERN ENGLAND ROSE, CARNATION & SWEET PEA SOCIETY, 38 Ridgewood Crescent, Newcastle-upon-Tyne.
ORCHID SOCIETY OF GREAT BRITAIN, 87 Brookmans Avenue, Brookmans Park, Hatfield, Hertfordshire.

Folk Dance & Song

BRITISH COUNTRY MUSIC ASSOCIATION, 38 Guycroft, Otley, Yorkshire.
COUNTRY MUSIC ASSOCIATION, c/o M. Conn Promotions Ltd, 45–46 Chandos Place, London WC2.
ENGLISH FOLK DANCE AND SONG SOCIETY, Cecil Sharp House, 2 Regent's Park Road, London NW1.
ROYAL SCOTTISH COUNTRY DANCE SOCIETY, 12 Coates Crescent, Edinburgh EH3 7AF.

Folklore (General)

FOLK-LORE SOCIETY, c/o University College Library, Gower Street, London WC1.
INSTITUTE OF DIALECT & FOLK-LIFE STUDIES, c/o University of Sussex, Falmer, Brighton, Sussex.
SOCIETY OF FOLK-LIFE STUDIES, c/o National Museum of Antiquities, Queen Street, Edinburgh 2, Scotland.
ULSTER FOLK-LIFE SOCIETY, c/o Ulster Folk Museum, Culha Manor, Holywood, Co. Down.

Folklore (Specific)

ENGLISH PLACE-NAME SOCIETY, University College, London WC1.
GIPSY COUNCIL, 14 Princess Avenue, London N3.
GIPSY-LORE SOCIETY, University Library, Liverpool.

237

Footpaths

CENTRAL RIGHTS OF WAY COMMITTEE, Suite 4, 166 Shaftesbury Avenue, London WC2.

COMMONS, OPEN SPACES & FOOTPATHS PRESERVATION SOCIETY, Suite 4, 166 Shaftesbury Avenue, London WC2.

THE RAMBLERS' ASSOCIATION, 1/4 Crawford Mews, London W1H 1PT.

SCOTTISH RIGHTS OF WAY SOCIETY, 32 Rutland Square, Edinburgh 1.

Gardens

EIRE GARDENS SCHEME, c/o Organising Secretary, Blackrock House, Blackrock, Dublin.

THE GARDENER'S ROYAL BENEVOLENT SOCIETY, Palace Gate, Hampton Court, East Molesey, Surrey.

GARDENERS SUNDAY, White Witches, Claygate Road, Dorking, Surrey.

GARDEN HISTORIC SOCIETY, 15 St Margaret's Close, Berkhamsted, Hertfordshire.

THE GOOD GARDENER'S ASSOCIATION, Arkley Manor, Arkley, Hertfordshire.

LONDON GARDENERS SOCIETY, 20 Buckingham Street, London WC2.

METROPOLITAN PUBLIC GARDENS ASSOCIATION, 58 Denison House, 296 Vauxhall Bridge Road, London SW1.

NATIONAL GARDENS GUILD, 'Sharnden', Fourth Avenue, Stanford-le-Hope, Essex.

NATIONAL GARDENS SCHEME, 57 Lower Belgrave Street, London SW1.

THE NATIONAL TRUST, 42 Queen Anne's Gate, London SW1.

THE NORTHERN HORTICULTURAL SOCIETY, Harlow Car, Harrogate, Yorkshire.

THE ROYAL HORTICULTURAL SOCIETY, Horticultural Hall, Vincent Square, London SW1.

SCOTLAND'S GARDENS SCHEME, 26 Castle Terrace, Edinburgh 1.

ULSTER GARDENS SCHEME, c/o General Organiser, The National Trust, 82 Dublin Road, Belfast BT2 7JA.

Health

THE BRITISH COLLEGE NATUROPATHY & OSTEOPATHY, 6 Netherhall Gardens, London NW3. *A society devoted to the use of natural remedies to heal sickness and disease.*

FRIENDS OF THE VEGETARIAN SOCIETY, c/o Mr T. Lane, 108 Bishop Road, Chelmsford, Essex.

HEALTH EATING SOCIETY, 21 Hanway Place, London W1.

THE IRISH ASSOCIATION FOR NATURAL HEALTH, 28 Cambridge Road, York Road, Dun Laoghaire, Ireland.

THE JEWISH VEGETARIAN SOCIETY, 'Bet Teva', 855 Finchley Road, London NW11 8LX.

RHYL NATURAL FOODS SOCIETY, Mrs Daphne Goodwin, 16 Castle Street, Ruthin, North Wales.

NATIONAL INSTITUTE OF MEDICAL HERBALISTS, c/o General Secretary, Mrs E. G. Merritt, 673 Barking Road, Plaistow, London E13.

NORTH WEST FEDERATION OF VEGETARIAN SOCIETIES, c/o Mr J. M. Raby, 21 Smithy Lane, St Annes-on-Sea, Lancashire.

THE SOCIETY FOR BOTANIC MEDICINE, 3 Littlecote, Petworth, Sussex.

THE SOCIETY OF HERBALISTS, Dept H.21, Bruton Street, Berkeley Square, London W1.

ULSTER VEGETARIAN SOCIETY, c/o Mr W. M. Capper, Westwinds, Craigavad, Holywood, Co. Down.

THE VEGETARIAN CATERING ASSOCIATION, c/o Mrs K. Keleny, Combe Lodge, Wotton-Under-Edge, Gloucestershire.

VEGAN SOCIETY, 47 Highlands Road, Leatherhead, Surrey.

VEGETARIAN SOCIETY, 53 Marloes Road, Kensington, London W8 6LD.

THE VEGETARIAN SOCIAL CLUB, Mrs E. Moore, 23 Sutherland House, Marloes Road, London W8 6LD.

THE VEGETARIAN SOCIETY OF IRELAND, c/o Miss B. Feeney, 10 Church Avenue, South Circular Road, Dublin.

YORKSHIRE VEGETARIAN FEDERATION, c/o Miss O. Robotham, 14 Wensley Road, Stockton-on-Tees TS18 4JQ.

YOUNG VEGAN SECTION, c/o Robert Colby, Vegro Organic Nurseries, Tyringham, Newport Pagnell, Buckinghamshire MK1 69ER.

Natural History (general)

ASSOCIATION OF SCHOOL NATURAL HISTORY SOCIETIES, c/o J. E. G. Morris, Strand School, Elm Park, London SW2.

BIRMINGHAM NATURAL HISTORY SOCIETY, 3/219 Brandwood Road, Kings Heath, Birmingham 4.

BRITISH JUNIOR EXPLORATION SOCIETY, c/o John Lodge, Great Ruffins, Wickham Bishops, Essex.

BRITISH NATURALISTS ASSOCIATION, Hawkshead, Tower Hill, Dorking, Surrey.

COUNCIL FOR NATURE, Zoological Gardens, Regents Park, London NW1 4RY.

FIELD STUDIES COUNCIL, 9 Devereux Court, Strand, London WC2.

FRESHWATER BIOLOGICAL ASSOCIATION, The Ferry House, Ambleside, Westmorland.

LONDON NATURAL HISTORY SOCIETY, 28 Hetherington Road, London SW4.

NATURAL HISTORY SOCIETY OF NORTHUMBERLAND, DURHAM & NEWCASTLE-UPON-TYNE, The Hancock Museum, Newcastle-upon-Tyne NE2 4PT.

NATURE CONSERVANCY, 19–20 Belgrave Square, London SW1X 8PY.

NOTTINGHAM & NOTTINGHAMSHIRE FIELD CLUB, 1a Trevelyan Road, West Bridgford, Nottingham NG2 5GY.

SCHOOL NATURAL SCIENCE SOCIETY, 2 Bramley Mansions, Berrylands Road, Surbiton, Surrey.

SCOTTISH FIELD STUDIES ASSOCIATION, 104 West George Street, Glasgow C2.

SOCIETY FOR THE BIBLIOGRAPHY OF NATURAL HISTORY, c/o The British Museum (Natural History), London SW7.

SOCIETY FOR THE PROMOTION OF NATURE RESERVES, The Manor House, Alford, Lincolnshire.

WEST WALES NATURALISTS TRUST, 4 Victoria Place, Haverfordwest, Pembrokeshire.

WILDLIFE SOUND RECORDING SOCIETY, Chadswell, Sandy Lane, Rushmoor, Tilford, Farnham, Surrey.

Natural History (specific)

BOTANICAL SOCIETY, c/o C. E. Allen, Department of Botany, British Museum (Natural History), London SW7.

BOTANICAL SOCIETY OF EDINBURGH, c/o Royal Botanical Garden, Inverleith Row, Edinburgh EH3 5LR.

BRITISH BRYNOLOGICAL SOCIETY, 2 Strathearn Road, Sutton, Surrey.

BRITISH LICHEN SOCIETY, c/o Department of Botany, British Museum (Natural History), London SW7.

BRITISH PHYLOLOGICAL SOCIETY, Department of Botany, Birkbeck College, Malet Street, London WC1.

BRITISH SPIDERS STUDY GROUP, c/o British Arachnological Society, Peare Tree House, Blennerhasset Green, Carlisle, Cumberland.

BRITISH TRUST FOR ENTOMOLOGY, Hope Department of Entomology, University Museum, Oxford.

CONCHOLOGICAL SOCIETY OF GREAT BRITAIN AND IRELAND, 58 Teignmouth Road, London NW2.

FAUNA PRESERVATION SOCIETY, Zoological Gardens, Regents Park, London N1.

MAMMAL SOCIETY OF THE BRITISH ISLES, c/o Institute of Biology, 41 Queensgate, London SW7.

ROYAL SOCIETY FOR THE PROTECTION OF BIRDS, The Lodge, Sandy, Bedfordshire.

WILD FLOWER SOCIETY, Mrs C. M. R. Schwerdt, Rams Hill House, Horsemonden, Tonbridge, Kent.

Railways

ASSOCIATION OF RAILWAY PRESERVATION SOCIETIES, 34 Templegate Road, Whitkirk, Leeds.

BAHAMAS LOCOMOTIVE SOCIETY, 36 Kirkham Road, Heald Green, Cheadle, Cheshire.

THE BATTLE OF BRITAIN LOCOMOTIVE PRESERVATION SOCIETY, c/o The Secretaries, '92 Squadron Appeal', c/o Midland Bank Ltd, 56 St Johns Avenue, Churchdown, Gloucester GL3 2BY.

DART VALLEY RAILWAY ASSOCIATION, Dept 1, Forelands, Redgewood Road, Sidmouth, Devon EX10 9AD.

GREAT WESTERN SOCIETY LTD, 196 Norwood Road, Southall, Middlesex.

THE LONDON & NORTH WESTERN SOCIETY, c/o Mr J. C. James, 'Solaby', 4 Longview Drive, Huyton, Liverpool L36 6EE.

THE MONMOUTHSHIRE RAILWAY SOCIETY, 1 Forest Close, Newport, Monmouthshire NPT 8LX.

RAILWAY & CANAL HISTORY SOCIETY, 174 Station Road, Wylde Green, Sutton Coldfield, Warwickshire.

RAILWAY CLUB, 112 High Holborn, London WC1.

RAILWAY CONVERSION LEAGUE, 51 Upper Richmond Road, London SW15.

THE RAILWAY CORRESPONDENCE & TRAVEL SOCIETY, c/o Lee Crowder, 24 Harborne Road, Edgbaston, Birmingham 15.

RAILWAY CORRESPONDENCE & TRAVEL SOCIETY, 'Rannock', Upper Way, Upper Longden, Rugely, Staffordshire.

WIGHT LOCOMOTIVE SOCIETY, c/o 106 Gordon Road, Fareham, Hampshire.

WIRRAL RAILWAY CIRCLE, P.O. Box 74, Bebington, Wirral, Cheshire.

WORCESTER LOCOMOTIVE SOCIETY, c/o Mr H. D. Wood, 24 Cecilia Avenue, Worcester WR2 6EN.

River and Sea Pollution

ASSOCIATION OF RIVER AUTHORITIES, Grosvenor Gardens House, Grosvenor Gardens, London SW1W 0BS.

CENTRAL COUNCIL FOR RIVERS PROTECTION, Fishmongers' Hall, London EC4R 9EL.

COASTAL ANTI-POLLUTION LEAGUE, Alverstoke, Greenway Lane, Bath.

INLAND WATERWAYS ASSOCIATION LTD, 114 Regent's Park Road, London NW1 8OQ.

WATER POLLUTION RESEARCH LABORATORY, Elder Way, Stevenage, Herts.

Rural Life Furtherment and Preservation

ASSOCIATION FOR THE PRESERVATION OF RURAL LIFE, Dyrham, Chippenham, Wiltshire.

ASSOCIATION FOR THE PRESERVATION OF RURAL SCOTLAND, 39 Castle Street, Edinburgh.

INSTITUTE OF RURAL LIFE AT HOME & OVERSEAS, 27 Northumberland Road, New Barnet, Hertfordshire.

NATIONAL FEDERATION OF VILLAGE PRODUCE ASSOCIATION, 36 North Road, Berkhamsted, Hertfordshire.

SAVE THE VILLAGE POND CAMPAIGN, 111 Lambeth Road, London SE1.

WWOOF (WORKING WEEKENDS ON ORGANIC FARMS), 143 Sabine Road, London, SW11.

The Soil & Soil Husbandry

BIO-DYNAMIC AGRICULTURAL ASSOCIATION, Broome Farm, Clent, Stourbridge, Worcestershire.

THE HENRY DOUBLEDAY ASSOCIATION, Bocking, Braintree, Essex.

THE SOIL ASSOCIATION, Walnut Tree Manor, Houghley, Stowmarket, Suffolk IP14 3RS.

Trams

TRAMWAY & LIGHT RAILWAY SOCIETY, 102 Marlborough Lane, London SE7.

TRAMWAY MUSEUM SOCIETY, 1 Griffith Road, Birmingham 23.

Trees and Forestry

ARBORICULTURE ASSOCIATION, 59 Blythwood Gardens, Stansted, Essex.

ASSOCIATION OF BRITISH TREE SURGEONS AND ARBORISTS, 11 Wings Road, Upper Hale, Farnham, Surrey.

ASSOCIATION OF TREE TRANSPLANTERS, 91A High Street, Great Missenden, Buckinghamshire.

FOREST PRODUCTS RESEARCH LABORATORY, Princes Risborough, Aylesbury, Buckinghamshire.

FORESTRY COMMISSION, 25 Savile Row, London W1X 2AY.

GLASGOW TREE LOVERS SOCIETY, 147 Blythswood Street, Glasgow C2.

MEN OF THE TREES, Leagate Centre, Bramley, Surrey.

ROYAL FORESTRY SOCIETY OF ENGLAND, WALES & NORTHERN IRELAND, 102 High Street, Trina, Hertfordshire.

ROYAL SCOTTISH FORESTRY SOCIETY, 26 Rutland Square, Edinburgh EH1 2BU.

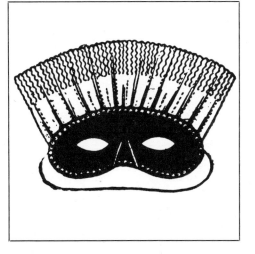

Miscellaneous

ASHTON CONKER CLUB, Ashton, nr Oundle, Northamptonshire. *World championship games held every second Sunday in October each year.*

BRITISH BEER MAT COLLECTORS SOCIETY, 142 Leicester Street, Wolverhampton WV6 0PS.

BRITISH MATCHBOX LABEL & BOOKLET SOCIETY, 283–5 Worplesdon Road, Guildford, Surrey.

THE BRITISH PANTOMIME ASSOCIATION, 170 Clarence Gate Gardens, London NW1.

BRITISH PUPPET & MODEL THEATRE GUILD, 90 Minories, London EC3.

CARTOPHILIC SOCIETY OF GREAT BRITAIN (including the Cameric Cigarette Card Club), 208 Vicarage Farm Road, Heston, Hounslow, Middlesex.

DESERTED MEDIEVAL VILLAGE GROUP, 67 Gloucester Crescent, London NW1.

DOLLS CLUB, 12 The Close, New Malden, Surrey.

FAIR ORGAN PRESERVATION SOCIETY, 65 Market Road, Thrapston, Northamptonshire.

HERALDRY SOCIETY, 28 Museum Street, London WC1.

NATIONAL TROLLEY BUS ASSOCIATION, 43 Quarry Rock Gardens, Claverton Down, Bath, Somerset.

SOCIETY OF CADDY-SPOON COLLECTORS, c/o E. Kramer, 5 Verulum Buildings, Gray's Inn, London WC1.

WINE LABEL CIRCLE, Stadhampton Vicarage, Oxford OX9 7TU.

YORKSHIRE FARM MACHINERY PRESERVATION SOCIETY, 42 Northgate, Walkington, Beverley, Yorkshire HU17 8ST.

Miscellaneous Bibliography

SPECIALIST BOOKSHOPS

ANSFORD BOOKS, Lower Ansford, Castle Cary, Somerset. *Specialists in natural history.*

CLEARWATER BOOKS, 130 Andover Road, Orpington, Kent. *Specialises in rural crafts, village life and husbandry.*

DESIGN CENTRE, 28 Haymarket, London WC1. *Books on art, design and crafts for sale, as well as registers and directories for reference.*

DRUMMOND, 30 Hart Grove, London W5. *Specialises in countrycrafts, horticulture and wild flowers.*

P. KENNEDY, 285 New Hall Lane, Preston, Lancashire. *Specialists in natural history and gardening. Second-hand books also available.*

LANDSMAN'S BOOKSHOP, Buckenhill, Bromyard, Hereford. *Specialises in farming, gardening and forestry. Second-hand books also available.*

THE ECOLOGY BOOKSHOP, 45 Lower Belgrave Street, London SW1.

ROBINSON & WATKINS, Cecil Court (off Charing Cross Road), London WC1. *An excellent environmental section.*

STOBART & SON LTD, 67–73 Worship Street, London EC2A 2EL. *Specialises in handicrafts. Catalogue on request.*

N.B. Sometimes quite useful and nostalgic craft and country books are out of print and difficult to obtain. If you have no luck in local jumble sales or second-hand book shops, try the following firm which, although it is one of the largest second-hand book dealers in the country, gives very good service :

RICHARD BOOTH (BOOKSELLERS) LTD, Hay Castle, Hay-on-Wye, via Hereford.

ANIMALS

ANIMAL HEALTH/Animal Health Trust, 24 Portland Place, London W1N 4HN. (Twice a year) Annual subscription: 37½p.

ANIMAL WAYS/The R.S.P.C.A., 105 Jermyn Street, London SW1Y 6LG. (Monthly) Annual subscription: 35p.

ANIMALS/Nigel Sitwell Ltd, 21–22 Great Castle Street, London W1. (Monthly) Price: 20p. Annual subscription: £3.00.

ANIMALS' DEFENDER AND ANTI-VIVISECTION NEWS/National Anti-Vivisection Society, 51 Harley Street, London W1W 1DP. (Alternate months) Price: 8p. Annual subscription: 50p.

THE ANIMALS' QUARTERLY/available c/o The Raystede Centre for Animal Welfare, Raystede, Ringmer, Sussex.

THE ARK/Catholic Study Circle for Animal Welfare, Catholic Rectory, Goring, Reading. (April, August and December) Price: 20p. Annual subscription: 75p.

AYRSHIRE CATTLE SOCIETY JOURNAL/available from 1 Racecourse Road, Ayr, Scotland. (Quarterly) Annual subscription: £1.00 (free to members).

BIRDS/Royal Society for the Protection of Birds, The Lodge, Sandy, Bedfordshire. (Bi-monthly) Annual subscription: £2.00.

BIRDS AND COUNTRY MAGAZINE/available from 79 Surbiton Hill Park, Surbiton, Surrey. (Quarterly) Price: 18p. Annual subscription: 90p.

BLUE CROSS ILLUSTRATED/available from 1 Hugh Street, London SW1. (Twice a year) Price: 15p. Annual subscription: 30p.

BRITISH FRIESIAN HERD BOOK/British Friesian Cattle Society of Great Britain & Ireland, Scotsbridge House, Rickmansworth, Hertfordshire WD3 3BB. (Annually) Price: £2.00.

BRITISH FRIESIAN JOURNAL/British Friesian Cattle Society of Great Britain & Ireland (as above). (Alternate months) Price: 25p. Annual subscription: £1.50.

BRITISH GOAT SOCIETY MONTHLY JOURNAL/British Goat Society, Rougham, Bury St Edmonds, Suffolk. Price: 15p. (Gratis to members).

BRITISH GOAT SOCIETY'S YEAR BOOK/British Goat Society (as above). (Annually in February) Price: 50p.

BRITISH RABBIT COUNCIL YEAR BOOK(The British Rabbit Council, 7 Kirkgate, Newark, Nottinghamshire. (March) Price: 25p.

THE CAT/The Cats Protection League, 29 Church Street, Slough, Buckinghamshire. (Alternate months) Annual subscription: £1.05.

CRUEL SPORTS AND WILDLIFE/League Against Cruel Sports Ltd, 1 Reform Row, London N17 9TW. (January, May and September) Price: 4p. Annual subscription: 50p.

DAIRY SHORTHORN JOURNAL/Shorthorn Society, Green Lodge, Great Bowden, Market Harborough, Leicestershire. (Monthly) Price: 21p. Annual subscription: £2.50.

DOG NEWS/Jodo Publicity, Green Castle, Goudhurst, Kent. (Bi-monthly) Price: 15p. Annual subscription: £1.00.

DOG TRAINING WEEKLY/available from 7 Greenwich South Street, Greenwich, London SE10 8BR. Price: 13p. Annual subscription: £8.66.

DOG WORLD/Dog World Ltd, P.O. Box 13, Ashford,

Kent. Price: 13p. Annual subscription: £10.00.

DOG WORLD ANNUAL(Dog World Ltd (as above). Price: £1.25.

FLOCK BOOK OF DEVON LONG-WOOLLED SHEEP/Devon Long-Woolled Sheep Breeders' Society, Drumlarrig, Lustleigh, Newton Abbot, Devon. (Every three years) Price: 72p.

FLOCK BOOK OF OXFORD DOWN SHEEP/Oxford Down Sheep Breeders' Association, St Michael's House, Malton, N. Yorkshire. (Annually in July) Price: £1.50.

FLOCK BOOK OF ROMNEY SHEEP BREEDERS' SOCIETY/Romney Sheep Breeders' Society, Station Road, Ashford, Kent. (Annually in July) Price: £1.05.

JOURNAL OF ANIMAL ECOLOGY/Blackwell Scientific Publications Ltd, Osney Mead, Oxford OX2 0EL. (February, June, October) Price: £5.25. Annual subscription: £14.00.

FRIENDS OF ANIMALS/Humane Education Society, Newgate, Wilmslow, Cheshire. (Alternate months) Price: 3p. Annual subscription: 27p.

FUR AND FEATHER/ Watmoughs Ltd, Idle, Bradford, Yorkshire. (Fortnightly) Price: 15p. Annual subscription: £4.75.

HOOFPRINT/available from 55 Cross Street, Manchester M2 4JN (Monthly) Price: 7p. Annual subscription: £1.50.

HORSE & PONY/Scottish Farmer Publications Ltd, 39 York Street, Glasgow, G2 8JL. (Monthly) Price: 16p.

HORSE WORLD/Horse World Publications, 17 Fleet Street, London EC4. (Monthly) Price: 25p. Annual subscription: £2.25.

MAMMAL REVIEW/Blackwell Scientific Publications Ltd, Osney Mead, Oxford OX2 0EL. (Quarterly) Price: £1.75. Annual subscription: £6.00.

ORYX/Fauna Preservation Society, c/o The Zoological Society, Regent's Park, London NW1 4RY. (Three times a year) Price: 50p. Annual subscription: £3.00.

OUR DOGS/Our Dogs Publishing Co. Ltd, Oxford Road Station Approach, Manchester M60 1SX. (Weekly) Price: 15p. Annual subscription: £11.30.

PIGEON RACING NEWS AND GAZETTE/Redferns, Weybridge, Surrey. (Monthly) Price: 14p. Annual subscription: £2.40.

R.S.P.C.A. TODAY/R.S.P.C.A., 105 Jermyn Street, London SW17 6EG. (Quarterly) Price: 5p. Annual subscription: 30p.

STABLE MANAGEMENT/Riding School and Stable Management Ltd, 1 Tahoma Lodge, Lubbock Road, Chislehurst, Kent BR7 5JS. (Alternate months) Annual subscription: £1.50.

TAIL-WAGGER AND FAMILY MAGAZINE/Tail-Waggers Club (Great Britain) Ltd, Old Charge House, Cannon Street, London EC4. (Monthly) Price: 12p. Annual subscription: £1.50.

THE ARMCHAIR NATURALIST/Poyntoniana Books, Poynton, Cheshire.

THE COUNTRYMAN ANIMAL BOOK, by Bruce and Margaret Campbell/David & Charles Ltd.

THE DEXTER COW, by W. R. Shrower/Faber & Faber Ltd.

GOAT HUSBANDRY, by David Mackenzie.

THE PIONEERING PIG, by Norman Blake.

THE PROVISIONAL ATLAS OF INSECTS OF THE BRITISH ISLES/The Biological Records Centre, Monks Wood. Obtainable from bookshops or direct from E. W. Classey, 353 Hanworth Road, Hampton TW12 3EN.

THE RIGHT WAY TO KEEP HENS, DUCKS, GEESE AND TURKEYS/Elliot Right Way Books, Kingswood Buildings, Kingswood, Todworth, Surrey.

THE SHELL BIRD BOOK, by James Fisher/Ebury Press. *The following publications are available from* THE FORESTRY COMMISSION, *25 Savile Row, London W1X 2AY:*

BADGERS IN WOODLANDS (Leaflet No. 34). Price: 10½p.

BLACKGAME (Forest Records No. 66). Price: 17½p.

BUTTERFLIES IN WOODLANDS (Forest Records No. 65). Price: 17½p.

THE CAPERCAILLIE (Leaflet No. 37). Price: 12½p.

THE CRESTED TIT (Leaflet No. 41). Price: 10½p.

CROSSBILLS (Leaflet No. 36). Price: 10p.

THE FALLOW DEER (Leaflet No. 52). Price: 20p.

HEDGEHOGS (Forest Records No. 77). Price: 15p.

TITMICE IN WOODLANDS (Leaflet No. 46). Price: 12½p.

VOLES AND FIELD MICE (Leaflet No. 44). Price: 10p.

WILDLIFE CONSERVATION IN WOODLANDS (Booklet No. 29). Price: 47½p.

WOODPECKERS IN WOODLANDS (Leaflet No. 42). Price: 10p.

BUILDING RENOVATION

BUILD YOUR OWN HOUSE, by Stuart Martin/Stanley Paul & Co. Ltd.

HOUSE & GARDEN Book of Cottages, by Joyce Lowrie/Collins Sons & Co. Ltd.

IMPROVE YOUR HOUSE ON A GRANT, by Robert Tattersall/Stanley Paul & Co. Ltd.

JOBS AROUND THE HOUSE, by Mike Smith/Stanley Paul & Co. Ltd.

READERS DIGEST REPAIR MANUAL/Hodder & Stoughton Ltd.

YOUR COUNTRY COTTAGE, by Robert Edmunds/David & Charles Ltd.

FLOWERS

CARNATION YEAR BOOK/available from E. Palmer, Roman Ridge, Brighton Road, Hassocks, Sussex. Price: 40p. (free to members of The British National Carnation Society).

FUSCHIA ANNUAL/British Fuschia Society, 72 Ash Lane, Hale, Altrincham, Cheshire. Price: £1.00.

GLADIOLUS ANNUAL/available from the Hon. Secretary, British Gladiolus Society, 9 The Drive, Shoreham, Sussex. Price: 75p. (plus membership subscription).

THE IRIS YEAR BOOK/British Iris Society, 72 South Hill Park, London NW3 2SN. Price: £1.50.

LILIES/The Royal Horticultural Society, Vincent Square, London SW1. (Annually) Price: 95p.

NATIONAL DAHLIA SOCIETY ANNUAL/National Dahlia Society, 26 Burns Road, Lillington, Leamington Spa, Warwickshire. Price: £1.00.

ORCHID REVIEW/Orchid Review Ltd, 62 Chaldon Common Road, Caterham, Surrey. (Monthly) Price: 40p. Annual subscription: £4.00.

RHODODENDRONS/The Royal Horticultural Society, Vincent Square, London SW1. (Annually) Price: 95p.

THE BOOK OF FLOWERS, by Alice M. Coats/Phaidon Press Ltd.

CONCISE BRITISH FLORA IN COLOUR, by Keeble-Martin/Michael Joseph Ltd.

AN ENGLISHMANS' FLORA, by Geoffrey Grigson/Phoenix House Publications. *A comprehensive guide to wild flower names in folk-lore.*

FLOWERS AND TREES OF TUDOR ENGLAND, by Clare Putnam/Hugh Evelyn Ltd.

GLOSSARY OF ENGLISH FLORA, by Gilbert Carter/Cambridge University Press. *An explanation of the Latin names of flowers.*

FOLK CULTURE

FOLKLORE/Folklore Society, c/o University College, Gower Street, London WC1E 6BT. (Quarterly) Price: 90p. Annual subscription: £3.25.

JOURNAL OF THE ENGLISH FOLK DANCE AND SONG SOCIETY/The English Folk Dance and Song Society, Cecil Sharp House, 2 Regent's Park Road, London NW1 7AY. (Annually) Price: £1.50 (free to members).

JOURNAL OF THE GYPSY LORE SOCIETY/available from D. E. Yates, The Gypsy Lore Society, The Library, The University, Liverpool. (January and July to members only) Annual subscription: £3.00.

JOURNAL OF THE LANCASHIRE DIALECT SOCIETY/available from Dr. S. Brook, Dept of English, The University, Manchester M13 9PL. (Annually) Price: 50p.

SAGA BOOK OF THE VIKING SOCIETY/The Viking Society, University College, Gower Street, London WC1. (Irregular) Price: £2.50.

CAMBRIDGESHIRE CUSTOMS & FOLK-LORE, by Enid Porter/Routledge and Kegan Paul Ltd.

THE COUNTRY DANCE BOOK, by Cecil J. Sharp/Educational Productions Ltd.

CUSTOMS & SAVAGE MYTHS, by R. M. Dorson/Routledge and Kegan Paul Ltd.

A DICTIONARY OF BRITISH FOLK TALES VOLUME 1 (A & B), VOLUME 2 (A & B), by Katherine M. Briggs/Routledge and Kegan Paul Ltd.

ENGLISH FOLK SONG & DANCE, by K. Kidson & M. Neal/Educational Productions Ltd.

A FENMAN'S STORY, by W. H. Barret/Routledge and Kegan Paul Ltd.

FOLK DANCE, by J. Tillman/Goodyear Publishing Co.

FOLK-LORE & LEGENDS OF ENGLAND/Educational Productions Ltd.

FOLK-LORE, MYTHS & LEGENDS OF BRITAIN/Readers Digest Publications Ltd.

FOLKLORE & DIALECT OF THE LOWER WYE VALLEY, by Ivor Waters/The Chepstow Society, 41 Hardwick Avenue, Chepstow.

THE FOLKLORE OF SUSSEX, by Jaqueline Simpson/B. T. Batsford Ltd.

GYPSIES, by Jeremy Sandford/Secker and Warburg Ltd.

HIGHLAND FOLK WAYS, by I. F. Grant/Routledge and Kegan Paul Ltd.

IN THE LIFE OF A ROMANY GYPSY, by Manfri F. Wood/Routledge and Kegan Paul Ltd.

MORE TALES FROM THE FENS, by W. H. Barret/Routledge and Kegan Paul Ltd.

ORAL FOLKTALES OF WESSEX, by Kingsley Palmer/David & Charles Ltd.

TALES FROM THE FENS, by W. H. Barret/Routledge and Kegan Paul Ltd.

TRADITION & FOLK LIFE, by I. C. Peate/Faber & Faber Ltd.

WEATHER LORE, by Richard Lowards/S.R. Publishers Ltd.

GARDENING AND GROWING (see also FLOWERS)

AMATEUR GARDENING/IPC Magazines Ltd. (Weekly) Price: 6p. Annual subscription: £6.00.

AMATEUR GARDENING ANNUAL/IPC Magazines Ltd. (September) Price: 40p.

BOTANICAL MAGAZINE/The Bentham Moxon Trust.

FARMERS WEEKLY/Agricultural Press Ltd, 161–166 Fleet Street, London EC4P 4AA. Price: 12p.

Annual subscription: £10.25.

FARM WEEK/Morton Publications Ltd, Lurgan, Co. Armagh. Price: 5p. Annual subscription: £4.42.

GARDEN NEWS/East Midland Allied Press Ltd, Park House, 117 Park Road, Peterborough PE1 2TS.

GARDENS TO VISIT/available from Mrs K. Collett, White Witches, Claygate Road, Dorking, Surrey. (Annually in March) Price: 10p.

GROWER/Grower Publications Ltd., 49 Doughty Street, London WC1. Price: 10p. Annual subscription: £5.00.

PLANT VARIETIES AND SEEDS GAZETTE/H.M.S.O., Atlantic House, Holborn Viaduct, London EC1P 1BN. (Monthly) Price: 9p. Annual subscription: £1.35.

POPULAR GARDENING(I.P.C. Magazines Ltd. (Weekly) Price: 6p. Annual subscription: £5.00.

PRACTICAL GARDENING/Mercury House, Waterloo Road, London SE1 8UL. (Monthly) Price: 15p. Annual subscription: £2.25.

ROYAL HORTICULTURAL SOCIETY JOURNAL/The Royal Horticultural Society, Vincent Square, London SW1P 2PE. (Monthly) Free to Fellows of the Society only.

THE BULB BOOK, by F. Doerflinger/David & Charles Ltd.

CAPABILITY BROWN & HUMPHREY REPTON, by Edward Hyams/J. M. Dent & Sons Ltd. *All about two of Britain's greatest landscape gardeners.*

THE COUNTRYMAN GARDENING BOOK/David & Charles Ltd.

THE DICTIONARY OF GARDEN PLANTS, by R. Hay & P. M. Synge/The Ebury Press.

DISCOVERING ENGLISH GARDENS, by Kay Sanecki/Shire Publications Ltd, 12B Temple Square, Aylesbury, Buckinghamshire.

THE ENCYCLOPAEDIA OF ORGANIC GARDENING/available from the Unicorn Bookshop.

EVERYMANS' ENCYCLOPAEDIA OF GARDENING, by Stanley B. Whitehead/J. M. Dent & Sons Ltd.

FOUR HEDGES—A GARDENERS CHRONICLE, by Clare Leighton/Victor Gollancz Ltd. *Beautifully illustrated by Agnes Miller.*

GARDENING WEEK BY WEEK, by Xenia Field/Octopus Books Ltd.

GARDENS OF ENGLAND & WALES/The National Gardens Scheme, 57 Lower Belgrave Street, London SW1.

GROWING THINGS, by Elizabeth Gundrey/Pan Books Ltd.

A HANDBOOK OF PLANT PROPAGATION, by R. C. M. Wright/Ward Lock Ltd.

A HISTORY OF BRITISH GARDENING, by Miles Hadfield/Hamlyn Ltd.

ORGANIC FARMING, by Hugh Chorley/Faber & Faber Ltd.

THE PIP BOOK, by Keith Mossman/Witherby & Co. Ltd, 15 Nicholas Lane, London EC4N 7BR. *A book devoted to those of us who cannot resist the temptation of burying pips, nuts, and berries in order to see whether they will grow.*

THE ROCHFORD BOOK OF HOUSEPLANTS, by Thomas Rochford & Richard Gorer/Faber & Faber Ltd.

THE SHELL GARDEN BOOK, by Peter Hunt/Phoenix House Publications.

VEGETABLES AND FRUIT BY THE ORGANIC METHOD, by J. I. Rodale/Rodale Books.

GENERAL CRAFTS

CRAFTSMAN/Moat House, Aborfield, Berkshire. (Monthly) Price: 15p. Annual subscription: £1.80.

THE ART & CRAFT BOOK, by Henry Pluckrose/Evans & Sons Ltd.

ART & CRAFT FROM FOUND MATERIALS, by Mary Lou Stribling/Allen & Unwin Ltd.

ART & CRAFT TODAY/Evans & Sons Ltd.

THE BOOK OF CRAFTS, by Henry Pluckrose/Evans & Sons Ltd.

CAKE DECORATION & SUGARCRAFT, by Evelyn Wallace/Hamlyn Ltd.

COUNTRY CRAFTS TODAY, by S. E. Manners, Laurel House, Great Cheverell, Devizes, Wiltshire.

COUNTRY CRAFT TOOLS, by Percy W. Blandford, Quinton House, Newbold-On-Stour, Stratford-On-Avon, Warwickshire.

COUNTRY WORKSHOPS/The Council for Small Industries in Rural Areas (CoSIRA), 35 Camp Road, Wimbledon Common, London SW19 4UP.

A CRAFT COLLECTION/Evans & Sons Ltd.

CREATIVE CRAFTS FOR TODAY, by John Portchmouth/Studio Vista.

GREAT CRAFTSMEN, by Raymond Lister/Bell & Sons Ltd.

GREAT WORKS OF CRAFTSMANSHIP, by Raymond Lister/Bell & Sons Ltd.

HANDBOOK OF COUNTRYCRAFTS/Drive Publications Ltd, for the AA.

NATURAL COLLAGE, by Sally Miles/Lutterworth Press.

SERENDIPITY/BBC Publications. *An illustrated introduction to a variety of simple home handicrafts.*

THE SHELL BOOK OF COUNTRYCRAFTS/Phoenix House Publications.

HEALTH & EATING (see also HERBS and WILD FOOD)

HEALTH FROM HERBS/available from 100 Portland Road, Worthing, Sussex.
GRACE/available from 736b Christchurch Road, Bournemouth, Hampshire. (Quarterly) Devoted to healing by natural methods.
PLANT FOODS FOR HUMAN NUTRITION/available from Dr S. Wokes, The Vegetarian Nutritional Centre, Elwood Gardens, Watford, Hertfordshire. (Quarterly) Price: £2.50. Annual subscription: £8.00.
SEED: THE JOURNAL OF ORGANIC LIVING/available from 269 Portobello Road, London W11.
THE JEWISH VEGETARIAN/The Jewish Vegetarian and Natural Health Society, Bet Teva, 855 Finchley Road, London NW11. (Quarterly) Price: 10p. Annual subscription: £1.00.
THE VEGETARIAN/The Vegetarian Society (U.K.) Ltd, Parkdale, Dunham Road, Altrincham, Cheshire. (Monthly) Price: 3p. Annual subscription: 66p.
VEGETARIAN HANDBOOK/The Vegetarian Society, 53 Marloes Road, London W8. (Every three years) Price: 15p.
WORLD FORUM/H. H. Greaves Ltd, 106–110 Lordship Lane, London SE22 8HG. (Quarterly) Price: 20p. Annual subscription: £1.00. Devoted to vegetarianism.
YOGA AND HEALTH/Astrian P.R. Ltd, 344–360 South Lamsett Road, London SW8. (Monthly) Price: 25p. Annual subscription: £3.75.
THE ALTERNATIVE FEASTBOOK/The Juniper Press, The Old Vicarage, Marshfield, nr Cardiff CF2 3UP. Price: 50p (including postage).
COOKING & CATERING THE WHOLEFOOD WAY, by Ursula M. Cavanagh/Faber & Faber Ltd.
COUNTRYMANS' COOKING, by W. M. W. Fowler/Arlington Books Ltd.
EATING YOUR WAY TO HEALTH, by Ruth Bircher/Faber & Faber Ltd.
FOLK MEDICINE, by D. C. Jarvis/Pan Books Ltd.
GET WELL NATURALLY, by Linda Clark/Arc Books Inc., New York.
HERBS FOR DAILY USE, by Mary Thorne Quelch/Faber & Faber Ltd.
INTERNATIONAL VEGETARIAN HEALTH FOOD HANDBOOK/The Vegetarian Society Publishing Co., Parkdale, Dunham Road, Altrincham, Cheshire. *A complete guide to vegetarian restaurants, retail shops and useful information.*

LET'S EAT RIGHT TO KEEP FIT, by Adelle Davis/Allen & Unwin.
THE NATURAL FOODS COOKBOOK, by Beatrice Trum Hunter/Pyramid Communications Inc., New York.
NATURE'S MEDICINES, by Richard Lucas/Award Books.
THE PURE HEALTHFOOD COOK BOOK, by Anne Marshal/Octopus Books Ltd.
VERMONT FOLK MEDICINE, by D. C. Jarvis/Fawcett Crest Books, New York.
THE WHOLE EARTH COOKBOOK, by Sharon Cadwaller & Judi Ohr/Penguin Books Ltd.
THE WHOLEFOOD COOKERY BOOK, by Ursula M. Cavenagh/Faber & Faber Ltd.
THE BEER DRINKER'S COMPANION/David & Charles Ltd.
DIRECTORY OF ENGLISH APPLES, by Muriel Smith/The Ministry of Agriculture. Available from any of Her Majesty's Stationery Offices.

HERBS

CULPEPPER'S COMPLETE HERBAL. *Now available in facsimile editions.*
HERBAL HANDBOOK FOR FARM & STABLE, by Juliette de Bairacli Levy/Faber & Faber Ltd.
HERBAL MANUAL, by Harold Ward/L. N. Fowler & Co. Ltd, 15 New Bridge Street, London EC4V 6BB.
THE HERBALIST, by Joseph E. Meyer/Oak Tree Press Ltd. *The other of the two great herbals.*
HERBS FOR DAILY USE, by Mary Thorne Quelch/Faber & Faber Ltd.
HERBS FOR HEALTH & COOKING, by Claire Loewenfeld & Philipa Back/Pan Books Ltd. *One of the two finest books on herbs around.*

GARDEN OF HERBS, by Eleanour Sinclair Rohde/Dover Publications Inc., New York. *A glorious pot pourri of recipes, cures, cosmetic preparations, culinary oddities and other delights.*
THE MAGIC OF HERBS, by C. F. Leyel/Jonathan Cape Ltd.
THE MAGIC OF HERBS, by Audrey Wynne Hatfield/Corgi Books Ltd.

RURAL LIFE

COUNTRY-SIDE/British Naturalists' Association, Hon. Secretary: Mrs K. L. Butcher, 'Willowfield', Boyneswood Road, Four Marks, Alton, Hampshire. (February, June and October) Price: 25p. Annual subscription: 50p.
THE COUNTRYMAN/The Countryman Ltd, 23–27 Tudor Street, London EC4. (Quarterly) Price: 35p. Annual subscription: £1.75.
COUNTRYWOMAN/Associated Country Women of the World, 17 Old Court Place, 40 Kensington High Street, London W8 4PR. (Alternate months) Annual subscription: 50p.
DALESMAN/Dalesman Publishing Co. Ltd, Clapham via Lancaster. (Monthly) Price: 12p. Annual subscription: £1.75.
FLOWER PATCH/c/o Anne and David Lazell, 127 Tower Road South, Warmley, Bristol BS15 5BT.
IN BRITAIN/The British Tourist Association, 64 St James Street, London SW1.
RURAL IRELAND/Muinter Na Tire Publications, H.Q., Tipperary. (Annually) Price: 15p.
AA BOOK OF THE BRITISH COUNTRYSIDE/Collins, Sons & Co. Ltd.
ASK THE FELLOWS WHO CUT THE HAY, by George Ewart Evans/Faber & Faber Ltd.
BRITISH INN SIGNS & THEIR STORIES, by Eric Delderfield/David & Charles Ltd.
THE COUNTRY BOOK, by Barbara Hargreaves/Countrywise Books.

A COUNTRY CAMERA 1844–1914, by Gordon Winter/ David & Charles Ltd.

THE ENGLISH LANDSCAPE, by W. G. Hoskins/BBC Publications.

THE FARMERS OF OLD ENGLAND, by Eric Kerridge/ Allen & Unwin Ltd.

A GUIDE TO COUNTRY LIVING/David & Charles Ltd.

A GUIDE OF ENGLISH COUNTRY HOUSES, by Gary Hogg/ Hamlyn Ltd.

THE HORSE IN THE FURROUGH, by George Ewart Evans/Faber & Faber Ltd.

HOW TO BUY AN ISLAND, by David McCormick/David & Charles Ltd.

LIFE AND TRADITIONS IN THE COTSWOLDS, by Edith Brill/J. M. Dent.

MAKING OF THE ENGLISH LANDSCAPE, by W. G. Hoskins/BBC Publications.

MAN MADE THE LAND, by Alan R. H. Baker & J. B. Harley/David & Charles Ltd.

THE PATTERN OF ENGLISH BUILDING, by Alec Clifton Taylor/Faber & Faber Ltd.

THE PATTERN UNDER THE FLOWER, by George Ewart Evans/Faber & Faber Ltd.

RESCUING THE PAST, by Ann Cripps/David & Charles Ltd. *An analysis and identification of unusual objects from our rural heritage.*

THE SHELL BOOK OF THE COUNTRYSIDE/Phoenix House Publications.

THE SHELL COUNTRY ALPHABET, by G. Grigson/ Michael Joseph Ltd.

THE SHELL NATURAL HISTORY OF BRITAIN/Michael Joseph Ltd.

THE SHELL NATURE BOOK, by G. Grigson & J. Fisher/ Phoenix House Publications.

THE SHELL TREASURY OF THE COUNTRYSIDE, by John Baker/Phoenix House Publications.

WHERE BEARDS WAG ALL, by George Ewart Evans/ Faber & Faber Ltd.

The following booklets are all available from The Council for the Protection of Rural England, 4 Hobart Place, London SW1W 0HY:

THE FUTURE OF OUR VILLAGE
HOMES IN THE COUNTRYSIDE
PLANNING SENSE
TREES IN THE VILLAGE

THE WEATHER

BRITAIN'S WEATHER/David & Charles Ltd.

INTERPRETING THE WEATHER, by Ingrid Holford/ David & Charles Ltd..

WEATHER LORE, by Richard Lowards/S. R. Publishers Ltd.

WATER-DIVINING

JOURNAL OF THE BRITISH SOCIETY OF DOWSERS/available from 19 High Street, Eydon, Daventry, Northamptonshire N11 6PP. (Quarterly) Price: 30p. Annual subscription: £1.20.

WILD FOOD

BRITAIN'S WILD LARDER, by Claire Lowenfield/ Collins Sons & Co. Ltd.

CONCISE BRITISH FLORA IN COLOUR, by Keeble-Martin/Michael Joseph Ltd. *Consult this to avoid poisoning yourself.*

FOOD FOR FREE, by Richard Mabey/Collins Sons & Co. Ltd.

WILD FOODS OF BRITAIN, by Jason Hill/A. C. Black Ltd.

In the many bibliographies in this book, we give the addresses of publishers only where the firm concerned may not be immediately familiar to readers. If you have difficulty in getting any of the books, the addresses of most British publishers can be found at your local reference library in: PUBLISHERS IN THE UNITED KINGDOM AND THEIR ADDRESSES/J. Whitaker & Sons Ltd. Prices of all publications mentioned are correct at time of going to press.

MUSEUMS

Most museums display examples of local craftwork, but these may vary in quality and extent. For a complete list of museums with a subject index of the collections they keep consult: MUSEUMS AND GALLERIES IN GREAT BRITAIN AND IRELAND/ABC Travel Guides Ltd, Oldhill, London Road, Dunstable. (Annually, published in July) Price: 30p.